- This book is intended to introduce a beginner level of using Microsoft Excel in civil engineering practices
- A direct translation

Copyright © Gunthar Pangaribuan 2016

PREFACE

Microsoft Excel learning is perceived as more attractive from time to time and it is probably the most widely software-learning topic written into books, websites, courses, tutorial videos, groups, etc. Favored by many people because Excel is relatively easy to operate and giving "complete" results by showing spreadsheet form (rows and columns), images, text, tables, charts, and so on. Talking about Excel for applied engineering calculation cannot be separated from a discussion on Visual Basic for Application (VBA) macro, which is the programming language of Microsoft Visual Basic for automation of certain tasks. This is due to macro like any other programming language capable of doing iterative calculations or repeating calculations with ease. There is a unique combination between worksheet as a user-interface and VBA, which turned out to be a lot makes it easy for users to create programs.

This book also discussed the depiction in AutoCAD software. Why? Because the drawing creation process can be done through Excel formulas or macros, and this will enhance a series of producing program. The advantage of an AutoCAD drawing creation is no doubt that relies on high image accuracy with a myriad of features it will certainly be a challenge to create drawings. With the ease of working with Excel, coupled with a lot of given examples in this book, it is expected to increase the interest of the readers to create new original application programs. Thus, each model or even a specific model of calculation will be an exciting challenge for a programming job is already enjoyable.

Jakarta, November, 2015

Gunthar Pangaribuan

CONTENTS

PREFACE ii

Chapter 1: BASICS OF EXCEL 1

    1.1   Worksheet and Workbook 1

    1.2   Data Type 2

    1.3   Formula 5

    1.4   Built-In Function 7

    1.5   Array Formula 9

    1.6   Data Formatting 11

    1.7   Error Message 11

    1.8   Printing 12

    1.9   Making Charts 13

    1.10   Engineering Drawing 15

    1.11   Visual Basic for Application 24

        1.11.1   Creating Macro 25

        1.11.2   Recording Macro 27

        1.11.3   Procedure 29

        1.11.4   Running Macro 31

        1.11.5   VBA Dictionary 32

Chapter 2: EXCEL FUNCTIONS 33

    2.1   Math and Trigonometry Functions 33

    2.2   Logical Functions 36

    2.3   Lookup Functions 38

    2.4   Text Functions 40

    2.5   Data Analysis Functions 43

        2.5.1   Linear Regression 43

        2.5.2   Polynomial Regression 52

        2.5.3   Interpolation 53

        2.5.4   Statistical Data 59

    2.6   Circular Reference 65

Chapter 3: CREATING MACRO ... 69

- 3.1 Function Procedure ... 69
- 3.2 Sub Procedure ... 74
- 3.3 Control Structures ... 76
  - 3.3.1 Looping ... 76
  - 3.3.2 Branching ... 79
- 3.4 User Defined Function Problems ... 83
- 3.5 Structure of Program ... 97
  - 3.5.1 Input Output Form ... 97
  - 3.5.2 Work With Modules ... 98
  - 3.5.3 Tips ... 100
- 3.6 Chart Macro ... 102
- 3.7 Manipulation on Program Steps ... 108

Chapter 4: MATRIX PROGRAM ... 112

- 4.1 Matrix Definition ... 112
  - 4.1.1 Types of Matrix ... 112
  - 4.1.2 Matrix Operation ... 115
- 4.2 Program for Matrix Operations ... 124
- 4.3 Matrix Method for Structural Analysis ... 132
  - 4.3.1 Upper Structure ... 132
  - 4.3.2 Sub Structure ... 134

Chapter 5: NUMERICAL METHOD ... 135

- 5.1 Numerical Integration ... 135
- 5.2 Numerical Differentiation ... 138

Chapter 6: PROGRAM FOR 2D FRAME STRUCTURE ANALYSIS ... 144

- 6.1 Case Example ... 144
- 6.2 Sign Convention for Diagram ... 160
- 6.3 Application ... 162

Chapter 7: PROGRAM FOR 2D TRUSS STRUCTURE ANALYSIS ... 163

- 7.1 Case Example ... 164
- 7.2 Application ... 176

Chapter 8: BEAM ON ELASTIC FOUNDATION 180

    8.1   Case Example 182

    8.1   Application 187

Chapter 9: LATERALLY LOADED STRUCTURE 189

    9.1   Case Example 189

    9.2   Application 196

Chapter 10: ONE DIMENSIONAL CONSOLIDATION 199

    10.1   Application 1 205

    10.2   Application 2 207

Chapter 11: AUTOCAD SCRIPT FILE 210

    11.1   Creating Scripts in Worksheet 210

    11.2   Creating Scripts in VBA 231

REFERENCES 240

ATTACHMENT: PROGRAM CODE 241

Gunthar Pangaribuan

Graduated from Indonesia Institute of Technology and earned a bachelor degree in Civil Engineering. Getting started with a career in geotechnical engineering services and became his major work which he has spent over 10 years. During the time, he has created numerous computer programs especially for completion of geotechnical problems using Excel-VBA-AutoCAD - the 'magic trio' he relies on. Some of the programs are presented in this book. In 2012, he joined the oil and gas company as a facility engineer.

CHAPTER 1

BASICS OF EXCEL

The work performed by Excel is basically the job of entering data which is then processed to obtain the desired results. It is, in principle, the same as entering data into an electronic calculator. However, the data entered here consists of various types and coupled with existing Excel facilities makes possible to present the appearance of numbers, text, tables, calculations, graphs, a database, etc. This makes Excel becomes a well-integrated sheet that allows users to make text writing and the problem analysis as well.

Each version of Excel to be developed to always make changes and additions of new facilities, while still maintaining compatibility with previous versions. However, the changes do not alter the basic features of this software for computing applications. In this book, we will be working with Microsoft Excel 2007.

1.1 WORKSHEET AND WORKBOOK

When opening Excel, by default Book1 is the name of the first workbook. This workbook consists of three worksheets, namely Sheet1, Sheet2 and Sheet3. The Excel worksheet is also referred to as a spreadsheet, that is, a sheet for processing text and numbers.

Figure 1.1 shows the elements of a workbook. At the top of the page, there is a title bar displays the workbook name. Underneath, there is a **Ribbon**, new interface introduced in Excel 2007, which is a navigation tool replaces the menu and tool bars in earlier Excel version as a tool of access to Excel commands. All commands are grouped and placed into tabs for particular tasks, thus a tab contains groups of commands.

Worksheet is divided into rows and columns. In Excel 2007, the numbers of columns and rows have been improved from previous versions. Columns are from A to Z, then AA, AB to XFD (16,384 columns), while the rows start from 1 to 1,048,576. The intersection point of column and row forms a cell as a place to fill data. Each cell has an address referred to by a column and a row, for example cell B4 is a cell in column B and 4th row. The address of a selected cell can be seen in the Name Box below the Ribbon.

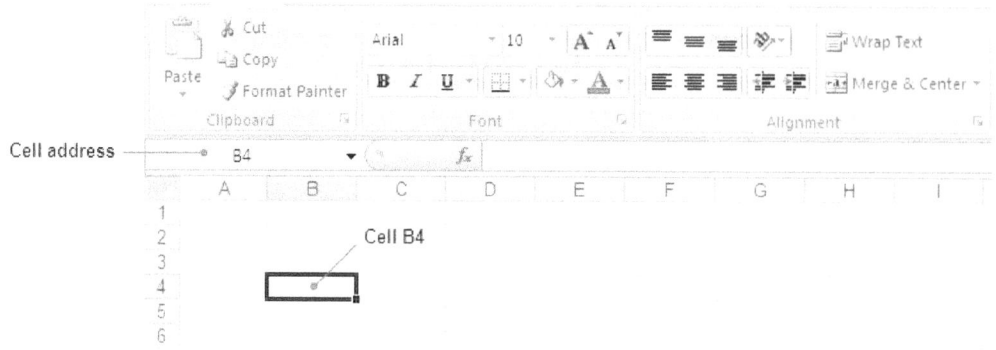

A collection of cells is called a cell range, forming an array that is extended horizontally or vertically. A collection of cells from A1 to A5 (generally written as a range A1:A5) is a collection of cells from A1 to A5 that forms an array of 5 x 1 (rows x columns); further, a range A1:C5 forms 5 x 3 array, and so on.

Name of a worksheet can be changed by any names by clicking twice on the sheet tab, press **Delete** to clear the current name, then write a new name; or by right-clicking on the sheet tab and then on the shortcut menu click **Rename** to change its name.

1.2 DATA TYPE

Input data in spreadsheets can be divided into some types as follows:

a. Text: alphabet characters and text: A, B, -Z, AB, A2, Computers...

b. Numbers: numerical data: 1,2,3,0, -1, -2,4,5.85...

c. Date: the date data typically refers to the setting of a computer calendar or formulated in the calculation.

d. Hours: data of hours is generally referred to computer time setting or formulated in calculation.

e. Formula: mathematical expressions that calculate two or more values produce a new value.

f. Function: functions that are used for various applications such as finance, mathematics and trigonometry, statistic, database and engineering.

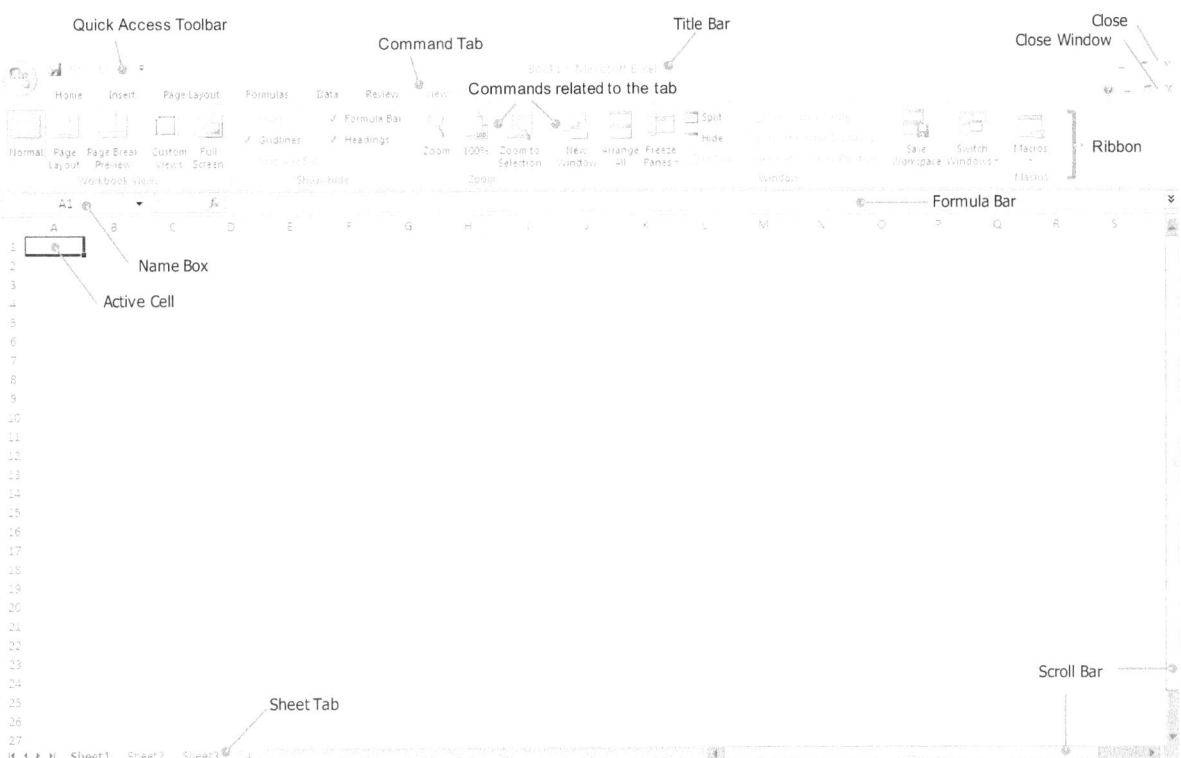

Figure 1.1: Excel 2007 Worksheet

Table 1.1: Excel Basic Commands

Name	Shortcut or Icon	Description
Office Button		Icon to the basic commands below:
Save		Save a file with the name of the workbook that is being done
Save As	Alt+FA	Store a file with another name into a folder and directory, or to a disc. By default, a file with extension of .xlsx is given (free macro). If a file contains macro (VBA) that needs to activate when the file is opened, the file is then saved with .xlsm extension
New		Open a new workbook
Open		Open an existing workbook
Print		Print a worksheet through the printer device
Close		Close a workbook (Close Window icon)

An Introduction to Excel for Civil Engineers

Exit	☒	Close the program and exit Excel (icon Close)
Quick Access Toolbar:		
Undo	↶	Cancel the last job
Redo	↷	Repeat the last job
Tab HOME		
Copy		Copy the data of a cell or range of cells to another location. To select the data copied or cut, click on the cell or range of cells where the data is, then press Ctrl+C
Cut	✂	Move the data to another location. Commands such as Cut, Copy and Paste can be found in the pop-up menu by clicking the right mouse button on the highlighted cells or by pressing Ctrl+X
Paste		Put the data into a new cell or range of cells. Paste command is done after preceding Cut or Copy. To place the data to a new location, press Enter or by pressing Ctrl+V
Insert > Cells	Alt+IE	Display Insert dialog box. It is used to insert a new cell, row or column at the pointer position (highlighted cell)
Insert > Sheet Rows	Alt+IR	Insert a new row at the pointer position
Insert > Sheet Columns	Alt+IC	Insert a new column at the pointer position
Format .> Row Height	Alt+HO (Home > Format)	Format row, which consists of the row height setting, to hide and unhide row
Format .> Column Width	Alt+HO (Home > Format)	Format column, which consists of the column width setting, automatic width (autofit selection), hides and shows columns, and showing information of the standard column width
Format > Cell	Alt+HO (Home > Format)	Format cell, such as numbers, text, font used, borders, colors and worksheet protection

An Introduction to Excel for Civil Engineers

Table 1.2 Operators and mathematical relationships

Operator	Description
+	Summation
−	Subtraction
*	Multiplication
/	Division
%	Percent
^	Exponentiation
Relationships	
=	Equal to
>	Greater than
<	Less than
<>	Not equal to
>=	Greater than or equal to
<=	Less than or equal to

1.3 FORMULA

By definition, a formula is a mathematical expression to calculate the results of two or more values. A formula can consist of numbers, mathematical operators, functions, reference cell or range of cells. Cells and cell range are often given a name, for example "A" to B2, or "B" for a range D2:D6. Naming cells will be discussed later in this section. All formulas begin with an equal sign (=), for example, the following formula is written in cell B4:

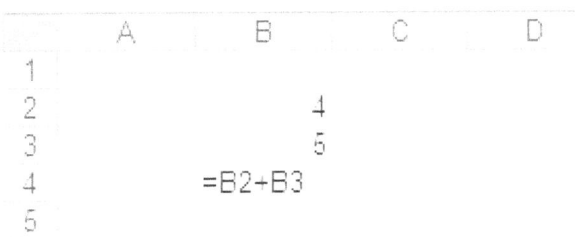

=B2+B3 summing the numbers in cell B2 and cell B3

=B4*B5 multiplying the numbers in cell B4 and cell B5

=SUM(D2:D4) summing all the numbers in cells D2, D3 and D4

When a formula to be copied, it must be considered cell references typed in the formula. If the cell address changes when it is copied to another cell, thus it is called relative cell reference. Cell C1 that contains formula =A1+B1 will be =C2+D2 in Cell E2. The result is as shown in Figure 1.2. By default, Excel uses relative reference.

If the cell address does not change when it is copied to another cell, it is called absolute cell reference. The notation is to add "$" sign before a column name and a row number, for instance: $A$4. Adding $ before any column names or row numbers will only change one of the column or row reference. Column A in "$A4" will remain when it is copied, but the row number will adjust to its new location and vice versa with "A$4". Such cell reference is called semi-absolute or mixed reference.

	A	B	C	D	E	F
1	20	30	=A1+B1			
2					=C2+D2	
3			=$A$1+B1			
4					=$A$1+D2	
5			=$A1+B1			
6					=$A2+D2	
7			=A$1+B7			
8					=C$1+D8	
9						
10						

Figure 1.2: Copied formula and the results in a spreadsheet

Formula stating cell relationships or range of cells, for example, =B4+C30 or =SUM (A4: C20) are more difficult to read than the mathematical relationship with a more practical variable name, for example, =x+n or SUM(B). Name of cell or cell range is created through **Formulas > Define Name**. By default, a name applies to all sheets in a workbook. To represent a specific sheet, you must select the specific sheet in the **Scope** field, for example, Sheet1!x means it refers to variable x in Sheet1. The names used and their locations can be seen in **Name Manager** where you can create, edit and delete a name. The use of variable is highly recommended because it will simplify a formula.

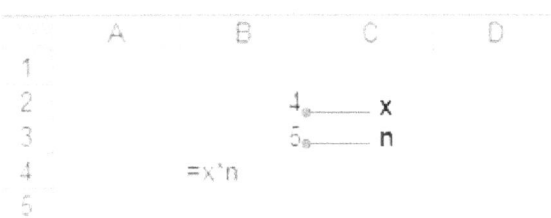

1.4 BUILT-IN FUNCTION

Excel has many built-in functions to build complex formulas; some of them are given in Table 1.3. Functions such as in mathematic and trigonometry or statistic category, for example, are the most common functions used in engineering practices e.g. to produce calculation data sheet in laboratory soil testing. Before using a function, one should have to know well the function and its arguments. The reference could be found the Help menu or by pressing F1.

Table 1.3 Excel Built-in Functions

A. Math and Trigonometry	
ABS(num)	Returns the absolute value of a number
ACOS(num)	Returns the arccosine of a number
ACOSH(num)	Returns the inverse hyperbolic cosine of a number
ATAN(num)	Returns the arctangent of a number
EXP(num)	Returns *e* raised to the power of a given number
FACT(num)	Returns the factorial of a number
INT(num)	Rounds a number down to the nearest integer
LOG(num, base)	Returns the logarithm of a number to a specified base
LOG10(num)	Returns the base-10 logarithm of a number
MDETERM(array)	Returns the matrix determinant of an array
MINVERS(array)	Returns the matrix inverse of an array
MMULT(array1,array2)	Multiplying of 2 arrays
PI()	Value of pi = 3.141592654
RAND()	Random value between 0 and 1
SIGN(num)	Sign of number. Sign 1, 0 or -1 if the number is respectively, positive, zero or negative.
SIN(num)	Returns the sine of the given angle

An Introduction to Excel for Civil Engineers

SINH(num)	Returns the hyperbolic sine of a number
SQRT(num)	Returns square root of a number
SUM (num1,num2,...)	Add the numbers
SUMPRODUCT(array1,array2)	Multiplies corresponding components in the given arrays
TAN(num)	Returns the tangent of a number
TANH(num)	Returns the hyperbolic tangent of a number
B. IS Function	
ISBLANK(value)	TRUE if value is empty
ISLOGICAL(value)	TRUE if value is logical value (TRUE or FALSE)
ISNUMBER(value)	TRUE if value is a number
ISTEXT(value)	TRUE if value is a text
C. Statistic	
AVERAGE(num1,num2,...)	Average value of numbers
COUNT(value1,value2,...)	Counts the number of cells that contain numbers within the list of arguments
COUNTA(value1,value2,...)	Counts the number of cells that are not empty within the list of arguments
LINEST(y's,x's,const,stats)	Returns the parameters of a linear trend. Const and stats are logical values (see in Excel Help)
MAX(num1,num2,...)	Maximum value in a list of arguments
MIN(num1,num2,...)	Minimum value in a list of arguments
SLOPE(y's,x's)	Returns the slope of the linear regression line
INTERCEPT(y's,x's)	Returns the intercept of the linear regression line on the Y-axis (Y-intercept)
TREND(y's,x's, new x's,const)	Returns values along a linear trend. Const is a logical value specifying whether to set the constant b = 0 in y = mx + b relationship
D. Lookup and Reference	
COLUMNS(reference)	Returns the column number of the given reference
INDEX(array,row_num,column_num)	To choose a value from a reference or array
ROWS(reference)	Returns the row number of the given reference

TRANSPOSE(array)	Returns the transpose of an array
HLOOKUP(value,table,row_in)	Search for a value based on the row index in the data table arranged horizontally
VLOOKUP(value,table,col_in)	Search for a value based on the column index in the data table arranged vertically
E. Logical	
AND(logical1,logical2,..)	Returns TRUE if all of its arguments are TRUE
IF(log_value,value_if_ true,value_if_false)	Specifies a logical test to perform
NOT(logical)	Reverses the logic of its argument: NOT(TRUE) = FALSE
OR(logical1,logical2)	TRUE if one of its argument is TRUE
F. Text	
CHAR(num)	Returns the character specified by the code number
EXACT(text1,text2)	Checks between two text strings and returns TRUE if they are exactly the same, otherwise returns FALSE
FIND(text1,text2,start_num)	Finds one text value within another with start number
LEFT(text, num_character)	Returns the first character based on the specified number of characters
LEN(text)	Returns the number of characters in a text string
RIGHT(text, num_character)	Returns the last character or characters in a text string, based on the specified number of characters
TRIM(text)	Removes spaces from text except for single spaces between words
UPPER(text)	Converts text to uppercase

1.5 Array Formula

By Excel definition, array formula is a formula that can perform multiple calculations and then return either a single result or multiple results. Array formulas act on two or more sets of values known as array arguments. Each array argument must have the same number of rows and columns. For example, **LINEST** function returns two results: the slope and the Y-intercept. This function calculates a linear regression line that best fits the given x and y-values. Figure 1.3 shows an array formula using the LINEST function.

	A	B
1	x	y
2	-1.0	-5.0
3	-0.5	0.0
4	1.0	5.0
5	2.0	4.0
6	3.0	0.5
7	4.0	-5.0
8	5.0	-12.0
9	Slope	Y-intercept
10	-1.204	0.537

	Slope	Y-intercept
9	Slope	Y-intercept
10	={LINEST(B2:B8,A2:A8)}	{=LINEST(B2:B8,A2:A8)}

Figure 1.3: Array formula for linear regression and the results

An array formula is entered into cells by pressing **Ctrl+Shift+Enter**. Excel will automatically insert the formula in brackets ({}). To display values returned by LINEST function, type **LINEST** formula in cell A10 as shown in Figure 1.3, and then select range A10:B10 > press **F2** > **Ctrl+Shift+Enter**.

The other examples of array formulas:

{=SUM(A2: B2*A3:B3)}   returns a single result

{=TREND(A2:A6,B2:B6)}   returns a separately 5 results

Alternatively, **INDEX** function can be combined with LINEST function to return the LINEST function results that are sequentially indexed for the slope and the Y-intercept. It shows as below:

	Slope	Y-intercept
9	Slope	Y-intercept
10	-1.204	0.537

	Slope	Y-intercept
9	Slope	Y-intercept
10	=INDEX(LINEST(B2:B8,A2:A8),1)	=INDEX(LINEST(B2:B8,A2:A8),2)

1.6 Data Formatting

Data and cells formatting can be done through the **Home** tab > **Format** (in Cells group) > **Format Cells**. In the **Format Cells** dialog box, there are several sheet tabs: **Number, Alignment, Font, Border, Fill** and **Protection**. Number formatting in **Number** tab is divided into several categories: general, number, date and others. The custom category or user preference for numbers is shown in Table 1.4. **Alignment** is the setting for layout of text in a cell such as vertical and horizontal alignment, control and orientation of text in a cell. **Fonts** is for the settings that relate to font appearance, such as font type (Arial, Times New Roman, Tahoma, ...), style (italic, bold ...), size, color and so on. **Border** is to apply borders, specify line styles (straight, dotted, thin, thick), and line color to the selected cells. **Fill** is to set background color, pattern style (horizontal, diagonal, dot, ...), pattern color and fill effects. **Protection** to prevent selected cells from being changed (locked or not) and hide formulas (hidden or not) when a sheet is protected. To protect a sheet, click the **Review** tab > in **Changes** group click **Protect Sheet**.

Table 1.4: Custom formats for numbers

Format	Displayed
0.00	2343.00
0.00E+00	2.34E+03
##0.0+0	2.3E+3
#,##0.00	2,343.00
#,##0.00%	234,300.00%
0.0 "m"	2343.0 m

Column width and row height can be adjusted through the several ways as follows. Move the pointer to the sides of column and row headings (so the pointer becomes two arrowheads) and drag the mouse (hold the left mouse button while moving) to make the column and row wider or smaller. The other way is to right click the mouse on the column or row heading and in the shortcut menu, click **Row Height** or **Column Width** and then enter the desired value in the textbox. You can also use the **Home** tab > **Format**.

1.7 Error Message

Error message will be appeared when a formula does not work as should it be, for examples, arguments in a formula are not complete, the data type does not match, or wrong in developing the logic. Another case, for example is division by zero (0) or the width of the column is not wide enough to display a result. The message started with the "#" sign followed by the type of error. Table 1.5 shows some error messages that may appear.

Table 1.5 Error Messages

Messages	Remarks
#####	Cell contains number, date or time that is wider than the cell width or minus result in the date and time format
#N/A	(Not Available) when a value is not available to a function or formula
#DIV/0!	Error due to division by zero (0)
#NAME?	Excel does not recognize text in a formula
#REF!	When a reference cell is not valid
#VALUE!	The types of arguments used in the function are wrong. The argument can be a numerical value, text, name, label, reference cell, cell range and function

1.8 PRINTING

Before printing an Excel sheet to a paper, you must set an area that will be printed by blocking the area. For this purpose, you can press **Shift** key + "→" or "↓" (hold Shift when pressing arrow keys) or by dragging the mouse. Then, click the **Page Layout** tab > **Print Area** > **Set Print Area**. The print area can be seen through the **Office Button** > **Print** > **Print Preview** or press the shortcut key **Ctrl+F2**. The printing is then performed through > **Print** > **OK** or pressing **Ctrl+P**.

To view page will break when printing, you can use Page Break Preview through the **View** tab > **Page Break Preview**. This will show all pages to be printed with page numbers. You can adjust the boundaries of the printed area by dragging the mouse on the blue line. Any changes made on the sheet affect the automatic page breaks.

Page configuration is then set through the **Page Layout** tab. Click the **Print Titles** in the **Page Setup** group, and a **Page Setup** dialog box will appear with several sheets tabs: **Page**, **Margins**, **Header/ Footer**, and **Sheet**. **Page** is to select the orientation and size of paper, and set the scale of the sheet on a paper; **Margins** is to set the margin sizes of the printed area on paper; **Header/Footer** is to make custom header and footer; and **Sheet** is to select print area, showing gridlines, print titles and page order.

1.9 MAKING CHARTS

A set of data can be well delivered and communicated through a chart image shown the correlation between the data. Excel provides many chart types such as Bar, Column, Line, Pie, Area plus 3-dimensional views. A chart is created through the **Insert** tab > **Chart**, and **Charts** group will appear as shown in Figure 1.4. For this example, say, the used data is selected from Figure 1.3. To proceed, select **Scatter** > **Scatter with Smooth Lines and Markers** to make smooth lines between points. Click the **Select Data** on the Ribbon to display the **Select Data Source** dialog box as shown below.

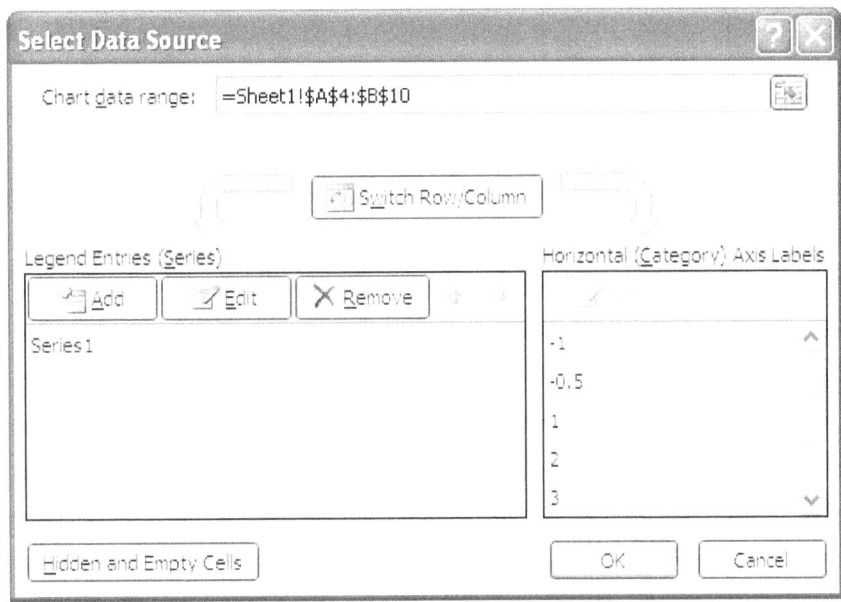

Enter x and y-values data in the **Chart Data Range** by clicking the button at the right side of the input box and then put the pointer to cell A2 and drag the mouse from cell A2 to cell B8. Click **OK**, and a chart will be created as shown in Figure 1.5. On the chart, a regression line is also presented with the associated equation. Regression line is created by clicking the mouse on the chart (at any points or a line), then right click > **Add Trendline** > **Linear** > checked the **Display Equation on Chart**. Furthermore, if you want to work with the chart thoroughly, click the graph area to display **Chart Tools** to add **Design**, **Layout** and **Format** tabs with the associated commands as shown on the Ribbon. You can use the commands to modify the chart.

Figure 1.4: Charts group displays chart type options

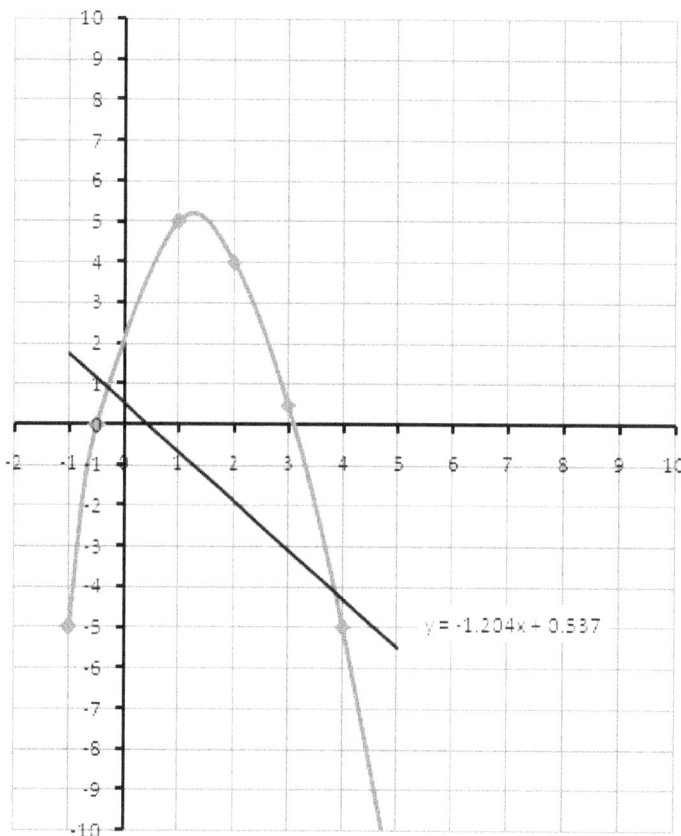

Figure 1.5: Example of Scatter with smooth lines chart type

Note:

As designed for office applications, Excel offers various types of charts for the respective purposes. However, we will not discuss many different types of charts here, and but only focus on **Scatter chart type with straight lines** that frequently used in this book.

1.10 Engineering Drawing

Chart type of **XY Scatter** is suitable for use in Civil engineering practices in giving a drawing presentation that forms lines or elements of structure. The reason is that every line can stand alone, so that easily modified and formulated for an intended drawing.

A straight line of **XY Scatter** chart type is determined by giving coordinates of both ends required for its input data. If both ends of the line are called joints, then the coordinates of two joints form a line segment. Thus, there will be a series of joint data put into a worksheet table to create straight lines.

To understand the intent and purpose of this section, below is given some examples of how to create engineering drawings.

Example 1

Create a drawing of 3 continuous lines through 4 points (1 to 4) as shown below.

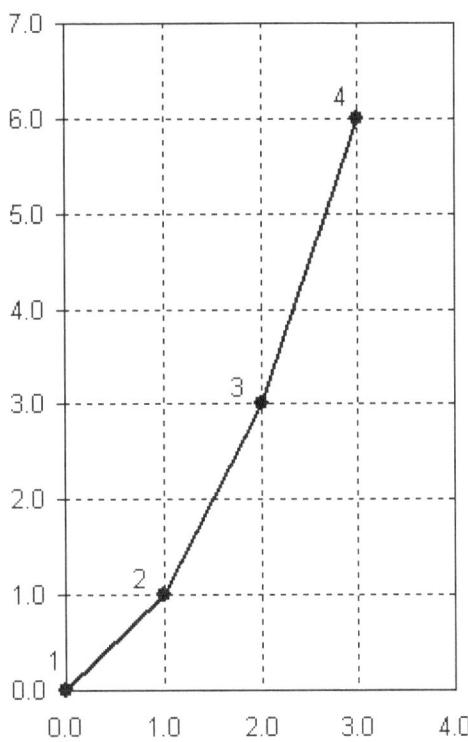

The coordinates of joints are as follows:

	x	y
Joint 1	0	0

An Introduction to Excel for Civil Engineers

Joint 2	1	1
Joint 3	2	3
Joint 4	3	4

To create continuous lines as shown in the figure above, take the following steps:

1. Click on the **Insert** tab > **Scatter** > **Scatter with Straight Lines and Markers**.

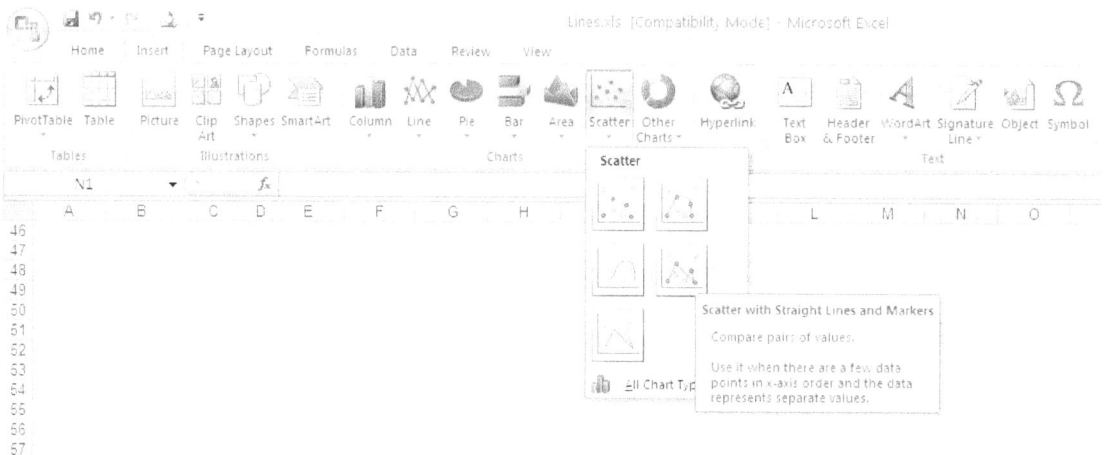

2. Here, **Chart Area** displays nothing because no data on it. Click **Select Data** on the Ribbon interface to display the **Select Data Source** dialog box.

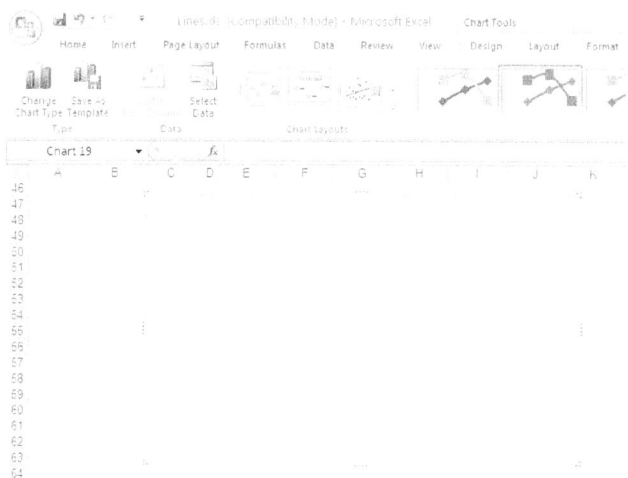

3. A **Select Data Source** dialog box is displayed in the figure below (left side). Click **Add** to display the **Edit Series** dialog box (right side). Each series that is added (by

An Introduction to Excel for Civil Engineers

clicking Add) represents **a line** that requires a **pair** of x and y values as inputs. Thus, a line series shall consist of coordinates of both ends of the line, the one to be (x1, y1) and the other is (x2, y2).

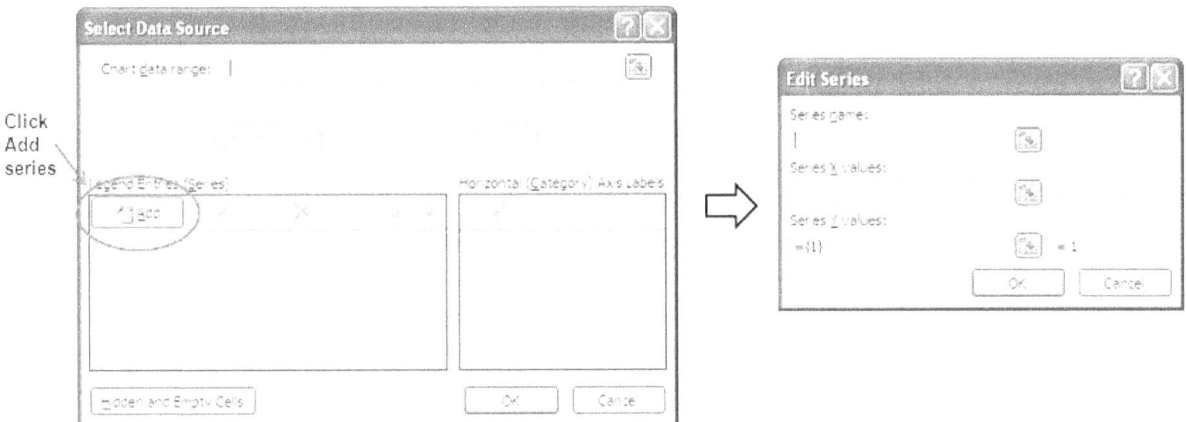

Click Add series

4. Following Step 3, enter the line coordinate i.e. series x and series y-values. When needed, give a name for the series in the **Series name** input box.
5. Click **OK** to end.

By using the Edit Series in this chart type, lines are inputted by giving first and second joint coordinates. From the above figure, the intended coordinates of joints for creating lines can be summarized as below:

Line	Joint	Coordinate			
		x1	y1	x2	y2
1	1	2	0.0	0.0	1.0	1.0
2	2	3	1.0	1.0	2.0	3.0
3	3	4	2.0	3.0	3.0	6.0

In step 4, what we do is to enter the column x1 and x2 (range of values is colored yellow) into the **Series X values** input box, while the **Series Y values** is filled by the column y1 and y2 (range of values is colored green). To enter x-coordinates, press **Ctrl+left mouse button click** at x1 column and repeat **left mouse button click** at x2 column to get the range of cells. Do the same way to enter y-coordinates.

Repeat step 3 to 5 to make 2nd and 3rd line. The result will be shown as below:

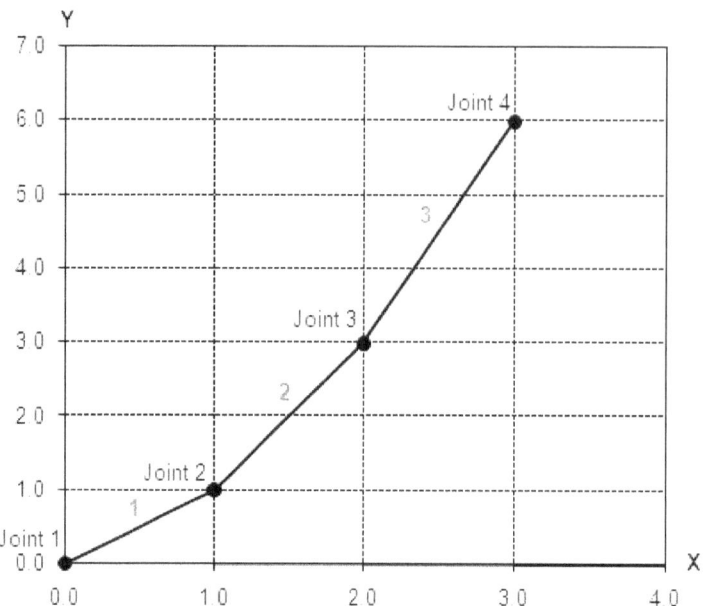

Example 2

Draw a simple one-floor building as shown below:

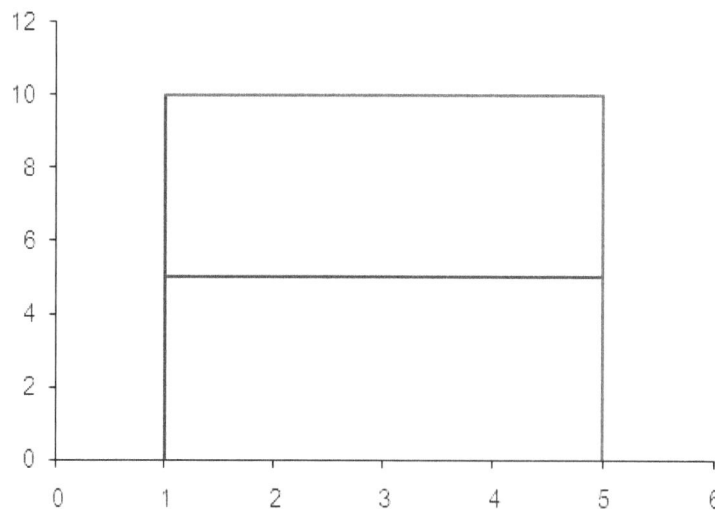

As in Example 1, to simplify the portrayal of the drawing we need to produce joints and lines coordinate tables. The building is composed of 6 joints and 6 straight lines that can be built-up with the following numbering system:

An Introduction to Excel for Civil Engineers

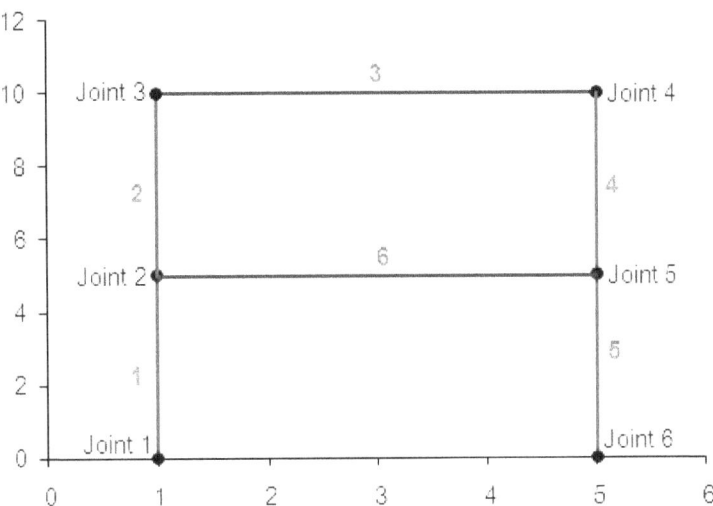

Based on the picture above, the following tables can be created:

	A	B	C	D	E	F	G	H	I	J	K
1											
2											
3			Coordinate						Coordinate		
4	Joint	x	y		Line	Joint		x1	y1	x2	y2
5	1	1.0	0.0		1	1	2	1	0	1	5
6	2	1.0	5.0		2	2	3	1	5	1	10
7	3	1.0	10.0		3	3	4	1	10	5	10
8	4	5.0	10.0		4	4	5	5	10	5	5
9	5	5.0	5.0		5	5	6	5	5	5	0
10	6	5.0	0.0		6	2	5	1	5	5	5
11											

The joints coordinates for assigning lines on the right table is obviously the repetition of inputting task of the previous joints coordinates on the left table. To avoid repeated data entry manually, **VLOOKUP** function can be used by adopting the x, y joint coordinates data of the left table as a reference table to obtain x1, y1, and x2, y2 lines coordinates of the right table. The formulas are written in a worksheet as follows:

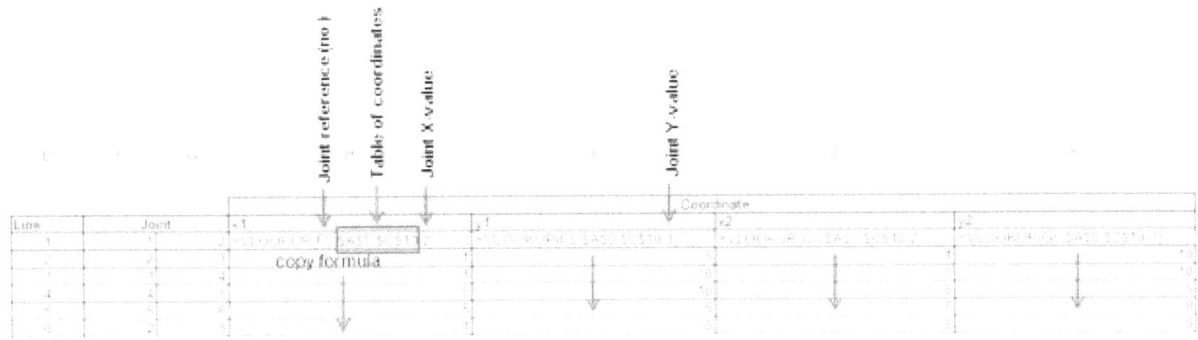

To get the drawing, do the sequence steps as shown in Example 1.

An Introduction to Excel for Civil Engineers

Example 3

Draw the following truss structure that consists of 21 lines and 12 joints. The coordinates of the joints are summarized in the table below.

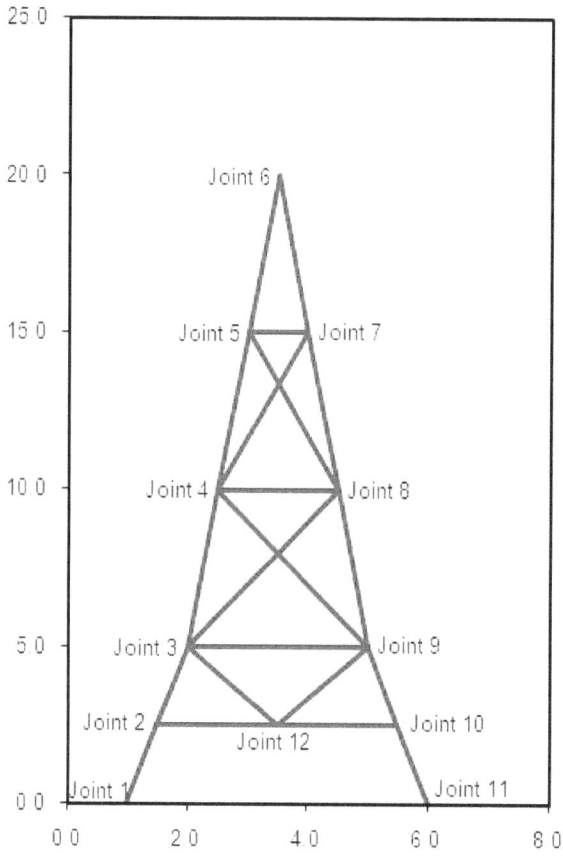

Joint	x	y
1	1.0	0.0
2	1.5	2.5
3	2.0	5.0
4	2.5	10.0
5	3.0	15.0
6	3.5	20.0
7	4.0	15.0
8	4.5	10.0
9	5.0	5.0
10	5.5	2.5

An Introduction to Excel for Civil Engineers

11	6.0	0.0
12	3.5	2.5

Before creating a drawing of the truss structure, it is convenient to form lines coordinates as required for **Series X** and **Series Y** input data. The coordinates of the truss lines are tabulated as shown below:

Line	Joint	x1	y1	x2	y2
1	1	2	1.0	0.0	1.5	2.5
2	2	3	1.5	2.5	2.0	5.0
3	3	4	2.0	5.0	2.5	10.0
4	4	5	2.5	10.0	3.0	15.0
5	5	6	3.0	15.0	3.5	20.0
6	6	7	3.5	20.0	4.0	15.0
7	7	8	4.0	15.0	4.5	10.0
8	8	9	4.5	10.0	5.0	5.0
9	9	10	5.0	5.0	5.5	2.5
10	10	11	5.5	2.5	6.0	0.0
11	2	12	1.5	2.5	3.5	2.5
12	12	10	3.5	2.5	5.5	2.5
13	3	12	2.0	5.0	3.5	2.5
14	12	9	3.5	2.5	5.0	5.0
15	3	8	2.0	5.0	4.5	10.0
16	3	9	2.0	5.0	5.0	5.0
17	4	9	2.5	10.0	5.0	5.0
18	4	8	2.5	10.0	4.5	10.0
19	4	7	2.5	10.0	4.0	15.0
20	5	8	3.0	15.0	4.5	10.0
21	5	7	3.0	15.0	4.0	15.0

An Introduction to Excel for Civil Engineers

The formulas writing are to follow the same manner as in Example 2, where the **VLOOKUP** function is used for coordinates data entry. To create the truss drawing, do the sequence steps as shown in Example 1.

Next example is to draw the previous truss structure subjected to a horizontal load such that after loading, each joints will be shifted as far as *n* units. Suppose that displacements at the joints vary from 0 to maximum of +0.5 units at joint 6 (will be in a range of $0 < n < 0.5$) or it increases by 0.1 units from the supports to the top. The table of joints coordinates is then modified for two conditions: before and after the loading, where *n* is used into calculation. The formulas are written as follows:

	A	B	C	D	E
4					
5		Coord Before		Coord After	
6	Joint	x	y	x	y
7	1	1.0	0.0	1.0	0.0
8	2	1.5	2.5	=B8+0.1	2.5
9	3	2.0	5.0	=B9+0.2	5.0
10	4	2.5	10.0	=B10+0.3	10.0
11	5	3.0	15.0	=B11+0.4	15.0
12	6	3.5	20.0	=B12+0.5	20.0
13	7	4.0	15.0	=B13+0.4	15.0
14	8	4.5	10.0	=B14+0.3	10.0
15	9	5.0	5.0	=B15+0.2	5.0
16	10	5.5	2.5	=B16+0.1	2.5
17	11	6.0	0.0	6.0	0.0
18	12	3.5	2.5	=B18+0.2	2.5
19					

It is noted that only the x-values will be changed by adding the horizontal displacement of *n*, which is 0 at Joint 1 up to a maximum of +0.5 units at Joint 6. Joint 1 and 11 are fixed supports so their positions remain in place before and after the loading.

After forming the joints coordinates table, next is to create lines coordinates table of **Series X** and **Y**. There are now 42 **Series X** and **Y** lines coordinates, before and after the loading as shown in the table below:

	F	G	H	I	J	K	L	M	N	O	P	Q	R
4													
5						Coord Before					Coord After		
6		Line		Joint	x1	y1	x2	y2		x1	y1	x2	y2
7		1	1	2	1.0	0.0	1.5	2.5		1.0	0.0	1.6	2.5
8		2	2	3	1.5	2.5	2.0	5.0		1.6	2.5	2.2	5.0
9		3	3	4	2.0	5.0	2.5	10.0		2.2	5.0	2.8	10.0
10		4	4	5	2.5	10.0	3.0	15.0		2.8	10.0	3.4	15.0
11		5	5	6	3.0	15.0	3.5	20.0		3.4	15.0	4.0	20.0
12		6	6	7	3.5	20.0	4.0	15.0		4.0	20.0	4.4	15.0
13		7	7	8	4.0	15.0	4.5	10.0		4.4	15.0	4.8	10.0
14		8	8	9	4.5	10.0	5.0	5.0		4.8	10.0	5.2	5.0
15		9	9	10	5.0	5.0	5.5	2.5		5.2	5.0	5.6	2.5
16		10	10	11	5.5	2.5	6.0	0.0		5.6	2.5	6.0	0.0
17		11	2	12	1.5	2.5	3.5	2.5		1.6	2.5	3.7	2.5
18		12	12	10	3.5	2.5	5.5	2.5		3.7	2.5	5.6	2.5
19		13	3	12	2.0	5.0	3.5	2.5		2.2	5.0	3.7	2.5
20		14	12	9	3.5	2.5	5.0	5.0		3.7	2.5	5.2	5.0
21		15	3	8	2.0	5.0	4.5	10.0		2.2	5.0	4.8	10.0
22		16	3	9	2.0	5.0	5.0	5.0		2.2	5.0	5.2	5.0
23		17	4	9	2.5	10.0	5.0	5.0		2.8	10.0	5.2	5.0
24		18	4	8	2.5	10.0	4.5	10.0		2.8	10.0	4.8	10.0
25		19	4	7	2.5	10.0	4.0	15.0		2.8	10.0	4.4	15.0
26		20	5	8	3.0	15.0	4.5	10.0		3.4	15.0	4.8	10.0
27		21	5	7	3.0	15.0	4.0	15.0		3.4	15.0	4.4	15.0
28													

The reference range of data table in **VLOOKUP** function is now at cell range A7 to E18. Thus, the coordinates of the lines before and after the loading are respectively referred to column BC and DE (column index 2,3,4 and 5).

The chart below shows the truss lines before and after the horizontal loading, which are drawn in blue and red, respectively.

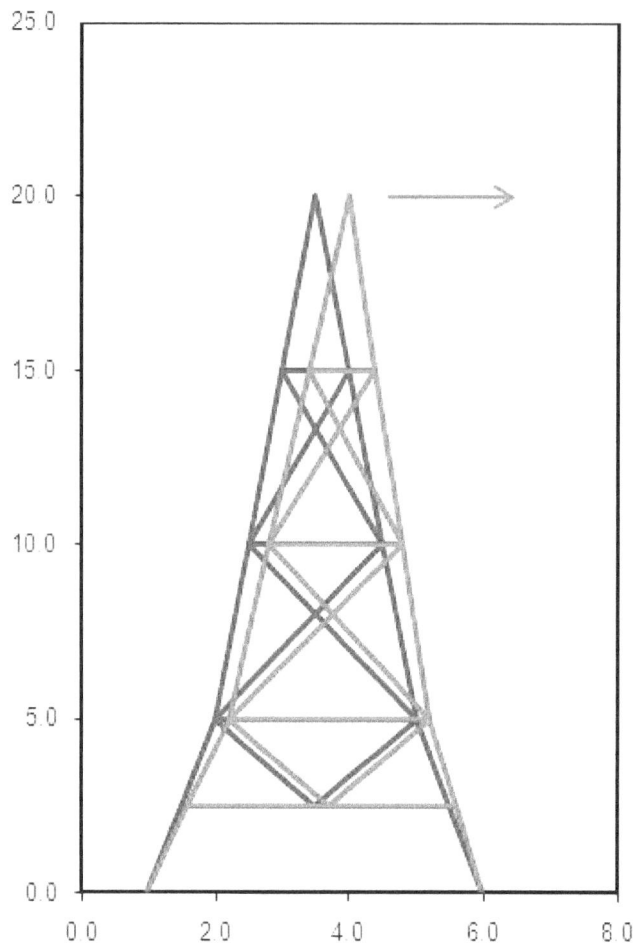

1.11 VISUAL BASIC FOR APPLICATION

One of the strong points of Excel is its macro capability of using macro-programming language to shorten and simplify repetitive works (automation tasks). It cannot be separated, however, from the presence of Microsoft Visual Basic application, which is by default embedded in as an Excel command menu. The Visual Basic application for repetitive tasks or macro in an application program (e.g. Excel or Word) is called **Visual Basic for Applications** (**VBA**). In addition to Microsoft Office, many of non-Microsoft software also use VBA, such as AutoCAD, CorelDraw, Visio and Norton.

VBA can also serve as a programming language to solve many problems in science and technology field, for instance to solve a "complex" iteration or an analysis of civil engineering structure that are not easily or cannot be done rely on Excel built-in functions and spreadsheet "standard" commands. In this respect, the analogy of using macro is therefore a way of automating repetitive tasks in an attempt to get new output when new input is entered.

VBA as well as Microsoft Visual Basic is an object oriented programming language. VBA reads and analyzes objects (and their properties and methods) exposed by Excel through an object library. The reference to these objects is stored in Microsoft Excel Object Library (EXCEL12.OLB). In a programming structure for a calculation application, Excel exposes the property of an object, which is the value of input data that to be processed by VBA and returns the result to a worksheet. Thus, writing the input data is actually storing an object value into a variable, or the value of the variable = value of cell property of the worksheet (that is, a Range object that will be mentioned next).

1.11.1 CREATING MACRO

To create a macro, activate the Developers tab through > **Excel Options** > **Popular** > **Show Developer tab in the Ribbon**, hence it looks like this:

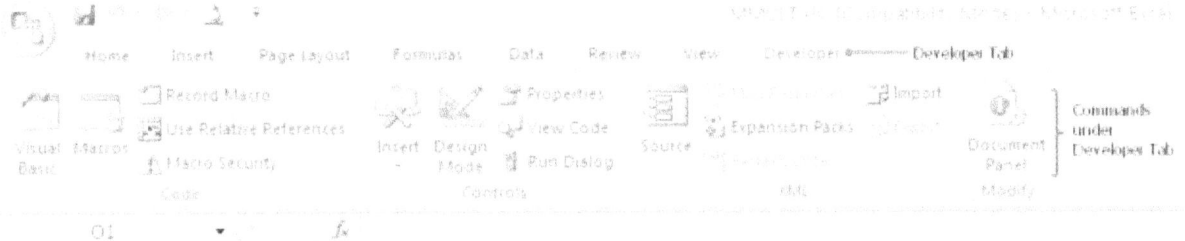

To go to the window where VBA programming language will be created, click **Visual Basic** to open **Visual Basic Editor** (**VBE**) window > click the **Insert** menu > **Module** to show the following window:

VBA programming language is written in a module (that has been added through **Insert** > **Module**). The example below shows VBA code in a procedure in a module:

An Introduction to Excel for Civil Engineers

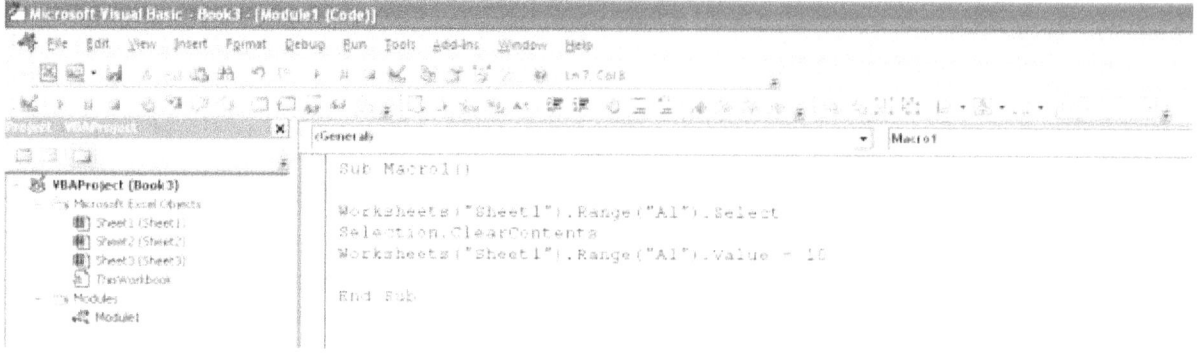

VBA code for an object is orderly composed of the object name, a period, followed by the property or method. The property is an attribute of an object and always accompanied by an equal sign (=), while the method is the action carried out with the object. VBA manipulates Excel's objects through their properties and methods.

In the code created above, Select and ClearContents are called **method**, while Selection in the second line is an **object** refers to the Range object in the first line. The value in the third line is a **property** of the Range object, which it equals 10. The code above is intended to remove the existing value of range A1 on Sheet1 and replace it with a new value of 10. The Worksheets ("Sheet1") code refers to the active sheet, that is, Sheet1.

To see the available objects in Excel, you can access through the **Object Browser** by clicking the icon on VBE toolbar or press **F2**. Selecting the Excel libraries in the pull down menu will show as below:

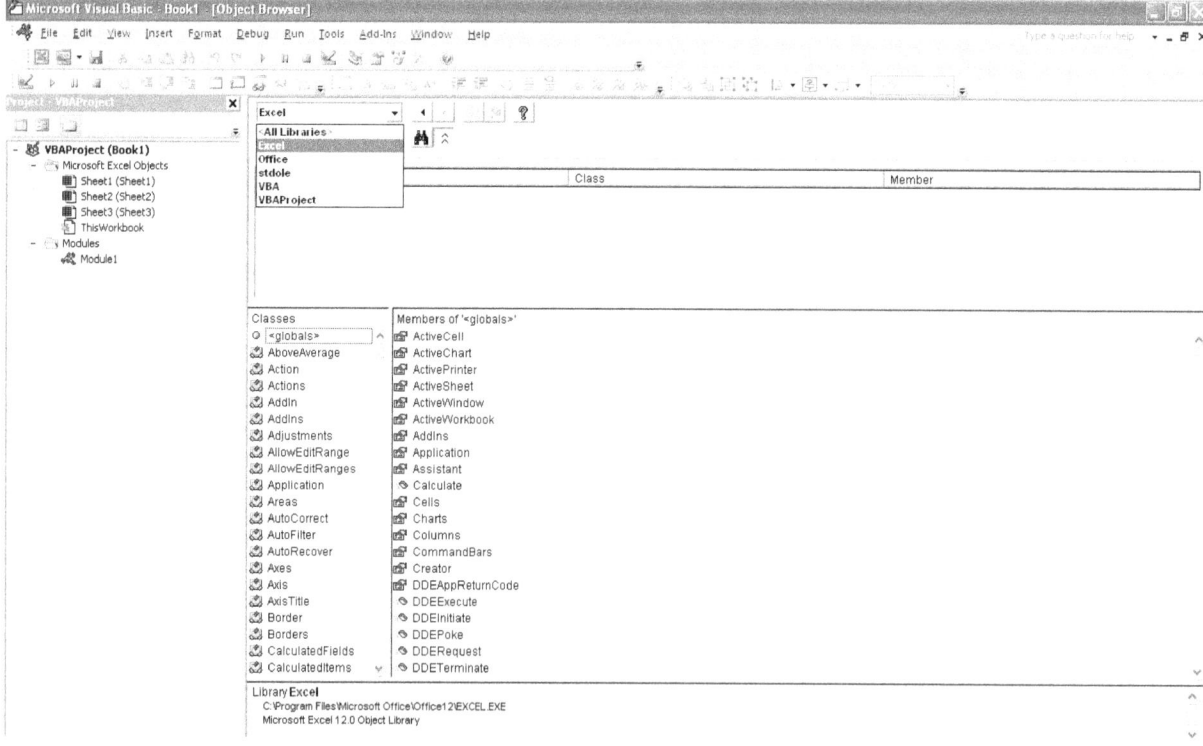

An Introduction to Excel for Civil Engineers

Objects in the Object Browser are classified into **Classes** as displayed on Class window. Their **Members** (displayed on Members window) could either be **properties**, **methods** or **constants**. For instance, Name, Cells and FormulaArray are the members of the Range class. Excel objects are arranged in a hierarchy; objects contain other objects from top level to down level. The code below shows an example of an object hierarchy from the Application object to the Range object:

```
Application.Workbooks("Book1.xls").Worksheets("Sheet1").Range("A1")
```

In the code, the Range property of the Worksheet object returns a Range object. It uses syntax: **object.Range(*cell1*)** where *cell1* is the name of the range (A1) to return a Range object that represents cell A1. Further, the Worksheets property of the Workbook object returns a Worksheet object, the Workbooks property of the Application object returns a Workbook object, and the top level of the hierarchy is the Application object, that is, Excel.

1.11.2 RECORDING MACRO

The best way to figure out how VBA communicates with Excel's objects is to record macros via the **Record Macro** command. This feature gives a quick introduction of all Excel's object as well as how to write code in VBA. For instance, say, we would like to record a macro to delete data on a range of cells A1 to E10. We need to create this automation to clean the existing data as the program produces a new one. The steps for recording macro are as follows:

1. Click the **Developer** tab > **Record Macro** to display the **Record Macro** dialog box with the default name of Macro1 for macro name as shown below:

2. Change macro name to *ClearOutput*

3. Move the pointer to cell A1 and drag the mouse to cell E10 to assign the range data that will be removed.

4. Press **Delete** to delete the contents of the range (cell A1 to E10) and then place the pointer in cell A1.

5. End the process by clicking **Stop Recording**.

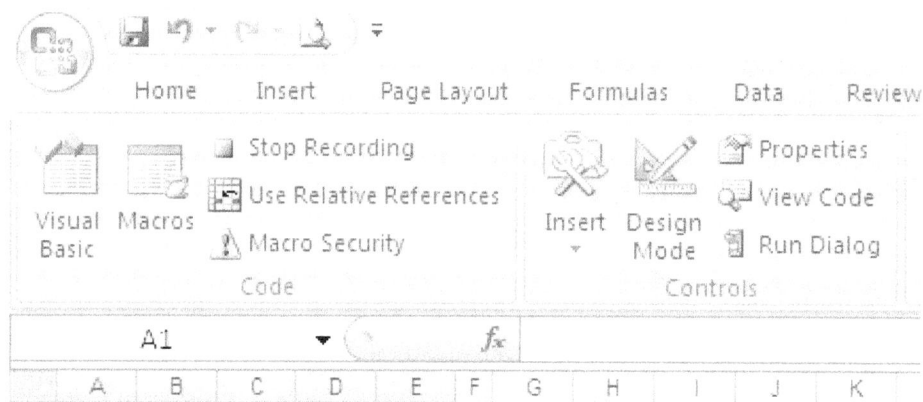

The recorded macro is stored in the workbook, and to see the code you have to open the **Visual Basic Editor** window through **Develope**r tab > **Visual Basic**. The code is created as the following:.

```
Sub ClearOutput ()
'
'Macro ClearOutput
'
    Range("A1:E10").Select
    Selection.ClearContents
End Sub
```

You may a bit familiar with VBA statements such as, Range (), Select, Selection and ClearContents in the recorded macro above. These statements have been presented in the previous section.

Recording macros is very useful when you have no idea where to start with VBA code, for instance how to manipulate a Chart object such as adding a new chart, chart formatting, create titles, set the marker fill, and an automation for adding lines. These can all be done without the need to understand in more detail about Excel object hierarchy that such "long" and may be a bit confused.

1.11.3 PROCEDURE

VBA macro is a programming language written in procedures, for instance, *ClearOuput* macro that is written in a *Sub* procedure. There are three commonly used procedures to create VBA macros:

- *Sub* procedure, procedure that begins with *Sub*, its name and ended with *End Sub*
- *Function* procedure, begins with *Function*, its name and ended with *End Function*
- *Event* procedure, works when there is a certain event, for example, open a workbook, click the button, activate the worksheet, and so on.

The syntaxes of the above procedures are as follows:

1. **Sub Procedure**

Syntax:

[Private | Public | Friend] [Static] Sub *name* [(*arguments*)]

[*statements*]

[Exit Sub]

[*statements*]

End Sub

Remarks:

Public	Optional. Indicates that the Sub procedure is accessible to all other procedures in all modules. If not defined, the procedure by default is Public
Private	Optional. Indicates that the Sub procedure is accessible only to other procedures in the module where it is declared
Friend	Optional. Used only in a class or object module. Can be accessed from other procedure in all modules in a workbook
Static	Optional. Indicates that the Sub procedure's local variables are preserved between calls

name	Required. Name of the Sub follows standard variable naming conventions
arglist	Optional. List of variables representing arguments that are passed to the Sub procedure when it is called. Multiple variables are separated by commas.
statements	Optional. Any group of statements to be executed within the Sub procedure.

2. Function Procedure

Syntax:

[Private | Public | [Static] Function *name* [(*arguments*)][**As** type]

[*statements*]

End Function

3. Event Procedure

Syntax:

Sub *expression.eventname* (*parameters*)

Remarks:

expression	variabel that refers to object
eventname	name of event
parameters	arguments used in *Event* procedure

The most frequently used of Event procedure is to click a button (command button) on a worksheet. Here is the example code:

```
Private Sub CommandButton1_Click()
    'call other procedure
    Call Pro_Sub1
End Sub
```

The use of the above procedures will be presented in the next chapters.

1.11.4 RUNNING MACRO

Macros can be executed in the two following ways:

1. Through the **Developer** tab > **Macros** > select the macro name > **Run**. Function procedure, Private Sub procedure and Sub procedure written with arguments (e.g. `Sub MyProcedure(x, y, z)`) can not be run by this way.

2. By clicking **Button** (Form Control) or the **Command Button** (Active X control) on the worksheet.

The second way is commonly used because it is done in only one-step. However, it can be done in two ways:

- Create a button through the **Developer** tab > **Insert** > **Form Controls** > **Button** > there is a "+" sign at the pointer, and place it on the worksheet by dragging the mouse, the same way to determine its size as well. The **Assign Macro** dialog box will be displayed as below. Enter a name for the macro in the **Macro name** box and then click **OK**.

- Macro is executed by clicking command button on a worksheet, which is associated with an event procedure. To a create command button, click the **Developer** tab> **Insert** > **Active X Controls** > **Command Button** > there is "+" sign at the pointer, and place it on the worksheet by dragging the mouse, the same way to determine its size as well. The result is shown below:

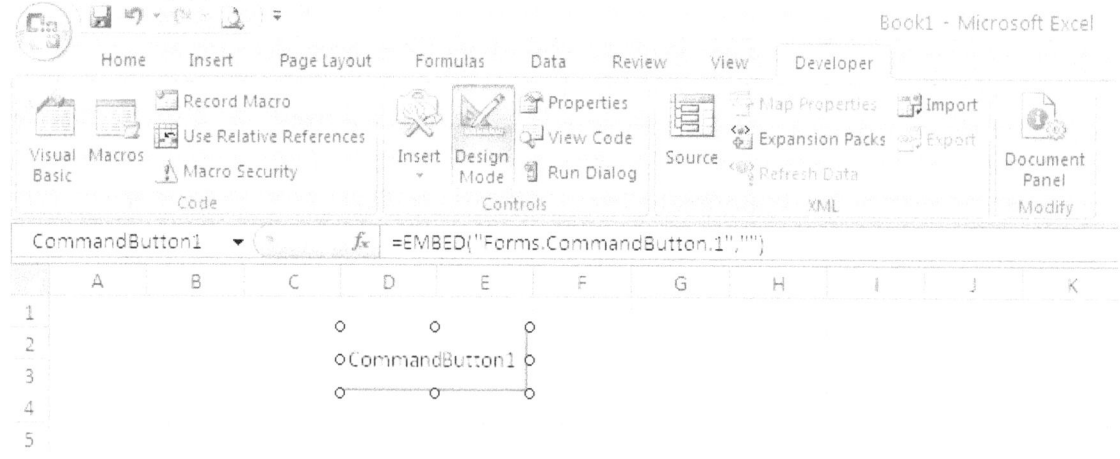

Double-click the command button to write code in the following procedure:

```
Private Sub CommandButton1_Click()

End Sub
```

Macro is inactive when a command button is created or where the Design Mode is enabled. Before run macro, click the Design Mode to disable (so it looks "unselected").

1.11.5 VBA Dictionary

Statements or words that are used in Excel-VBA are too many because the capability VBA to support Excel for diverse goals. Some statements are similar to those used by Excel, for examples, operator and mathematical relationships, some strings functions and math functions. However, not all statements related to this book will be placed in a special section, but it will be discussed on each topic in its section, respectively.

CHAPTER 2

EXCEL FUNCTIONS

Almost identical to the definition of a function in mathematics, a function in Excel works based on the given arguments and can be written as follows:

$$y = f(a,b,c,\ldots)$$

where y is the Result, f is the Name, and $(a,b,c,\ldots)$ are the Argument/s.

Arguments are written after the function name, between parentheses, which are the values used to perform the operation. The argument can be a numerical value, text, reference or range of cell, name, label or a function.

Excel functions are listed by category such as math and trigonometry, statistical, financial, and logical. In addition, Excel also provides macrosheet and Visual Basic for Applications (VBA) to create functions defined by the user (user-defined functions).

2.1 MATH AND TRIGONOMETRY FUNCTIONS

ABS

Returns the absolute value of a number.

Syntax:

ABS(number)

Example:

ABS(4) = 4

ABS(-4) = 4

SQRT(ABS(-81)) = 9

INT

Rounds a number down to the nearest integer

Syntax:

INT(number)

Example:

INT(8.9) = 8

INT(-8.9) = -9

TRUNC

Makes a number to an integer by removing the fractional part of the number. To specify the precision of the truncation, enter a specified number of digits after the number.

Syntax:

TRUNC (number,number_digits)

Example:

TRUNC(8.9) = 8

TRUNC(-8.9) = -8

TRUNC(PI ()) = 3

TRUNC(PI (), 3) = 3,141

ROUND

Rounds a number to a specified number of digits.

Syntax:

ROUND(number,num_digits)

Example:

ROUND(3.25,1) = 3.3

ROUND(3.247,1) = 3.2

ROUND(3.247,0) = 3

ROUND(32.47,-1) = 30

ROUNDOWN

Rounds a number down to a specified number of digits.

Syntax:

ROUNDDOWN (number,number_digits)

Example:

ROUNDDOWN(3.3,0) = 3

ROUNDDOWN(66.8,0) = 66

ROUNDDOWN(3.14159,3) = 3,141

ROUNDDOWN(-5.24621,2) = -5.24

ROUNDDOWN(1550.24621,-2) = 1500

ROUNDUP

Rounds a number up to the desired number of digits.

Syntax:

ROUNDUP (number, num_digits)

Example:

ROUNDUP (3.3, 0) = 4

ROUNDUP (66.8, 0) = 67

ROUNDUP (3.14159, 3) = 3,142

ROUNDUP (-5.24621, 2) = -5.25

ROUNDUP (1550.24621,-2) = 1600

SUMPRODUCT

The number resulted by multiplying corresponding components of arrays

Syntax:

SUMPRODUCT(array1,array2,...)

Example

SUMPRODUCT(1,2,3) = 1 x 2 x 3 = 6

SUMPRODUCT({1,2,3},{4,5,6}) = 1 x 4 + 2 x 5 + 3 x 6 = 36

SUMPRODUCT({1,2,3,"hello"},{4,5,6,5}) = 36

2.2 Logical Functions

IF

This function has two results, TRUE and FALSE, with logical test, if met will do the TRUE value. If the result returns a text, then the text must be between quotes ("text").

Syntax:

IF(logical_test,value_ if true,value_if_ false)

Example 1:

In an examination, students that score below or equal to (<=) 55 will FAIL the exam, and above the value will PASS the exam. Find students with the criteria above.

Name	Score	Remark
V. Magda	51	FAIL	← =IF(B3<=55,"FAIL","PASS")
Y. Artist	93	PASS
L. Money	90	PASS
M. House	70	PASS
H. Aunt	37	FAIL

Result of copying cell from C3 to C4:C7

Example 2: Nested IFs with two logical tests

Students who FAIL with scores > 45 have a chance to take a supplementary exam (re-exam) to increase their scores. Find students with the criteria above.

	A	B	C
2	Name	Score	Remark
3	V. Magda	51	RE-EXAM ← =IF(B3<=45,"FAIL",IF(B3<=55,"RE-EXAM","PASS"))
4	Y. Artist	93	PASS
5	L. Money	90	PASS
6	M. House	70	PASS
7	H. Aunt	37	FAIL

Result of copying cell from C3 to C4:C7

AND

Returns TRUE if all of its arguments are TRUE, and returns FALSE if one of its argument is FALSE. Generally nested with IF function.

Syntax:

AND(logical_1, logical_2, ...)

Example 1:

AND(2*2=4,2+2=4)   Returns TRUE

AND(2<100,4<100,102<100)   Returns FALSE

Example 2:

Now, with the same class and the same students as in Example 1, but with different examination subject where an extracurricular course score can improve the scores > 40 and <= 55. The given formula = (2 x Exam score + 1 x Course score) / 3.

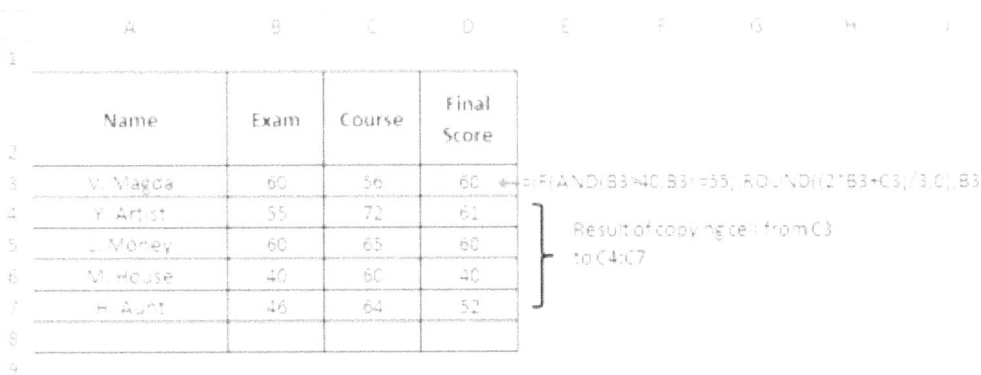

	A	B	C	D
2	Name	Exam	Course	Final Score
3	V. Magda	60	56	60 ← =IF(AND(B3>40,B3<=55),ROUND((2*B3+C3)/3,0),B3)
4	Y. Artist	55	72	61
5	L. Money	60	65	60
6	M. House	40	60	40
7	H. Aunt	46	64	52

Result of copying cell from C3 to C4:C7

COUNTIF

Counting the number of cells in a range of cells according to given criteria.

Syntax:

COUNTIF(range,criteria)

Example 1

Looking for the number of students with specified value for Example 2 above:

COUNTIF(D2: D6,60) = 2

COUNTIF(D2: D6,> 60) = 1

OR

The result is TRUE if one of its arguments is TRUE. Generally nested the IF function.

Syntax:

OR(logical1,logical2, ...)

Example:

OR(2*2 = 4,2+2=4)   Returns TRUE

OR(2<100,4<100,102<100)   Returns TRUE

2.3 Lookup Functions

VLOOKUP

Search for a value based on the column index in the data table arranged vertically

Syntax:

VLOOKUP(value,table,col_index,range_lookup)

Example

The experimental result of laboratory test is affected by the size and weight of the used tools. This example shows how to use VLOOKUP function to read the size and weight of rings based on the **Ring Calibration** table. Suppose it is intended to search the diameter and weight of ring no. 3 and 7. The data table refers to cell range A4 to F11, ignoring the column heading.

	A	B	C	D	E	F
1	RING CALIBRATION					
2						
3	Ring No.	Height (cm)	Diameter (cm)	Weight (gram)	Area (cm^2)	Volume (cm^3)
4	1	1.950	5.000	32.850	19.635	38.288
5	2	2.000	5.000	32.000	19.635	39.270
6	3	2.000	5.000	33.440	19.635	39.270
7	4	2.000	5.000	34.980	19.635	39.270
8	5	1.950	5.000	33.700	19.635	38.288
9	6	1.925	4.985	32.000	19.517	37.571
10	7	2.000	5.000	33.000	19.635	39.270
11	8	1.975	5.125	34.000	20.629	39.711

VLOOKUP result:

	A	B	C	D	E	F
14	Ring No.	Diameter (cm)	Weight (gram)			
15	3	5.000	33.440			
16	7	5.000	33.000			

Formula in cell B15 to C16:

	A	B	C
14	Ring No.	Diameter (cm)	Weight (gram)
15	3	=VLOOKUP(A15,$A$4:$F$11,3)	=VLOOKUP(A15,$A$4:$F$11,4)
16	7	=VLOOKUP(A16,$A$4:$F$11,3)	=VLOOKUP(A16,$A$4:$F$11,4)

Range_lookup is a logical value that specifies whether VLOOKUP finds an exact match or an approximate match. If TRUE (or omitted), the values in the first column of table_array must be in ascending sort order (-2, -1,0,1,2, ..) because VLOOKUP may return an incorrect result. If FALSE, the table_array values do not need to be sorted. For TRUE condition, if the lookup_value does not match with table_array, VLOOKUP returns the next largest value that is less than lookup_value. Otherwise, if FALSE, VLOOKUP will find an exact match, if it is not found, VLOOKUP returns #N/A (error).

HLOOKUP

Search for a value based on the row index in the data table arranged horizontally. The application of HLOOKUP are almost identical to VLOOKUP, in exception that row index is used to lookup the value.

Syntax:

HLOOKUP(value,table,row_index,range_lookup)

Example

Transpose (**Copy** > **Paste Special** > **Transpose**) the Ring Calibration table to arrange data table as shown below. Further, use HLOOKUP the same way as VLOOKUP example above to search the diameter and weight of ring no. 3 and 7.

Ring No.	1	2	3	4	5	6	7	8
Height (cm)	1.95	2.00	2.00	2.00	1.95	1.93	2.00	1.98
Diameter (cm)	5.00	5.00	5.00	5.00	5.00	4.99	5.00	5.13
Weight (gram)	32.85	32.00	33.44	34.98	33.70	32.00	33.00	34.00
Area (cm^2)	19.64	19.64	19.64	19.64	19.64	19.52	19.64	20.63
Volume (cm^3)	38.29	39.27	39.27	39.27	38.29	37.57	39.27	39.71

2.4 TEXT FUNCTIONS

LEFT, RIGHT, MID

Returns characters in a text string based on the specified number of characters

=**LEFT**(text,num_chars)

Returns the first character

=**RIGHT**(text,num_chars)

Returns the last character

=**MID**(text,start_num,num_chars)

Returns characters starting at specified position

Example

	A	B	
1	ENGINEERING	ENG	=LEFT(A1,3)
2	745.56	RING	=RIGHT(A1,4)
3		ENGINEER	=MID(A1,1,8)
4		745.5	=LEFT(A2,5)

CONCATENATE

Combines two or more strings from different cells into one string

Example

	A	B	C	D
1				
2	Civil	Engineer		Civil Engineer
3				
4		Point		Coordinate
5	x	y	z	
6	2.0	4.0	0.0	2,4,0
7	2.0	4.0	-1.5	2,4,-1.5
8	2.0	4.0	-1.5	(2,4,-1.5)

	D	
1		
2	Civil Engineer	=CONCATENATE(A2," ",B2)
3		
4	Coordinate	
5		
6	2,4,0	=CONCATENATE(A6,",",B6,",",C6)
7	2,4,-1.5	=CONCATENATE(A7,",",B7,",",C7)
8	(2,4,-1.5)	=CONCATENATE("(",A8,",",B8,",",C8,")")

Another way is to use the way of writing as the following:

numeric **&** "text" **&** numeric

Example

	A	B	C	D
1				
2	Civil	Engineer		Civil Engineer
3				
4		Point		Coordinate
5	x	y	z	
6	2.0	4.0	0.0	2,4,0
7	2.0	4.0	-1.5	2,4,-1.5
8	2.0	4.0	-1.5	(2,4,-1.5)

	D	
1		
2	Civil Engineer	=A2&" "&B2
3		

4	Coordinate	
5		
6	2,4,0	=A6&","&B6&","&C6
7	2,4,-1.5	=A7&" "&B7&","&C7
8	(2,4,-1.5)	="("&A8&","&B8&","&C8&")"

2.5 DATA ANALYSIS FUNCTIONS

Excel has many built-in functions that are used to analyze data obtained from experimental results. The objective of the analysis is to obtain theoretical parameters that give the best relationship between theories and the experimental results. Three methods will be discussed here: linear regression, polynomial regression and interpolation.

2.5.1 LINEAR REGRESSION

Linear regression is to determine a straight line that best fits or the most closely fits a number of data points, providing a linear relationship between two variables. The method used to obtain the line is by using the least squares method. Thus, linear regression consists of a series of points that fit to a number (n) of data points (x_i, y_i) written into a straight line equation:

$$y = Ax + B \tag{2.1}$$

where:

A = slope of the line,

B = the intersection of the straight line to the Y-axis

The accuracy of the straight line over a number of data points is evaluated by a total deviation (E), which is the sum of squares of distance (**e**) between the data points and the fitted points:

$$E = \sum_{i=1}^{n} e_i^2 = \sum_{i=1}^{n} (Ax_i + B - y_i)^2 \tag{2.2}$$

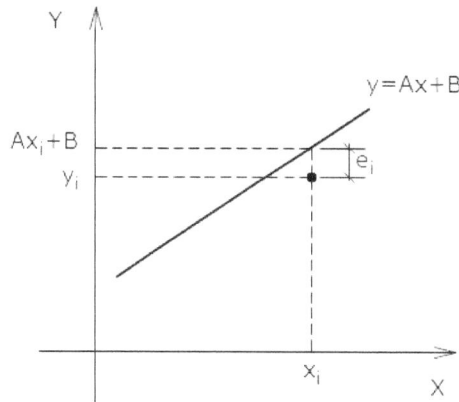

By making E to minimum, A and B values can therefore be determined to write Equation 2.1. Beside E, R^2 value is also used for the accuracy measurement, where:

$$R^2 = 1 - \frac{\sum_{i=1}^{n}[y_i - f(x_i)]^2}{\sum_{i=1}^{n}y_i^2 - \frac{1}{n}\left(\sum_{i=1}^{n}y_i\right)^2} \qquad (2.3)$$

R^2 values vary from 0 to 1. $R^2 = 1$ is when the regression line coincides with the data. In polynomial regression, the higher-order of polynomial, the closer R^2 value to = 1.

Regression in Excel can be obtained by using the **TREND**, **SLOPE**, **INTERCEPT** and **LINEST** functions or using the **Trendline** option, which is a graphic presentation of trends in data series. The Trendline is created by the following steps: right-click the mouse when the pointer at any data points in the chart to display the shortcut menus > click **Add Trendline** to display the **Format Trendline** dialog box > select **Linear** for linear regression.

Example 1: Linear Regression

The soil shear strength determination in a laboratory obtains the result as shown in Figure 2.1. In general, the depiction of data generated from the test is rarely a straight line to show failure envelope, therefore it needs a fitted straight line to represent the data. Regression is used to represent shear strength parameters (that is, cohesion (c) and friction angle (ϕ)) of the soil mass.

In direct shear test, the failure envelope is a straight line expressed as:

$\tau = c + \sigma_n \tan \phi$

where, τ shear strength

         c cohesion intercept

         σ_n normal stress

         ϕ friction angle, is given by the slope of the failure envelope

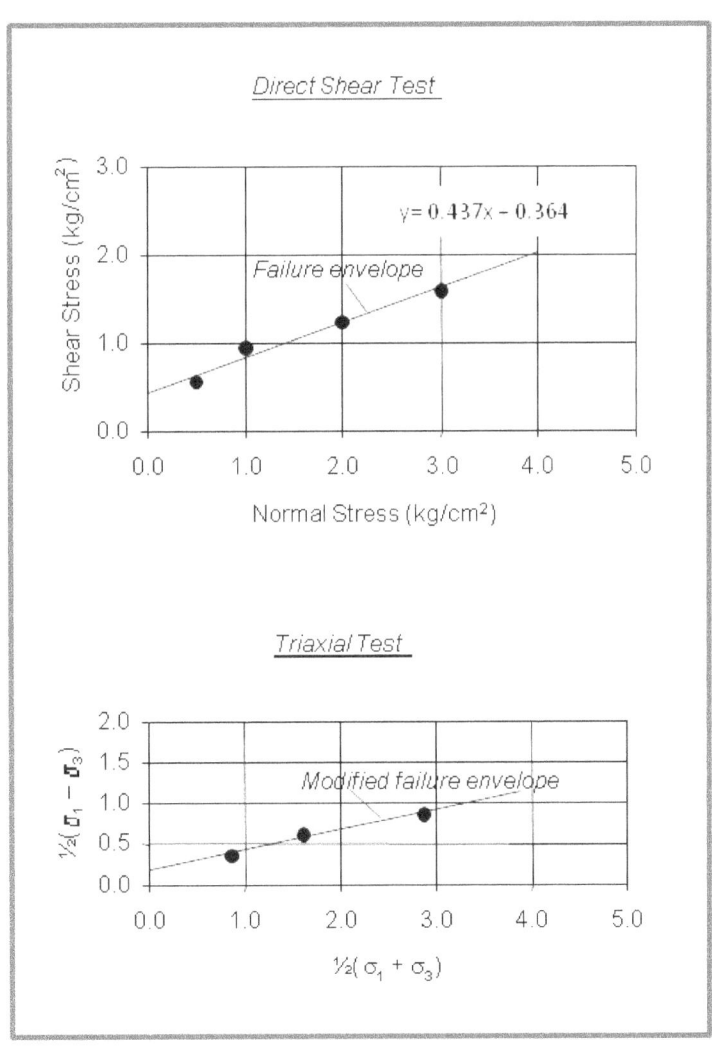

Figure 2.1: Regression on Excel Chart

Shear strength in this model is a linear function of the normal stress, where c and tan ϕ, respectively, expresses Y-axis intercept and slope of the line.

To display the failure envelope lines shown in Figure 2.1, right-click the mouse when the pointer at any data points in the chart to display the shortcut menu, and then select **Add Trendline** to display the **Format Trendline** dialog box > **Linear** > **Backward** to intercept Y-axis > click **Display Equation on Chart**.

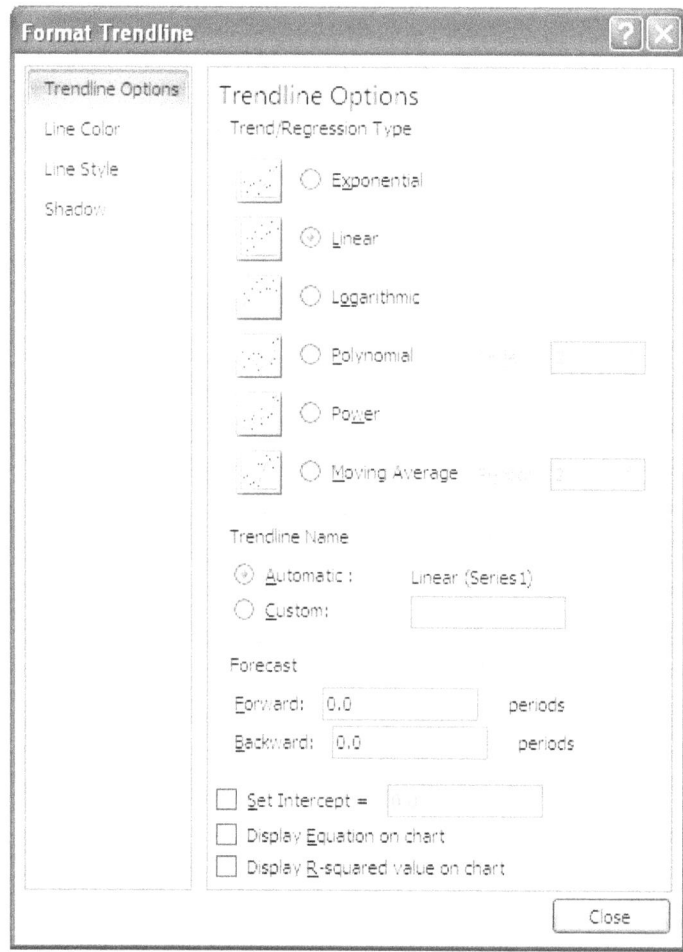

The values of A and B in equation y = Ax + B resulted from the direct shear test (Figure 2.1) can also be obtained using the following functions:

A = slope of the line = tan ϕ = SLOPE(Y,X)

B = Y-intercept = INTERCEPT(Y,X)

Moreover, friction angle ϕ can be calculated using ATAN function (in degree):

=ATAN(SLOPE(Y,X))*180/PI()

Another option is using LINEST and TREND functions that are written as follows:

=INDEX(LINEST(Y,X),1) to obtain Slope,

=INDEX(LINEST(Y,X),2) to obtain Y-intercept

The TREND function is commonly used on a data series made in a worksheet to obtain fitted points based on a number of known Y and X values. The formulas are as follows:

	A	B	C	D	E
1	Direct Shear Test				
2		Normal Stress	Shear Stress	Fitted Shear	
3					
4		0.50	0.50	0.583	=TREND($C$4:$C$7,$B$4:$B$7,B4)
5		0.90	1.00	0.802	
6		1.25	2.00	1.239	Result of copying cell from D4 to D5..D8
7		1.65	3.00	1.676	
8	Y-Intercept =		0.00	0.364	
9					

Shear strength of a soil can also be expressed in major σ_1 and minor σ_3 principal stresses in a laboratory triaxial test by plotting ½($\sigma_1 - \sigma_3$) against ½($\sigma_1 + \sigma_3$). The stress condition that fits a number of data points is referred to as modified failure envelope, which is given by the following equation:

$$½(\sigma_1 - \sigma_3) = a + ½(\sigma_1 + \sigma_3) \tan \alpha$$

where a and α are the modified shear strength parameters. The parameters c and ϕ are then given by:

$$\phi = \sin^{-1}(\tan \alpha)$$

$$c = \frac{a}{\cos \phi}$$

Example 2: Logarithmic Regression

It is also often presented that the X-axis is made in log scale as shown Figure 2.2. In log scale, re-write Equation 2.1 becomes,

$$y = A \ln(x) + B \tag{2.4}$$

where A and B are constants

In this example, we adopt laboratory liquid limit (LL) test, i.e. to determine soil moisture content at 25 blows. See the descriptions below:

- Moisture content (Wn) = [(weight of wet soil - weight of dry soil) / (weight of dry soil)] x 100%.
- Water content' (Wn') = fitted Wn in semi-log relationship.
- N = number of blows

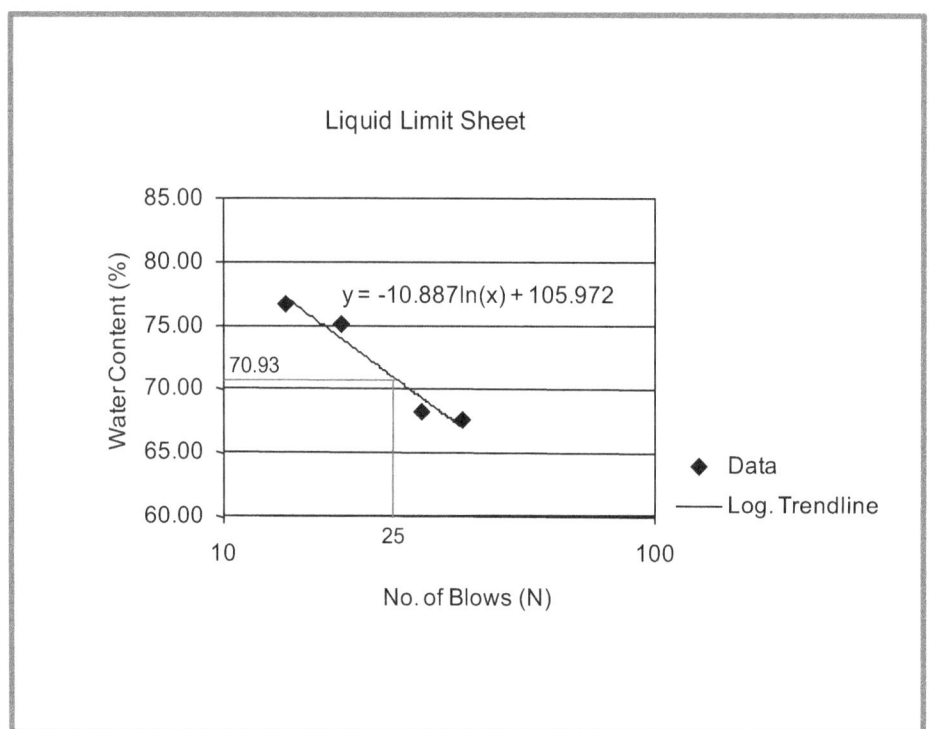

Figure 2.2: Regression on Semi-log Liquid Limit Test

Figure 2.2 shows the LL test result and a regression line created through **Add Trendline** command. The fitted Wn values (Wn') that represent a number of Wn for each N value can be obtained through the equation below:

y = -10.887ln(x) + 105.972

Using the equation, at N = 25 blows, the related fitted Wn = 70.93%.

The calculation sheet of LL test is made in a worksheet as follows:

	A	B	C	D	E	F	G
1		**LIQUID LIMIT TEST**					
2							
3	No.	Weight of	Can +	Can +		Water	Fitted
4	Set	Can (gr)	Soil (gr)	Dry Soil (gr)	Blows	Content (%)	Wn (%)
5		Wc	Ws	Wd	N	Wn	Wn'
6	1	8.3	52.46	33.29	14	76.71	77.24
7	2	2.8	55.61	32.96	19	75.10	73.92
8	3	2.8	57.14	35.12	29	68.13	69.31
9	4	7.8	52.72	34.62	36	67.49	66.96

Liquid Limit (%) = 70.93

3	Water	Fitted
4	Content (%)	Wn (%)
5	Wn	Wn'
6	=100*(C6-D6)/(D6-B6)	=TREND(Wn,LOG10(N),LOG10(E6))
7	=100*(C7-D7)/(D7-B7)	=TREND(Wn,LOG10(N),LOG10(E7))

Liquid Limit (%) =TREND(Wn,LOG10(N),LOG10(25))

Based on data provided in the calculation sheet above, we can draw a regression line as shown in Figure 2.2.

Example 3: Log-log Regression

In the third example, we will examine regression on the data that is formed in log-log scale in an XY coordinate system. The given data is the standard sieve size (US) used for the particle size distribution of granular material as shown in Figure 2.3.

An Introduction to Excel for Civil Engineers

	A	B	C	D
1	Sieve	Sieve	Fitted	
2	No.	Size	Sieve Size	
3	(US)	(mm)	(mm)	
4	N	S		Formula :
5	4	4.750	5.142	=10^TREND(LOG10(S),LOG10(N),LOG10(A5))
6	5	4.000	4.031	=10^TREND(LOG10(S),LOG10(N),LOG10(A6))
7	6	3.350	3.305	=10^TREND(LOG10(S),LOG10(N),LOG10(A7))
8	7	2.800	2.794	Copy the formula down...
9	8	2.360	2.415	
10	10	2.000	1.894	
11	12	1.700	1.552	
12	14	1.400	1.312	
13	16	1.180	1.134	
14	18	1.000	0.998	
15	20	0.850	0.889	
16	25	0.710	0.697	
17	30	0.600	0.572	
18	35	0.500	0.483	
19	40	0.425	0.418	
20	45	0.355	0.367	
21	50	0.300	0.328	
22	60	0.250	0.268	
23	70	0.212	0.227	
24	80	0.180	0.196	
25	100	0.150	0.154	
26	120	0.125	0.126	
27	140	0.106	0.107	
28	170	0.090	0.086	
29	200	0.075	0.072	
30	230	0.063	0.062	
31	270	0.053	0.052	
32	325	0.045	0.043	
33	400	0.038	0.034	
34	500	0.025	0.027	

Figure 2.3: Formulas for Log-log data relationship

Regression in log-log data relationship can be obtained using formulas as given in Figure 2.3, or adding the Trendline by the following steps: click the **Add Trendline > Power > Display equation on chart and the R-squared value on the graph**, and the result will be shown in Figure 2.4. The general equation of Power Trendline is:

$$y = 10^c X^a, \quad c \text{ and } a = \text{constant} \tag{2.5}$$

Slope and Y-intercept are respectively the constants a and c in equation 2.5. The formulas for this series are, respectively:

=SLOPE(LOG (S),LOG (N)) = -1.09022

=INTERCEPT(LOG (S),LOG (N)) = 1.36749

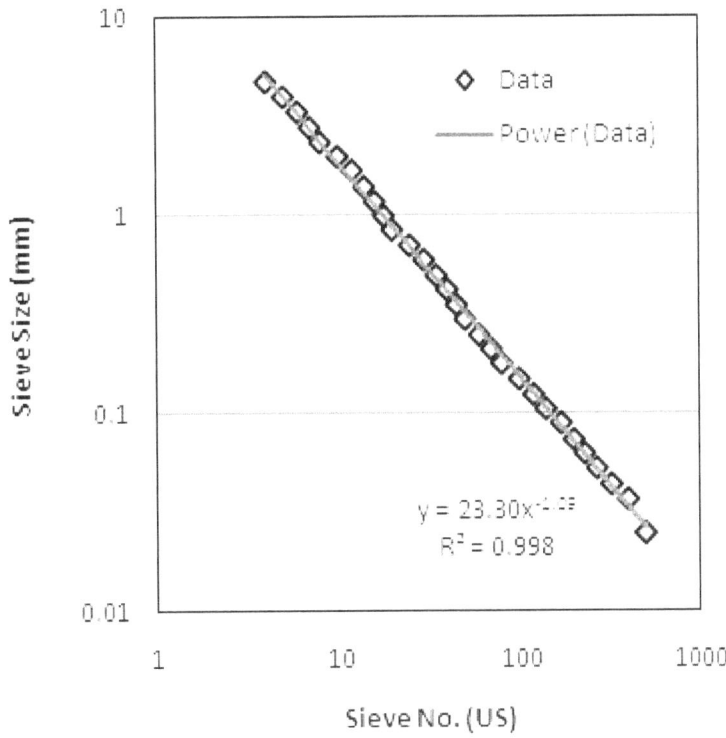

Figure 2.4: Chart from Figure 2.3 data series where TREND function is used to obtain the fitted points

2.5.2 Polynomial Regression

Polynomial regression is used to obtain fitted points of a number of data points, which have a curve (nonlinear) trend in XY coordinate system. Thus, polynomial regression consists of fitted points of a number (n) of data points (x_i, y_i) into a polynomial function form:

$$f(x) = a_m x^m + a_{m-1} x^{m-1} + \ldots + a_1 x + a_0 \qquad (2.6)$$

The polynomial 2.6 is called a polynomial function of order m, where m = a positive integer. Linear regression is a polynomial regression of the first degree (the exponent m = 1).

	A	B
1	Temp (°C)	Unit Mass (gr/cm³)
2	X	Y
3	4	1.00000
4	16	0.99897
5	17	0.99880
6	18	0.99862
7	19	0.99844
8	20	0.99823
9	21	0.99802
10	22	0.99780
11	23	0.99757
12	24	0.99733
13	25	0.99708
14	26	0.99682
15	27	0.99655
16	28	0.99627
17	29	0.99598
18	30	0.99568

Figure 2.5: Example of a data series for polynomial regression

Example

Figure 2.5 shows a data series from the relationship between water density and temperature, where X-coordinate is the temperature (°C) and the Y-coordinate is the water density (g/cm³). By plotting Y-values against X-values, it is apparently visible that the result is a curve trend.

Figure 2.6 shows a chart of the plotted data from Figure 2.5. Regression lines are created using **Trendline**, that is, to obtain Linear and Polynomial regressions. It is apparently seen that the polynomial regression is much better than the linear regression for this data series. The fitted points produced from polynomials of order 2 and 3 seem like really coincide with the data and are only distinguished by the value of R^2, where for order 3 (red curve) the value of $R^2 = 1$. Excel 2007 provides polynomial regression up to order 6.

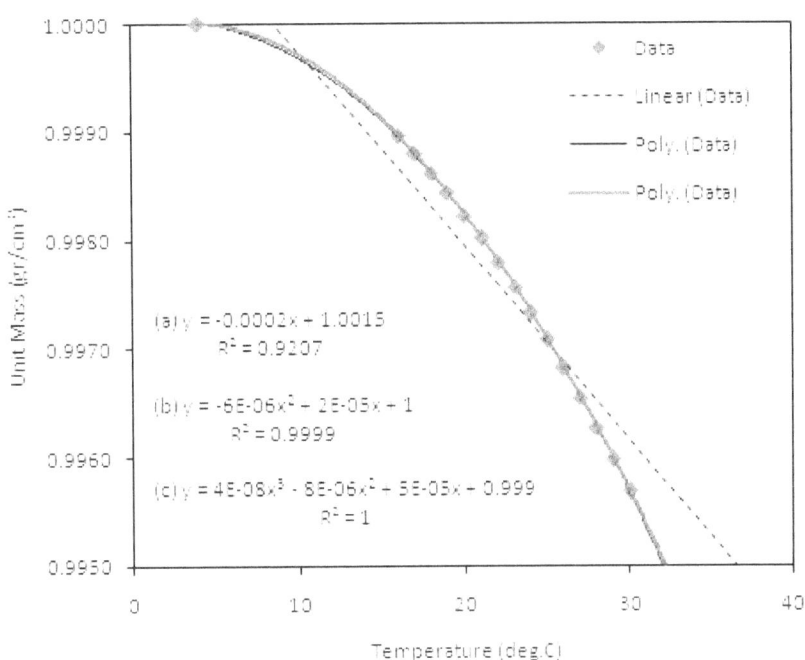

Figure 2.6: Regression analysis using Trendline for data series in Figure 2.5

2.5.3 INTERPOLATION

In an engineering calculation, sometimes we need to perform interpolation of data points without resolve the data into regression analysis. Here is to find a y-value that corresponds to known x-values of a line segment, based on a number of data (x_i, y_i) tabulation, where x_i may continuously be increased or decreased. Linear interpolation of the y-value that corresponds to the x-values is:

$$y = y_i + \frac{y_{i+1} - y_i}{x_{i+1} - x_i}(x - x_i) \tag{2.7}$$

where $(x - x_i)(x - x_{i+1}) \leq 0$ and $x_i \neq x_{i+1}$

If y and x-axis are made in linear and log scale, respectively (semi-log), thus equation 2.7 becomes:

An Introduction to Excel for Civil Engineers

$$\ln(y) = \ln(y_i) + \frac{\ln(y_{i+1}) - \ln(y_i)}{x_{i+1} - x_i}(x - x_i) \qquad (2.8)$$

where $(x - x_i)(x - x_{i+1}) \leq 0$ and $x_i \neq x_{i+1}$

Equation 2.8 can also be written:

$$\ln\frac{y}{y_i} = \frac{x - x_i}{x_{i+1} - x_i} \ln\frac{y_{i+1}}{y_i} \qquad (2.9)$$

Or,

$$y = y_i \left(\frac{y_{i+1}}{y_i}\right)^{(x - x_i)/(x_{i+1} - x_i)} \qquad (2.10)$$

In Excel, the linear interpolation can be performed using **TREND** function. Data series for this function is a line segment formed by x_i, y_i and x_{i+1}, y_{i+1}.

Example 1: Linear Interpolation

Given below is a data series of X and Y-array for interpolation:

Table 2.1: Data Series for Linear Interpolation

Data X	Data Y
0	-1
1	0
2	4
3	5
4	-1
5	-2
6	0
7	3

Plotted in a chart:

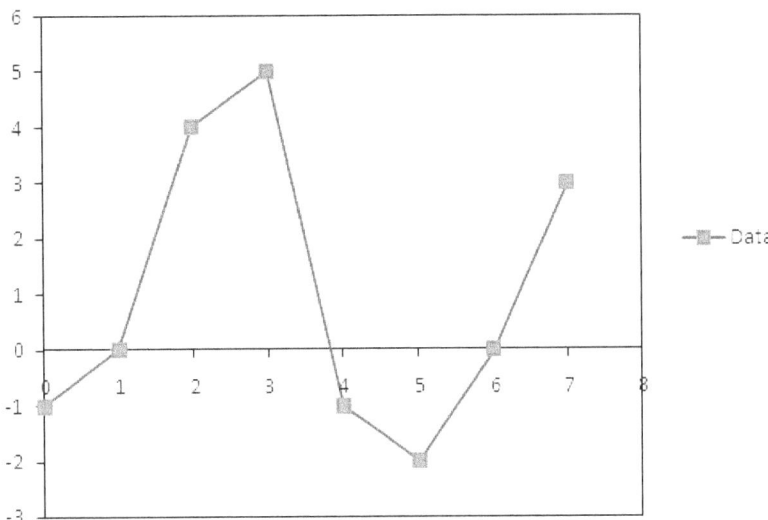

The worksheets below show formulas to obtain the interpolation of data presented in Table 2.1 by using TREND function and Equation 2.7, respectively.

Using the TREND function:

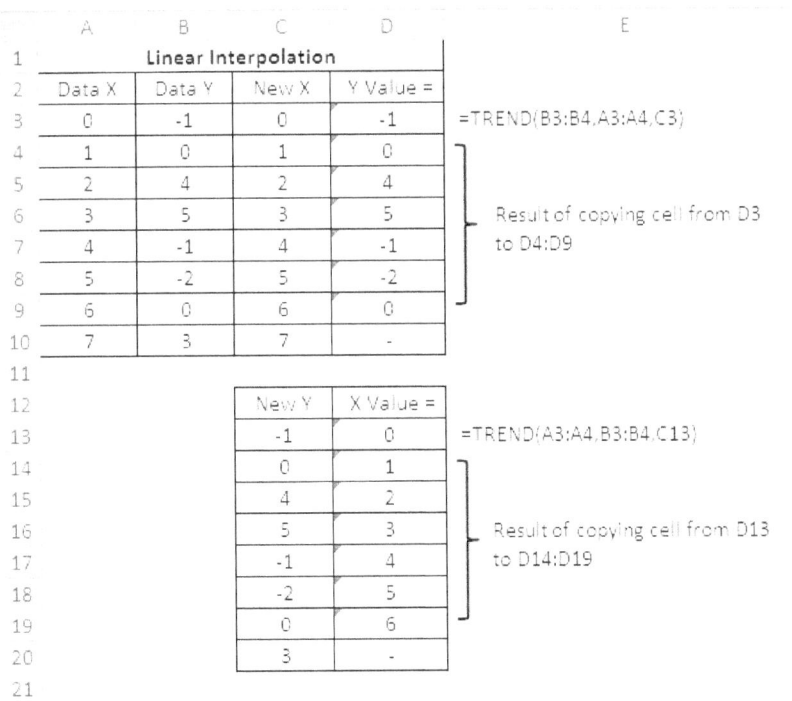

Using Equation 2.7:

An Introduction to Excel for Civil Engineers   55

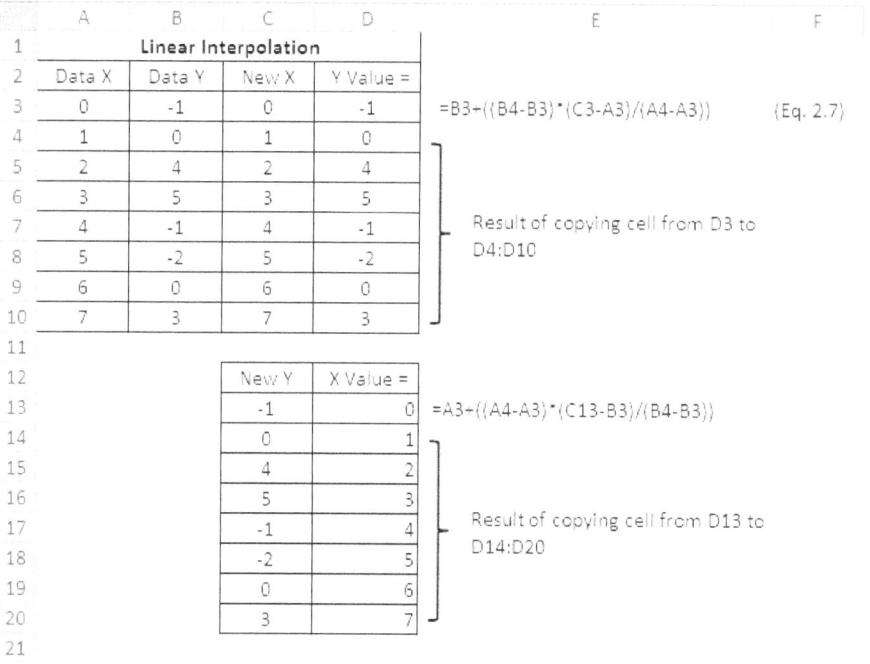

The interpolated values are shown in column D, which correspond to new values entered in column C. More specific, the y-value that corresponds to x-value that lies between 0 - 1 in cell C3 is shown in cell D3; the y-value that corresponds to x-value that lies between 1 - 2 in cell C4 is shown in cell D4, and so forth.

TREND function and Equation 2.7 can also be used to interpolate x-values from known y-values by replacing the variable x with y and vice versa in Equation 2.7, or by switching x and y-argument in the TREND function. The formulas are shown in the table at row 12 to row 20, columns C and D, in the worksheet above.

Example 2: Logarithmic Interpolation

A sands soil sample of 1,000 grams weight is taken and placed in a sieving machine for the sieve analysis test. The data presented in Table 2.2 shows the used sieve size and percent finer results. The percent finer (or percent passing) is calculated based on cumulative weight of soil retained on each sieve. Figure 2.7 shows a chart of log grain sizes versus percent finer of the soil.

Table 2.2: Sieve Analysis Results

	A	B
1	Sieve Size	Finer
2	(mm)	%
3	9.50	100.00
4	4.75	97.80
5	2.36	95.48
6	1.18	88.50
7	0.60	70.60
8	0.30	24.10
9	0.15	2.40
10		0.00

Logarithmic interpolation for this data series, for an example, is to obtain grain size distribution in percentage of weight of the sample that corresponds to 60 percent finer (D60). The corresponding value can be obtained using Equation 2.10, and formulas for semi-log interpolation are made in a worksheet as follows:

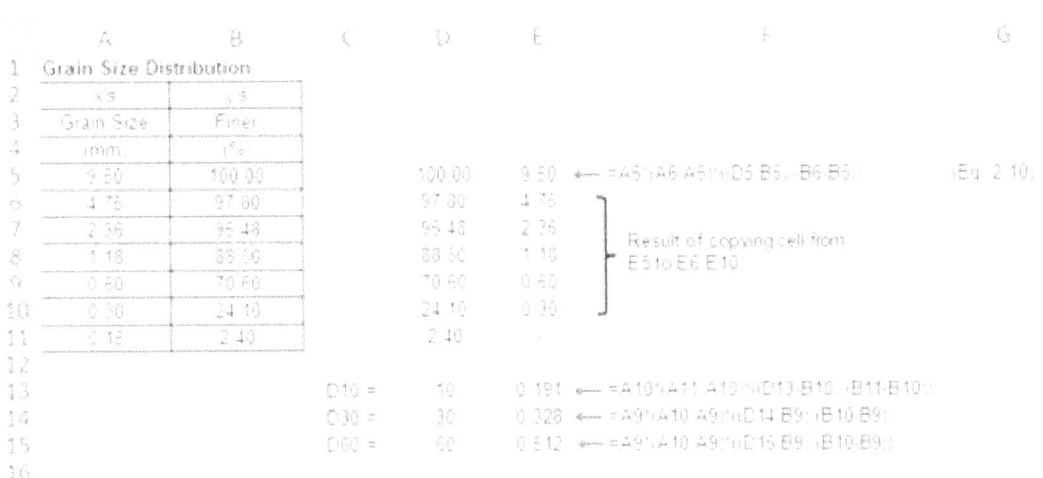

Plotted in a chart:

An Introduction to Excel for Civil Engineers

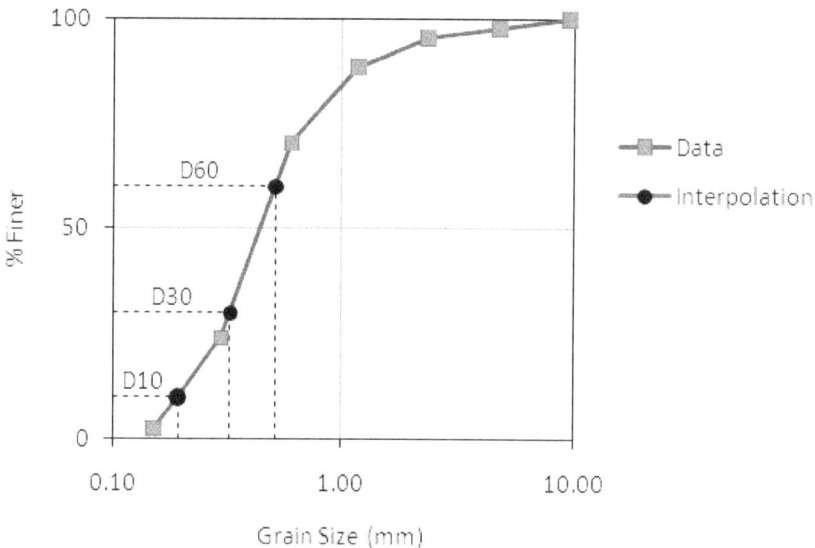

Figure 2.7: Semilog interpolation for the data of Table 2.2

Notes:

- There is however a more-more flexible way to obtain the data interpolation, which to resolve them with macros (custom functions) based on Equation 2.7 or 2.10. When entered into a macro, formulas can be "shortened" and simply replaced by a looping, as it does not "depend" on a line segment where a known value is placed. The discussion of creating custom function macros will be in the following chapter, on the topic of user-defined function.
- The interpretation on sieve analysis result includes a determination of how "well" the gradation of sands soil. The gradation of grained particles (silt to gravel) can be measured by the coefficient of uniformity (C_U) and the curvature coefficient (C_C) defined as follows:

$$C_U = \frac{D_{60}}{D_{10}}, \quad C_C = \frac{D_{30}^2}{D_{60} D_{10}}$$

The greater the value of C_U, the greater the range of grain sizes in the sample, where a well graded soil usually has C_C value between 1 and 3.

2.5.4 STATISTICAL DATA

Histogram and Cumulative Distribution

In a presentation of statistical data, it is convenient to make a data from observation into histogram to see the data distribution. In histogram, the observed data is plotted against its frequency distribution in giving a visual summary on the observed data and a quick impression on the distribution.

Example

The following is concrete compressive strength data selected randomly from 40 samples obtained from the characteristics compressive strength test:

Concrete compressive strength test result (kg/cm^2)			
376.28	399.30	375.41	370.41
394.43	409.47	393.53	371.43
387.19	374.34	386.30	372.44
390.35	392.29	389.46	390.30
401.27	386.78	390.37	384.82
379.95	361.23	379.08	362.28
380.97	402.90	380.10	400.86
389.33	368.22	388.44	366.35
384.64	399.20	383.76	407.46
396.34	365.36	398.83	363.51

To simplify the distribution, the results are divided into several classes with an interval (taken) of 5 kg/cm^2, and then tabulated in Table 2.3. The score from each class is called class frequency, which is represented by height of the bar. To ease data distribution process into classes, it is common to be done using a function macro or custom function. The discussion of creating custom functions will be presented in the next chapter on the topic of user-defined functions.

Table 2.3: Data distribution to create a histogram

Class Interval kg/cm²	Mid Point kg/cm²	Frequency N	Percent (%)	Cumulative (%)
360-365	362.5	3	7.5	7.5
365-370	367.5	3	7.5	15.0
370-375	372.5	4	10.0	25.0
375-380	377.5	4	10.0	35.0
380-385	382.5	5	12.5	47.5
385-390	387.5	6	15.0	62.5
390-395	392.5	6	15.0	77.5
395-400	397.5	4	10.0	87.5
400-405	402.5	3	7.5	95.0
405-410	407.5	2	5.0	100.0
		40	100.0	

The histogram chart shown in Figure 2.8 presents the data in Table 2.3.

To create a histogram, take the following steps: click the **Insert** tab > **Column** > **Column clusterd** > **Select Dat**a > **Add** > **Series Values**: select range "Percentage" > **OK**. Click **Edit for Horizontal Axis Labe**ls > insert range "Mid Point".

To create cumulative frequency chart as shown in Figure 2.9, select **XY scatter chart with smoothlines and markers** > **Select Data** > **Add** > **Series X values**: select range "Mid Point" > **Y-values**: select range "Cumulative".

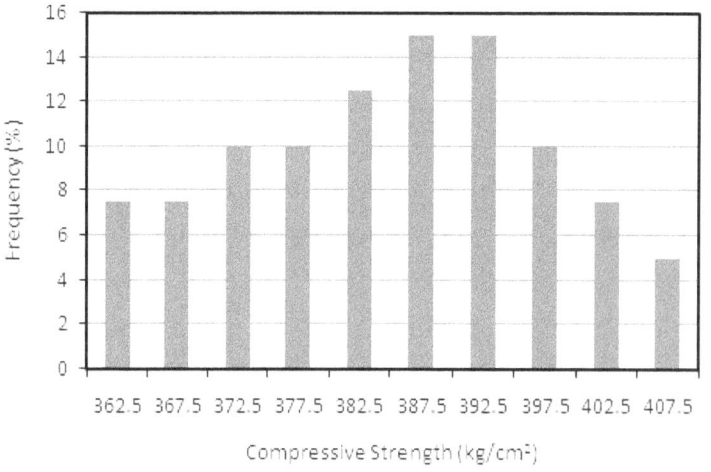

Figure 2.8: Histogram of concrete compressive strength

An Introduction to Excel for Civil Engineers

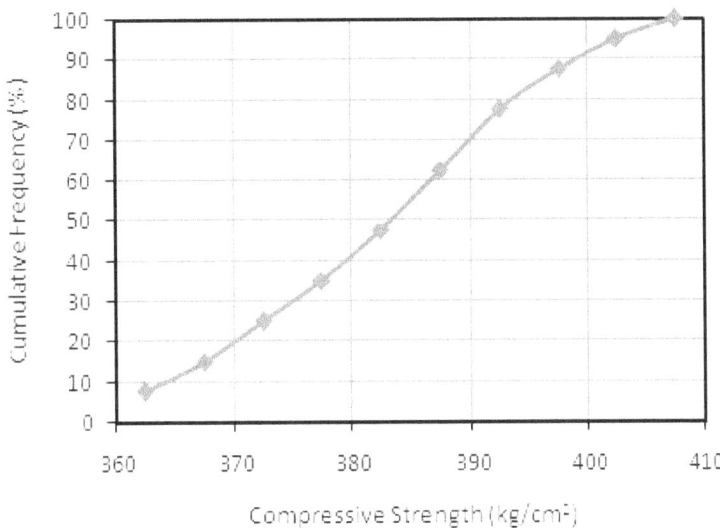

Figure 2.9: Cumulative frequency of concrete compressive strength

Range, Mean and Standard Deviation

The classification or data distribution is generally defined into three statistical parameters, namely range, mean and standard deviation. Range is the difference between the lowest and the highest value of data. The concrete compressive strength test above results the range = 48.24 kg/cm², that is, from the lowest of 361.23 to the highest of 409.47 kg/cm². Mean or average is the sum of all the data values divided by the total number of data (n). From the test, the mean is obtained = 384.87 kg/cm². If a set of data values divided into M classes, the mean formula is written:

$$\bar{x} = \frac{\sum_{i=1}^{M} m_i x_i}{n} \qquad (2.11)$$

Where,

m_i = frequency of class interval i

x_i = mid point of class interval i

The mean is a value that commonly used to represent values of a set of data. In consistent with this, several measurements are made to state deviation, and one of them is a formulation of mean square deviation (MSD). The MSD is also called variance given by the following formula:

An Introduction to Excel for Civil Engineers

$$\frac{\sum_{i=1}^{M} m_i (x_i - \bar{x})^2}{n} \tag{2.12}$$

Another measurement that commonly used is the standard deviation (S), which is the square root of MSD:

$$S = \sqrt{\frac{\sum_{i=1}^{M} m_i (x_i - \bar{x})^2}{n}} \tag{2.13}$$

According to Equation 2.13, the standard deviation of the sample data presented in Table 2.3 is equal to 12.49 kg/cm² and for divisor = n - 1 (calculated from the sample), MSD and S is respectively equal to 394.74 and 16.12 kg/cm². The standard deviation is a measure of dispersion of a set of data values from the Mean; where a big or small of the value indicates the quality of job execution.

Normal Distribution

From the histogram data and measurement of statistical parameters above, a normal distribution curve can be made. The normal distribution function is,

$$f(x, S, \bar{x}) = \frac{1}{S\sqrt{2\pi}} e^{-\frac{1}{2}\left(\frac{x-\bar{x}}{S}\right)^2} \tag{2.14}$$

The log-normal distribution is given by replacing x with ln(x) in Equation 2.14.

Figure 2.10 and 2.11 respectively show normal distribution curves that fit the frequencies and the cumulative frequencies data given in Table 2.3. Figure 2.12 shows the formulas used in presentation of the result.

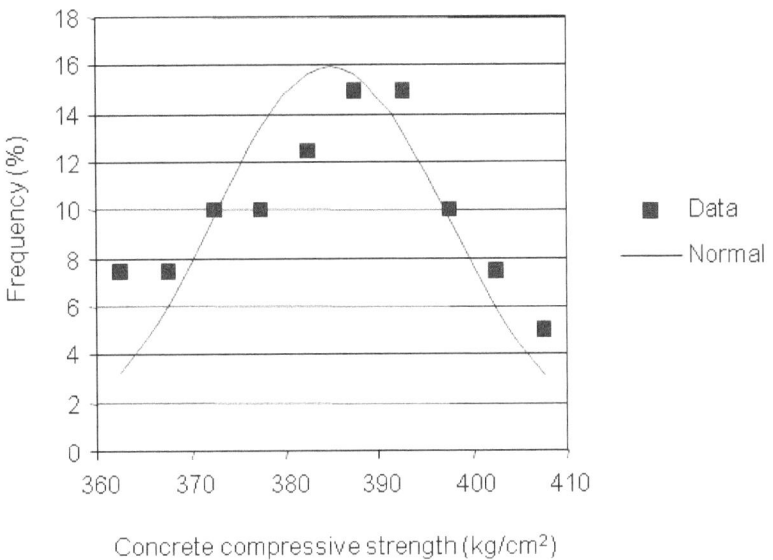

Figure 2.10: Normal distribution curve that fits the frequencies

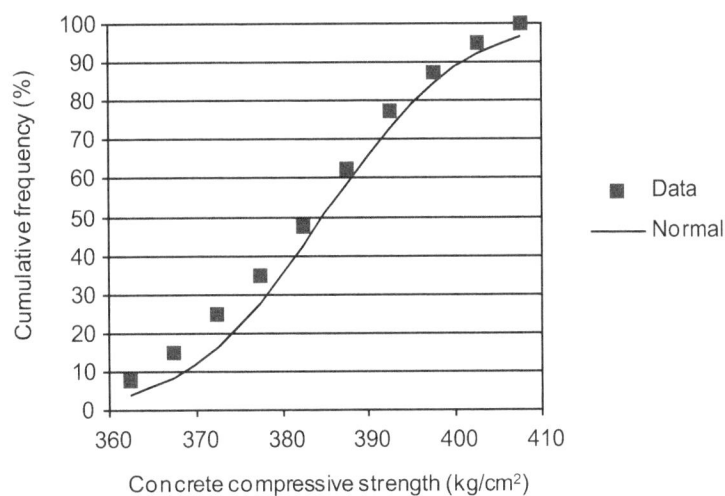

Figure 2.11: Normal distribution curve that fits the cumulative frequencies

An Introduction to Excel for Civil Engineers

	A	B	C	D	E	F	G
1	Class Interval	Mid Point	Frequency	Percent	Cumulative	Normal	Normal
2	kg/cm²	Kg/cm²		(%)	(%)		Cum.
3		k	N	f			
4	360-365	362.5	3	7.5	7.5	3.2	3.7
5	365-370	367.5	3	7.5	15.0	6.1	8.2
6	370-375	372.5	4	10.0	25.0	9.8	16.1
7	375-380	377.5	4	10.0	35.0	13.4	27.8
8	380-385	382.5	5	12.5	47.5	15.7	42.5
9	385-390	387.5	6	15.0	62.5	15.6	58.3
10	390-395	392.5	6	15.0	77.5	13.2	72.9
11	395-400	397.5	4	10.0	87.5	9.6	84.4
12	400-405	402.5	3	7.5	95.0	5.9	92.1
13	405-410	407.5	2	5.0	100.0	3.1	96.5
14			40	100.0			
15							
16				Mean =	384.87	kg/cm²	
17				S =	12.49	kg/cm²	

	F	G
1	Normal	Normal
2		Cumulative
3		
4	=500/($E$17*SQRT(2*PI()))*EXP(-0.5*((k-$E$16)/$E$17)^2)	=NORMDIST(k,$E$16,$E$17,TRUE)*100
5	=500/($E$17*SQRT(2*PI()))*EXP(-0.5*((k-$E$16)/$E$17)^2)	=NORMDIST(k,$E$16,$E$17,TRUE)*100

	D	E	F
15			
16	Mean =	=SUMPRODUCT(k,n)/SUM(n)	kg/cm²
17	S =	=SQRT(SUMPRODUCT(n,(k-E16)^2)/SUM(n))	kg/cm²

Figure 2.12: Data presentation from the test result to obtain normal distribution and the formula used in a spreadsheet

Formulas used as follows:

Mean : =SUMPRODUCT(k,n)/SUM(n)

S : =SQRT(SUMPRODUCT(n,(k-Mean)^2)/SUM(n))

Normal : =500/(S*SQRT(2*PI()))*EXP(-0.5*((k-Mean)/S)^2)

Normal Cumulative : =NORMDIST(k,Mean,S,TRUE)*100

Mean and standard deviation are respectively derived from Equation 2.11 and 2.13. The actual scale for the Normal function (Equation 2.14) is determined from the interval used, in this case were taken 5 kg/cm2. Multiply by 100 to get depiction in percent (%).

There are also several ways to make distributions in Excel, such as Exponential, Weibull, Gamma and Poisson.

2.6 CIRCULAR REFERENCE

When a formula in a cell refers to its own cell either directly or indirectly, it is called a circular reference. Excel by default can not process a formula that contains a circular reference until we select **Enable Iterative calculation** by the following steps: **Office Button > Excel Options > Formulas**. Iteration is the repetition of numerical calculation until a condition is met. The process is executed based on iterations number entered in the textbox **Maximum iterations** and **Maximum Change** for the maximum change resulting from the last two iterations. Excel will stop counting when one of the conditions is met, or whichever comes first.

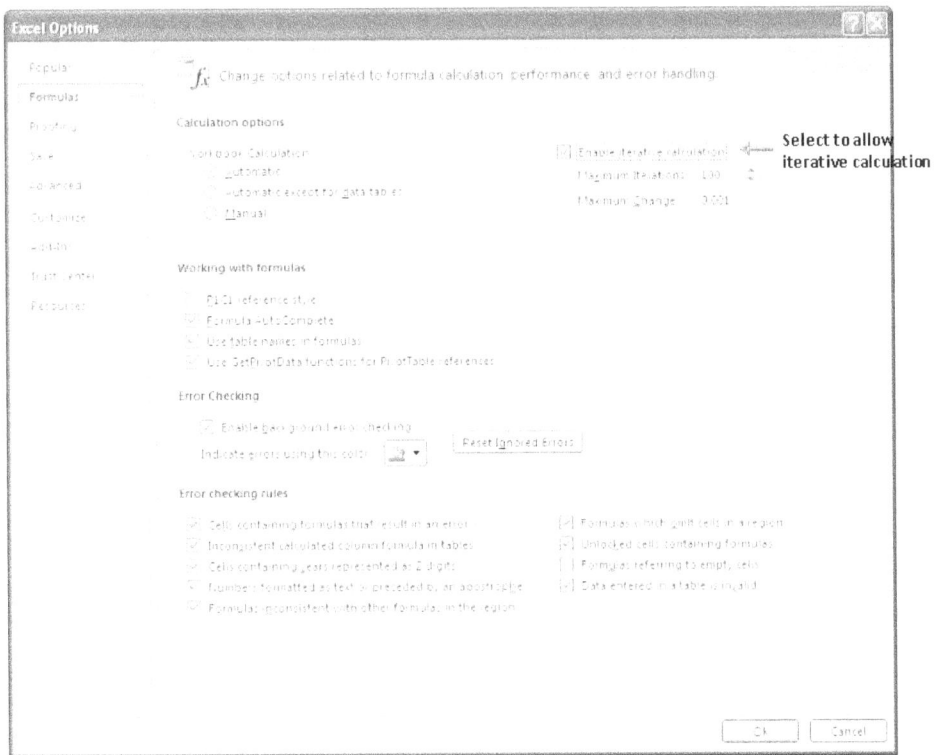

An Introduction to Excel for Civil Engineers

Cells with circular reference are shown as below:

Example 1

	A	B
1	4	
2	=B2	=(A1+A2)/3

Result: 1 x iteration

	A	B
1	4	
2	0	1.33333

5 x iterations

	A	B
1	4	
2	1.97531	1.99177

100 x iterations

	A	B
1	4	
2	2	2

In short, it can be explained herein about the iteration method to describe the way of Excel executes Example 1. Formulas in cell A2 and B2 are interrelated and have a form x = f(x) or is written as,

$x_{n+1} = f(x_n)$,

where: x_n = predicted value of x at iteration n^{th}

x_{n+1} = predicted new value of x at iteration n^{th} + 1

n = number of iterations

Formula in cell A2 and B2 can be written: $x_{n+1} = (4 + x_n)/3$.

At first iteration (n =1), x_1 is taken = 0 → x_2 = (4 + 0)/3 = 1.33333

At n = 2, x_2 is taken = 1.33333 → x_3 =1.77778

At n = 5, x_5 = 1.97531 → x_6 = 1.99177

And so on.

Excel will do this process based on the number of iterations (n) and the maximum change $|x_{n+1} - x_n|$ that you specify, and will stop if one condition is met. This analogy is found in the process of Newton-Raphson Method function in Chapter 3, but of course with the different method.

The Excel iteration can also be applied to solve system of linear equations, that is, to obtain unknown variables of equations. The following is an example to obtain values of x and y that satisfy the equations below:

2x + 3y = 7

3x - 2y = 4

At first, expressing each equation into x and y forms:

2x + 3y = 7   → x = (7 – 3y)/2; y = (7 – 2x)/3

3x – 2y = 4   → x = (4 + 2y)/3; y = (4 – 3x)/2

Further, convert the formed x and y into formulas, and placed them in cell B2 to C3 as shown in the worksheet below. In order to perform iteration, the cells must be linked which is in this operation the formulas in cell B3 and C2 are to be interrelated.

	A	B	C	D
1		Eq.1	Eq.2	
2	x =	=(7-3*B3)/2	=(4+2*B3)/3	
3	y =	=(7-2*C2)/3	=-(4-3*C2)/2	
4				

10 x iterations

	A	B	C	D
1		Eq.1	Eq.2	
2	x =	1.999	2.000	
3	y =	1.000	1.001	
4				

11 x iterations

	A	B	C	D
1		Eq.1	Eq.2	
2	x =	2.000	2.000	
3	y =	1.000	1.000	
4				

An Introduction to Excel for Civil Engineers

Values of x and y that satisfy both equations are obtained at iteration 11, where: x = 2 and y = 1.

Example 2

	A	B	C
1	0	10	10
2	10	=(B1+B3+A2+C2)/4	=B2
3	10	=(B2+B4+A3+C3)/4	=B3
4	0	0	0

1 x iteration

	A	B	C
1	0	10	10
2	10	5	5
3	10	3.75	3.75
4	0	0	0

5 x iterations

	A	B	C
1	0	10	10
2	10	8.64128	8.64128
3	10	6.18032	6.18032
4	0	0	0

100 x iterations

	A	B	C
1	0	10	10
2	10	8.75	8.75
3	10	6.25	6.25
4	0	0	0

The initial value for B3 and C2 in the formula in cell B2 are taken = 0. The value of B2 will be used as an initial value in the formula in cell B3, where C3 = 0. The result is then used as a predicted new value in the next iteration.

In practice, Excel iterative calculation or circular reference can be used, for examples, for solutions of simultaneous linear equations, slope stability analysis using the Bishop method (where safety factor is on both sides of the equation) and seepage below dam using finite difference method.

CHAPTER 3

CREATING MACRO

3.1 FUNCTION PROCEDURE

In addition to the functions that already exist in Excel, it is often to create a function to perform calculation that is determined by the user. Such function is called user-defined (UD) function. This function will be added into a collection of Excel function and can be used as a built-in function.

Some UD functions are built up by combining formulas and built-in functions. UD function is written in macrosheet or using Visual Basic Application (VBA). Macrosheet is a sheet where a macro is created by XLM language, which is the original Excel macro language that is still maintained at least until Excel 2007. Figure 3.1 shows the UD functions to obtain cosine of an angle in macrosheet and VBA.

	A
1	COSD
2	=RESULT(1)
3	=ARGUMENT("X",1)
4	=RETURN(COS(PI()*X/180))

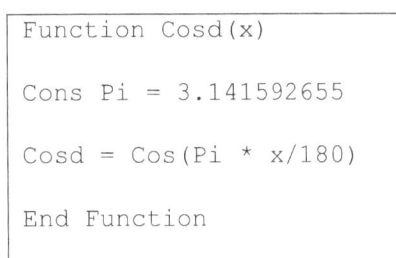

```
Function Cosd(x)

Cons Pi = 3.141592655

Cosd = Cos(Pi * x/180)

End Function
```

Figure 3.1: Function in Macrosheet (left) and VBA (right)

Creating Functions in Macrosheet

To insert a macrosheet in worksheet, right-click on the sheet tab to display the shortcut menu, click **Insert** > **MS. Excel 4.0 Macro** > **OK** to insert a macrosheet named **Macro1** as shown below:

An Introduction to Excel for Civil Engineers   69

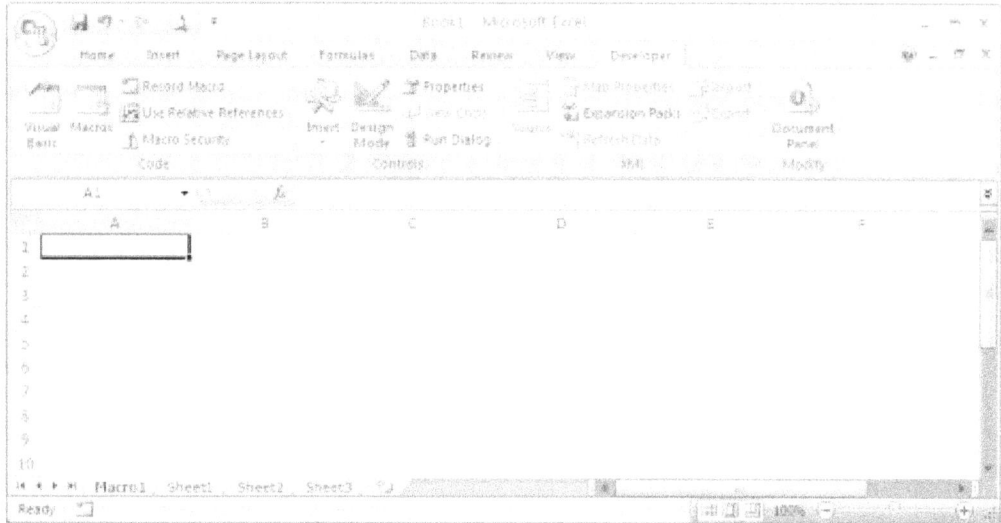

This sheet is seemingly similar to a worksheet, but there are columns that are wide enough to write a function. The first row is to write the name of function, for example, COSD in Figure 3.1. The second row is to define types of output refer to Table 3.1, for example, number, text or an array, using **RESULT** statement and followed by data type. The next row (or rows) is to define a variable as input data using **ARGUMENT** statement followed by its name and data type between parentheses.

Further, the user has to write formulas used for the operation of a function based on the given variables in the ARGUMENT. A variable can refer to a name or cell reference of a worksheet, such as "x" of COSD that refers to a cell in a worksheet. A formula can be given a name to simplify macro writing. The sequence of creating macro is ended by **RETURN** statement, which returns the function value. Below is an example of a macro in macrosheet to calculate the volume of a cube:

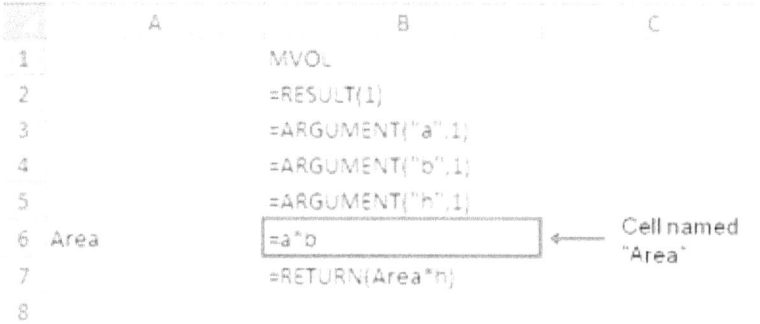

MVOL function is used in a worksheet as follows:

An Introduction to Excel for Civil Engineers

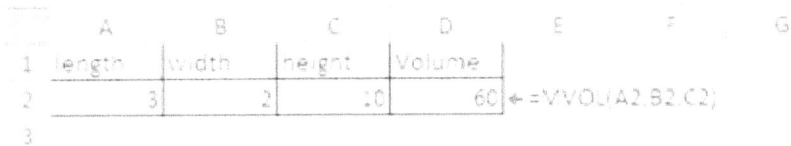

Table 3.1: Data Types in Macrosheet

Value	Data Type
1	Number
2	Text
4	Logical
8	Reference
16	Error
64	Array

Creating Visual Basic for Application (VBA) Functions

A VBA function (UD function) is created in a module that is inserted through the **Insert** tab > **Module** (see in Chapter 1). A VBA function is a set of statements that begins with **Function** statement followed by a name, argument list in parentheses and ends with **End Function** statement. The type of a function can be Single, Double or all data types of Variant, depends on what it would be produced, a number, a text or an array. Data types in VBA are presented in Table 3.2.

The selection on these data types, in addition to defining a function and its arguments, it relates to allocation of computer memory which depends on the range of data types (the greater the value, the greater memory allocation). If an argument is not defined, it will be classified as a Variant, which consumes computer memory more than any other data types. Defining data types in a program is highly recommended because it saves computer memory consumption, accelerates the VBA process in recognizing the data types and hence accelerates macro execution.

Table 3.1: Data Types in VBA

Data Type	Range
Integer	-32,768 to 32,767
Long (long integer)	-2,147,483,648 to 2,147,483,647

An Introduction to Excel for Civil Engineers

Single (single precision)	-3.402823E38 to -1.401298E-45 (- values)
	1.401298E-45 to 3.402823E38 (+ values)
Double (double precision)	-1.79769313486231E308 to -4.94065645841247E-324 (-)
	4.94065645841247E-324 to 1.79769313486232E308 (+)
Currency	-922,337,203,685,477.5808 to 922,337,203,685,477.5807
String (variable length)	0 to approx.2 billion characters
String (fixed length)	1 to approx. 65,400 characters
Byte	0 to 255
Boolean logic	TRUE or FALSE
Date	1 January 100 to 31 December 9999
Object	Any object reference
Variant (with numbers)	Any numeric value up to the range of Double
Variant (with characters)	0 to approx.2 billion characters

Such as Excel, VBA also has many built-in functions. Some have names similar to Excel built-in functions, say, Cos function (as seen in Figure 3.1) or Abs to find the absolute value of a number. Some Excel built-in functions can also be used in VBA by using the prefix Application. Figure 3.2 shows an example where Excel built-in functions are used in the UD function MLIN to obtain linear regression parameters. MLIN returns an array result (multiple results), which calculates the slope of the regression line and the intersection with the Y-axis (Y-intercept).

```
Function MLIN(Y, X) As Variant
    Slope = Application.Slope(Y, X)
    Intercept = Application.Intercept(Y, X)
MLIN = Array(Slope, Intercept)
End Function
```

Figure 3.2: Excel built-in functions in VBA

Notes:

- A module with Option Explicit statement requires all variables are to be declared. If do not, an error occurs at the execution showing a message "Variable not defined". To declare variables, use Dim, ReDim, Private, Public and Static statements.

    Example

```
Option Explicit
Sub OptEx1()
Dim myVar as Integer
     MyInt = 5 'error: variable not defined
     myVar = 10
End Sub
```

- Dim declares size of variables, which are stated at the beginning of the program. ReDim is to change the size of variables that could be changed during the execution of program. Variables declared by Dim or Redim at procedure level (between the Sub – End Sub statements) are available only to the procedure where the variables are declared.

Example

```
Sub OptEx2()
Dim myVar as Integer
Dim myString(1 to 3) as String
Dim n As Integer
n = 3 'an input

ReDim MyInt(n) As Integer
     MyInt(1) = 1
     MyInt(2) = 3
     MyInt(3) = 5
     myVar = 10
     myString(3) = "Hello"
End Sub
```

- Use **Type**...**End Type** to create user-defined data types.

```
Type FamilyTree
    Name As String
    Address As String
    Phone As Long
    Numsiblings As Byte
End Type

Sub GetRecord()
    Dim TheFirst As FamilyTree
    TheFirst.Name = "Johan"
```

An Introduction to Excel for Civil Engineers

```
        TheFirst.Address = "Street 123"
        TheFirst.Phone = 1234
        TheFirst.Numsiblings = 3
    End Sub
```

3.2 SUB PROCEDURE

Macros that are previously used to create UD functions can also be used for engineering calculation programs to solve more complex problems, such as civil engineering structural analyses. In VBA, such programs are generally created within Sub procedures (see in Chapter 1).

It is common to present macro process into three main parts:

1. Read – read input data from a worksheet
2. Execute – execute the data or program execution
3. Print – print the results back to the worksheet

In Excel-VBA programming, the input values refer to the given values of cells (or range of cells) on a worksheet, that is, a Range object where the values set in Value property. Therefore, typing a value, such as number or text into a cell is actually to set a value in the Value property of the cell. Cells property is commonly used to return a Range object with syntax: Cells (row_index, column_index), for example, Cell (1,1) used to return a Range object that represents cell A1.

Here is an example how to set a number to a cell in VBA code, which sets the value of cell A1 = 10:

```
Worksheets("Sheet1").Cells(1,1).Value = 10
```

If no object qualifier or an object before the period (is the Worksheet object above), then the range is in the active sheet from which the macro runs, for example via the command button click on the worksheet. You should provide an object qualifier before the range if the data is not located in the active sheet, for example: Worksheets("Sheet2") that refers to Sheet2. The Value property is a default property of a Range object, therefore can be omitted without the need for writing it.

The following is an example of a Sub procedure named Pro_Sub1:

```
Sub Pro_Sub1()
Dim Length As Double
Dim Width As Double
```

```
Dim Area As Double
   Length = Cells(2, 1)
   Width = Cells(3, 1)
'Determine Area
   Area = Length * Width
   Cells(4, 1) = Area
End Sub
```

The above procedure is to calculate the area of a rectangle by multiplying the length by the width. All the variables are declared using the Dim statement and the data types are defined as double precision (Double). The Cells property is created without an object qualifier; therefore, the range of cells is on the active sheet, that is, the (open) active sheet when the code is executed.

Sign apostrophe (') is a sign where program ignores the comments that follow it. This sign is used to insert explanations. The default color of the text is green.

The process of input-output of Pro_Sub1 procedure is illustrated as below:

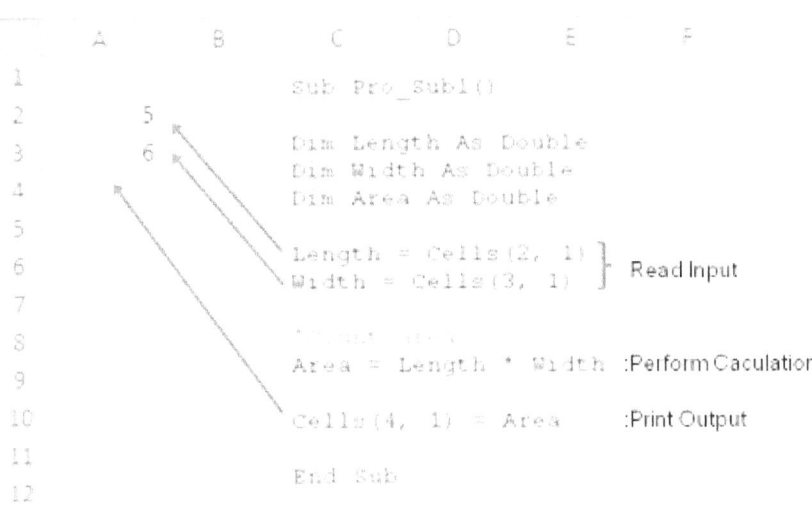

If the procedure is executed, value of cell A4 or Cells (4,1) will be = 30. To run the macro, perform the steps as described in Chapter 1.11.4.

In creating large-scale application program, normally, the program is divided into several sub-programs or Sub procedures with Function procedures where each Sub or Function handles a specific task then is called using the Call statement or by the function name. The

An Introduction to Excel for Civil Engineers

advantages of this division are to make a programming is more focused, more readable and if an error occurs, it can quickly be addressed. Such computer programmings are given in the next chapters.

3.3 Control Structures

A program is created to be able to handle any changes either from the input data or that are occurred during program execution. Therefore, it is necessary to involve control structures in order to make the program remains on its specified steps. Such controls are looping and branching or a combination of both.

3.3.1 Looping

Do While...Loop or Do...Loop While

Repeats a set of statements while a condition is TRUE. If the condition becomes FALSE, the program will exit the looping and move to the next code.

Syntax:

Do While condition

    [statements]

    [Exit Do]

    [statements]

Loop

Example

```
Sub exLoop1()
    i = 1
    Do While i <= 5
        Cells(1 + i, 1) = i
    i = i + 1
    Loop
End Sub
```

Do Until...Loop or Do...Loop Until

Repeats a set of statements until a condition becomes TRUE. If the condition becomes FALSE, the looping will be discontinued.

Syntax:

Do Until condition

    [Statements]

    [Exit Do]

    [Statements]

Loop

Example

```
Sub exLoop2()
    i = 1
    Do Until i >= 5
        Cells(1 + i, 1) = i
      i = i + 1
    Loop
End Sub
```

For...Next

Repeats a set of statements a given number of times

Syntax:

For counter = start **To** end [**Step** step]

    [statements]

    [Exit For]

    [statements]

Next [counter

Example

```
Sub exLoop3()
j = 1
    For i = 1 To 5
        Cells(1 + i, 1) = j
    j = j + 1
    Next i
End Sub
```

For Each...Next

Repeats a set of statements a number of elements in an array. It helps if the number is unknown. It is written in the function below:

Syntax:

For Each element **In** array

    [statements]

    [Exit For]

    [statements]

Next [element]

Example

```
Function exLoop4(Yarray, Xarray) As Variant
Dim n As Integer, x As Single, y As Single
    n = 0
    x = 0
    y = 0
    For Each c In Xarray
        n = n + 1
        x = x + Xarray(n)
        y = y + Yarray(n)
    Next
    a = x * x
    b = y * x
    exLoop4 = Array(a, b)
End Function
```

An Introduction to Excel for Civil Engineers

3.3.2 BRANCHING

Select Case

Executes several set of statements depends on the value of an expression

Syntax:

Select Case testexpression

[**Case** expressionlist-n

[statements-n]]

 [**Case Else**

[elsestatements]]

End Select

Example

```
Sub exLoop5()
Dim Number
Number = Cells(1, 1) 'a number
Select Case Number
Case 1 To 5
    Cells(2, 1) = "Between 1 and 5"
Case 6, 7, 8
    Cells(2, 1) = "Between 6 and 8"
Case Else
    Cells(2, 1) = "Greater than 8"
End Select
```

If…Then…Else

Executes a set of statements because of certain condition, when it is not appropriate then move to another state of condition.

Syntax:

If condition (1) **Then**

statement(1)

ElseIf condition(2) **Then**

statement(2)

Else

    statement(3)

End If

Branching is usually nested within a looping. If the condition is met, the program will exit the looping using Exit command. If...Then...Else branching can also be combined with the And, Or, or Not statements to state the relation between two expressions.

Syntax:

For...or **Do Until**...

    statement(1)

    If statement(1) **And** or **Or** expression(2) **Then**

        statement(2)

        Exit For or **Exit Do** or **Exit Function** or **Exit Sub**

    End If

Next...or **Loop**

Goto...Gosub...Return

GOSUB...RETURN statement is used in a procedure that consists of one or more subroutines (blocks of statements that are made for particular tasks or calculations). It branches to and returns from a subroutine. Use GOTO statement to go to specified lines, line labels or subroutines, before proceeding with the next code.

Example

```
Sub exBranch()
Dim myNum As Double
myNum = Cells(2, 1)
    If myNum >= 0 Then
```

```
        GoSub MyRoutine
        GoTo 10
    Else 'means myNum < 0
        GoTo 20
    End If
MyRoutine:
    myNum = Sqr(myNum) 'determine square root of number >=0
    Return
10 Cells(3, 1) = myNum
    Exit Sub
20 Cells(3, 1) = "#NUM!" 'error message
End Sub
```

Call…Sub

Calls a procedure from another procedure.

Syntax

[**Call**] name [argument]

Example 1: Calling Sub procedure from function procedure

```
Sub Area(x, y, L)
    L = x * y
End Sub

Function Volume(a, b, t) As Single
    Call Area(a, b, L)
    Volume = L * t
End Function
```

Example 2: Calling Sub procedure from another Sub procedure.

```
Sub Area(x, y, L)
    L = x * y
End Sub
Sub Pro_Vol()
```

```
Dim a As Single, b As Single, t As Single
Dim volume As Single

a = Cells(2, 2)
b = Cells(3, 2)
t = Cells(4, 2)

Call Area(a, b, L)
    volume = (L * t)
    Cells(5, 2) = volume
End Sub
```

In addition to looping and branching statements defined above, there is also a useful statement, that is, the **With…End With** statement.

With

Execute a series of statements on the same object.

Syntax:

With object

[*statements*]

End With

Example:

```
With MyObject
    .HorizontalAlignment = xlCenter
    .VerticalAlignment = xlCenter
    .Position = xlLabelPositionRight
    .Orientation = xlHorizontal
        With .Font
            .Name = "Arial"
            .FontStyle = "Regular"
            .Size = 8
        End With
End With
```

3.4 USER DEFINED FUNCTION PROBLEMS

Problem 1

Create a macro to determine a rectangular area where the area = the length x the width of the rectangular.

Solution

If a and b express the length and the width respectively, the area can be expressed as a function (a, b) = a x b. If the function name is Area, thus:

Area (a, b) = a x b.

We can solve this problem by writing it in macrosheet language. Insert a macrosheet by right-clicking on the worksheet **Sheet** tab > **Insert** > **MS. Excel 4.0 Macro** > **OK** and type these statements:

```
        A                  B
1   AREA
2   =RESULT(1)
3   =ARGUMENT("a",1)
4   =ARGUMENT("b",1)
5   =RETURN(a*b)
6
```

Further, we have to define a name for the function so that it can be recognized by Excel and added as an Excel function. The steps for this purpose are:

1. Click cell A1 where the name of the function (Area) is placed.

2. Click the **Formula** tab > **Define Name** to show the **New Name** dialog box as below. Enter a name in the name text box. Macro name will automatically be referred to cell A1 with step 1 above.

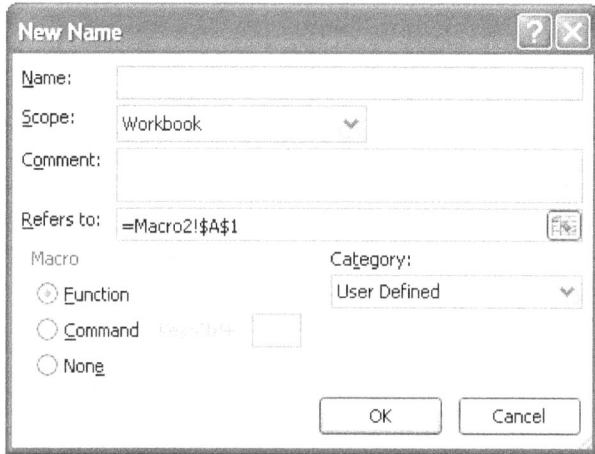

3. Select **Function** in the option button, so the function (by default) is categorized as **User Defined** or you can choose a category for your function.

4. Click **OK**.

Now, go to the worksheet. The use of **Area** function is as follows:

	A	B	C	D	E
1	a (length)	b (width)	Area		
2	3	2	6←=Area(a,b)		
3					
4					

Cells A2 and B2 are named a and b, respectively. We can name cells on a worksheet by following the Step 1 and 2 above. Here, there is no option (option button) for Macro category in the **New Name** dialog box.

Problem 2

Find the area between a straight line y = mx + c and the X-axis, between x = a and x = b (c ≥ 0). This problem will be solved using integration formula:

$$\text{Area} = \int_a^b (mx+c)dx$$

Macro for finding the area can be formulated as follows:

function(m,c,a,b) = (½.mb² + cb) - (½ma² + ca)

Using the macro, find the area between y = x + 2, X-axis, between a = -1, b = 3.

Solution

The macro is named **INAREA**, and written in a macrosheet as follows:

	A	B
1	INAREA	
2	=RESULT(1)	
3	=ARGUMENT("m",1)	
4	=ARGUMENT("c_",1)	
5	=ARGUMENT("a",1)	
6	=ARGUMENT("b",1)	
7	=-c_/m	
8	=IF(m<0,IF(OR(a>A7,b>A7),RETURN(#VALUE!)))	
9	=IF(m>0,IF(OR(a<A7,b<A7),RETURN(#VALUE!)))	
10	=1/2*m*a^2+(c_*a)	
11	=1/2*m*b^2+(c_*b)	
12	=RETURN(A11-A10)	

Problem 2 in a chart as below:

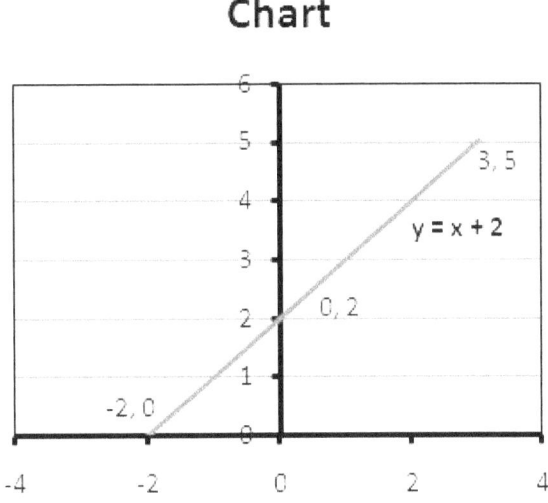

Before applying the function, perform Step 1 to 4 as shown in Problem 1 to define the function name. The use of the function will be as follows:

	A	B	C	D	E	F
1	m	c	a	b	Area	
2	1	2	-1	3	12	← =INAREA(A2,B2,C2,D2)
3	1	2	-3	3	#VALUE!	← =INAREA(A3,B3,C3,D3)
4	-0.5	2	1	5	#VALUE!	← =INAREA(A4,B4,C4,D4)
5						

An Introduction to Excel for Civil Engineers

Problem 3

Create a VBA macro to assign letter grade for a course with score range 0 – 100, where A represents scores from 80 - 100, B: 65 - 79, C: 51 - 64, D: 40 - 50 and F: for scores below 40. Moreover, macro will return literal grade with sign + and – at the given numerical value.

Solution

```
Function VBGrade(g, a, b, c, d) As String
    Select Case g
        Case Is >= 2 * (100 - a) / 3 + a
            VBGrade = "A+"
        Case Is >= (100 - a) / 3 + a
            VBGrade = "A"
        Case Is >= a
            VBGrade = "A-"
        Case Is >= 2 * (a - b) / 3 + b
            VBGrade = "B+"
        Case Is >= (a - b) / 3 + b
            VBGrade = "B"
        Case Is >= b
            VBGrade = "B-"
        Case Is >= 2 * (b - c) / 3 + c
            VBGrade = "C+"
        Case Is >= (b - c) / 3 + c
            VBGrade = "C"
        Case Is >= c
            VBGrade = "C-"
        Case Is >= 2 * (c - d) / 3 + d
            VBGrade = "D+"
        Case Is >= (c - d) / 3 + d
            VBGrade = "D"
        Case Is >= d
            VBGrade = "D-"
        Case Else
            VBGrade = "F"
    End Select
End Function
```

Functions that created in VBA will automatically be added into collection of Excel functions. The use of the function in a worksheet will be as follows:

If you use a new assessment for the scoring, it is simply done by changing the values of the VBGrade arguments.

Problem 4

Create a VBA macro to find a vertical stress distribution below a foundation using elastic equation given by Boussinesq - Newmark (1935). The equation to get the vertical stress (σ) below a corner of a rectangular area b x l at depth y is:

$$\sigma_y = \sigma_0 \frac{1}{4\pi} \left[\frac{2MN\sqrt{V}}{V+V_1} \cdot \frac{V+1}{V} + \tan^{-1}\left(\frac{2MN\sqrt{V}}{V-V_1}\right) \right]$$

where,

M = b/y

N = l/y

V = M² + N² + 1

$V_1 = (MN)^2$

b, l and y refer to Figure 3.3

If $V_1 > V$, then the arctan in the equation needs to be added with π.

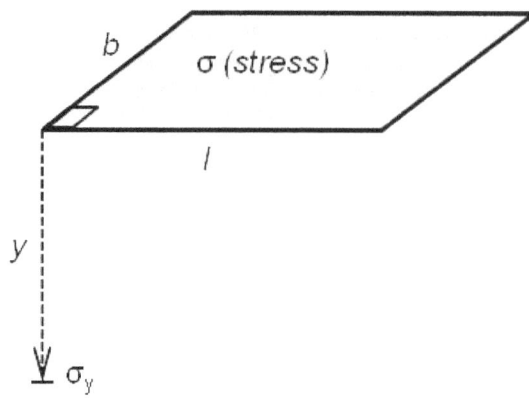

Figure 3.3: Vertical stress below a corner of a rectangular area

Solution

```
Function Bous(q, b, l, y) As Double
Const pi = 3.141593
Dim m, n, v, vs, rad, at
    m = b / y
    n = l / y
    v = m ^ 2 + n ^ 2 + 1
    vs = (m * n) ^ 2
    rad = (2 * m * n * Sqr(v)) / (v - vs)
    If vs > v Then
        at = Atn(rad) + pi
    Else
        at = Atn(rad)
    End If

    Bous = q / (4 * pi) * (((2 * m * n * Sqr(v) / (v + vs)) * ((v + 1) / v)) + at)
End Function
```

The advantage of converting an equation into a user-defined VBA function instead of worksheet formula is that it greatly simplifies the writing of the equation. The above equation with a condition $V_1 > V$ certainly would be very lengthy and requires a lot "attention" if it is converted into worksheet formula.

Below is given a foundation with size of 3 x 3 m subjected to a uniform pressure of 10 ton/m². The computation result of vertical stress below the **center** of the foundation made for depth interval of 0.5 meters is presented in the worksheet below:

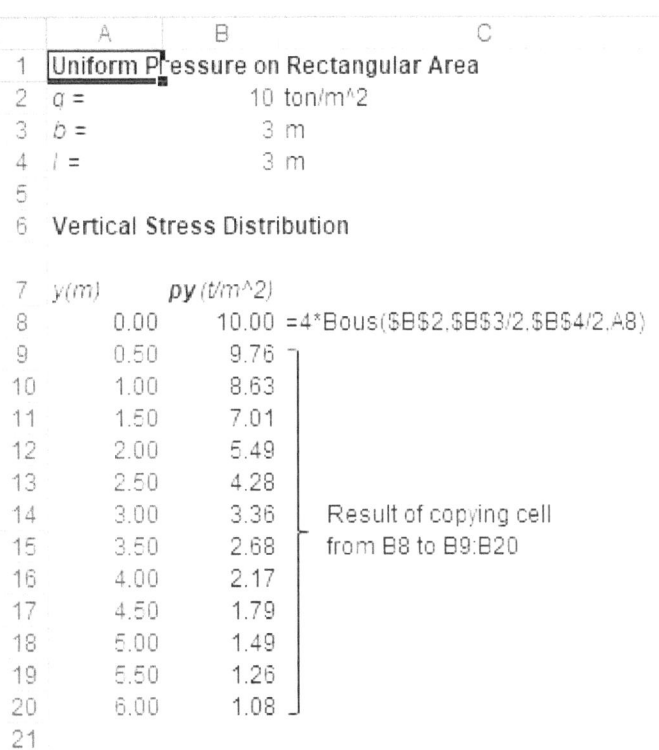

- Boussinesq - Newmark equation is used to find vertical stress below a corner of a rectangular area, therefore, below a center a foundation of 3 x 3 m obtains 4 area with the same size, with dimension of 1.5 x 1.5 m. Further, for the contribution of four corners it is equal to = 4 σ_y. See Figure 3.3.
- Division by 0 is not allowed in the calculation, therefore the value entered in cell A8 shall be an approach = 0. Take, for example, y = 0.0001.

A chart of the stress versus the depth is shown below:

An Introduction to Excel for Civil Engineers 89

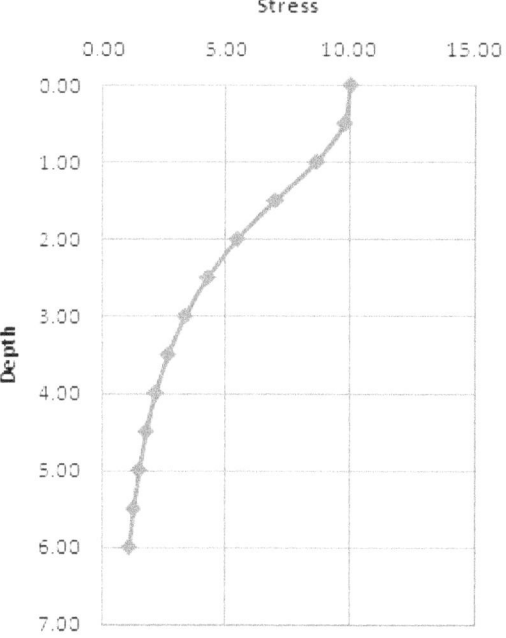

Chart is created through the **Insert** tab> **Scatters with smoothlines and markers** > **Select Data** > **Add** and then select x and y-data. To modify the chart, click once on chart area then click the **Chart Tools** tab > **Chart Layout** > **Layout 1** to select a chart layout, and add chart titles by clicking once on the title, select **Edit Text** to type titles. The depth orientation is made to increase downward and for this purpose, right click on the Y-axis > **Format Axis** > **Axis Option** > **Values in reverse order**.

Problem 5

Find root x in equation: $ax^4 + bx^3 + cx^2 + dx + c = 0$

Solution

This problem will be solved numerically by Newton-Raphson method. The process of calculation is done in an iterative technique, which root x is gradually approached. Function of equation is depicted in the figure below and exemplified intercepts the X-axis at point p and $f(x) = 0$ or $(p, 0)$. In the first step, it is taken x_1-value to get tangent line at $y = f(x)$ which intercepts the X-axis at point $(x_2, 0)$. Here, x_2 is a new approach to p. The next approach is done using x_2 value (value to get x_3) and so on until $x_n \to p$.

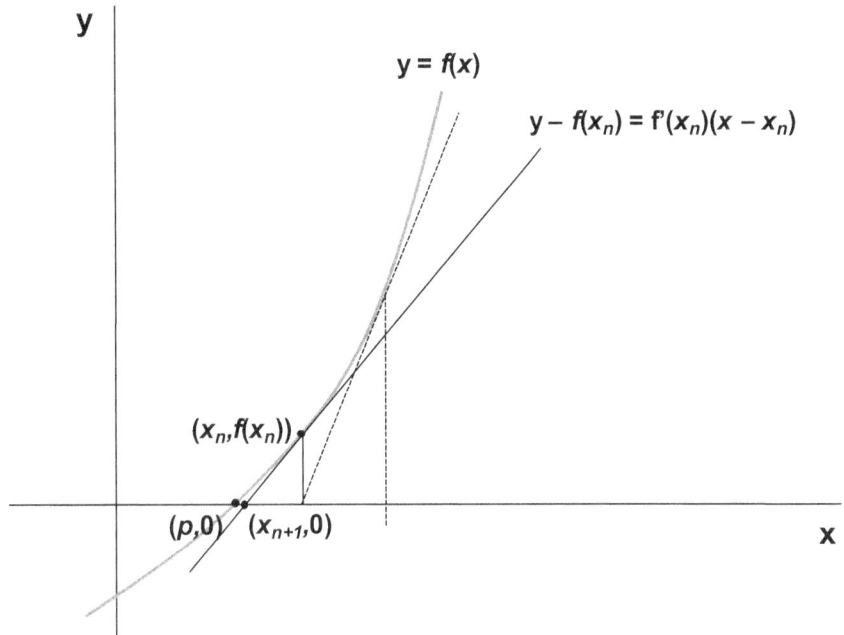

Thus, by induction it obtains tangent line: y - f(x$_n$) = f '(x$_n$) (x - x$_n$) which intercepts X-axis at point (x$_{n+1}$,0), where:

$$x_{n+1} = x_n - \frac{f(x_n)}{f'(x_n)}$$

Macro

```
Function NRM(a, b, c, d, e) As Double
Dim funct, deriv, x, xn
Dim n As Integer, i As Integer
n = 1000
i = 1
x = 100
    Do
        funct = (a * x ^ 4) + (b * x ^ 3) + (c * x ^ 2) _
        + (d * x) + e
        deriv = (4 * a * x ^ 3) + (3 * b * x ^ 2) + _
        (2 * c * x) + d
        xn = x - (funct / deriv)
```

An Introduction to Excel for Civil Engineers

```
            If funct = 0 Or Abs(xn - x) < 0.00001 Then
                NRM = xn
                Exit Function
            End If
            i = i + 1
            x = xn
        Loop Until i = n
        NRM = "Divergen!"
End Function
```

Function NRM (stands for Newton-Raphson Method) is now used to find the value of x in the equation below:

$-2.79x^3 - 12.11x^2 + 24.51x + 36.68 = 0$.

The use of the function in a worksheet is as below:

Note: this equation form can be found in the geotechnical engineering to find the embedment depth of retaining wall with Free-Earth Support Method.

Problem 6

Table X is a number of random numeric data from 0 - 100. Create a macro to calculate the amount of the data in Table X with a range of values from Y to Z.

	A	B	C	D	E	F	G
1	Table X						
2	77.58	73.27	22.21	70.40	81.40	52.57	98.34
3	68.58	21.86	62.37	37.61	51.24	12.41	18.55
4	60.92	22.26	35.01	23.76	63.34	32.81	83.16
5	98.27	63.85	30.97	34.98	64.44	70.49	17.96
6	71.23	79.63	74.21	100.00	37.95	3.94	95.27
7	10.62	20.69	5.82	74.81	95.09	37.48	0.74

Solution

Macro

```
Function DNUM(Xarray, Y, Z) As Integer
Dim n As Integer, Num As Integer
Dim c
n = 0
    For Each c In Xarray
    n = n + 1
        If Xarray(n) >= Y And Xarray(n) <= Z Then Num = Num + 1
    Next
DNUM = Num
End Function
```

The use of the function in a worksheet is as below:

	I	J	K	Formula at Column K
2	0.0	50.0	19	=DNUM(X,I2,J2)
3	50.0	100.0	23	=DNUM(X,I3,J3)
4	0.0	100.0	42	=DNUM(X,I4,J4)

Argument **X** is an array argument and it is the name that has been defined for the data table in cell range A2 to G7. Argument X in DNUM can also be written as A2:G7, or can refer to a certain range, for example, B2:C7, A7:G7 and so on. One of the advantages of using function in Excel is that it enables to create variable names, writing functions and put the results together in a worksheet.

Problem 7

Create a macro for linear interpolation example presented in Chapter 2.5.3. Use Equation 2.7 to solve.

Solution (Macro)

```
Function Linter(Xrange, Yrange, nval) As Double
    Dim i As Integer
    Dim c, x
    x = Xrange(1)
    i = 1
    For Each c In Xrange
        If nval = c Then
```

```
            Linter = Yrange(i)
            Exit Function
        'find a new value satisfying the given condition
        ElseIf (nval - c) * (nval - x) <= 0 And c <> x Then
            'Eq. 2.7:
              Linter = Yrange(i - 1) + (Yrange(i) - Yrange(i - 1)) _
    * (nval - x) / (c - x)
            Exit Function
        End If
        x = c
    i = i + 1
    Next
End Function
```

The use of the function in a worksheet is as below:

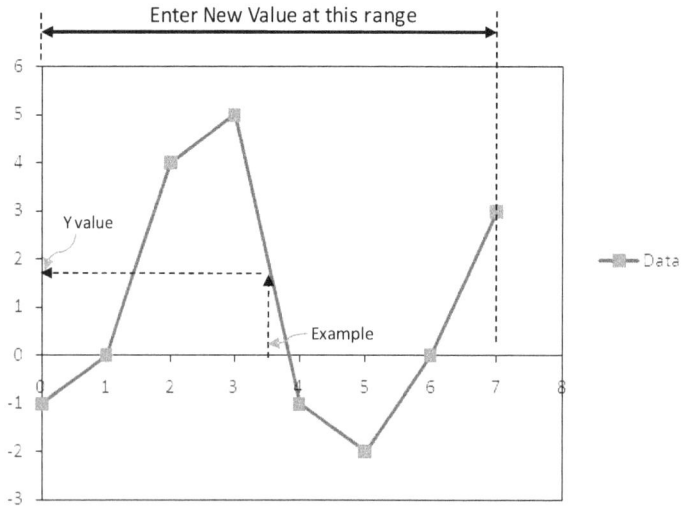

The interpolation in a chart:

Problem 8

Create a macro for semilog interpolation example presented in Chapter 2.5.3. Use Equation 2.10 to solve.

Solution

Macro

```
Function Loginter(Xrange, Yrange, nval) As Double
    Dim i As Integer
    Dim c, x
    x = Xrange(1)
    i = 1

    For Each c In Xrange
        If nval = c Then
            Loginter = Yrange(i)
            Exit Function
        'find a new value satisfying the given condition
        ElseIf (nval - c) * (nval - x) <= 0 And c <> x Then
            'Eq 2.10:
        Loginter = Yrange(i - 1) * (Yrange(i) / Yrange(i -1)) _
          ^ ((nval - x) / (c - x))
            Exit Function
        End If
        x = c
    i = i + 1
    Next
End Function
```

The use of the function in a worksheet is as below:

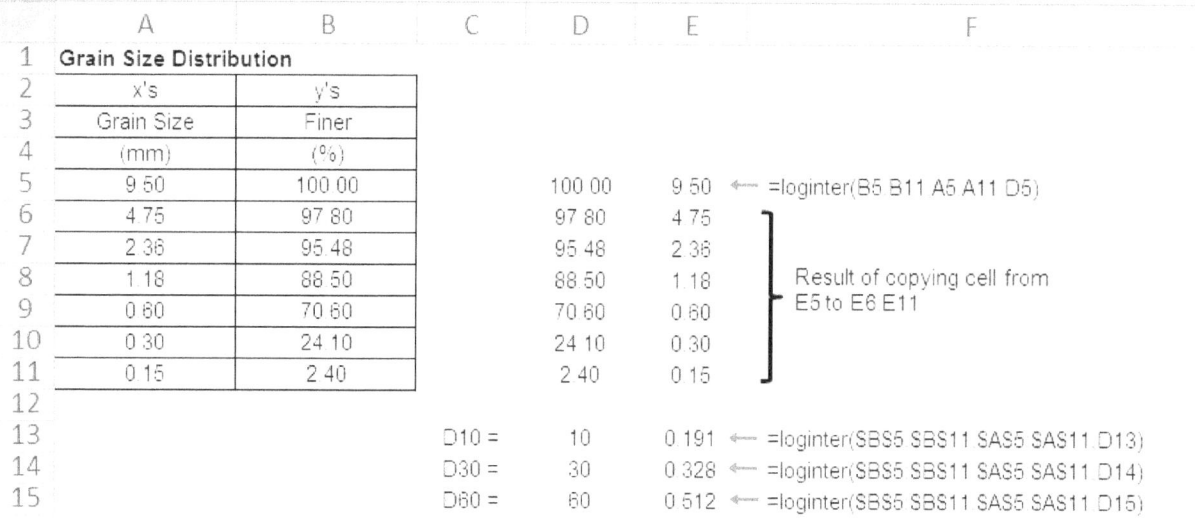

The interpolation in a chart:

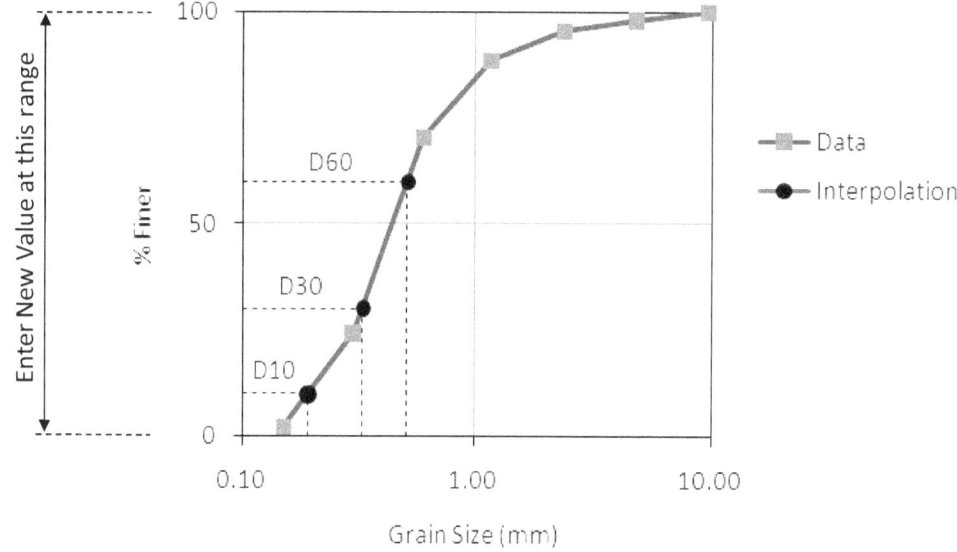

Note:

- Character "c" and "r" can not be used for variable names in macrosheet, because C and R stand for column and row, respectively. However, you can define a variable name such as "c_" or "r_", "cx" or "rx" and so on.
- **Linear**, **log** and also **polynomial** (order 3) interpolation functions are probably the **most useful** functions in civil engineering or at least based on the Author's experience on geotechnical problems. They are used to obtain fitted points on a set of experimental or theoritical data. These functions are already included in the excercise file, written in VBA and Excel 4.0 macro code.

An Introduction to Excel for Civil Engineers

3.5 Structure of Program

Data processing in Excel-VBA program is a sequence of steps; **read – execution – print** as described previously in Section 3.2, that is:

1. Read input data from a worksheet
2. Execute the data
3. Print the results to the worksheet

In creating a computer program that involves a large data (either from the input data or comes from program execution), the code writing must be well planned. The goal is obvious: to make the program flow as simple as possible, well structured and it is easy to solve if an error occurs. An introduction to the three steps above will be presented here, include some tips that are helpful when designing a macro. The codes for data processing are presented in the rest of this subchapter.

3.5.1 Input Output Form

In Excel-VBA programming structure, the input-output form is worksheet itself and can be made in the same sheet, e.g. on Sheet1 for storing input and output data. For a large data inputted into cells, for example as shown in Figure 3.4, it would be better to extend the input data to the next columns. By doing this way, the locations (read: rows) of the output data can be specified in the program. This form model is adopted from a civil engineering structural analysis program.

Figure 3.4: Input-Output Form Example

An Introduction to Excel for Civil Engineers

The form "shows" that no matter how much the data inputted into cells, it does not change the row numbers assigned for output data. Therefore, we obtain a fixed input-output form that does not depend on the size of the input data and hence the read - print steps can be specified in the program.

Contrary to the input form arrangement, it is possible to extend the output data downward because end of row is not a boundary that has to be specified. Therefore, the form presented here follows the common way of presenting results of a program (extending downward and hence improve readability).

3.5.2 WORK WITH MODULES

A large data processing such as in an application program generally consists of several smaller programs or sub-programs that are well structured and united into one unit. The sub-programs meant here are VBA Sub-procedures (that may include one or more functions) placed in modules with given scope of their respective tasks.

For the convenience, the Author classifies each procedure into three modules according to their tasks as follows:

Module 1: Main Module

Module 1 consists of data provision from input-output form, which if we refer to Figure 3.4 comes mainly from the geometry data, materials data, determination of nodal supports, and loads data. Module 1 is the main module, which controls the process of read - execution – print.

Module 2: Calculation Process (Analysis)

Procedures in module 2 are associated with the theory of the structure and the analytical methods used, e.g. to assemble structural stiffness matrix, generate load matrix, and compute nodal displacements. Module 2 works based on data provided by Module 1.

Module 3: Creating Charts

Procedures in module 3 are associated with the presentation of data in graphical form, e.g. related to, 1). Input data: geometry of the structure and load magnitudes, and 2). Output data: displacements, moments and shear forces distribution. Module 3 works based on data provided by Module 1 and Module 2.

Figure 3.5 shows the depiction of Excel-VBA programming structure. Figure 3.6 shows a chart of programming structure for a specified task consists of main procedures (abbreviated to facilitate in writing) in TRUSS2D, a program for truss structural analysis as presented in Chapter 7.

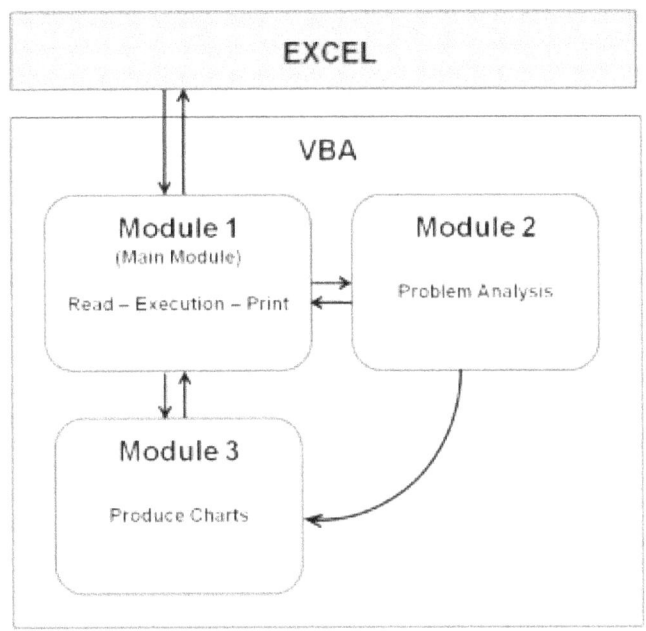

Figure 3.5: Excel-VBA programming structure

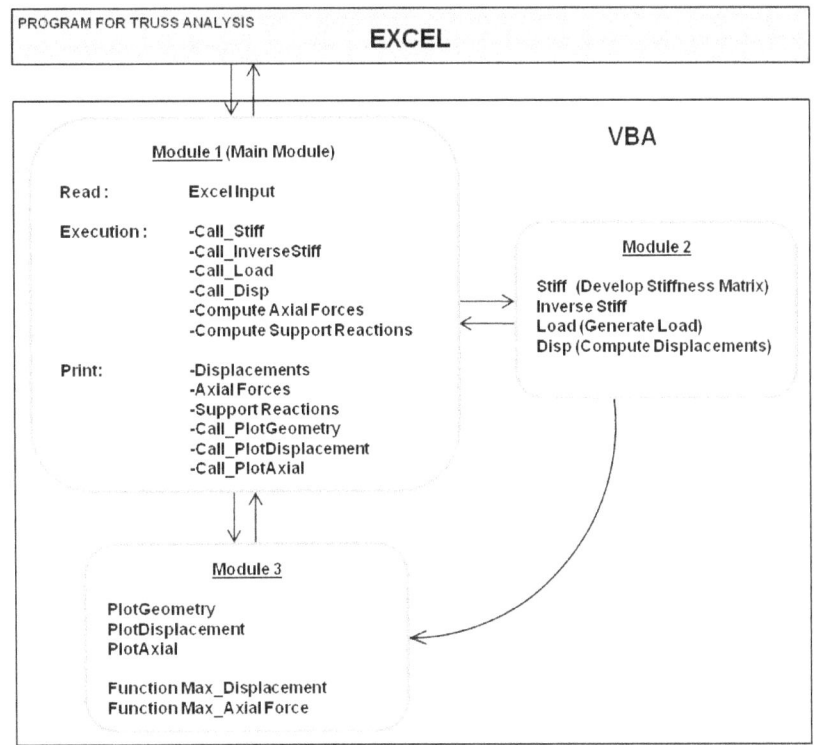

Figure 3.6: Excel-VBA programming structure for truss analysis (TRUSS2D)

3.5.3 Tips

In designing macros, the movements between a worksheet and Visual Basic Editor (VBE) window is often done as both windows are interconnected. To launch the VBE, click on the **Visual Basic** icon (in the **Developer** tab) and if you wish to go back to the worksheet, click **Microsoft Excel** icon in VBA menu. The other way is by using shortcut **Alt+F11** on both windows. Actually, to accelerate of displaying both windows is to place them together in a monitor screen as shown in Figure 3.7. Thus, if VBA code is executed, its interaction with the worksheet can be seen at the same time.

Below are the steps to put a worksheet and VBE in one screen and commands to execute a code line by line:

1. In the worksheet window, click **Restore Down** icon at the top right corner and drag the top sheet to move it to the left side of the monitor screen. Point to the sheet border so the pointer becomes two arrowheads, and then drag the worksheet border to change its size to approximately half size of the monitor screen.

2. Go to the VBE window and use the same way to place it on the right side of the monitor screen. Now, both windows are viewed at the same time.

3. Next, go to the VBE by clicking its window. Click **Close** icon in the **VBA Project** window, so only VBA module is now visible (to display the VBA Project window back, click icon **Project Explorer** or press **Ctrl+R**). To run a code line by line, press **F8** and press F8 again to continue to the next line. To jump to the desired line, place the cursor at the desired line and press **Ctrl+F8**. Each line to be executed is marked in yellow.

4. You can set a breakpoint to suspend program execution at a selected line. Place the cursor at the selected line and press **F9**. To run macro, click **Run Macro** (**F5**). The other way is to click the left bar at the line that you want to set the breakpoint, so a red dot appears. Click on the red dot to remove.

5. A variable value computed during program execution can be seen its value by attaching the pointer on a variable, as shown in Figure 3.8. This variable "reads" a

cell value in a worksheet. Hold the mouse for a second until the value displays. It shows the cell value in the worksheet.

Through step 1 and 2, the movement between worksheet - VBE is simply done by clicking one window without losing another window. It is very helpful if you wish to run the program and see the results at once (through step 3 and 4).

Performing all the steps above is very helpful in developing flow of a program and solve errors as well. Step 3 and 4 is actually the process of tracing errors (debugging) by using commands in the **Debug** menu, and the process for program verification (testing) by running code line by line. Testing and debugging is a routine activity when creating a program that requires a number of control structures (branching and looping). A condition where a program is paused for developing code is called **break mode**.

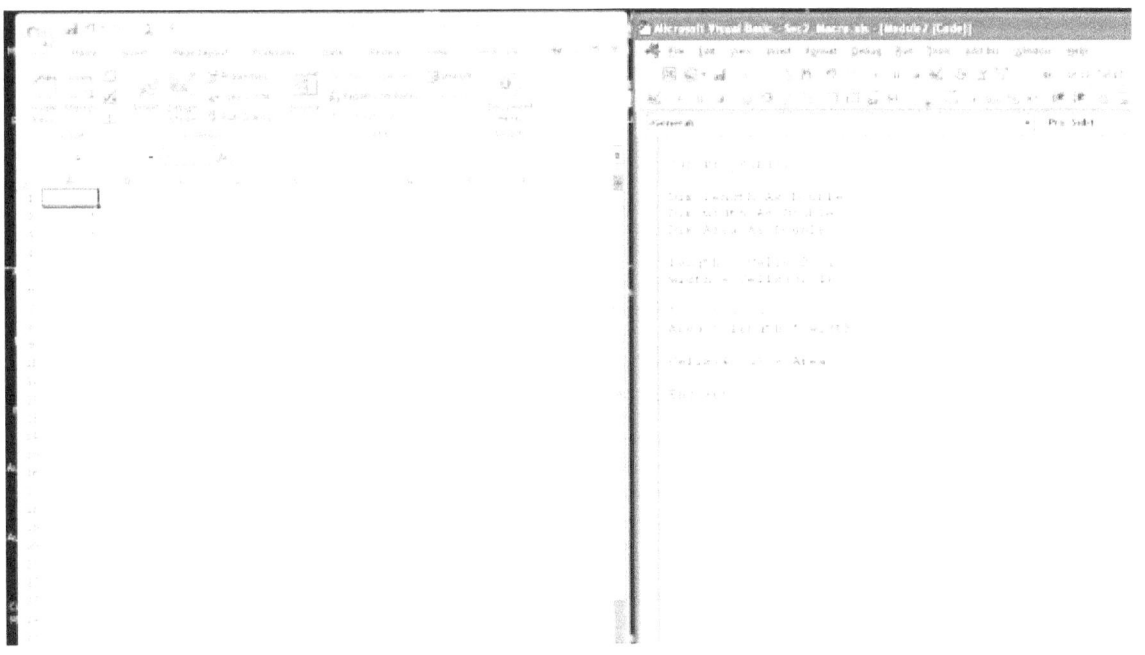

Figure 3.7: Worksheet – VBA windows are placed in one screen

One of error types that may occur is when attempting to access elements of an array with subscripts exceed the range that has been specified, so when the code is running, a "subscript out of range" error message appears. For example, in a looping where the number of process exceeds maximum subscript of an element. To get to the location where an error occurs, click **Debug**, and **Reset** to stop the program.

An Introduction to Excel for Civil Engineers

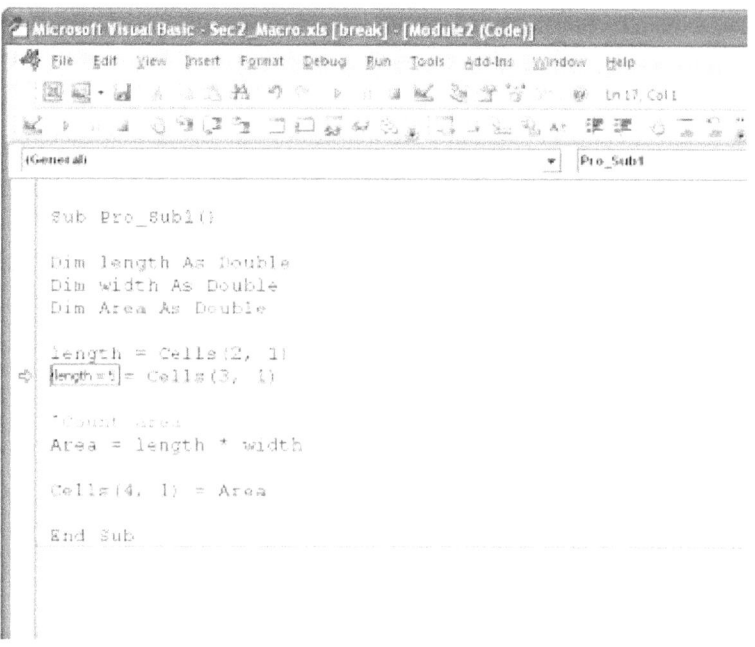

Figure 3.8: To see a variable value by attaching pointer

3.6 CHART MACRO

Excel chart is an object that can be manipulated by VBA through its methods and properties, for examples, in an aim of adding some lines (**Select Data Source > Add**); to set border style and color; to set line style and color. Using VBA macro to create and manipulate charts makes the job becomes easy, faster, and advances to the most difficult level, which may not be done manually.

In Chapter 1, we have discussed how to make lines in a worksheet with given tables and formulas. Instead of that has done manually, it can be created using a macro. For a case, Example 3 of Chapter 1.10 will be presented here, that is to create a drawing of truss structure with the joint and line coordinates given below:

Table of joints

Joint	x	y
1	1.0	0.0
2	1.5	2.5
3	2.0	5.0
4	2.5	10.0
5	3.0	15.0
6	3.5	20.0

7	4.0	15.0
8	4.5	10.0
9	5.0	5.0
10	5.5	2.5
11	6.0	0.0
12	3.5	2.5

Table of Coordinates

Line	Joint		x1	y1	x2	y2
1	1	2				
2	2	3				
3	3	4				
4	4	5				
5	5	6				
6	6	7				
7	7	8				
8	8	9				
9	9	10		Data is programmed		
10	10	11				
11	2	12				
12	12	10				
13	3	12				
14	12	9				
15	3	8				
16	3	9				
17	4	9				
18	4	8				
19	4	7				
20	5	8				
21	5	7				

By creating a macro, the formulas to obtain (x1, y1) and (x2, y2) coordinates in the sheet above are no longer required, as the program will automatically read the data. The macro is as follows:

```
Sub MChart1()
Dim npt, nln, i
npt = 12 'no. of joint
nln = 21 'no. of line
```

An Introduction to Excel for Civil Engineers

```
ReDim x(npt), y(npt)
ReDim x1(nln), y1(nln), x2(nln), y2(nln)
'Read joint coord
For i = 1 To npt
   x(i) = Cells(4 + i, 2)
   y(i) = Cells(4 + i, 3)
Next i
'Read line coordinates
For i = 1 To nln
   x1(i) = x(Cells(4 + i, 6))
   y1(i) = y(Cells(4 + i, 6))
   x2(i) = x(Cells(4 + i, 7))
   y2(i) = y(Cells(4 + i, 7))
Next i
    ActiveSheet.ChartObjects("Chart 1").Activate
    ActiveChart.ChartArea.Select
    Selection.ClearContents
'creating lines
For i = 1 To nln
    With ActiveChart
        .SeriesCollection.NewSeries
        .SeriesCollection(i).XValues = Array(x1(i), x2(i))
        .SeriesCollection(i).Values = Array(y1(i), y2(i))
        .SeriesCollection(i).Name = "="""""
    End With
    ActiveChart.SeriesCollection(i).Select
Next i
End Sub
```

Now, we focus on three blocks of statements enclosed by a red line, as below. The blocks description will be given thereafter.

```vba
Sub XYChart()

Dim npt, nln, i

npt = 11 'no. of joint
nln = 21 'no. of line

ReDim x(npt), y(npt)
ReDim x1(nln), y1(nln), x2(nln), y2(nln)

'Read joint coordinates
For i = 1 To npt
    x(i) = Cells(4 + i, 2)
    y(i) = Cells(4 + i, 3)
Next i

'Read line coordinates
For i = 1 To nln
    x1(i) = x(Cells(4 + i, 6))
    y1(i) = y(Cells(4 + i, 6))
    x2(i) = x(Cells(4 + i, 7))
    y2(i) = y(Cells(4 + i, 7))
Next i                                              1

    ActiveSheet.ChartObjects("Chart 1").Activate
    ActiveChart.ChartArea.Select                    2
    Selection.ClearContents

'Drawing lines
For i = 1 To nln
    With ActiveChart
        .SeriesCollection.NewSeries
        .SeriesCollection(i).XValues = Array(x1(i), x2(i))   3
        .SeriesCollection(i).Values = Array(y1(i), y2(i))
        .SeriesCollection(i).Name = ""
    End With
    ActiveChart.SeriesCollection(i).Select
Next i

End Sub
```

Description:

- Block 1 is a code to read input data. It replaces what we have done using VLOOKUP function in Chapter 1, here are blank cells in the Table of Coordinates above. Figure out this "effectiveness", formulas as many as 21 rows x 4 columns (84 spreadsheet formulas) for defining 21 lines are simply replaced with only 6 *rows* of VBA code without limit of line that will be created, to tens, hundreds and more.
- Block 2 is a code to activate chart object that to be manipulated, in this case is Chart1. Note that, we will never (ever) create a new chart using VBA statement (**Charts.Add**), because there will be long "extra" code for chart formatting. Instead, we will proceed manually (through **Insert** > **Charts** > **Scatters**) and format the chart as desired! To identify a chart name, right-click the mouse on the **Chart Area** > **Assign Macro**, and then see the name in the **Macro Name** text box. Chart name identification is necessary especially if you work with many charts.
- Block 3 is the same steps if we use the **Add Series** in the **Select Data Source** dialog box for lines coordinates data entry in a worksheet. Yes, that is right; this block does a great *job* of saving a lot of time!

Excel input form for the chart macro above as below:

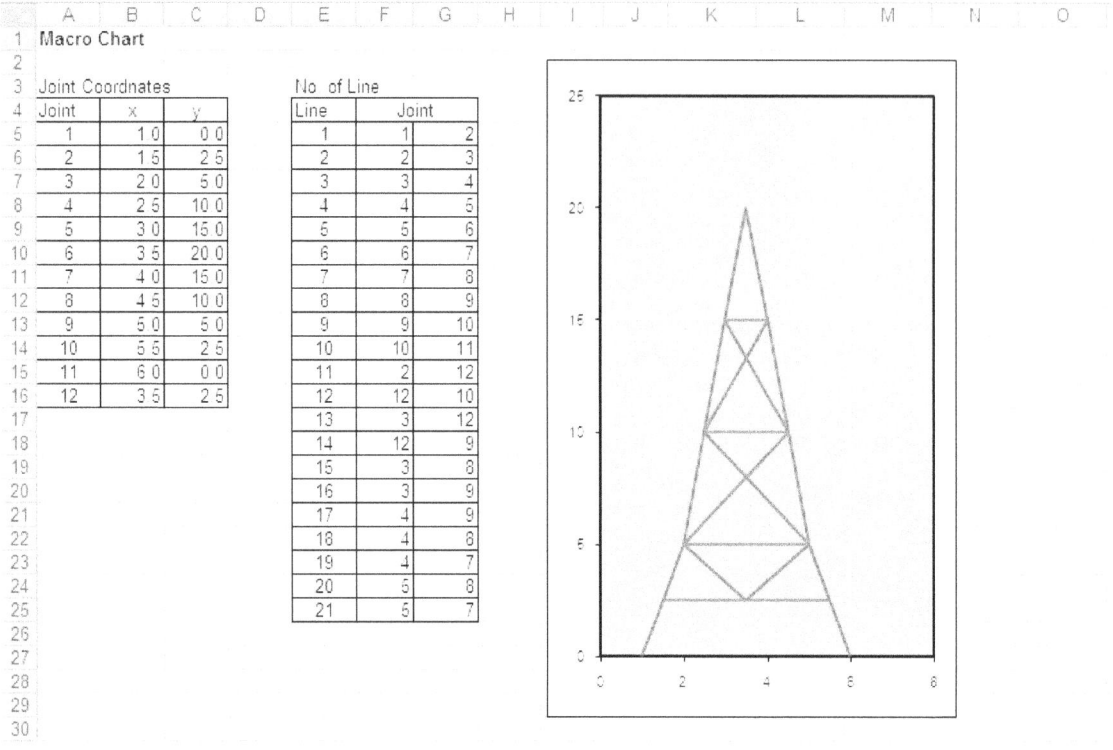

If you want to go further in creating chart, you may proceed by setting its properties, such as line color, marker style and color, or line style (continuous or dashed). The following code is to set (values of) the Chart properties (code is enclosed by red lines):

```
Sub MChart1()
Dim npt, nln, i
npt = 12 'no. of joint
nln = 21 'no. of line
ReDim x(npt), y(npt)
ReDim x1(nln), y1(nln), x2(nln), y2(nln)

'Read joint coordinates
For i = 1 To npt
   x(i) = Cells(4 + i, 2)
   y(i) = Cells(4 + i, 3)
Next i
```

An Introduction to Excel for Civil Engineers

```
'Read line coordinates
For i = 1 To nln
    x1(i) = x(Cells(4 + i, 6))
    y1(i) = y(Cells(4 + i, 6))
    x2(i) = x(Cells(4 + i, 7))
    y2(i) = y(Cells(4 + i, 7))
Next i
    ActiveSheet.ChartObjects("Chart 1").Activate
    ActiveChart.ChartArea.Select
    Selection.ClearContents

'creating lines
For i = 1 To nln
    With ActiveChart
        .SeriesCollection.NewSeries
        .SeriesCollection(i).XValues = Array(x1(i), x2(i))
        .SeriesCollection(i).Values = Array(y1(i), y2(i))
        .SeriesCollection(i).Name = "="""""
    End With

    ActiveChart.SeriesCollection(i).Select
    With Selection
        .MarkerBackgroundColorIndex = xlNone
        .MarkerForegroundColorIndex = xlNone
        .MarkerStyle = xlNone
        .Smooth = False
    End With
    With Selection.Border
        .ColorIndex = 3 'red
        .Weight = xlMedium
        .LineStyle = xlContinuous
    End With
Next i

End Sub
```

The code (enclosed by red lines) is to set the chart properties, such as marker style, line type and line border. It uses the Border property of the Selection object to return a Border object with its properties: ColorIndex, Weight and LineStyle. In this example, line style and color properties are respectively set to "continuous" (xlcontinuous) and red (color index = 3). The Selection object represents the SeriesCollection(index) object of the ActiveChart object, that is, an active chart named Chart 1.

3.7 Manipulation on Program Steps

An application program (that is, a program for specific application) is built through a sequence of steps that take long process. It starts from defining problems, developing a model, building an algorithm and steps analysis, testing and debugging until it is published. An algorithm is a sequence of logical steps in problem solving.

Algorithm is closely related to the use of programming control structures such as branching and looping, which have been discussed earlier. In array data basis used in most civil engineering structural analysis program, it is necessary to have a little bit of knowledge of how to "manipulate" program steps or dictating the program flow using the programming control structure to read and print data, change the composition of elements of an array, create integer variables for storing data, and etc.

Example 1

Below is an example of array of numbers in a worksheet that has 6 rows and 6 columns. Change the array of numbers on the left side become the arrangement as seen on the right side, where only the main diagonal value will still remain, while the other = 0.

	A	B	C	D	E	F	G	H	I	J	K	L	M
1													
2	INPUT							OUTPUT					
3	1	7	13	19	25	31		1	0	0	0	0	0
4	2	8	14	20	26	32		0	8	0	0	0	0
5	3	9	15	21	27	33		0	0	15	0	0	0
6	4	10	16	22	28	34		0	0	0	22	0	0
7	5	11	17	23	29	35		0	0	0	0	29	0
8	6	12	18	24	30	36		0	0	0	0	0	36
9													
10													

Below is a code to solve Example 1. It starts (always) with reading the data, and then manipulate the steps (code inside the red line) and finally print the results:

```
Sub ExSTEP1()
Dim i, j, n
ReDim myArray(6, 6) As Integer

'Read input data
For i = 1 To 6
    For j = 1 To 6
        myArray(i, j) = Cells(2 + i, j)
    Next j
Next i
```

```
'Manipulate steps
For i = 1 To 6
n = myArray(i, i)
    For j = 1 To 6
        myArray(i, j) = 0
    Next j
myArray(i, i) = n
Next i
```

```
'Print ouput data
For i = 1 To 6
    For j = 1 To 6
        Cells(2 + i, 7 + j) = myArray(i, j)
    Next j
Next i
End Sub
```

Note that, the code (inside the red line) is the Author's version. Every programmer has own steps based on his/her interpretation in this problem. Similarly, if you are a programmer or whose accustomed to use Excel-VBA.

Example 2

Change elements arrangement of the left side array in Example 1 become in reverse order from the bottom to the top of the array. Thus, it simply starts by replacing the largest subscript value [myArray (6,6)] with the smallest subscript value [myArray (1,1)] and vice versa.

An Introduction to Excel for Civil Engineers

	A	B	C	D	E	F	G	H	I	J	K	L	M
1													
2	INPUT							OUTPUT					
3	1	7	13	19	25	31		36	30	24	18	12	6
4	2	8	14	20	26	32		35	29	23	17	11	5
5	3	9	15	21	27	33		34	28	22	16	10	4
6	4	10	16	22	28	34		33	27	21	15	9	3
7	5	11	17	23	29	35		32	26	20	14	8	2
8	6	12	18	24	30	36		31	25	19	13	7	1

The code (the Author's version):

```
Sub ExSTEP2()
Dim i, j, m, n
ReDim myArray(6, 6) As Integer
ReDim rvArray(6, 6) As Integer

'Read input data
For i = 1 To 6
    For j = 1 To 6
        myArray(i, j) = Cells(2 + i, j)
    Next j
Next i
```

```
'Manipulate steps
m = 0
n = 0
For i = 6 To 1 Step -1
    n = n + 1
    For j = 6 To 1 Step -1
        m = m + 1
        rvArray(j, i) = myArray(m, n)
    Next j
m = 0
Next i
```

```
'Print data
For i = 1 To 6
    For j = 1 To 6
        Cells(2 + i, 7 + j) = rvArray(i, j)
```

An Introduction to Excel for Civil Engineers

```
    Next j
Next i
End Sub
```

Example 3

Assemble the upper triangular on the left side array become the arrangement shown on the right side array, as shown in the worksheet below.

	A	B	C	D	E	F	G	H	I	J	K	L	M	N
1														
2	INPUT							OUTPUT						
3		1	7	13	19	25	31		1	7	13	19	25	31
4		2	8	14	20	26	32		8	14	20	26	32	
5		3	9	15	21	27	33		15	21	27	33		
6		4	10	16	22	28	34		22	28	34			
7		5	11	17	23	29	35		29	35				
8		6	12	18	24	30	36		36					
9														
10														

This example is made as an exercise for the readers to make their own code. As previous examples, the data manipulation in this example is done and completed within two looping. Use always the **Debug** menu to verify the program steps. Hopefully, all these examples are helpful to develop your Excel-VBA programming skill.

Note:

> An algorithm or in the (Author's) other words is a manipulation on program steps (flow) is basic procedure to tell computer how the program will be executed step by step. Although it may be formally a guideline to be followed but everything is gained from experiences and exercises. Therefore, the successful VBA programming "more depends" on instinct or interpretation of an author on the problems faced. Further, it was still agreed that the **fewer steps** needed to solve a problem, the better a program created, means the faster execution time needed by computer. Thus, it is **not** because of the **fewer code** lines created.

A Note for Beginners:

If you are a beginner in program algorithm, it is fine because your lesson has just started here. Run the code in Example 1 and 2 **step by step** using the **Debug** menu (for example, by pressing **F8**) and be focused on the code inside the red line. In **break mode**, see how the algorithm for both examples and try to understand the idea behind those codes writing. After you have understood, try to solve Example 3 or any problems you define by yourself or that are developed from Example 1 and 2.

An Introduction to Excel for Civil Engineers

CHAPTER 4

MATRIX PROGRAM

The calculation using matrix operation is very suitable and easy to be performed by a computer. Thus, in line with rapidly growth of computer usage, matrix method is becoming very popular and widely used instead of the analysis with manual method. It is widely used in mathematical sciences or in civil engineering field.

4.1 MATRIX DEFINITION

A matrix is a rectangular array, which involves a series of numbers of constituent components or elements.

Example:

$$A = \begin{bmatrix} a_{11} & a_{12} & \cdots & a_{1n} \\ a_{21} & & & \\ a_{31} & & & \\ - & & & \\ - & & & \\ a_{m1} & a_{m2} & & a_{mn} \end{bmatrix}$$

A matrix is generally written in [] or {} for row and column matrix. For example, [A] = [a_{ij}], where a_{ij} is element of the matrix, i = 1,2, .. m and j = 1,2, ... n. Subscript m indicates the number of rows and n indicates the number of column, or called has order (m x n). If a matrix has m = n, then it is called a square matrix.

4.1.1 TYPES OF MATRIX

1. Row matrix or row vector, where m = 1.

    Example: {1 2 3 4}

2. Column matrix or column vector, where n = 1.

Example: $\begin{Bmatrix} 1 \\ 2 \\ 3 \\ 4 \end{Bmatrix}$

3. Square Matrix

Diagonal matrix

All elements = 0, except in the main diagonal.

$$\begin{bmatrix} 1 & 0 & 0 & 0 \\ 0 & 2 & 0 & 0 \\ 0 & 0 & 3 & 0 \\ 0 & 0 & 0 & 4 \end{bmatrix}$$

Upper Triangular Matrix

All elements under the main diagonal = 0.

$$\begin{bmatrix} a_{11} & a_{12} & a_{13} & a_{14} & \ldots & a_{1n} \\ 0 & a_{22} & a_{23} & a_{24} & \ldots & a_{2n} \\ 0 & 0 & a_{33} & a_{34} & \ldots & a_{3n} \\ 0 & 0 & 0 & a_{44} & \ldots & a_{4n} \\ - & - & - & - & \ldots & - \\ 0 & 0 & 0 & 0 & \ldots & a_{nn} \end{bmatrix}$$

Lower Triangular Matrix

All elements above the main diagonal = 0.

$$\begin{bmatrix} a_{11} & 0 & 0 & 0 & \ldots & 0 \\ a_{21} & a_{22} & 0 & 0 & \ldots & 0 \\ a_{31} & a_{32} & a_{33} & 0 & \ldots & 0 \\ a_{41} & a_{42} & a_{43} & a_{44} & \ldots & 0 \\ - & - & - & - & \ldots & 0 \\ a_{m1} & a_{m2} & a_{m3} & a_{m4} & \ldots & a_{mn} \end{bmatrix}$$

An Introduction to Excel for Civil Engineers

Scalar matrix

Scalar matrix is a diagonal matrix where the diagonal elements are the same number.

$$\begin{bmatrix} 4 & 0 & 0 & 0 \\ 0 & 4 & 0 & 0 \\ 0 & 0 & 4 & 0 \\ 0 & 0 & 0 & 4 \end{bmatrix}$$

Unit matrix

Unit matrix is a scalar matrix in which the value of elements = 1. This matrix is also called identity matrix and generally denoted by [I]. Multiplying by [I] will return the origin matrix.

$$\begin{bmatrix} 1 & 0 & 0 & 0 \\ 0 & 1 & 0 & 0 \\ 0 & 0 & 1 & 0 \\ 0 & 0 & 0 & 1 \end{bmatrix}$$

Band Matrix

Band matrix is a square matrix (n x n) where the non-zero elements are grouped and form a diagonal elements band.

$$\begin{bmatrix} a_{11} & a_{12} & 0 & 0 & \ldots & 0 & 0 \\ a_{21} & a_{22} & 0 & 0 & \ldots & 0 & 0 \\ 0 & 0 & a_{33} & a_{34} & \ldots & 0 & 0 \\ 0 & 0 & a_{43} & a_{44} & \ldots & 0 & 0 \\ 0 & 0 & 0 & 0 & \ldots & a_{n-1,n-1} & a_{n-1,n} \\ 0 & 0 & 0 & 0 & \ldots & a_{n,n-1} & a_{n,n} \end{bmatrix}$$

Symmetric matrix

A matrix [A] is announced symmetric if,

$[A]^T = [A]$ or $a_{ij} = a_{ji}$

Example:

$$\begin{bmatrix} 1 & 4 & -5 \\ 4 & 2 & 6 \\ -5 & 6 & 3 \end{bmatrix}$$

4.1.2 Matrix Operation

Matrix Addition and Subtraction

If [A] and [B] are two matrices that have equal dimension, then they can be added.

If [A] = [a_{ij}] and [B] = [b_{ij}] returns [C] = [C_{ij}], it is written:

[C] = [A] + [B]

$c_{ij} = a_{ij} + b_{ij}$ for each *i* dan *j*.

Example

$$[A] = \begin{bmatrix} 2 & 4 & 3 \\ 1 & 5 & 4 \end{bmatrix}, [B] = \begin{bmatrix} 0 & -3 & 2 \\ 4 & 2 & -3 \end{bmatrix}$$

$$[A] + [B] = \begin{bmatrix} 2+0 & 4-3 & 3+2 \\ 1+4 & 5+2 & 4-3 \end{bmatrix} = \begin{bmatrix} 2 & 1 & 5 \\ 5 & 7 & 1 \end{bmatrix}$$

Subtract [B] from [A] is equal to add [A] with [-B] or written: [A] - [B] = [A] + [-B].

Matrix Multiplication

Multiplication of two matrices, [A] (m x n) by [B] (n x p) will return [C] of order (m x p). When do the matrix multiplication the number of columns [A] must be equal to the number of rows [B].

If [A] = [a_{ij}], [B] = [b_{ij}] and [C] = [C_{ij}] then,

$c_{ij} = a_{i1}b_{1j} + a_{i2}b_{2j} + ... + a_{im}b_{mj}$

or written as,

$$c_{ij} = \sum_{k=1}^{m} a_{ik} b_{kj}$$

Example 1

$$[A] = \begin{bmatrix} a_{11} & a_{12} \\ a_{21} & a_{22} \\ a_{31} & a_{32} \end{bmatrix}, [B] = \begin{bmatrix} b_{11} & b_{12} \\ b_{21} & b_{22} \end{bmatrix}$$

$$[C] = [A] \times [B] = \begin{bmatrix} a_{11} & a_{12} \\ a_{21} & a_{22} \\ a_{31} & a_{32} \end{bmatrix} \begin{bmatrix} b_{11} & b_{12} \\ b_{21} & b_{22} \end{bmatrix}$$

$$= \begin{bmatrix} a_{11}b_{11} + a_{12}b_{21} & a_{11}b_{12} + a_{12}b_{22} \\ a_{21}b_{11} + a_{22}b_{21} & a_{21}b_{12} + a_{22}b_{22} \\ a_{31}b_{11} + a_{32}b_{21} & a_{31}b_{12} + a_{32}b_{22} \end{bmatrix}$$

Example 2

$$[A] = \begin{bmatrix} 2 & 3 \\ 4 & 1 \\ 7 & 4 \end{bmatrix}, [B] = \begin{bmatrix} 3 & 3 \\ -1 & 5 \end{bmatrix}$$

$$[C] = [A] \times [B] = \begin{bmatrix} 2 & 3 \\ 4 & 1 \\ 7 & 4 \end{bmatrix} \begin{bmatrix} 3 & 3 \\ -1 & 5 \end{bmatrix}$$

$$= \begin{bmatrix} 2.3 + 3.-1 & 2.3 + 3.5 \\ 4.3 + 1.-1 & 4.3 + 1.5 \\ 7.3 + 4.-1 & 7.3 + 4.5 \end{bmatrix}$$

$$= \begin{bmatrix} 3 & 21 \\ 11 & 17 \\ 17 & 41 \end{bmatrix}$$

Matrix Inverse

Division is not defined in a matrix operation; it uses the inverse of a matrix. Matrix inversion is only done on a square matrix and written with notation [ ]$^{-1}$. Multiplication by matrix inverse is a division by the matrix. For example: [A] x [B] = [C] where [A] is a square matrix, the equation can be written into a division operation: [B] = [A]$^{-1}$ [C]. [A]$^{-1}$ is called the inverse of [A].

Matrix Transpose

If [A] is a matrix of order (m x n), then the transpose of [A] is a matrix of order (n x m) or written as $[A]^T$. Rows and columns of [A] become the columns and the rows of $[A]^T$.

$[B] = [A]^T$

$b_{ij} = a_{ji}$

Example

$$[A] = \begin{bmatrix} 1 & 2 & 3 \\ 4 & 5 & 6 \end{bmatrix}$$

$$[A]^T = \begin{bmatrix} 1 & 4 \\ 2 & 5 \\ 3 & 6 \end{bmatrix}$$

Some properties associated with matrix transpose:

$([A]^T)^T = [A]$

$([A]+[B])^T = [A]^T + [B]^T$

$([A][B])^T = [B]^T [A]^T$

System of Linear Equations

Many problems in civil engineering are represented by systems of "m" linear equations with "n" unknown number and this can be solved using matrix methods. It is often, the number of equations is equal to the number of unknowns.

Example: two systems of equations

3x + 2y = 9

5x − y = 2

When expressed in matrix form it becomes:

$$\begin{bmatrix} 3 & 2 \\ 5 & -1 \end{bmatrix} \begin{bmatrix} x \\ y \end{bmatrix} = \begin{bmatrix} 9 \\ 2 \end{bmatrix}$$

In the general form, "m" linear equations with "n" unknown number can be expressed as:

$$\begin{bmatrix} a_{11} & a_{12} & a_{13} & \cdots & a_{1n} \\ a_{21} & a_{22} & a_{23} & \cdots & a_{2n} \\ a_{31} & a_{32} & a_{33} & \cdots & a_{3n} \\ \vdots & \vdots & \vdots & \vdots & \vdots \\ a_{m1} & a_{m2} & a_{m3} & \cdots & a_{mn} \end{bmatrix} \begin{bmatrix} x_1 \\ x_2 \\ x_3 \\ \vdots \\ x_n \end{bmatrix} = \begin{bmatrix} b_1 \\ b_2 \\ b_3 \\ \vdots \\ b_m \end{bmatrix} \qquad (4.1)$$

and simplified into:

$[A].\{X\} = \{B\}$ (4.2)

where,

[A]   square matrix represents coefficients of Equation 4.2

{X}   unknowns column vector

{B}   constants column vector

It is simply to say that the solution of systems of "m" linear equations in matrix form as expressed in Equations 4.2 is finding unknowns {X}, where [A] and [B] are known values. There are many methods used to solve Equation 4.2, and some will briefly be discussed in the examples below.

1. Elimination Method

    Example

    $2x + 3y = 7$ ...(1)

    $3x - 2y = 4$ ...(2)

    This is an example of two linear equations with 2 unknowns, x and y.

    Elimination

    Eliminate x from both equations by subtracting Equation 2 from Equation 1 that has been given a multiplying factor (Eq. B1):

    $$2x + 3y = 7 \ldots (1) \times \frac{3}{2} \quad \rightarrow \quad 3x + \frac{9}{2}y = \frac{21}{2} \quad \ldots(B1)$$

$$3x - 2y = 4 \quad \ldots(2)$$

$$\frac{13}{2}y = \frac{13}{2}$$

$$y = 1$$

Back Substitution

Substituting this value of y back into either Eq.1 or Eq.2, we get x = 2.

Thus, solution for the unknowns {X}: $\begin{Bmatrix} x \\ y \end{Bmatrix} = \begin{Bmatrix} 2 \\ 1 \end{Bmatrix}$

2. Get directly the inverse of [A] or [A]$^{-1}$

From Equation 4.2:

[A]{X} = {B}

Multiply both matrices by [A]$^{-1}$:

[A]$^{-1}$[A]{X} = [A]$^{-1}${B}, it is known [A]$^{-1}$[A] = [I]

[I]{X}=[A]$^{-1}${B}

{X}=[A]$^{-1}${B}   (4.3)

Thus, if [A]$^{-1}$ is known, Equation 4.3 can be solved.

Example

Below is given a system of two linear equations:

2x + 3y = 7

3x − 2y = 4

In this example, the Gauss-Jordan method is used for finding matrix inverse. The solution is to put the unit matrix [I] next to coefficient matrix [A] such that when the process is finished [A] becomes [I] and the previous [I] becomes matrix inverse [A]$^{-1}$. The overall process can be written by:

[A ⋮ I] → [I ⋮ [A]$^{-1}$]

The process is done simultaneously on [A] and [I] through elementary row operations in order to reduce [A] to [I], that is, elements of [A] become ones on the main diagonal and zeros everywhere else. The example is given below:

$$[A] = \begin{bmatrix} 2 & 3 \\ 3 & -2 \end{bmatrix}$$

Put [I] next to [A]:

$$\begin{bmatrix} 2 & 3 \\ 3 & -2 \end{bmatrix} \begin{bmatrix} 1 & 0 \\ 0 & 1 \end{bmatrix}$$

Step 1: divide row 1 by 2 in the matrix above

$$\begin{bmatrix} 1 & \frac{3}{2} \\ 3 & -2 \end{bmatrix} \begin{bmatrix} \frac{1}{2} & 0 \\ 0 & 1 \end{bmatrix}$$

Step 2: Add row 2 to row 1 times -3

$$\begin{bmatrix} 1 & \frac{6}{2} \\ 0 & \frac{-13}{2} \end{bmatrix} \begin{bmatrix} \frac{1}{2} & 0 \\ -\frac{3}{2} & 1 \end{bmatrix}$$

Step 3: Multiply row 2 by $-\frac{2}{13}$

$$\begin{bmatrix} 1 & \frac{3}{2} \\ 0 & 1 \end{bmatrix} \begin{bmatrix} \frac{1}{2} & 0 \\ \frac{6}{26} & -\frac{2}{13} \end{bmatrix}$$

Step 4: Add row 1 to row 2 times $-\frac{3}{2}$

$$\begin{bmatrix} 1 & 0 \\ 0 & 1 \end{bmatrix} \begin{bmatrix} \frac{8}{52} & \frac{6}{26} \\ \frac{6}{26} & -\frac{2}{13} \end{bmatrix}$$

Thus,

$$[A]^{-1} = \begin{bmatrix} \dfrac{8}{52} & \dfrac{6}{26} \\ \dfrac{6}{26} & -\dfrac{2}{13} \end{bmatrix}$$

Enter $[A]^{-1}$ into Equation 4.3

$\{X\} = [A]^{-1}.\{B\}$

$$\begin{Bmatrix} x \\ y \end{Bmatrix} = \begin{bmatrix} \dfrac{8}{52} & \dfrac{6}{26} \\ \dfrac{6}{26} & -\dfrac{2}{13} \end{bmatrix} \begin{Bmatrix} 7 \\ 4 \end{Bmatrix}$$

$$\begin{Bmatrix} x \\ y \end{Bmatrix} = \begin{Bmatrix} \dfrac{104}{52} \\ \dfrac{26}{26} \end{Bmatrix}$$

So, the solution to this system,

$$\begin{Bmatrix} x \\ y \end{Bmatrix} = \begin{Bmatrix} 2 \\ 1 \end{Bmatrix}$$

3. Iterative Method

This method is actually an approach by taking an initial value of unknown and is corrected or refined to enter the next value. We have examined an iterative method for the example above in Chapter 2.6. Here is now an example of a system of three linear equations:

$5x + 4y + 3z = 12$ (4.4)

$4x + 7y + 4z = 15$ (4.5)

$3x + 4y + 4z = 11$ (4.6)

The iterative process is quite long, so in this example we will be working with help of a computer using Excel iteration.

Re-write Equation 4.4, 4.5 and 4.6 into forms below:

Equation 4.4: $x = 12/5 - 4y/5 - 3z/5 = (12 - 4y - 3z)/5$

Equation 4.5: $y = 15/7 - 4x/7 - 4z/7 = (15 - 4x - 4z)/7$

Equation 4.6: $z = 11/4 - 3x/4 - 4y/4 = (11 - 3x - 4y)/4$

Further, convert the equations into worksheet formulas and enter the formulas in cell B2, C3 and D4. However, until this stage no iteration to be done because the formulas still stand on their own equations.

	A	B	C	D	E	F
1		Eq.1	Eq.2	Eq.3		
2	x	=(12-4*B3-3*B4)/5				
3	y		=(15-4*C2-4*C4)/7			
4	z			=(11-3*D2-4*D3)/4		
5						
6						

The iterative process will be carried out after the following connections:

The value of y, z of Equation 4.4 = value y, z of Equation 4.5

The value of x, z of Equation 4.5 = value x of Equation 4.4 and z of Equation 4.6

The value of x, y of Equation 4.6 = value x, y of Equation 4.5

The above equations are written in the worksheet as follows:

	A	B	C	D	E
1		Eq.1	Eq.2	Eq.3	
2	x	=(12-4*B3-3*B4)/5	=B2	=C2	
3	y	=C3	=(15-4*C2-4*C4)/7	=C3	
4	z	=C4	=D4	=(11-3*D2-4*D3)/4	
5					
6					

The iteration steps shown in the worksheet below:

1 x iteration:

	A	B	C	D	E
1		Eq.1	Eq.2	Eq.3	
2	x	2.40000	2.40000	2.40000	
3	y	0.00000	0.77143	0.77143	
4	z	0.00000	0.00000	0.17857	
5					

5 x iterations:

	A	B	C	D	E
1		Eq.1	Eq.2	Eq.3	
2	x	1.29890	1.29890	1.29890	
3	y	1.07655	1.16637	1.16637	
4	z	0.40995	0.56703	0.60945	
5					

10 x iterations:

	A	B	C	D	E
1		Eq.1	Eq.2	Eq.3	
2	x	1.01854	1.01854	1.01854	
3	y	1.03905	1.02231	1.02231	
4	z	0.94242	0.95086	0.96379	
5					

20 x iterations:

	A	B	C	D	E
1		Eq.1	Eq.2	Eq.3	
2	x	1.00597	1.00597	1.00597	
3	y	1.01594	1.00960	1.00960	
4	z	0.97723	0.98348	0.98592	
5					

50 x iterations:

	A	B	C	D	E
1		Eq.1	Eq.2	Eq.3	
2	x	1.00046	1.00046	1.00046	
3	y	1.00172	1.00097	1.00097	
4	z	0.99784	0.99848	0.99868	
5					

The iteration process of finding {X} of Equation 4.4 is actually to make x, y, z to become equal (same value) on column B, C and D in satisfying the given equations. It appears that they are very close at 50th iteration and by rounding obtained:

$$\begin{Bmatrix} x \\ y \\ z \end{Bmatrix} = \begin{Bmatrix} 1 \\ 1 \\ 1 \end{Bmatrix}$$

4.2 PROGRAM FOR MATRIX OPERATIONS

Multiplication and inversion of matrix are two main operations in matrix equations found in most of engineering calculations using matrix method. This section will show some programs (macros) for multiplication and inversion of matrix.

Matrix Multiplication

The following is an example of program to calculate a multiplication of two matrices. The program is named MMULT1, where input data and the results are placed on Sheet1.

Example

Find the multiplication of two matrices with the following equation:

[C] = [A].[B]

where,

$$[A] = \begin{bmatrix} 2 & 3 \\ 4 & 1 \\ 7 & 4 \end{bmatrix}, [B] = \begin{bmatrix} 3 & 3 \\ -1 & 5 \end{bmatrix}$$

We know that the multiplication of a matrix = the multiplication of rows elements in the first matrix by columns elements of the second matrix. It has previously been shown in Section 4.1.2 example. VBA code to get [C] is:

```
Sub MMULT1()
Dim MA(3, 2) As Double
Dim MB(2, 2) As Double
Dim MC(1 To 3, 1 To 2) As Double


'===============
'Read Input Data
'===============
'[A] or MA
MA(1, 1) = Cells(6, 2)
MA(2, 1) = Cells(7, 2)
MA(3, 1) = Cells(8, 2)
MA(1, 2) = Cells(6, 3)
MA(2, 2) = Cells(7, 3)
MA(3, 2) = Cells(8, 3)
```

An Introduction to Excel for Civil Engineers

```
'[B] or MB
MB(1, 1) = Cells(6, 5)
MB(2, 1) = Cells(7, 5)
MB(1, 2) = Cells(6, 6)
MB(2, 2) = Cells(7, 6)
'=============
'Multiplying
'[C] = [A].[B]
'=============
MC(1, 1) = MA(1, 1) * MB(1, 1) + MA(1, 2) * MB(2, 1)
MC(2, 1) = MA(2, 1) * MB(1, 1) + MA(2, 2) * MB(2, 1)
MC(3, 1) = MA(3, 1) * MB(1, 1) + MA(3, 2) * MB(2, 1)
MC(1, 2) = MA(1, 1) * MB(1, 2) + MA(1, 2) * MB(2, 2)
MC(2, 2) = MA(2, 1) * MB(1, 2) + MA(2, 2) * MB(2, 2)
MC(3, 2) = MA(3, 1) * MB(1, 2) + MA(3, 2) * MB(2, 2)
'==========
'Print [C]:
'==========
Range(Cells(12, 2), Cells(14, 3)).FormulaArray = MC
End Sub
```

Worksheet form that relates to the above code is as below:

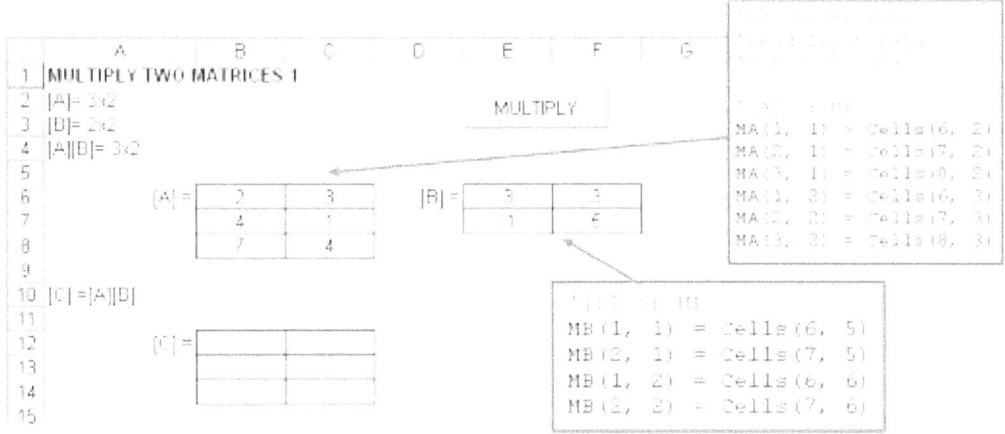

In this example, [A] has order 3 x 2 and [B] has order 2 x 2 to return [C] of order 3 x 2. Input data of element [A] is on the cell range B6:C8 or Cells (6,2) to Cells (8,3), while element [B] is on the cell range Cells (6,5) to Cells (7,6). To run the program, click the embedded

An Introduction to Excel for Civil Engineers

command button on the worksheet. The results are printed on the cell range Cells (12,2) to Cells (14,3) using statement **FormulaArray** = [C] as shown below:

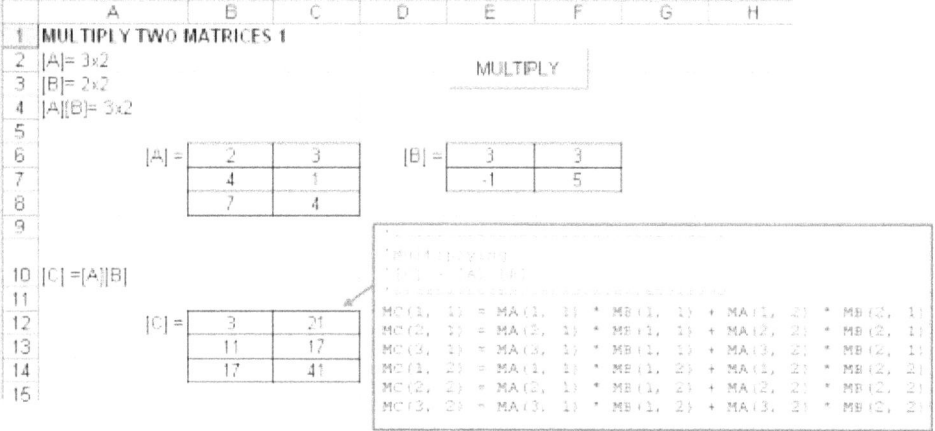

For a large-sized matrix, the given MMULT1 example is ineffective in term of that many code lines have to write which equal to a number of rows of the matrix. Instead, it would be better to use **For...Next** looping to read input data, to process and print the results. This way saves a lot of code writing.

The code above is then modified by giving the row and column indexes (i, j and k) to [A], [B] and [C], and the process is done in three looping as shown below:

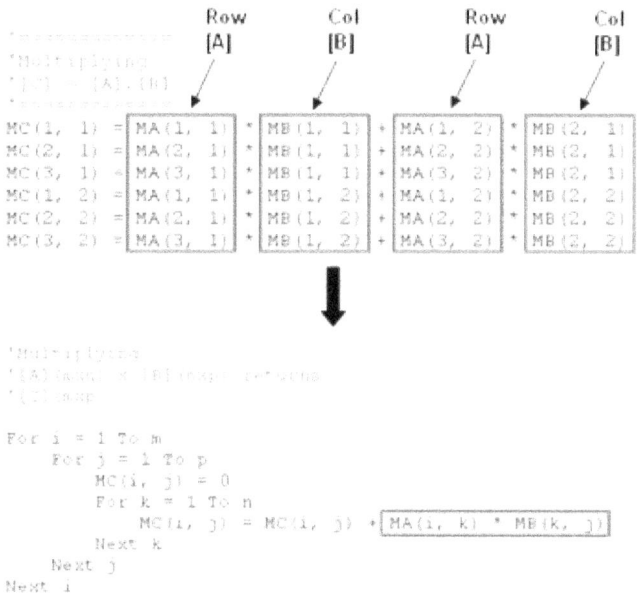

In the looping above, m and n represents number of rows and columns of [A], respectively, while n and p represents number of rows and columns of [B], respectively. The following example is a modified matrix multiplication code used to multiply a 6x6 matrix by a 6x3 matrix. The program is named MMULT2.

An Introduction to Excel for Civil Engineers

```
Sub MMULT2()
Dim m, n, p As Integer
m = Cells(2, 5)
n = Cells(3, 5)
p = Cells(4, 5)
ReDim MA(1 To m, 1 To n) As Double
ReDim MB(1 To n, 1 To p) As Double
ReDim MC(1 To m, 1 To p) As Double

'Input data [A]
For i = 1 To m
    For j = 1 To n
        MA(i, j) = Cells(5 + i, 1 + j)
    Next j
Next i

'Input data [B]
For i = 1 To n
    For j = 1 To p
        MB(i, j) = Cells(5 + i, 9 + j)
    Next j
Next i

'Multiplying
'[A](mxn) x [B](nxp) returns
'[C](mxp)

For i = 1 To m
    For j = 1 To p
        MC(i, j) = 0
        For k = 1 To n
            MC(i, j) = MC(i, j) + MA(i, k) * MB(k, j)
        Next k
    Next j
Next i

'Print result
```

```
For i = 1 To m
    For j = 1 To p
        Cells(15 + i, 1 + j) = MC(i, j)
    Next j
Next i
End Sub
```

	A	B	C	D	E	F	G	H	I	J	K	L
1												
2	[A] =	mxn		m =	6							
3	[B] =	nxp		n =	6							
4	[C] =	mxp		p =	3							
5												
6	[A] =	20	5	0	0	0	0		[B] =	0.25	0	0
7		5	20	0	0	0	0			0.25	1	0
8		0	0	30	10	0	0			-0.50	1	0
9		0	0	10	30	0	0			-0.50	0	1
10		0	0	0	0	12	6			0.25	0	1
11		0	0	0	0	6	12			0.25	0	0
12												
13												
14	[C] =[A].[B]											
15												
16	[C] =	6.25	5	0								
17		6.25	20	0								
18		-20	30	10								
19		-20	10	30								
20		4.5	0	12								
21		4.5	0	6								
22												

Printing the results that previously used *FormulaArray* statement is replaced by two orders of For…Next looping in MMULT2. The first and second looping are respectively for printing rows and columns of [C]. This way is much better in term of automating the print job, because we do not need to calculate a range of the array that will be generated, as it has been known = m x p.

Matrix multiplication can also be done in a worksheet using Excel built-in function **MMULT** (*array1*, *array2*). For this example, a formula can be written as follows:

= MMULT(B6:G11,J6:L11).

To print the result, use the **INDEX** function or you can enter the formula above as an array formula. See about an array formula in Chapter 1.5.

Matrix Inversion

One of the most common methods of finding an inverse of matrix is the The Gauss-Jordan method with a process that has been described in the previous section. The steps are in attempts to turn a matrix that to be found its inverse (e.g. [A]) becomes an identity matrix [I] and at the same time, the previous [I] becomes $[A]^{-1}$. These are done by elementary row operations as ever shown in the previous example.

$$[A \vdots I] \rightarrow [I \vdots [A]^{-1}]$$

In programming, it can be done by taking a matrix e.g. [C] such that at the end of the process [C] turns into $[A]^{-1}$. A looping through [C] rows carries out this process. In the beginning, values in the first row of [C] are divided by element **a11** of [A] in an attempt to turn a11 = 1, therefore c11 = 1 / a11. This process is an analogy from that performed in [I]. At the end of the first looping, the values of [C] of order 3x3 will be:

$$[C] = \begin{bmatrix} \dfrac{1}{a_{11}} & \dfrac{a_{12}}{a_{11}} & \dfrac{a_{13}}{a_{11}} \\ -\dfrac{a_{21}}{a_{11}} & a_{22} + \dfrac{a_{12}}{a_{11}}.-a_{21} & a_{23} + \dfrac{a_{13}}{a_{11}}.-a_{21} \\ -\dfrac{a_{31}}{a_{11}} & a_{32} + \dfrac{a_{12}}{a_{11}}.-a_{31} & a_{33} + \dfrac{a_{13}}{a_{11}}-a_{31} \end{bmatrix}$$

Program for finding inverse of matrix is created in VBA and provided here. It notes that matrix inversion requires a square matrix, say, of order *m* x *m*, and the determinant of a matrix must not be zero. For the purpose of creating an input form, the order *m* inputted in the worksheet should be limited = 6.

An Introduction to Excel for Civil Engineers

Example 1

Find the inverse of [A] = [5].

Solution for Example 1:

Example 2

Find the inverse of,

$$[A] = \begin{bmatrix} 2 & 3 \\ 3 & -2 \end{bmatrix}$$

Solution for Example 2:

Example 3

Find the inverse of,

$$[A] = \begin{bmatrix} 1 & 3 & 3 \\ 1 & 4 & 3 \\ 1 & 3 & 4 \end{bmatrix}$$

Solution for Example 3:

The inverse of matrix can also be determined in a worksheet by using the built-in function **MINVERSE**. The way to use it is the same as **MMULT**.

VBA code:

```
Sub Inverse()
On Error Resume Next
m = Cells(3, 2)
ReDim MA(1 To m, 1 To m) As Double
Range("k5:p10").ClearContents

'Read input data
For i = 1 To m
    For j = 1 To m
        MA(i, j) = Cells(4 + i, j)
    Next j
Next i

'Find inverse []
  For i = 1 To m
   For j = 1 To m
       If j <> i Then MA(i, j) = MA(i, j) / MA(i, i)
   Next j
   For n = 1 To m
       If n = i Then GoTo 10
   For j = 1 To m
       If j <> i Then MA(n, j) = MA(n, j) - MA(i, j) * MA(n, i)
   Next j
10 Next n
   For n = 1 To m
       If n <> i Then MA(n, i) = -MA(n, i) / MA(i, i)
   Next n
```

```
      MA(i, i) = 1 / MA(i, i)
        For ii = 1 To m
          For ij = 1 To m
              Cells(4 + ii, 10 + ij) = MA(ii, ij)
          Next ij
        Next ii
     Next i

'Print output data
For i = 1 To m
    For j = 1 To m
        Cells(4 + i, 10 + j) = MA(i, j)
    Next j
Next i

End Sub
```

4.3 MATRIX METHOD FOR STRUCTURAL ANALYSIS

Structure can be analyzed as a series of structural elements, which are connected to each other at endpoints called nodes. Solution to this system of arrangement of elements can be expressed by simultaneous linear equations that are made in a matrix form. In matrix form, then the calculation of the structure becomes easier to be solved with the help of a computer.

4.3.1 UPPER STRUCTURE

The method that will be adopted here is **direct stiffness method**. A brief introduction to the basics of this method will be given here; the readers are encouraged to read other references to supplement the discussion of this topic. The aim using of this method is to obtain **external forces – displacements** relationship expressed as:

$\{P\} = [K]\{X\}$ (4.7)

where, $\{P\}$ vector of external nodal forces

$[K]$ structure stiffness matrix

$\{X\}$ vector of nodal displacements

By deriving [K], thus the relationship between the external nodal forces and nodal displacements as expressed by Equation 4.7 can be obtained. It begins by deriving stiffness matrix of an element, then applies for other elements and put together to build stiffness matrix of a whole structure. To meet the compatibility of displacement between adjacent elements is by superposing the corresponding "force-displacement" components.

Further, to simplify the calculation we can partition the elements of [K], at the nodes that are free to displace (free nodes) and fixed (at the supports where displacement = 0). If X_b represents the displacements vector at the supports, X_f represents the displacements vector at the free nodes, P_f and P_b are the external forces vector, which correspond to their displacements, Equation 4.7 can be written as follows:

$$\begin{Bmatrix} P_f \\ P_b \end{Bmatrix} = \begin{bmatrix} K_{ff} & \vdots & K_{fb} \\ \cdots & \cdots & \cdots \\ K_{bf} & \vdots & K_{bb} \end{bmatrix} \begin{Bmatrix} X_f \\ X_b \end{Bmatrix}$$

(4.8)

If nodal displacements vector $\{X_b\} = 0$, then Equation 4.8 can be written:

$\{P_f\} = [K_{ff}]\{X_f\}$ (4.9)

And

$\{P_b\} = [K_{bf}]\{X_f\}$ (4.10)

The nodal displacements vector at the free nodes are then obtained using Equation 4.9 that becomes $\{X_f\} = [K_{ff}]^{-1}\{P_f\}$. Further, use the known $\{X_f\}$ to find the internal forces of each element. Here, the internal forces of element i are expressed in local coordinate system and given by:

$\{P\}i = \{P_o\} + [K]i\{X\}i$ (4.11)

where,

   $\{P_o\}$ fixed-end forces: reactions at end of element i due to external load that directly acting on element i

   $[K]i$ stiffness matrix of element i in local coordinate system

   $\{X\}i$ deformations matrix = $[T]i\{X_f\}$

   $[T]i$ transformation matrix of element i

The support reactions can be directly obtained in the global coordinate system of the structure using Equation 4.10 that becomes:

$\{R_b\} + \{P_b\} = [K_{bf}]\{X_f\}$

or $\quad \{R_b\} = [K_{bf}]\{X_f\} - \{P_b\}$ (4.12)

4.3.2 Sub Structure

The structure analysis in this subject is to obtain forces – displacements relationship of soil-structure interaction, which is by the means of **beam on elastic foundation** solution. Generally, it is solved with the finite element method where the soil-structure system is modeled by a series of finite elements connected at endpoints called nodes.

Some equations are developed through a sequence of steps where in the process satisfy: 1. Equilibrium relation that relates external nodal forces and internal element forces (are respectively represented by **P** and **F**); 2. Stress-strain relation that relates F and element deformations (**d**); 3. Compatibility relation that relates d and nodal displacements (**X**). Equating P with F using a bridging constant A in matrix form, we may write,

$$\{P\} = [\mathbf{A}]\{F\} \quad (4.13)$$

An equation relating $\{d\}$ at any node to $\{X\}$ is:

$\{d\} = [B]\{X\}$, and from reciprocal theorem it can be written,

$$\{d\} = [A]^T\{X\} \quad (4.14)$$

An equation relating $\{F\}$ to $\{d\}$ is:

$$\{F\} = [\mathbf{S}]\{d\} \quad (4.15)$$

Substituting Equation 4.14 into 4.15 to get,

$$\{F\} = [S]\{d\} = [S][A]^T\{X\} \quad (4.16)$$

Substituting Equation 4.16 into 4.13 to get,

$$\{P\} = [A]\{F\} = [\mathbf{A}][\mathbf{S}][\mathbf{A}]^T\{X\} \quad (4.17)$$

$\{X\}$ is the unknown displacements to be obtained, thus

$$\{X\} = ([A][S][A]^T)^{-1}\{P\} \quad (4.18)$$

Substituting $\{X\}$ back to Equation 4.16 to find the internal element forces $\{F\}$.

The $[A][S][A]^T$ matrix is also called a global stiffness matrix and it represents the system of equations for each P or X entry. Equations 4.16, 4.17 and 4.18 are the fundamental equations in the analysis using finite element method (J.E. Bowles, 1982).

CHAPTER 5

NUMERICAL METHOD

Many problems in science and technology involve the use of integral and differential equations. If the mathematical equation model is quite simple, then it can be solved by means of analytical method. However, many of those equations are difficult or may be impossible to be solved analytically. Instead, it must be solved numerically or using numerical methods.

The result of the numerical method is an approach to its exact value by means of analytically. Thus, it is just an approximate calculation with an estimated accuracy. Numerical methods will provide many benefits if done by a computer.

5.1 NUMERICAL INTEGRATION

The integral of a function f(x) from a to b is written:

$$y = \int_a^b f(x)dx$$

It has a broad sense as the area bounded by the curve y = f(x) and the X-axis, between x = a and x = b.

Analytical or exact solution to an integral is given by:

$$y = \int_a^b f(x)dx = \left[F(x)\right]_a^b = F(a) - F(b) \qquad (5.1)$$

where, F(x) is an anti-derivative of f(x) such that F'(x) = f(x).

Numerical integration of an integral to calculate area under the curve uses the concept of approach whereby the area is divided into smaller pieces of area such that if combined the total area of the pieces approaching the exact result. In this example we can use trapezoidal method where the area under the curve is divided into small pieces of area with sides $f(x_n)$ and $f(x_{n-1})$ that resembles a trapezoid as shown in Figure 5.1.

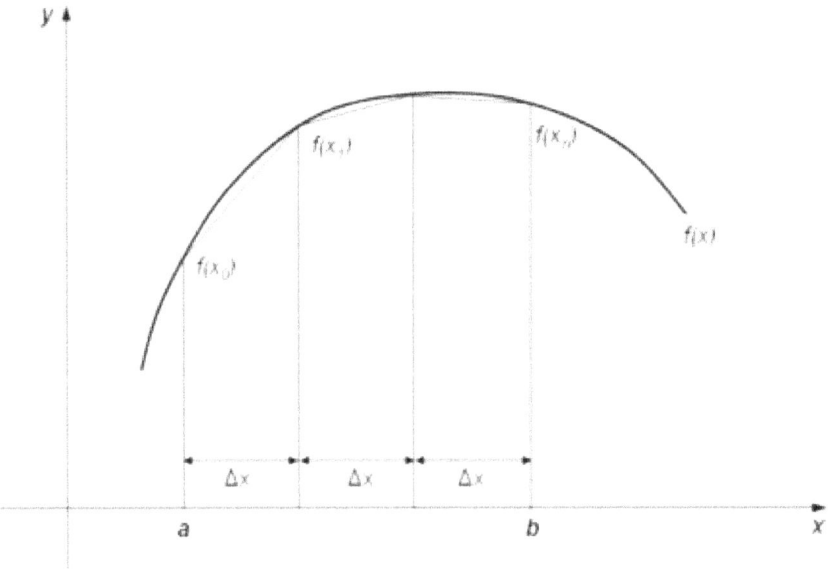

Figure 5.1: Trapezoidal method for approximating area

Trapezoids are having the same width Δx, and if there are n intervals (or n trapezoids) from a to b, then the Δx = (b - a)/n. Figure 5.2 shows the comparison of areas between that obtained from the total area of the trapezoids and the exact results obtained using Equation 5.1. The formula to find total area (L) is given by:

$$L_{total} = \frac{\Delta x}{2}((f(x_o)+f(x_1))+(f(x_1)+f(x_2))+...+(f(x_{n-1})+f(x_n))) \quad (5.2)$$

$$= \frac{\Delta x}{2}(f(x_o)+2f(x_1)+2f(x_2)+2f(x_3))+...+2f(x_{n-1})+f(x_n)) \quad (5.3)$$

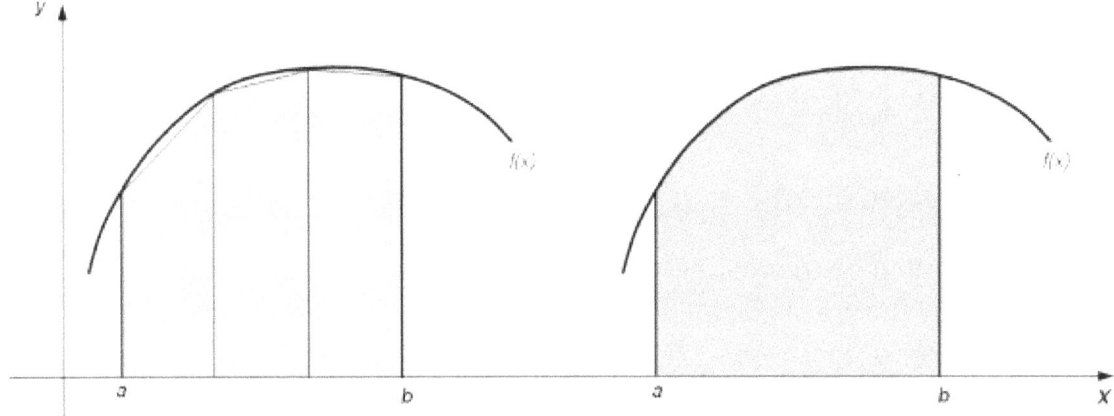

Figure 5.2: The comparison of areas resulted from trapezoids (left) and the exact result (right)

Figure 5.1 and 5.2 show that the calculation by means of trapezoidal method is getting closer to the exact result when more trapezoids are taking into account, or by making the Δx smaller.

Further, to complement this discussion we will examine the given example, where VBA is used to solve it.

Example

Find the area bounded by the parabola y = 4x - x^2, the X-axis, from x = a and x = b. Find also the exact value.

Solution

VBA code

```
Function Trapez(a, b, n)
a = Cells(3, 2)
b = Cells(4, 2)
n = Cells(5, 2)

Dx = (b - a) / n
x = a
    For i = 2 To n - 1
        x = x + Dx
        Sum = Sum + 2 * f(x)
    Next i

Sum = Sum + f(a) + f(b)
Trapez = Sum * Dx / 2
End Function

Function f(x)
    f = 4 * x - x ^ 2
End Function

Function integf(x)
    integf = 2 * x ^ 2 - 1 / 3 * x ^ 3
End Function
```

In this experiment, we take a = 0 and b = 4 for n = 10 and 100, respectively. The values of a, b and n are then used as arguments of **Integf** and **Trapez**. The use of the functions and the results are shown as below:

USING FUNCTION:

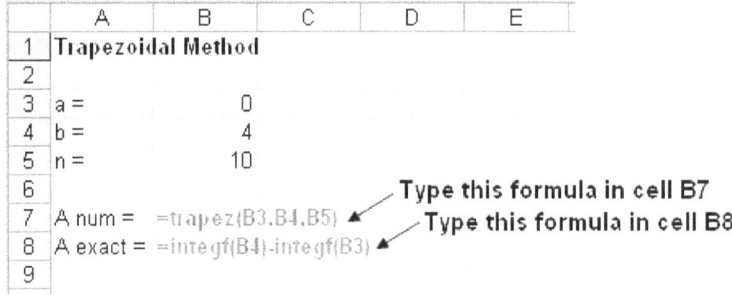

RESULT:

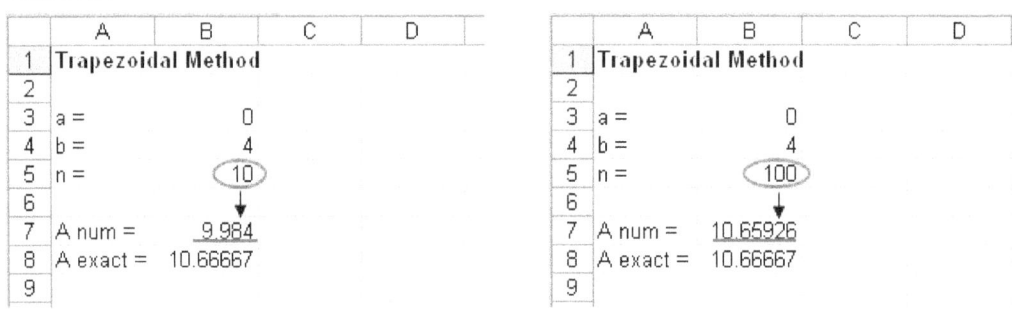

In the worksheet above, A_num and A_exact are respectively the magnitude area calculated using trapezoidal method and its exact value. This experiment shows that the smaller width of trapezoids taken with n = 100, the closer A_num to A_exact, compared with the result with n = 10. However, the more thorough result requires a longer calculation process and it is certainly suitable done only with the help of computer.

There are a number of methods for approaching areas, for examples, the Simpson method and Gauss quadrature rule.

5.2 NUMERICAL DIFFERENTIATION

Differential equation is any equation that contains derivatives of function.

Examples:

$$F = m.a = m\frac{dv}{dt} = m\frac{d^2x}{dt^2} \tag{5.4}$$

$$\frac{d^2v}{dx^2} = \frac{M}{EI} \tag{5.5}$$

$$\frac{\partial u}{\partial t} = c_v \frac{\partial^2 u}{\partial z^2} \tag{5.6}$$

Description:

- Equation 5.4 is Newton's second law of motion that states force (F) acting on an object = mass (m) of the object multiplied by its acceleration (a) where, acceleration (a) is the first derivative of velocity (v) with respect to time (t) and the second derivative of position (x).
- Equation 5.5 shows the relationships between bending moment (M) at any point on the X-axis and transverse deflection (v) of a beam. EI is flexural rigidity of the beam.
- Equation 5.6 is a partial differential equation of one-dimensional consolidation of a clay layer, where u, t, z are respectively, excess pore-water pressure, time and the depth of clay layer. Cv is a coefficient of consolidation where the value is assumed to be constant.

Numerical differentiation solution is an approach to continuous differential form into discrete or finite model. In this section, we adopt Taylor approach for it is among the most popular and widely used in introducing numerical approximation. Taylor theorem for approaching a function is graphically shown in Figure 5.3.

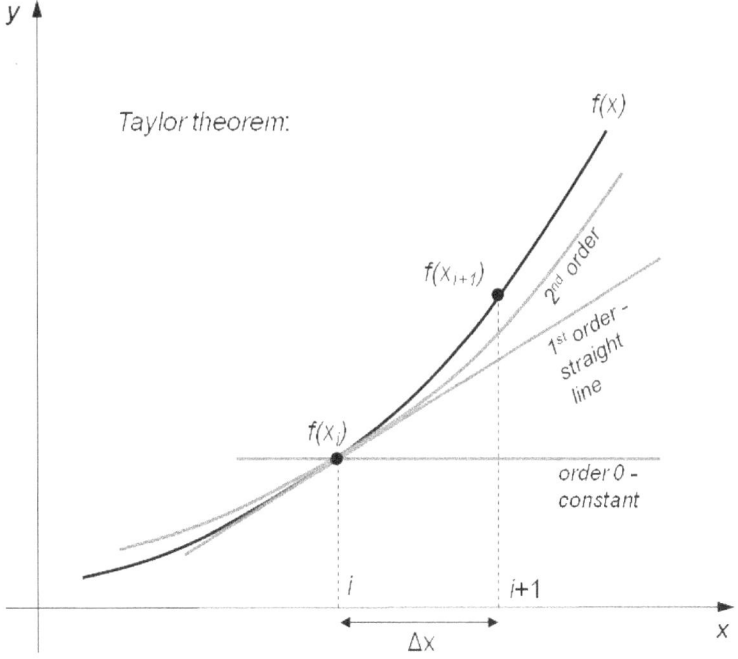

Figure 5.3: Taylor theorem for approximating a function

An Introduction to Excel for Civil Engineers

The value of a function at point x_{i+1} located at a distance Δx from point x_i can be approximated by Taylor series below:

$$f(x_{i+1}) = f(x_i) + f'(x_i)\frac{\Delta x}{1!} + f''(x_i)\frac{\Delta x^2}{2!} + f'''(x_i)\frac{\Delta x^3}{3!} + ... f^n(x_i)\frac{\Delta x^n}{n!} + Rn \qquad (5.7)$$

where,

- All derivatives of the function through the point $(x_i, f(x_i))$.

- Rn: truncation error when the series is counted up to n-order.

Taylor series will give an estimation of the function correctly if all derivatives in the series are taken into account, where n = infinite number. However, in practice, the use of Taylor series is done by simply taking the first few terms of the series.

Equation 5.7 of the Taylor series can be made into the discrete form (finite) as shown in Figure 5.4. The estimation of the first derivative of a function f'(x) is approached through several slope of the line through the value f(x) at x = x_{i-1} (point A), x = x_i (point B) and x = x_{i+1} (point C). From Equation 5.7 for the first derivative:

$$f(x_{i+1}) = f(x_1) + f'(x_i)\Delta x + Rn$$

or,

$$\frac{\partial f}{\partial x} = f'(x_i) = \frac{f(x_{i+1}) - f(x_i)}{\Delta x} - Rn \qquad (5.8)$$

Equation 5.8 is called forward difference formula.

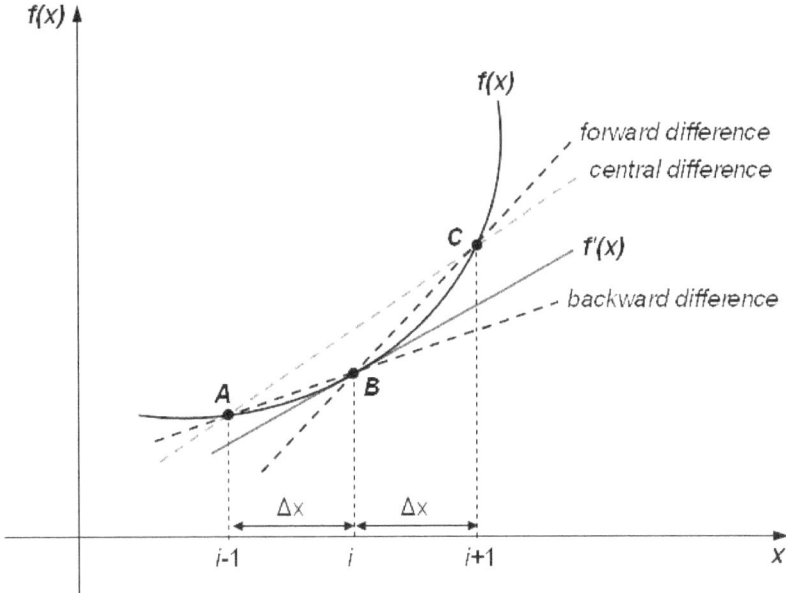

Figure 5.4: Estimation of first derivative of a function

Further, backward difference formula is given by:

$$\frac{\partial f}{\partial x} = f'(x_i) = \frac{f(x_i) - f(x_{i-1})}{\Delta x} + Rn \qquad (5.9)$$

Central difference formula is given by:

$$\frac{\partial f}{\partial x} = f'(x_i) = \frac{f(x_{i+1}) - f(x_{i-1})}{2\Delta x} + Rn \qquad (5.10)$$

If a function contains two independent variables such as f(x, y), then the derivatives in the Taylor series will have the following form:

$$f(x_{i+1}, y_{j+1}) = f(x_i, y_j) + \frac{\partial f}{\partial x}\frac{\Delta x}{1!} + \frac{\partial f}{\partial y}\frac{\Delta y}{1!} + \frac{\partial^2 f}{\partial x^2}\frac{\Delta x^2}{2!} + \frac{\partial^2 f}{\partial y^2}\frac{\Delta y^2}{2!} + \ldots \frac{\partial^n f}{\partial y^n}\frac{\Delta y^n}{n!} \qquad (5.11)$$

Equation 5.11 can be written into the following:

Forward difference formula of first derivative is:

$$\frac{\partial f}{\partial x} \approx \frac{f_{i+1,j} - f_{i,j}}{\Delta x}$$

An Introduction to Excel for Civil Engineers

$$\frac{\partial f}{\partial y} \approx \frac{f_{i,j+1} - f_{i,j}}{\Delta y}$$

Central difference formula of first derivative is:

$$\frac{\partial f}{\partial x} \approx \frac{f_{i+1,j} - f_{i-1,j}}{2\Delta x}$$

$$\frac{\partial f}{\partial y} \approx \frac{f_{i,j+1} - f_{i,j-1}}{2\Delta y}$$

Central difference formula of **second** derivative is:

$$\frac{\partial^2 f}{\partial x^2} \approx \frac{f_{i-1,j} - 2f_{i,j} + f_{i+1,j}}{\Delta x^2}$$

$$\frac{\partial^2 f}{\partial y^2} \approx \frac{f_{i,j-1} - 2f_{i,j} + f_{i,j+1}}{\Delta y^2}$$

Subscript i, j on the function $f_{i,j}$ is a simplification of f(xi, yj) form. Grid points of a function values in an XY coordinate system is shown in Figure 5.5. It is used to estimate partial derivative of $f_{i,j}$ with respect to x and y.

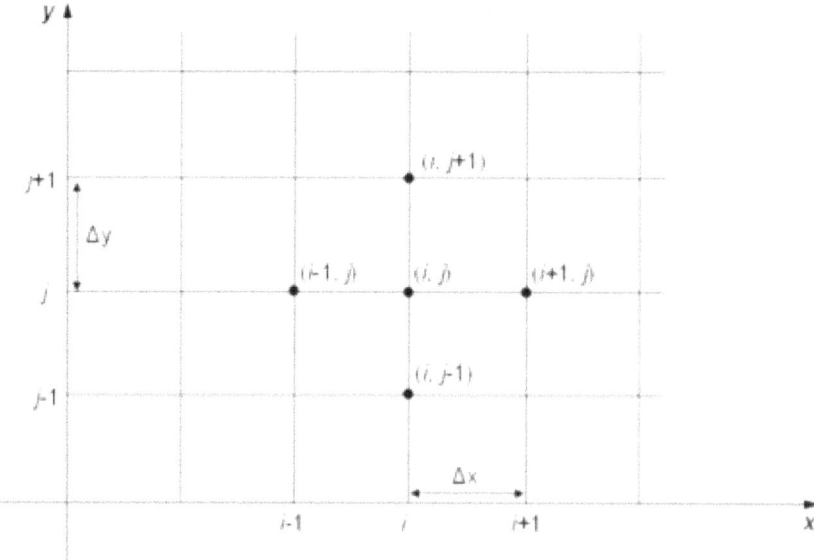

Figure 5.5: Two dimensional grid points of a function

Taylor's discretization method whereby derivative of a function is approached as the difference value of a function between the given independent variable (e.g. x_1) and a small increment (e.g. $x_1+\Delta x$), is called the **Finite Difference Method** (Gilberto E.U, 2004). An approach using the finite difference method implies that the smaller Δx used the better the result, means closer to the exact value as presented by an approach of the slope of lines in Figure 5.4.

In Chapter 10, we will build a program for one-dimensional consolidation solution based on Equation 5.6. In the calculation, it is necessary to put a multiplier into input data to divide interval of the independent variable (e.g. Δx) to be smaller so that the solution is expected close to exact result. The program is created by using VBA including chart automation to present the result.

CHAPTER 6

PROGRAM FOR 2D FRAME STRUCTURE ANALYSIS

The matrix program as described in Chapter 4 is now implemented in structural analyses in this chapter and the next few chapters. It is expected that these series of references for Excel-VBA programming will be complementary as a basic knowledge to make another application program.

Please differentiate between the purpose of Excel-VBA programming and the aim to build an executable program (using Visual Basic or C++ programming language). Using Excel means a program as a whole becomes convenient and practical for it is created case by case. Each case is packed in such a way to utilize spreadsheet facilities and then presented as in creating a technical report. This is consistent with the nature of working with Excel.

6.1 CASE EXAMPLE

Structure of plane frame is composed of 3 members with 4 m long each. The stiffness of member BC is 2 times of the stiffness of members AB or CD. Point B, and C are the free nodes, each has 3 displacement components.

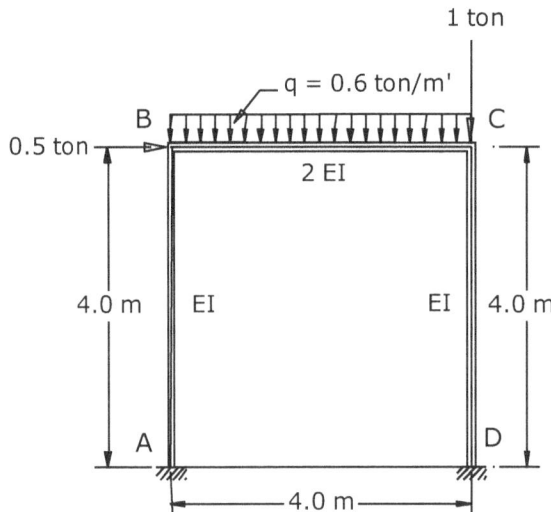

All members of the frame are made of the same linear elastic material with modulus of elasticity, E = 2.1 x 10⁶ ton/m². Dimension of member AB = BC = CD = 30 cm.

The given load as the following:

- Known external load:

  H at node B = 0.5 ton

  V at node C = 1 ton

  Uniform load, q at member BC = 0.6 tom/m'

- Uniform load, q is converted to equivalent nodal loads at B and C

  $P_{BC(M)} = - P_{CB(M)} = 1/12.q.L^2 = -0.8$ ton.m.

  $P_{B(V)} = P_{C(V)} = - \frac{1}{2}.q.L = -1.2$ ton.

  Sign convention refers to Figure 6.1.

The sign convention represents the direction of nodal forces, moments and displacements with reference to either global coordinate or local coordinate system. It is set as follows: the axial and shear forces follow the right-hand rule while the moments follow the right-hand screw rule, or in the easy way it is evident from Figure 6.1, that is, positive when in the direction of the positive axis.

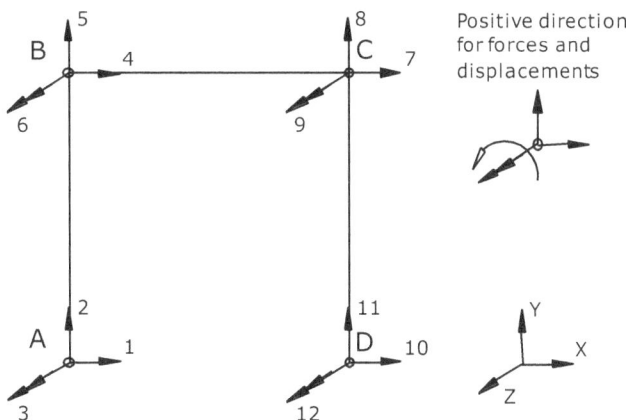

Figure 6.1: Force and displacement components at nodes in global coordinate system

An Introduction to Excel for Civil Engineers

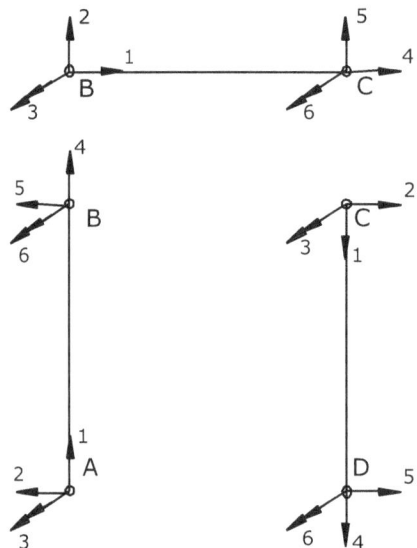

Figure 6.2: Member force and displacement components in local coordinate system

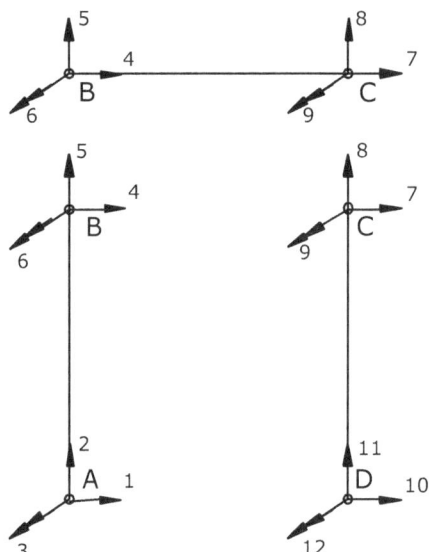

Figure 6.3: Member force and displacement components that conform to global coordinate system

The process of the frame analysis is written into the following steps:

1. Stiffness matrix for plane frame member is derived as the following:

An Introduction to Excel for Civil Engineers

$$[K]_i = \begin{bmatrix} \dfrac{EA}{L} & 0 & 0 & -\dfrac{EA}{L} & 0 & 0 \\ 0 & \dfrac{12EI}{L^3} & \dfrac{6EI}{L^2} & 0 & -\dfrac{12EI}{L^3} & \dfrac{6EI}{L^2} \\ 0 & \dfrac{6EI}{L^2} & \dfrac{4EI}{L} & 0 & -\dfrac{6EI}{L^2} & \dfrac{2EI}{L} \\ -\dfrac{EA}{L} & 0 & 0 & \dfrac{EA}{L} & 0 & 0 \\ 0 & -\dfrac{12EI}{L^3} & -\dfrac{6EI}{L^2} & 0 & \dfrac{12EI}{L^3} & -\dfrac{6EI}{L^2} \\ 0 & \dfrac{6EI}{L^2} & \dfrac{2EI}{L} & 0 & -\dfrac{6EI}{L^2} & \dfrac{4EI}{L} \end{bmatrix} \qquad (6.1)$$

2. Transformation matrix to convert vector components from local to global coordinate system is as the following:

For 6 force - displacement vector components of each member,

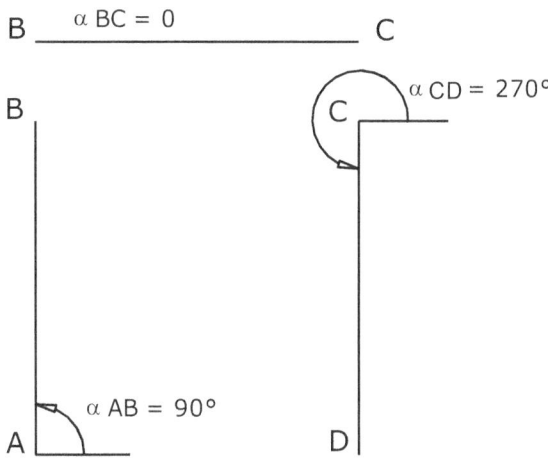

$$[T]_i = \begin{bmatrix} \cos\alpha & \sin\alpha & 0 & 0 & 0 & 0 \\ -\sin\alpha & \cos\alpha & 0 & 0 & 0 & 0 \\ 0 & 0 & 1 & 0 & 0 & 0 \\ 0 & 0 & 0 & \cos\alpha & \sin\alpha & 0 \\ 0 & 0 & 0 & -\sin\alpha & \cos\alpha & 0 \\ 0 & 0 & 0 & 0 & 0 & 1 \end{bmatrix} \qquad (6.2)$$

An Introduction to Excel for Civil Engineers

3. Member stiffness matrix in the global coordinate system:

   $$[K]s = [T]i^T[K]i[T]i \tag{6.3}$$

   Member stiffness matrix of one member is then superposed with other members, which is altogether form global stiffness matrix or called [K] structure. This process is written:

   $$\text{Superpose } [K]s \rightarrow [K] \text{ structure} \tag{6.4}$$

4. Displacements at the free nodes are obtained from Equation 4.9 that becomes:

   $$\{X_f\} = [K_{ff}]^{-1}\{P_f\} \tag{6.5}$$

5. Internal forces on each member can be found by firstly transforming displacements from global coordinate back to local coordinate,

   $$\{X\}i = [T]i\{X_f\}$$

   After the displacements of members $\{X\}i$ are obtained, then the internal forces on each member can be obtained from Equation 4.11:

   $$\{P\}i = \{P_o\} + [K]i\{X\}I \tag{6.6}$$

6. Support reactions are obtained from Equation 4.12:

   $$\{R_b\} = [K_{bf}]\{X_f\} - \{P_b\} \tag{6.7}$$

From the sequence of process above, we can create a simple program in Excel-VBA for frame structure analysis named FRAME2D.

Programming:

In designing matrix program, it is convenient to mastering design-build in matrix-based data. In this relation, is how to make matrix variables of Equation 6.3 to 6.7. A few things in coding actually require a little imagination of a programmer.

For instance is how to assemble [K] structure. For this purpose, it requires to manipulate program steps such that [K] members can be stored on "their position" in [K] structure. The idea is simply creating an integer variable, namely **dindex**, to "equalize" the subscripts of [K] members. **Dindex** reads index (numbering) of member deformations in the global coordinate system and is used to store [K] members in [K] structure and do the superposition at once.

The code is as follows:

```
'Member end-displacements index:
For i = 1 To NM
    With Member(i)
        dindex(1, i) = 3 * .J1 - 2
        dindex(2, i) = 3 * .J1 - 1
        dindex(3, i) = 3 * .J1
        dindex(4, i) = 3 * .J2 - 2
        dindex(5, i) = 3 * .J2 - 1
        dindex(6, i) = 3 * .J2
    End With
Next i


'Storing members and superposition
For i = 1 to NM 'NM= no. of member
    For j = 1 To 6
        For n = 1 To 6
            S(Idm(j, i), Idm(n, i)) = S(Idm(j, i), Idm(n, i)) + M(j, n, i)
        Next n
    Next j
Next i
```

Notes:

- **Idm** variable is the same nodal displacement indexes as stated by **dindex** variable, but declared at a different level. **Idm** is at public-level, while **dindex** is at procedure-level. For more clearly understand how these variables are proceeded, you can see in the FRAME2D code provided in the Attachment.
- The above code is for completion of the description 6.4 (p.148).

Another thing to be considered is how to partition or separation the structure stiffness matrix, that is, to form $[K_{ff}]$ and $[K_{bf}]$ as written in Equation 4.8. We can use two integer variables namely **Ifr** and **Ifx** to form $[K_{ff}]$ and $[K_{bf}]$, respectively.

The steps to partition the structure stiffness matrix is as follows:

1. Creating displacement index at the free nodes and the supports:

    ```
    'Joint free displacement index, IFr and restraint index, IFx:
    ```

An Introduction to Excel for Civil Engineers

```
Sub Mindex(dindex() As Integer, IFr() As Integer, IFx() As Integer)
n = 1
j = 1
For i = 1 To NP
    If Rs(i) = 0 Then IFr(n) = i: n = n + 1
Next i


n = 1
For i = 1 To NS
n = Cells(22, 1 + i)
    IFx(3 * i - 2) = 3 * n - 2
    IFx(3 * i - 1) = 3 * n - 1
    IFx(3 * i) = 3 * n
Next i
```

2. Code to form sub-matrix [K_{ff}]:

```
'submatrix Stiffness, KFF
For i = 1 To DOF
    For j = 1 To DOF
        SD(i, j) = GS(Idj(i), Idj(j))
    Next j
Next i
```

3 Code to form sub-matrix [K_{bf}]:

```
'submatrix Stiffness, KBF
For i = 1 To DOF
    For j = 1 To 3 * NS
        SR(j, i) = GS(Irj(j), Idj(i))
    Next j
Next i
```

Notes:

- Rs represents joint displacements condition at the supports, where: 1 = fixed, 0 = free.

- NS = number of supports

An Introduction to Excel for Civil Engineers

- Variable *Idj = Ifr*, *Irj = Ifx*, but they are declared at different level which is at *public* and *procedure level*, respectively. See FRAME2D code provided in the Attachment.

The input and output data form of FRAME2D is presented in Figure 6.4. Below are the results of each step in the analysis.

Member AB

[K] (member stiffness matrix)

47250.00	0.00	0.00	-47250.00	0.00	0.00
0.00	265.78	531.56	0.00	-265.78	531.56
0.00	531.56	1417.50	0.00	-531.56	708.75
-47250.00	0.00	0.00	47250.00	0.00	0.00
0.00	-265.78	-531.56	0.00	265.78	-531.56
0.00	531.56	708.75	0.00	-531.56	1417.50

[T] (member transformation matrix from local to global coordinate system)

0.00	1.00	0.00	0.00	0.00	0.00
-1.00	0.00	0.00	0.00	0.00	0.00
0.00	0.00	1.00	0.00	0.00	0.00
0.00	0.00	0.00	0.00	1.00	0.00
0.00	0.00	0.00	-1.00	0.00	0.00
0.00	0.00	0.00	0.00	0.00	1.00

$[K]s = [T]i^T[K]i[T]i$ (member stiffness matrix in global coordinate system)

265.78	0.00	-531.56	-265.78	0.00	-531.56
0.00	47250.00	0.00	0.00	-47250.00	0.00
-531.56	0.00	1417.50	531.56	0.00	708.75
-265.78	0.00	531.56	265.78	0.00	531.56
0.00	-47250.00	0.00	0.00	47250.00	0.00
-531.56	0.00	708.75	531.56	0.00	1417.50

Member BC

[K]

59850.00	0.00	0.00	-59850.00	0.00	0.00
0.00	540.15	1080.29	0.00	-540.15	1080.29
0.00	1080.29	2880.78	0.00	-1080.29	1440.39
-59850.00	0.00	0.00	59850.00	0.00	0.00
0.00	-540.15	-1080.29	0.00	540.15	-1080.29
0.00	1080.29	1440.39	0.00	-1080.29	2880.78

[T]

1.00	0.00	0.00	0.00	0.00	0.00
0.00	1.00	0.00	0.00	0.00	0.00
0.00	0.00	1.00	0.00	0.00	0.00
0.00	0.00	0.00	1.00	0.00	0.00
0.00	0.00	0.00	0.00	1.00	0.00
0.00	0.00	0.00	0.00	0.00	1.00

[K]s

59850.00	0.00	0.00	-59850.00	0.00	0.00
0.00	540.15	1080.29	0.00	-540.15	1080.29
0.00	1080.29	2880.78	0.00	-1080.29	1440.39
-59850.00	0.00	0.00	59850.00	0.00	0.00
0.00	-540.15	-1080.29	0.00	540.15	-1080.29
0.00	1080.29	1440.39	0.00	-1080.29	2880.78

Member CD

[K]

47250.00	0.00	0.00	-47250.00	0.00	0.00
0.00	265.78	531.56	0.00	-265.78	531.56
0.00	531.56	1417.50	0.00	-531.56	708.75
-47250.00	0.00	0.00	47250.00	0.00	0.00
0.00	-265.78	-531.56	0.00	265.78	-531.56
0.00	531.56	708.75	0.00	-531.56	1417.50

[T]

0.00	-1.00	0.00	0.00	0.00	0.00
1.00	0.00	0.00	0.00	0.00	0.00
0.00	0.00	1.00	0.00	0.00	0.00
0.00	0.00	0.00	0.00	-1.00	0.00
0.00	0.00	0.00	1.00	0.00	0.00
0.00	0.00	0.00	0.00	0.00	1.00

[K]s

265.78	0.00	531.56	-265.78	0.00	531.56
0.00	47250.00	0.00	0.00	-47250.00	0.00
531.56	0.00	1417.50	-531.56	0.00	708.75
-265.78	0.00	-531.56	265.78	0.00	-531.56
0.00	-47250.00	0.00	0.00	47250.00	0.00
531.56	0.00	708.75	-531.56	0.00	1417.50

An Introduction to Excel for Civil Engineers

[K] Structure

	1	2	3	4	5	6	7	8	9	10	11	12
1	265.78	0.00	-531.56	-265.78	0.00	-531.56	0.00	0.00	0.00	0.00	0.00	0.00
2	0.00	47250.00	0.00	0.00	-47250.00	0.00	0.00	0.00	0.00	0.00	0.00	0.00
3	-531.56	0.00	1417.50	531.56	0.00	708.75	0.00	0.00	0.00	0.00	0.00	0.00
4	-265.78	0.00	531.56	60115.78	0.00	531.56	-59850.00	0.00	0.00	0.00	0.00	0.00
5	0.00	-47250.00	0.00	0.00	47790.15	1080.29	0.00	-540.15	1080.29	0.00	0.00	0.00
6	-531.56	0.00	708.75	531.56	1080.29	4298.28	0.00	-1080.29	1440.39	0.00	0.00	0.00
7	0.00	0.00	0.00	-59850.00	0.00	0.00	60115.78	0.00	531.56	-265.78	0.00	531.56
8	0.00	0.00	0.00	0.00	-540.15	-1080.29	0.00	47790.15	-1080.29	0.00	-47250.00	0.00
9	0.00	0.00	0.00	0.00	1080.29	1440.39	531.56	-1080.29	4298.28	-531.56	0.00	708.75
10	0.00	0.00	0.00	0.00	0.00	0.00	-265.78	0.00	-531.56	265.78	0.00	-531.56
11	0.00	0.00	0.00	0.00	0.00	0.00	0.00	-47250.00	0.00	0.00	47250.00	0.00
12	0.00	0.00	0.00	0.00	0.00	0.00	531.56	0.00	708.75	-531.56	0.00	1417.50

An Introduction to Excel for Civil Engineers

Partition at the free nodes → [K_ff]

	4	5	6	7	8	9
4	60115.78	0.00	531.56	-59850.00	0.00	0.00
5	0.00	47790.15	1080.29	0.00	-540.15	1080.29
6	531.56	1080.29	4298.28	0.00	-1080.29	1440.39
7	-59850.00	0.00	0.00	60115.78	0.00	531.56
8	0.00	-540.15	-1080.29	0.00	47790.15	-1080.29
9	0.00	1080.29	1440.39	531.56	-1080.29	4298.28

Partition at the support nodes → [K_bf]

	4	5	6	7	8	9
1	-265.78	0.00	-531.56	0.00	0.00	0.00
2	0.00	-47250.00	0.00	0.00	0.00	0.00
3	531.56	0.00	708.75	0.00	0.00	0.00
10	0.00	0.00	0.00	-265.78	0.00	-531.56
11	0.00	0.00	0.00	0.00	-47250.00	0.00
12	0.00	0.00	0.00	531.56	0.00	708.75

Nodal displacements at the free nodes: $\{X_f\} = \begin{Bmatrix} 0.00000 \\ 0.00000 \\ 0.00000 \\ 0.00117 \\ -0.00002 \\ -0.00039 \\ 0.00117 \\ -0.00005 \\ 0.00017 \\ 0.00000 \\ 0.00000 \\ 0.00000 \end{Bmatrix}$

Member deformations are calculated using the following equation:

An Introduction to Excel for Civil Engineers

$\{X\}i = [T]i\{X_f\}$

Internal member forces are obtained from Equation 6.6:

$\{P\}i = \{P_o\} + [K]i\{X\}i$

Support reactions are obtained from Equation 6.7:

$\{R_b\} = [K_{bf}]\{X_f\} - \{P_b\}$

The result of the analysis is presented in FRAME2D input-output form shown in Figure 6.4 and 6.5 below:

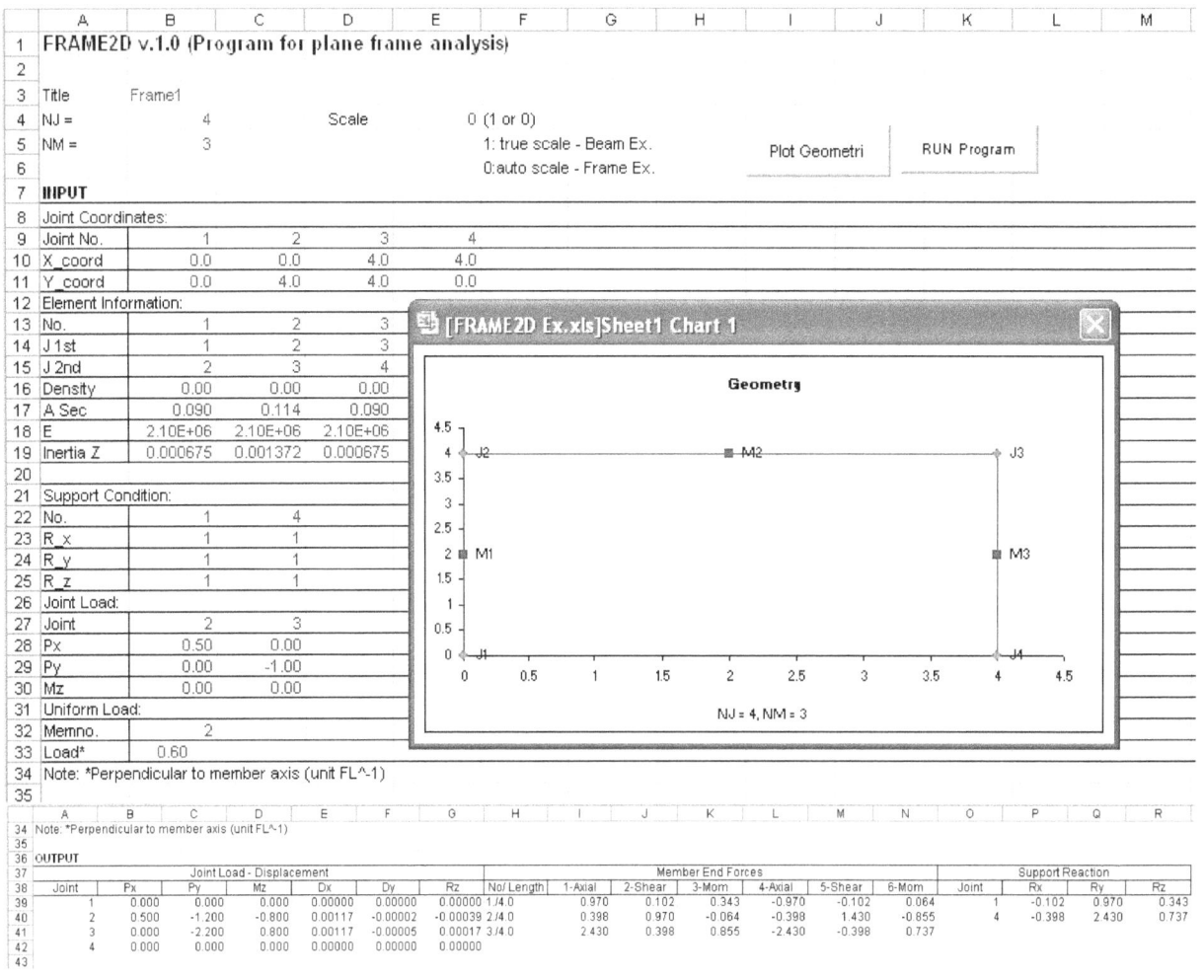

Figure 6.4: FRAME2D input-output form

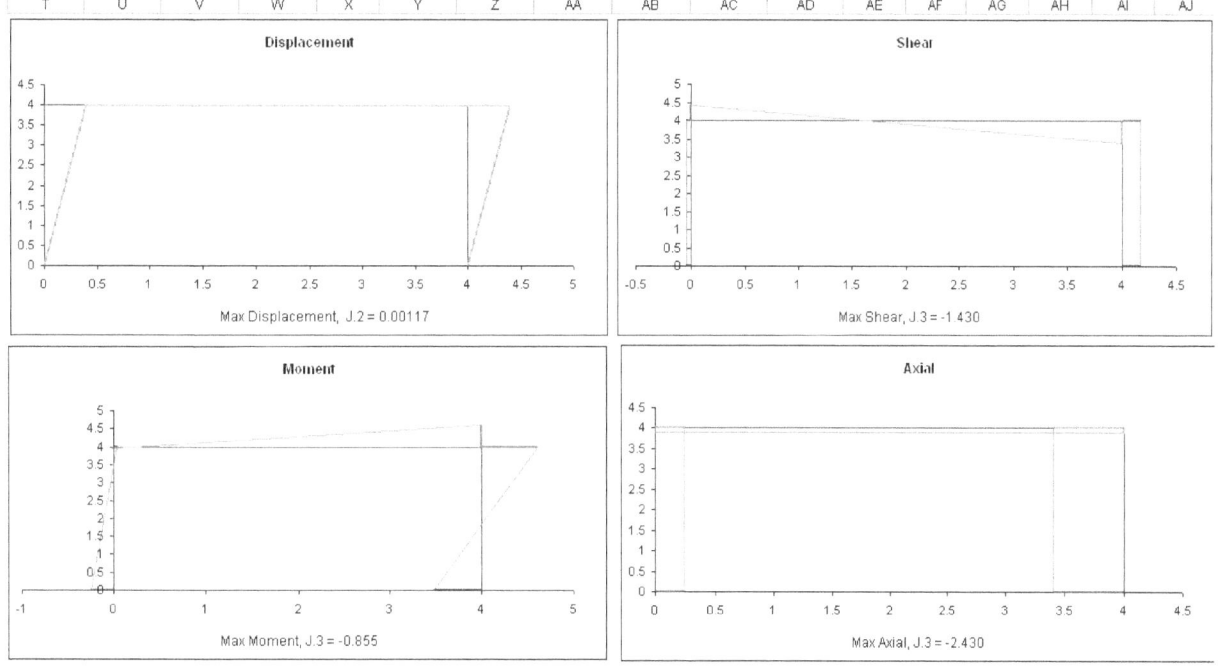

Figure 6.5: Charts of displacement, bending moment, shear force and axial force diagrams

Notes for FRAME2D input and output form:

- Data input is **blue** text.
- Scale for presenting the output data is divided into 2 cases: **true** scale for beam members (continuous beam) and **auto** scale for frame structure.
- NM: number of structural members
- NJ: number of joints or nodes
- FRAME2D distinguishes 3 types of loading: **selftweights** by inputting material density (row 16), **nodal loads** (row 27 to 30), and **uniform loads** (row 32 to. 33).
- When **Plot Geometry** button is clicked it shows the Chart Window. It presents the geometry of structure to allow user to check it (for quick verification) prior executing the program by clicking **RUN Program** button. Thus, it is expected to minimize errors arise from incorrect numbering system of members and joints.
- Chart Window command used in Plot Geometry is only compatible with **Excel 2003** and earlier, which is the version where FRAME2D was created and also the next few programs. When running it in Excel 2007, chart window (as shown in Figure 6.4) will not be displayed. However, the presented chart can be seen before displacement chart in the input-output form.

- Figure 6.5 shows the chart of displacements and the diagrams of moment, shear and axial force drawn automatically by the program. The maximum values of displacement, moment, shear and axial force occur on nodes are also shown. Sign convention used for presenting the diagrams is described in Chapter 6.2.
- The results shown in Figure 5 are however not presented the finest results as the displacement of the second member looks like a straight line contrary to the fact that the member is subjected to uniform load of 0.6 t/m'. Therefore, it is necessary to expose the result thoroughly by dividing all members into smaller members.
- With intention of the above point, the frame members and joints are therefore re-inputted, for example, by taking NM = 12 and NJ = 13. The results can be seen in Figure 6.6 and 6.7.

The displayed geometry in the chart window (only available in Excel 2003) from re-inputted data is shown below:

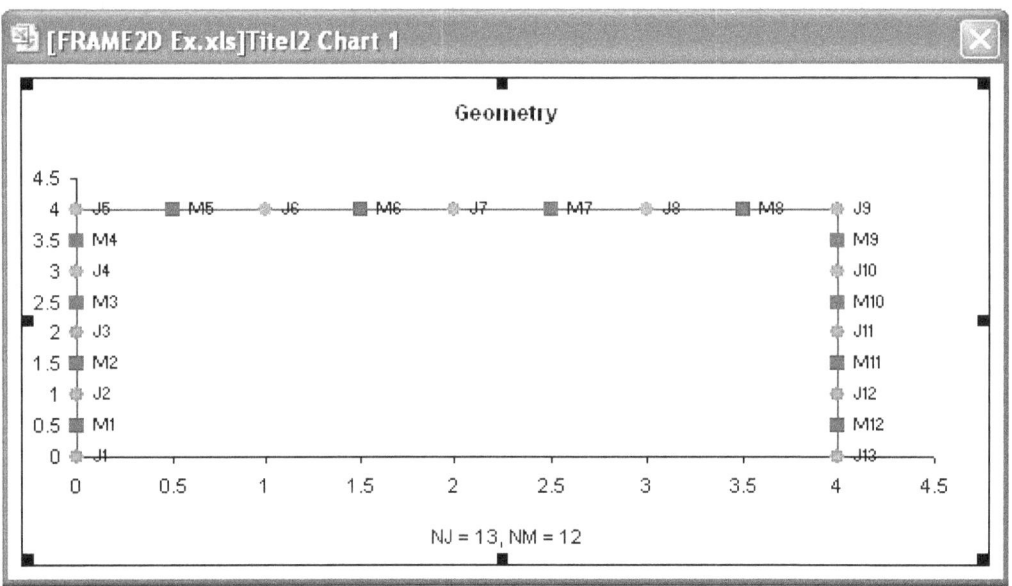

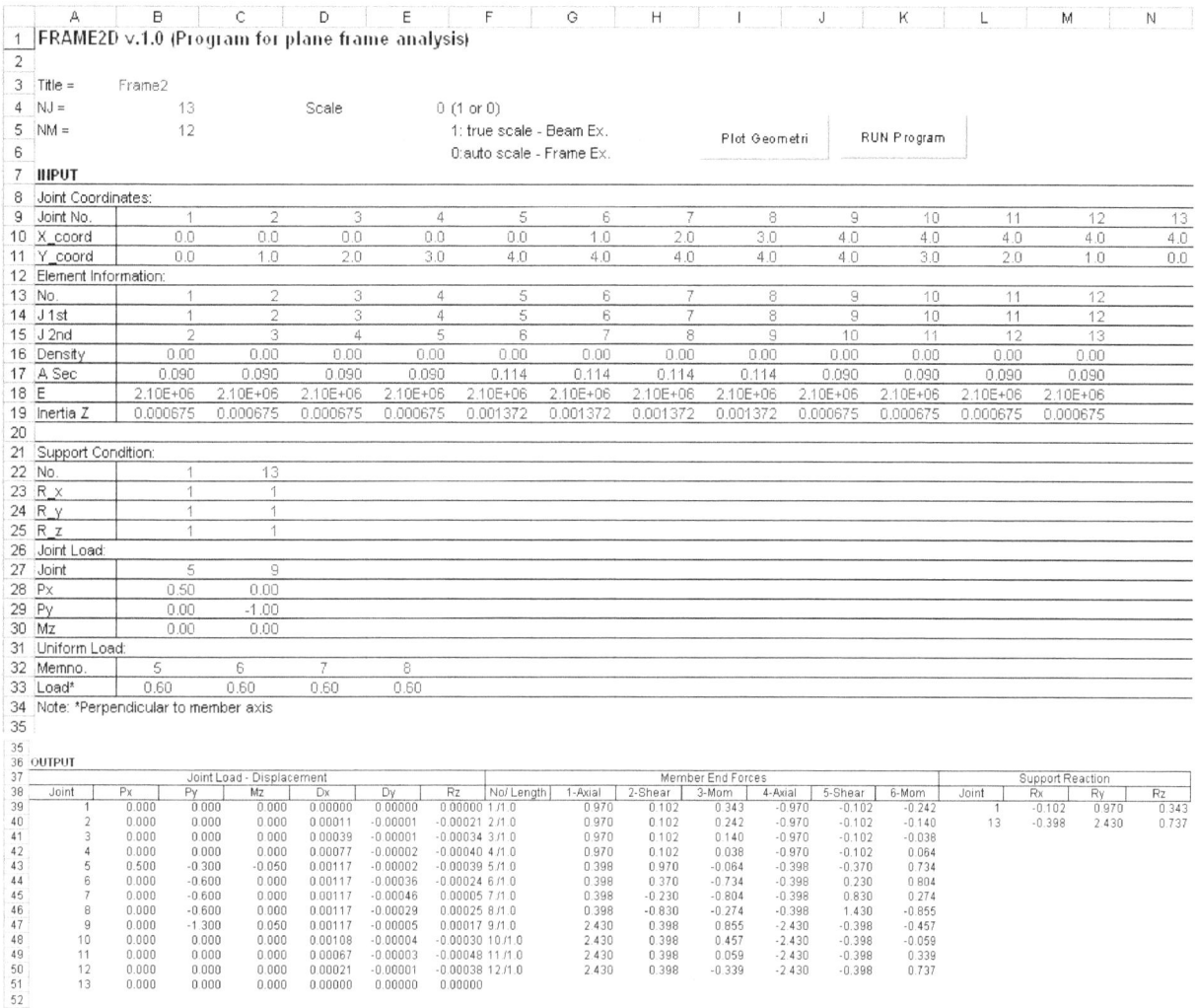

Figure 6.6: FRAME2D input-output form – Re-inputted

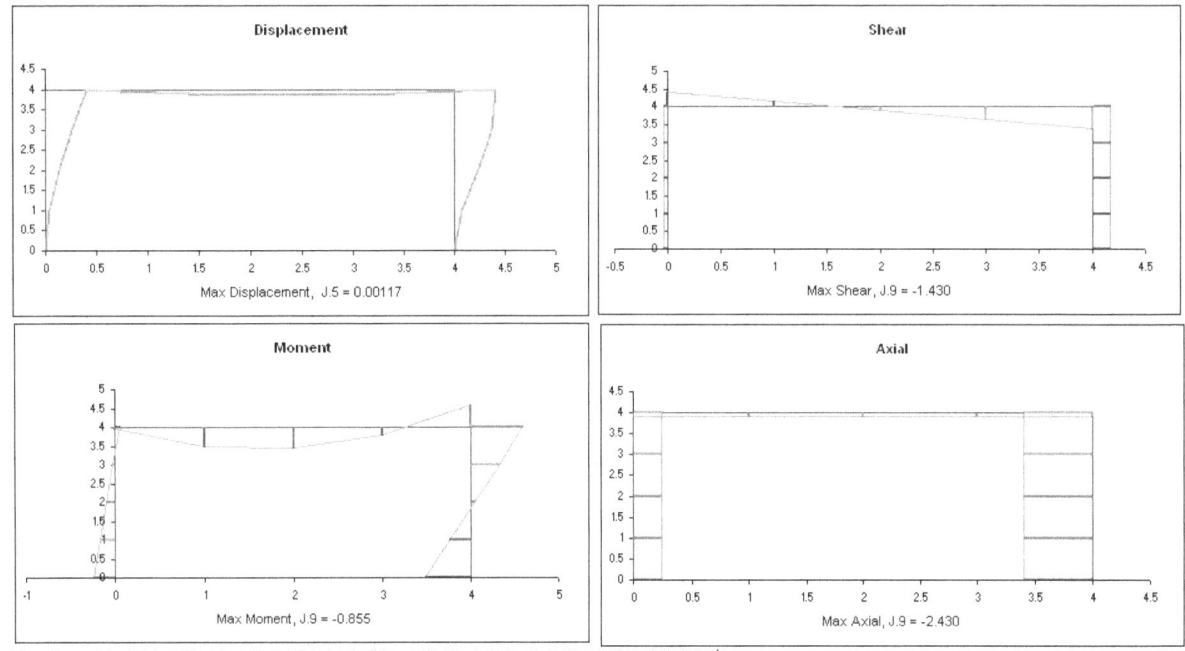

Figure 6.7: Charts of displacement, bending moment, shear force and axial force diagrams – Re-inputted

The program results shown in Figure 6.7 and 6.8 are much better than in Figure 6.5 and 6.6. Thus, in this case it is convenient to divide all frame members into smaller members at least 4 each with equal lengths. Avoid odd divisors (e.g. 5, 7, 9 etc.) so that the results in the middle of span can be exposed.s

6.2 Sign Convention for Diagram

To depict moment, shear force and axial force diagrams in structural members, the programs refer to a sign convention. Positive direction is as shown in the picture below and ruled as follows.

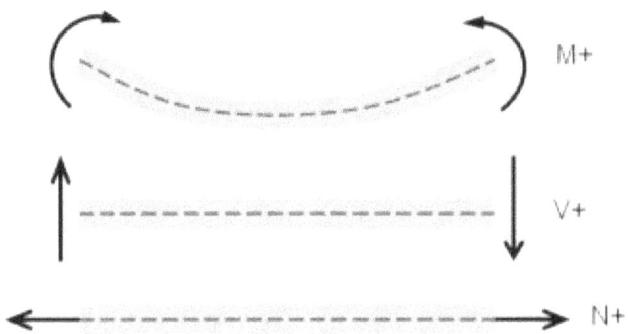

An Introduction to Excel for Civil Engineers

- Bending moment (M) is given a positive sign if causing the upper fibers of members is compressed or to curve upward, and is given a negative sign if to curve downward.

- Shear force (V) is given a positive sign if rotates the member clockwise and is given a negative sign if rotates the member counter-clockwise.

- Axial force (N) is given a positive sign if pulls the member apart, and is given a negative sign if pushes the member.

The sign convention is also used in order to give the same interpretation to the diagrams resulted from FRAME2D and the other programs in the next few chapters, thus it is easily interpreted and design-oriented as well. The program automatically differentiates the direction of moments and forces occur in structural members, which is **blue line** inside the curve for the **positive** direction and **red** for the **negative** direction. Figure below shows the coloring for the bending moment result:

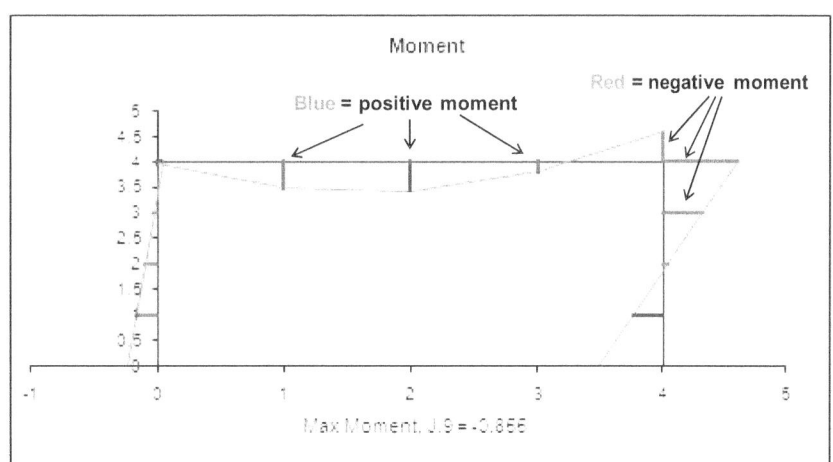

An Introduction to Excel for Civil Engineers

6.3 Application

FRAME2D is now applied to the following beam problem:

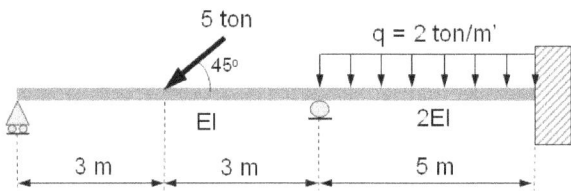

The beam is considered to consist of three main members: *roll-load* segment, *load-roll* segment and *roll-fixed node* segment that have lengths 3, 3 and 5 meters, respectively. In practice, however we need to divide the beam into smaller members for exposing the result thoroughly.

All main members are divided into 4 equal parts, thus, there are 11 members and 12 joints inputted into FRAME2D form. When the program has run, the results are shown on the charts below.

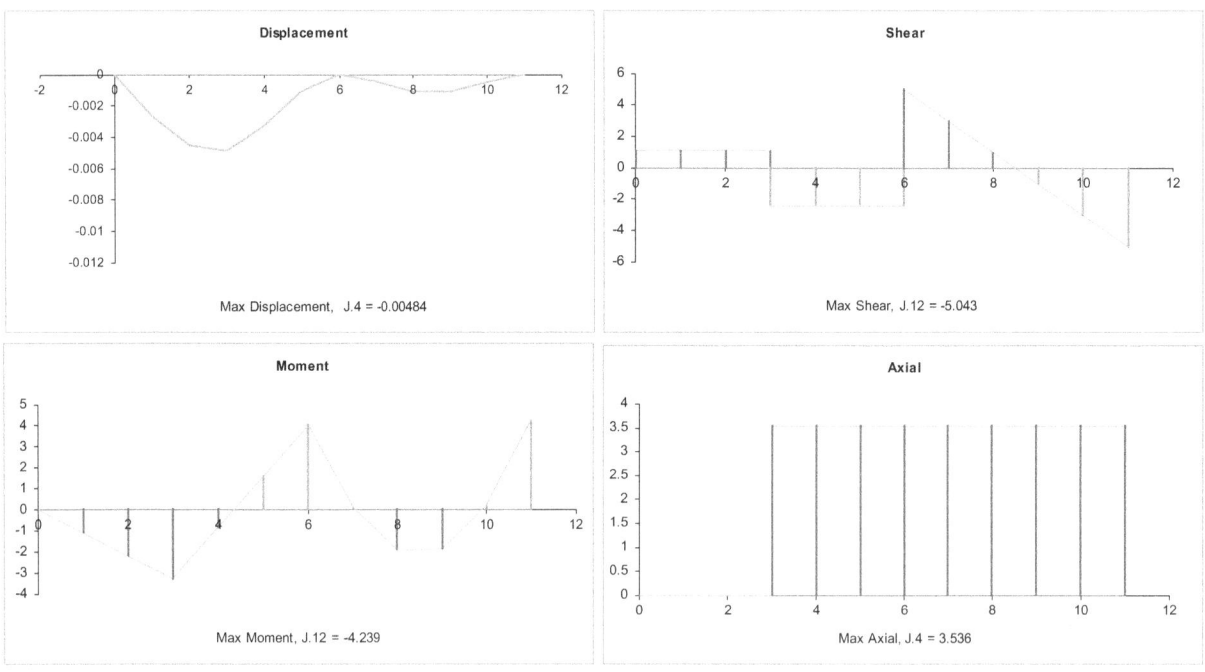

An Introduction to Excel for Civil Engineers

CHAPTER 7

PROGRAM FOR 2D TRUSS STRUCTURE ANALYSIS

Member of a truss structure is analyzed with consideration that each member carries only axial force, thus, there are two associated displacement components at both ends with respect to axial force. Truss member is generally made of steel or aluminum connected one to another as pin connection.

Stiffness matrix for plane truss member is derived as the following:

$$[K]i = \begin{bmatrix} \frac{AE}{L} & 0 & -\frac{AE}{L} & 0 \\ 0 & 0 & 0 & 0 \\ -\frac{AE}{L} & 0 & \frac{AE}{L} & 0 \\ 0 & 0 & 0 & 0 \end{bmatrix}$$

Transformation matrix to convert vector components from local to global coordinate is as the following:

$$[T]i = \begin{bmatrix} \cos\alpha & \sin\alpha & 0 & 0 \\ -\sin\alpha & \cos\alpha & 0 & 0 \\ 0 & 0 & \cos\alpha & \sin\alpha \\ 0 & 0 & -\sin\alpha & \cos\alpha \end{bmatrix}$$

The equation of member stiffness matrix in global coordinate system:

$$[K]s\,i = [T]i^T[K]i[T]i \qquad (7.1)$$

[K]s of the member is then superposed on the corresponding force-deflection components to get global stiffness matrix called [K] structure. The internal member forces and the support reactions can be obtained by firstly partitioning [K] structure at the free nodes and at the supports according to Equation 4.8.

7.1 CASE EXAMPLE

The following example shows a sequence of steps in the plane trusses analysis based on matrix method described in Chapter 4. It includes some notes relate to VBA code writing. This section is a complement explanation for the previous FRAME2D example.

Figure 7.1 shows an example of a truss structure and its numbering system shown in Figure 7.2 to 7.4. Each of member are made of the same linear elastic material, with E = 2,100,000 kg/cm² and cross-sectional area A = 68.4 cm².

The truss structure has only two degrees of freedom (DOF) which is at vector components 3 and 4, while both supports are pinned-pinned, thus will have no any translations.

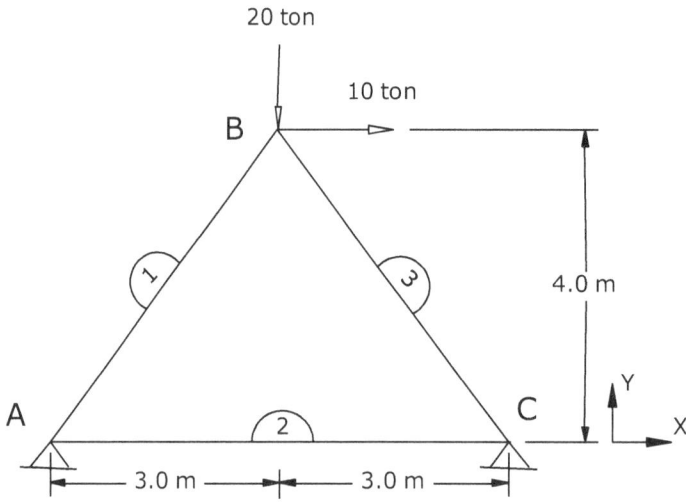

Figure 7.1: Geometry and loading condition on plane truss

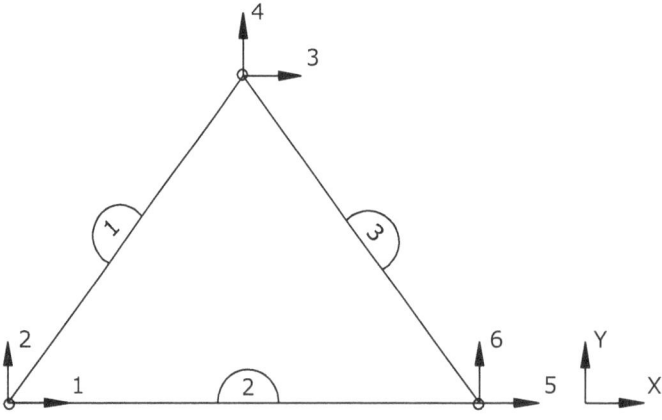

Figure 7.2: Force and displacement components at nodes in global coordinate system

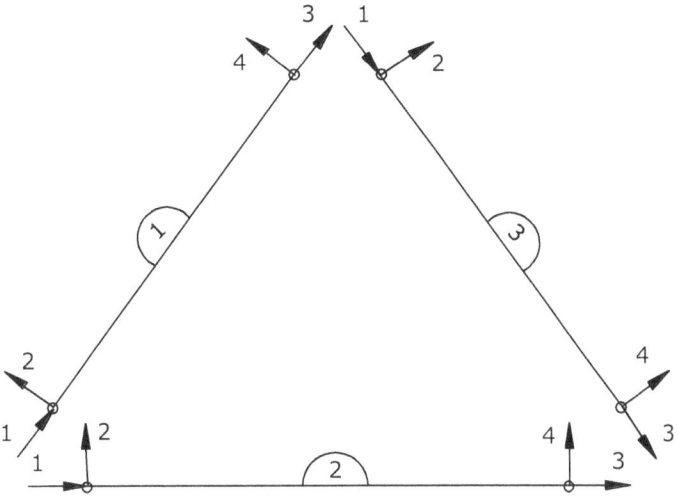

Figure 7.3: Member force and displacement components in local coordinate system

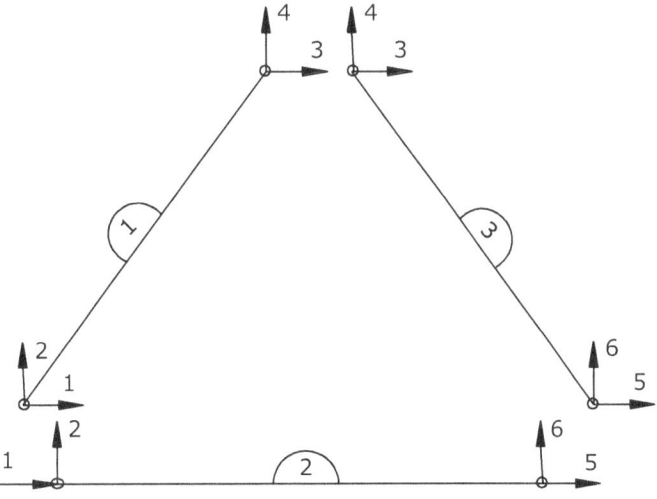

Figure 7.4: Member force and displacement components that conform to global coordinate system

The first step in the analysis is to build **member stiffness matrices** with reference to either local or global coordinate system. This is done within For…Next statement, to loop through a number of the members and made in a separate procedure (Module 2).

The code:

```
Sub Stiff_Mtx(MK() As Double, S() As Double)
Dim sms As Double
```

An Introduction to Excel for Civil Engineers

```vba
ReDim M(4, 4, NM) As Double

'Building global stiffness matrix
For i = 1 To NM
    With Member(i)
    sms = .Ax * .E / .Lh
    'Member stiffness
    MK(1, 1, i) = sms: MK(1, 3, i) = -sms
    MK(3, 1, i) = -sms: MK(3, 3, i) = sms


    'Member global stiffness
        M(1, 1, i) = sms * .Cx * .Cx: M(1, 2, i) = sms * .Cx * .Cy: M(1, 3, i) = -M(1, 1, i): M(1, 4, i) = -M(1, 2, i)
        M(2, 1, i) = M(1, 2, i): M(2, 2, i) = sms * .Cy * .Cy: M(2, 3, i) = M(1, 4, i): M(2, 4, i) = -M(2, 2, i)
        M(3, 1, i) = M(1, 3, i): M(3, 2, i) = M(2, 3, i): M(3, 3, i) = M(1, 1, i): M(3, 4, i) = M(1, 2, i)
        M(4, 1, i) = M(1, 4, i): M(4, 2, i) = M(2, 4, i): M(4, 3, i) = M(3, 4, i): M(4, 4, i) = M(2, 2, i)
    'Storing members and superposition
    For j = 1 To 4
        For n = 1 To 4
            S(Idm(j, i), Idm(n, i)) = S(Idm(j, i), Idm(n, i)) + M(j, n, i)
        Next n
    Next j
    End With
Next i

End Sub
```

Notes:

- The code above is about to build the member stiffness matrix according to Equation 7.1, and then to store them to assemble [K] structure and at the same time do the superposition.
- Each of member stiffness matrix (variable M) has three subscripts; the first and second subscripts state row and column indexes, respectively, while the third subscript states stiffness matrix of member i.

- Idm is an integer variable that reads nodal displacement indexes of member ends, which is the same as used in FRAME2D.

Program for truss structural analysis is modified from FRAME2D, and named TRUSS2D. Below are the given results from each step in the analysis.

Member Stiffness Matrix

[K]AB

28728.00	0.00	-28728.00	0.00
0.00	0.00	0.00	0.00
-28728.00	0.00	28728.00	0.00
0.00	0.00	0.00	0.00

[K]AC

23940.00	0.00	-23940.00	0.00
0.00	0.00	0.00	0.00
-23940.00	0.00	23940.00	0.00
0.00	0.00	0.00	0.00

[K]BC

28728.00	0.00	-28728.00	0.00
0.00	0.00	0.00	0.00
-28728.00	0.00	28728.00	0.00
0.00	0.00	0.00	0.00

Transformation Matrix

[T]AB

0.60	0.80	0.00	0.00
-0.80	0.60	0.00	0.00
0.00	0.00	0.60	0.80
0.00	0.00	-0.80	0.60

[T]AC

1.00	0.00	0.00	0.00
0.00	1.00	0.00	0.00
0.00	0.00	1.00	0.00
0.00	0.00	0.00	1.00

[T]BC

0.60	-0.80	0.00	0.00
0.80	0.60	0.00	0.00
0.00	0.00	0.60	-0.80
0.00	0.00	0.80	0.60

Member Stiffness Matrix in Global Coordinate System

$[K]s = [T]i^T[K]i[T]i$

[K]s AB

10342.08	13789.44	-10342.08	-13789.44
13789.44	18385.92	-13789.44	-18385.92
-10342.08	-13789.44	10342.08	13789.44
-13789.44	-18385.92	13789.44	18385.92

[K]s AC

23940.00	0.00	-23940.00	0.00
0.00	0.00	0.00	0.00
-23940.00	0.00	23940.00	0.00
0.00	0.00	0.00	0.00

[K]s BC

10342.08	-13789.44	-10342.08	13789.44
-13789.44	18385.92	13789.44	-18385.92
-10342.08	13789.44	10342.08	-13789.44
13789.44	-18385.92	-13789.44	18385.92

Structure Stiffness Matrix

	1	2	3	4	5	6
1	34282.08	13789.44	-10342.08	-13789.44	-23940.00	0.00
2	13789.44	18385.92	-13789.44	-18385.92	0.00	0.00
3	-10342.08	-13789.44	20684.16	0.00	-10342.08	13789.44
4	-13789.44	-18385.92	0.00	36771.84	13789.44	-18385.92
5	-23940.00	0.00	-10342.08	13789.44	34282.08	-13789.44
6	0.00	0.00	13789.44	-18385.92	-13789.44	18385.92

Next is to partition [K] structure at the free nodes and the supports. Manipulation on program steps to establish [K_{ff}] has been discussed earlier in FRAME2D example.

$$[K]\text{ structure} = \begin{array}{c}3\\4\\1\\2\\5\\6\end{array}\begin{bmatrix} K_{ff} & \vdots & K_{fb} \\ \cdots & \cdots & \cdots \\ K_{bf} & \vdots & K_{bb} \end{bmatrix}$$
$$\phantom{[K]\text{ structure} = }\quad\quad 3\ 4\ 1\ 2\ 5\ 6$$

$$[K_{ff}] = \begin{bmatrix} 20684.16 & 0.00 \\ 0.00 & 36771.84 \end{bmatrix}$$

From Equation 4.9,

$\{P_f\} = [K_{ff}]\{X_f\}$

$\{X_f\} = [K_{ff}]^{-1}\{P_f\}$

$\{X_f\} = \begin{Bmatrix} 0.00048 \\ -0.00054 \end{Bmatrix}$

After the displacements of the free nodes are known, internal member forces of each member can be obtained from the equation:

$\{P\}i = \{Po\} + [K]i([T]i\{X_f\})$

$[T]i\{X_f\}$ is displacements vector transformed from local to global coordinate system.

In this case, no external load directly acting on each member thus $\{P_o\} = 0$. Thus, the equation to obtain the internal member forces becomes:

$\{P\}i = [K]i([T]i\{X_f\})$

The internal member forces are equal to:

$\{P\}AB$: $\quad\quad\quad$ $\{P\}AC$: $\quad\quad\quad$ $\{P\}BC$:

4.167
0.00
-4.167
0.00

0.00
0.00
0.00
0.00

20.833
0.00
-20.833
0.00

The magnitude of support reactions can be found using Equation 4.12:

$\{R_b\} = [K_{bf}]\{X_f\} - \{P_b\}$

There is no external load directly acting on supports thus $\{P_b\} = 0$. The equation to obtain the support reactions becomes:

$\{R_b\} = [K_{bf}]\{X_f\}$

In this stage, at first we have to establish $[K_{bf}]$. It is the same way as to establish $[K_{ff}]$, which is to partition $[K]$ structure using integer variables. The completed code is similar to that in FRAME2D:

```
'Indexing for matrix subscript
Sub Mindex(index() As Integer, IFr() As Integer, IFx() As Integer)
```

```
'Member end-displacements index:
For i = 1 To NM
    With Member(i)
    dindex(1, i) = 2 * .J1 - 1
    dindex(2, i) = 2 * .J1
    dindex(3, i) = 2 * .J2 - 1
    dindex(4, i) = 2 * .J2
    End With
Next i
'Joint free displacement index, IFr and
'restraint (support) index, IFx
n = 1
j = 1
For i = 1 To NP
    If Rs(i) = 0 Then IFr(n) = i: n = n + 1
Next i

n = 1
For i = 1 To NS
    n = Cells(22, 1 + i)
    IFx(2 * i - 1) = 2 * n - 1
    IFx(2 * i) = 2 * n
Next i
End Sub


Sub MInvers(SR() As Double, SD() As Double)
…
'submatrix Stiffness, KBF
For i = 1 To DOF
    For j = 1 To 3 * NS
        SR(j, i) = GS(Irj(j), Idj(i))
    Next j
Next i
…
End Sub
```

An Introduction to Excel for Civil Engineers

We know that variable *Idj* = *Ifr*, *Irj* = *Ifx* but they are declared at different level, which is at *public* and *procedure level*, respectively. With the code above, the subscript i,j of $[K_{bf}]_{i,j}$ associated with this example are:

$$[K_{bf}] = \begin{bmatrix} 1,3 & 1,4 \\ 2,3 & 2,4 \\ 5,3 & 5,4 \\ 6,3 & 6,4 \end{bmatrix}$$

And the values of its elements are:

$$[K_{bf}] = \begin{bmatrix} -10342.08 & -13789.44 \\ -13789.44 & -18385.92 \\ -10342.08 & 13789.44 \\ 13789.44 & -18385.92 \end{bmatrix}$$

The magnitudes of the support reactions are equal to:

$$\{R_b\} = \begin{Bmatrix} 2.500 \\ 3.333 \\ -12.500 \\ 16.667 \end{Bmatrix} \text{ ton}$$

Figure 7.5 shows the internal member forces in every member and the support reactions calculated by the program. Negative sign indicates compression state along the member, and positive sign indicates tension state.

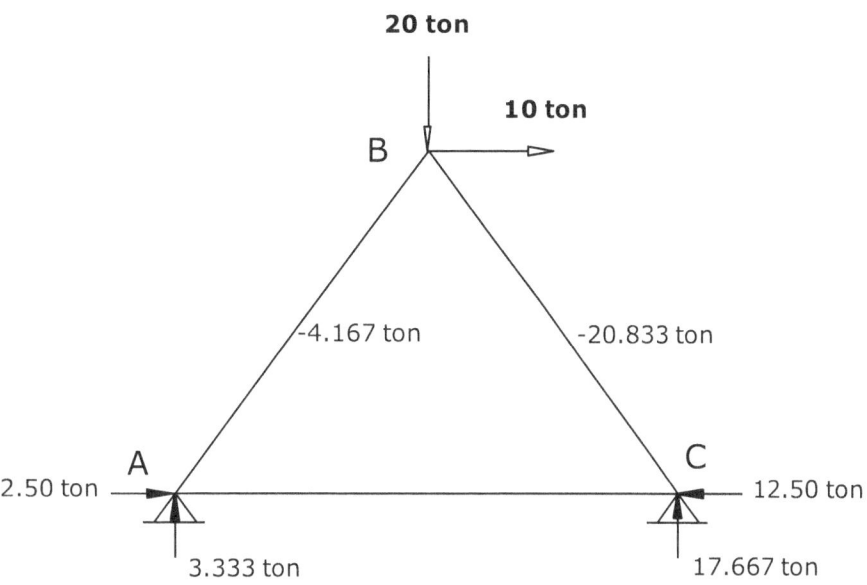

Figure 7.5: An example of 2D truss analysis

Check balance of forces at point B:

$\Sigma F_H = 10 + 4.167 \times 3/5 - 20.833 \times 3/5 = 0$

$\Sigma F_V = 20 - 4.167 \times 4/5 - 20.833 \times 4/5 = 0$ ...OK!

Check balance of forces of the whole structure:

$\Sigma F_H = 10 + 2.50 - 12.50 = 0$

$\Sigma F_V = 20 - 3.333 - 17.667 = 0$ ...OK!

The input and output form of TRUSS2D for the given truss example is shown below:

An Introduction to Excel for Civil Engineers

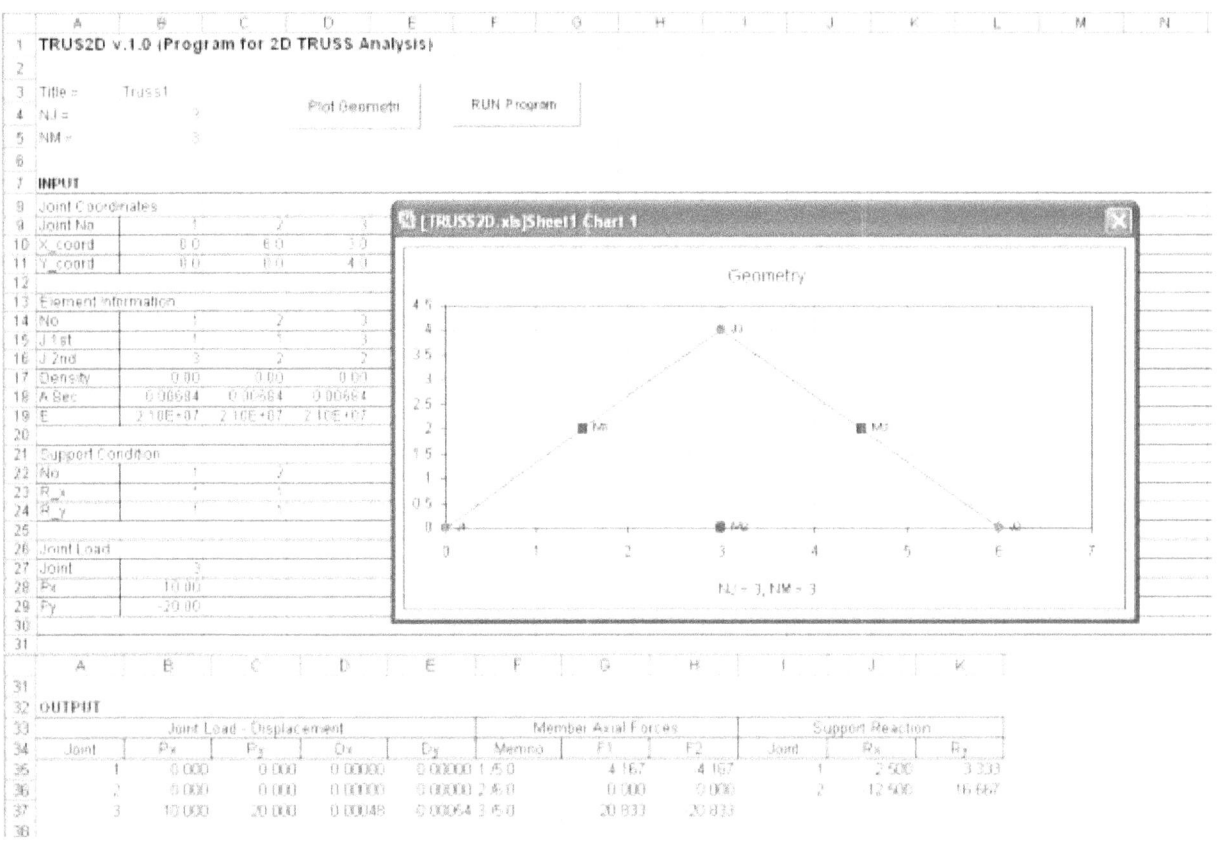

Figure 7.6: Input-output form of TRUSS2D

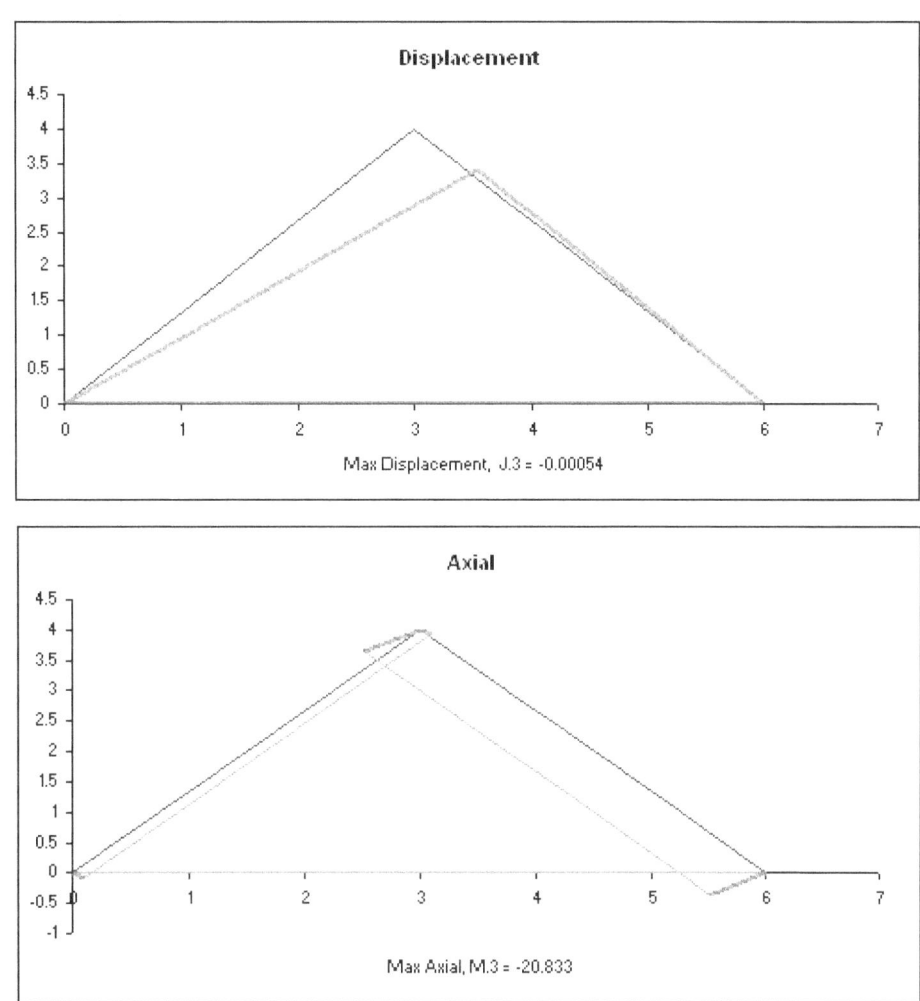

Figure 7.7: Charts of nodal displacement and axial force diagram

Note:

- Color coding for axial forces is the same as used in FRAME2D. Lines (that is, the lines that perpendicular to long section) of member 1 and 3 are red; it means negative axial forces occur or members in compression state.

An Introduction to Excel for Civil Engineers

7.2 APPLICATION

Now, TRUSS2D will be used to analyze a truss bridge with geometry as shown in Figure 7.8. The given number of bridge joints = 8, number of members = 12, which are supported by a pin and a roll support. Each member of truss is made of the same linear elastic material with E = 2,100,000 kg/cm² and cross-sectional area A = 132 cm². The loading data is given as follows:

- Vertical load = 40 tons and horizontal load = 2 tons, at the joint shown in Figure 7.8.
- Selfweight of all the members.

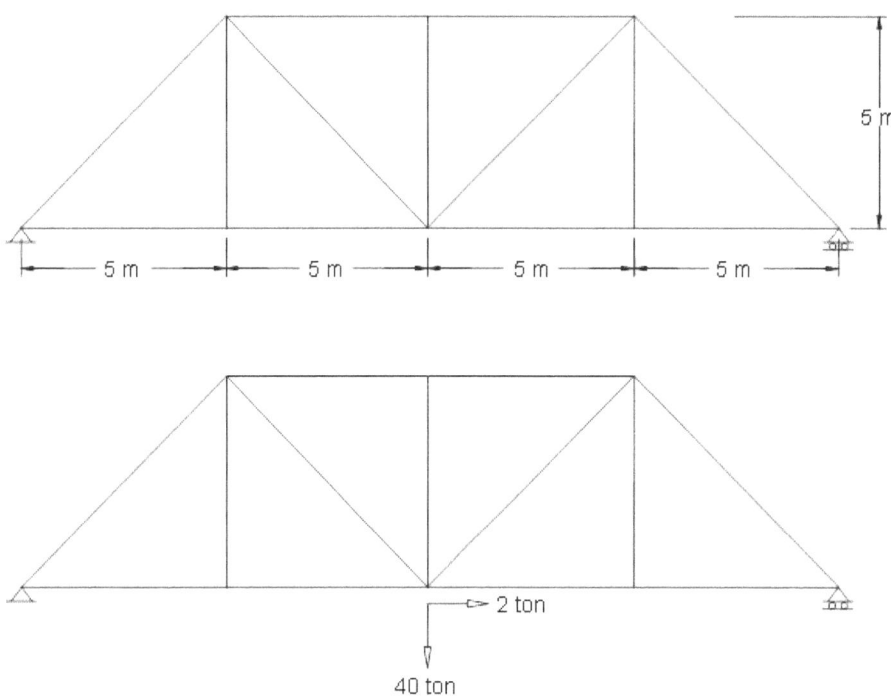

Figure 7.8: A truss bridge structure

The data of geometry, used material and loading are then inputted into the TRUSS2D input-output form as shown in Figure 7.9. The numbering system of the given truss bridge can be seen in the chart window (only available in Excel 2003). Figure 7.10 shows the program results on charts.

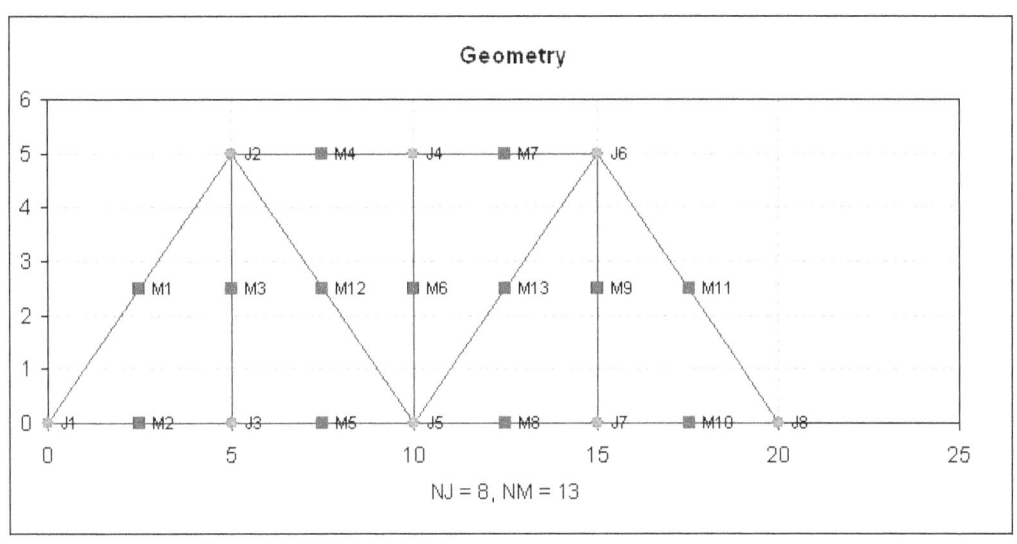

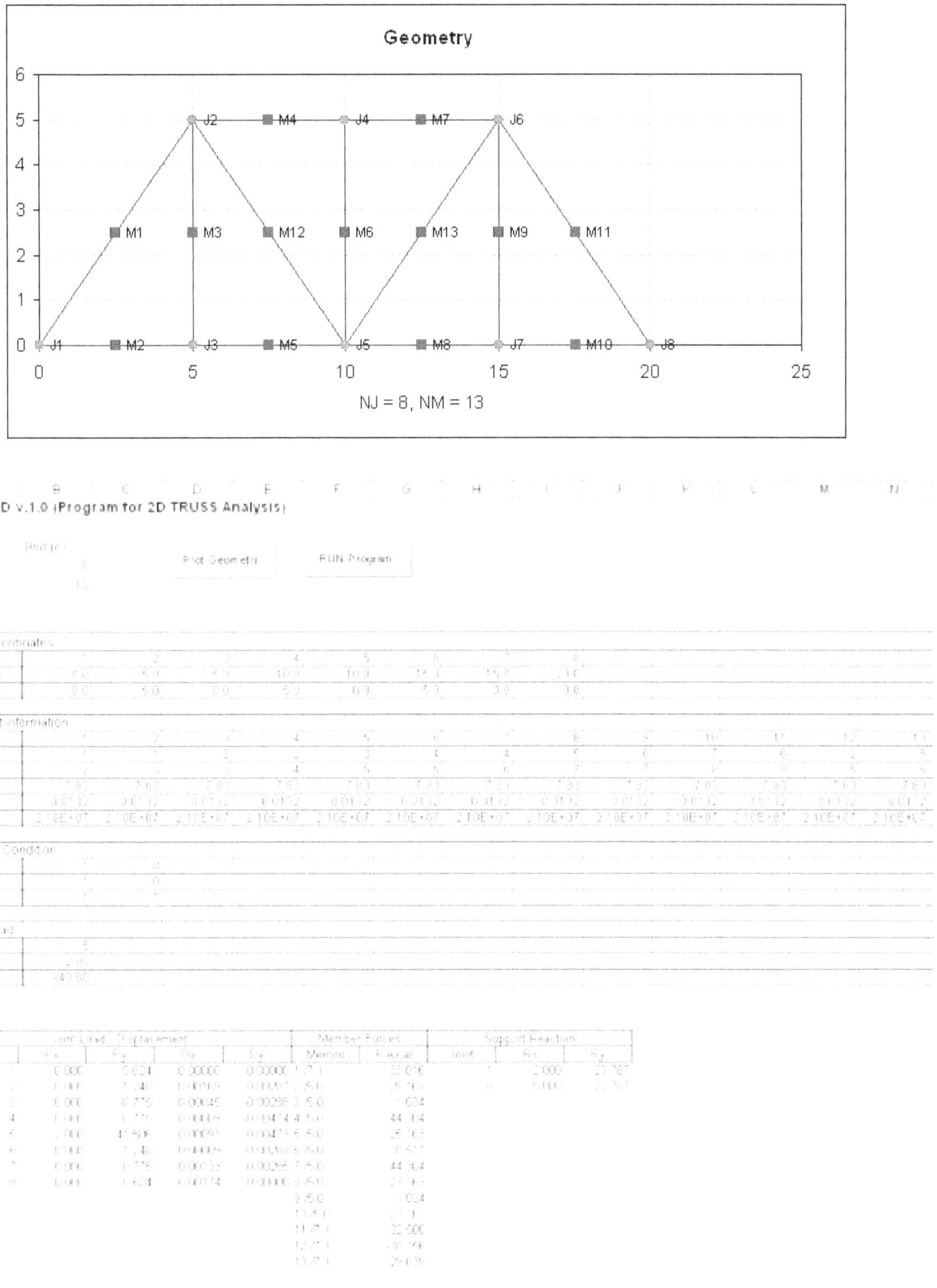

Figure 7.9: Input-output form of TRUSS2D for the given truss bridge

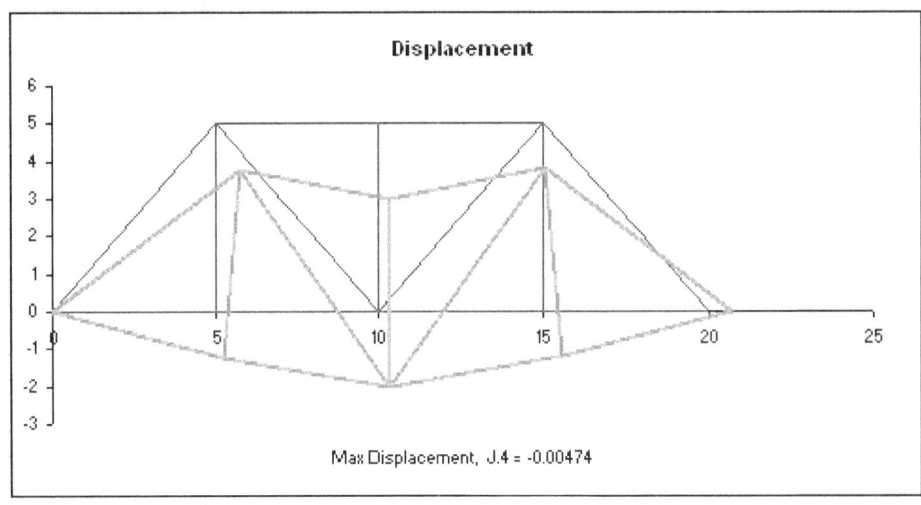

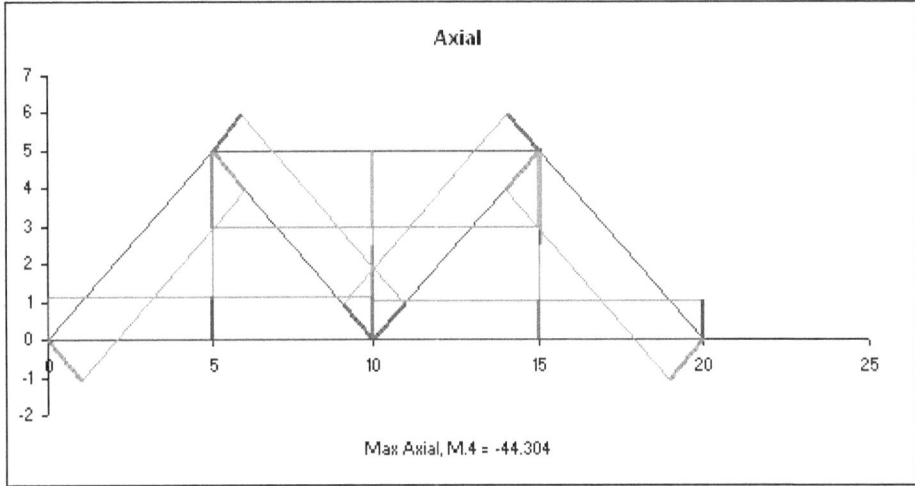

Figure 7.10: Charts of nodal displacement and axial force diagram for the given truss bridge

For a kind of drawing like a truss tower, it may require a chart that is extended upward or downward so you need to resize the chart by changing its aspect ratios. To do this, take the following steps:

- Click the mouse a chart > point to a sizing handle at the corners and sides of the chart > drag the sizing handle to be sizes as the charts below.
- The other way is to click the mouse on a chart > **Format** tab > in the **Size** group > enter a value in **Shape Height** and **Shape Width**.
- If font sizes change during chart resizing, click the mouse when the pointer on the chart or at any text, and then set the font size through the **Font Size** setting on the **Ribbon**.

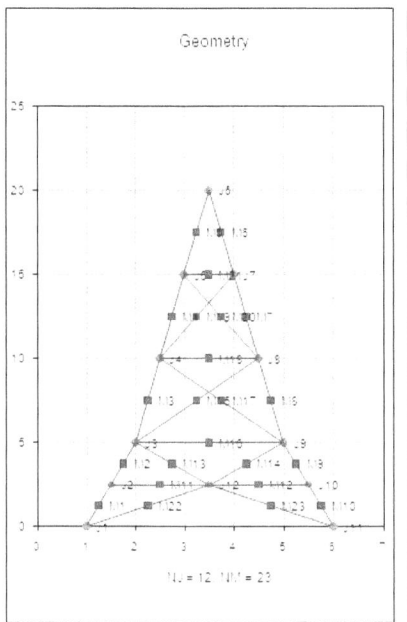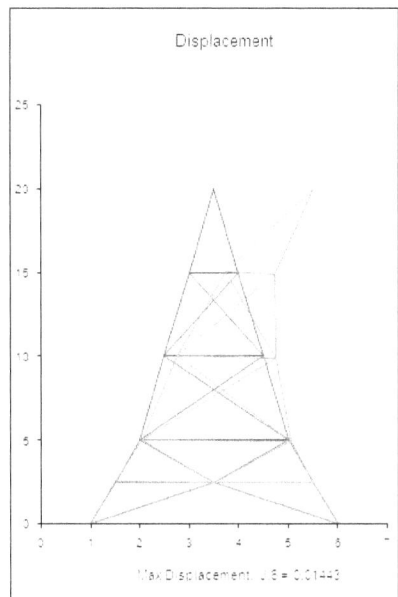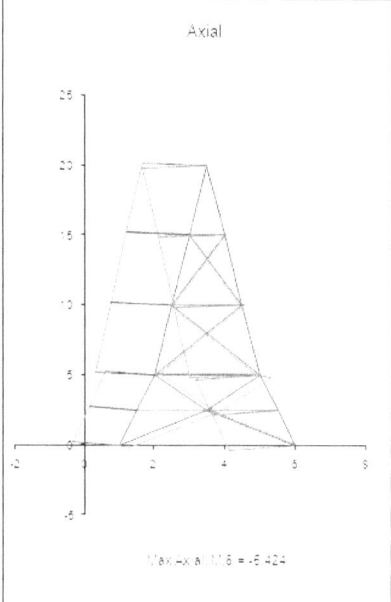

CHAPTER 8

BEAM ON ELASTIC FOUNDATION

Beam loaded on elastic foundation (BOF) is a theory that is often used in force - displacement prediction for analysis of structure that interacts directly with the ground. Elastic foundation is an approach to soil behavior as a collection of linear elastic springs, independent and one with another are unrelated (Winkler soil). This theory is often solved using numerical methods, especially by finite element method (FEM).

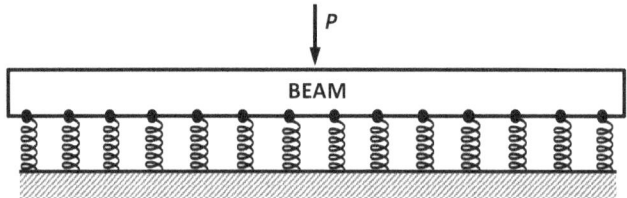

Here, the FEM for the solution of BOF adopts the sequence of steps given by Equation 4.13 to 4.18 that are developed by considering the coding of finite elements shown in Figure 8.1. The steps presented here are the steps used to develop a computer program for the solution of BOF.

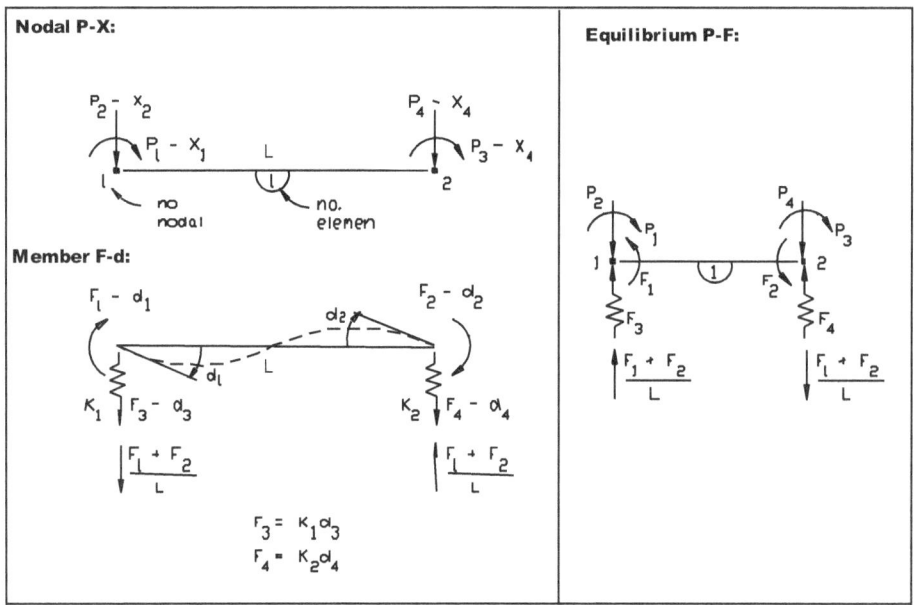

Figure 8.1: External force-displacement components at nodes and internal force-deformation components on elements of finite element

The external forces and moments {P} are related to the internal member forces {F} using a bridging constant [A] as {P} = [A]{F}, where:

$$[A] = \begin{bmatrix} 1 & 0 & 0 & 0 \\ \dfrac{1}{L} & \dfrac{1}{L} & 1 & 0 \\ 0 & 1 & 0 & 0 \\ -\dfrac{1}{L} & -\dfrac{1}{L} & 0 & 1 \end{bmatrix}$$

The internal member forces {F} are related to member deformations {d} and contributing member stiffnesses [S] as {F} = [S]{d}, where:

$$[S] = \begin{bmatrix} \dfrac{4EI}{L} & \dfrac{2EI}{L} & 0 & 0 \\ \dfrac{2EI}{L} & \dfrac{4EI}{L} & 0 & 0 \\ 0 & 0 & K_1 & 0 \\ 0 & 0 & 0 & K_2 \end{bmatrix} \begin{matrix} \dots F_1 \\ \dots F_2 \\ \dots F_3 \\ \dots F_4 \end{matrix}$$

with columns d_1, d_2, d_3, d_4.

Notes:

- E modulus of elasticity of element (beam)
- I moment of inertia of element
- K_1, K_2 soil spring constant = $(L/2).B.K_s$
- B width of beam
- K_s modulus of subgrade reaction
- P and F are used for either forces or moments; d and X are used for either translations or rotations

Hence, the nodal displacements {X} and the internal member forces {F} can be obtained from Equation 4.16 and 4.18:

$$\begin{Bmatrix} X_1 \\ X_2 \\ X_3 \\ X_4 \end{Bmatrix} = \{[A][S][A]^T\}^{-1} \begin{Bmatrix} P_1 \\ P_2 \\ P_3 \\ P_4 \end{Bmatrix} \begin{matrix} M \\ V \\ M \\ V \end{matrix}$$

$$\begin{Bmatrix} F_1 \\ F_2 \\ F_3 \\ F_4 \end{Bmatrix} \begin{matrix} M \\ M \\ V \\ V \end{matrix} = [S][A]^T \begin{Bmatrix} X_1 \\ X_2 \\ X_3 \\ X_4 \end{Bmatrix}$$

Notes:

- $\{[A][S][A]^T\}^{-1}$ inverse of global stiffness matrix
- $[S][A]^T$ element matrix
- M, F_1, F_2 moment components
- V, F_3, F_4 vertical force components

Moreover, in developing the program it is convenient to give boundary condition that restricts displacement by means of giving fixed supports at selected nodes. The magnitude of displacement at this node = 0.

The advantage of FEM over classical solution of BOF is that properties of elements and soil that are not constant such as weights, dimensions, flexural rigidities (EIs) and Ks along the beam can be easily incorporated into calculation.

8.1 Case Example

An application program for the solution of beam on elastic foundation is named BOF. It uses the same programming structure as the previous TRUSS2D or FRAME2D. BOF is now used for analysis of a footing foundation on the ground with a soil modulus Ks, and the footing geometry and loading condition as shown in Figure 8.2.

Given example:

Modulus of elasticity of the footing, E = 217000 ton/m^2

Height x width x length of the footing = 0.3 x 2 x 2 m

Ks = 1800 ton/m^3

Vertical load = 20 tons and moment load = 4 ton.m, acting in the column axis, right in the center of the footing.

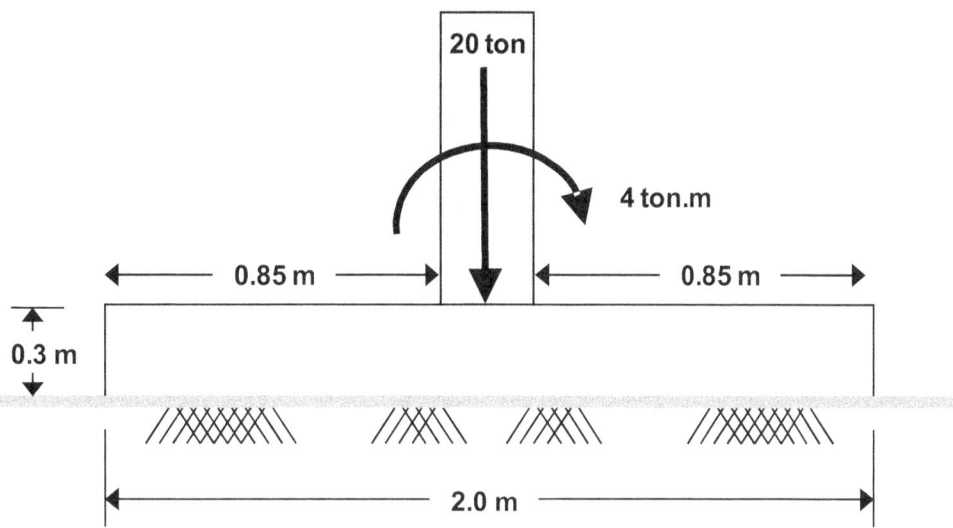

Figure 8.2: Footing on elastic foundation analysis

The input and output data of the given example is presented in the BOF input-output form in Figure 8.3. The footing structure consists of 10 members, with a continuous numbering system shown in the following chart:

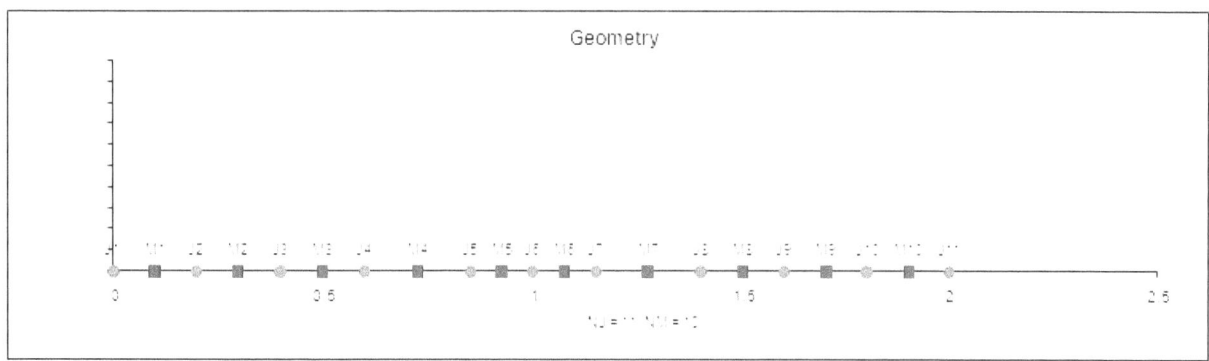

An Introduction to Excel for Civil Engineers

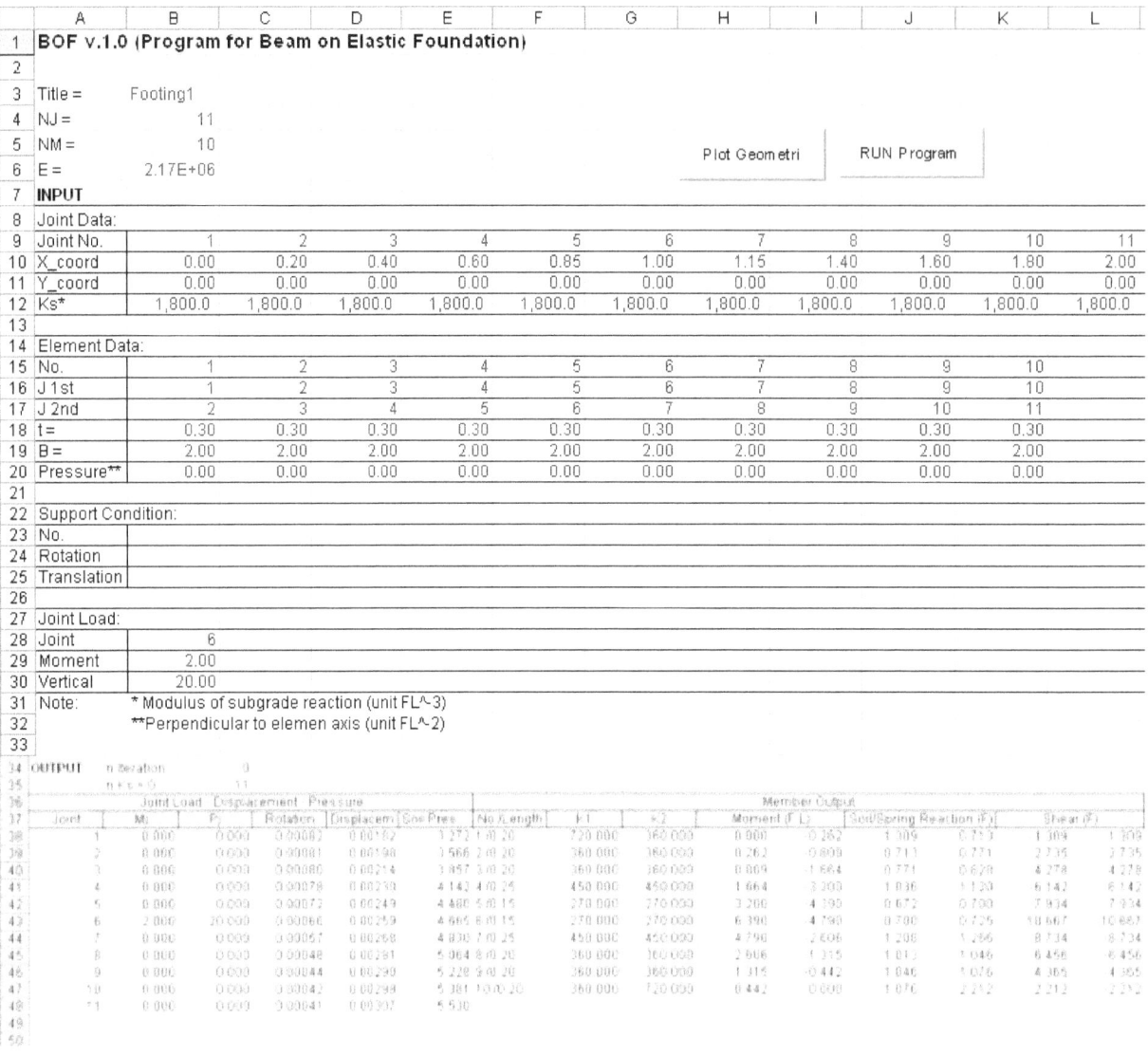

Figure 8.3: Input-output form of BOF for footing example

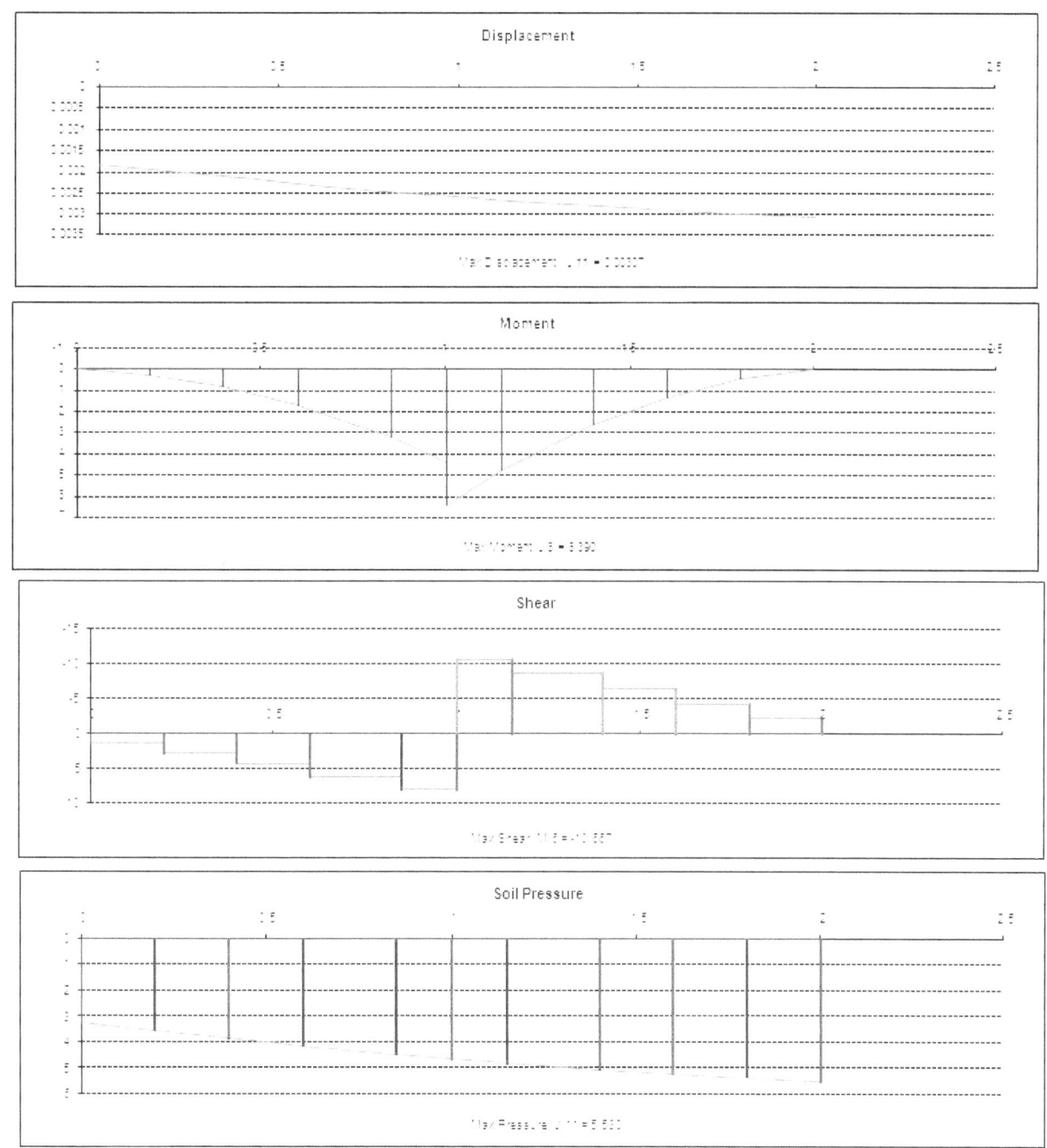

Figure 8.4: Charts of displacements, diagram of moment, shear and soil pressure

Notes:

- The output of BOF gives soil pressures that are plotted on the last chart. In practice, the soil pressures result must be checked whether the given loading on a foundation does not exceed the allowable bearing capacity of soil (qa). Thus, the maximum pressure obtained from the program should not exceed qa.
- Unlike FRAME2D and TRUSS2D, BOF has an iterative process to check if there are nodes that tend to separate from soil (x < 0), with a notion that soil springs only "accept" compressions. At the nodes where x < 0, ASA^T matrix needs to be rebuilt with Ks = 0 at those nodes. Here, the foundation selfweight shall be incorporated into the calculation. The result is then checked and it is necessary to repeat this step until convergence is achieved, where,

  Convergence → number $As(n)$ = number $As(n-1)$ at iteration n^{th},

  where *As* is active spring at X positive.

- For a case of retaining wall or pile foundation where the soil spring is modeled on both sides of the structure, the soil spring would always "work" where the one will be active while the other will be non-active. Thus, it is convenient to give an option to select limits on nodes where iteration will be performed. The intended limits can be found in Chapter 8, where BOF is modified for vertical structures.
- Sign convention of moments and shear forces for graphic depiction is to follow the sign convention described in Chapter 6.2 that is, based on the changes of structure shape after loading. It uses convention; blue line in a curve is for positive direction and red line for negative direction.

8.1 Application

The following example is just program verification on a beam problem shown in Figure 8.5, and the result is then compared with the output of FRAME2D for the same problem. Both programs should provide the same result because they use the same analysis method and theory of structure as well.

Here, no soil property is involved, thus Ks = 0. There are 3 supports along the beam, which is fixed at point A (input: R = 1, T = 1), pinned at point B (R = 0, T = 1) and fixed at point C (R = 1, T = 1).

The given data as below:

Beam:

Length = 18 m

Width = 2 m

Height = 0.5 m

Load:

Uniform load = 0.6 ton/m'/m width of the beam

The output of BOF is presented in Figure 8.6.

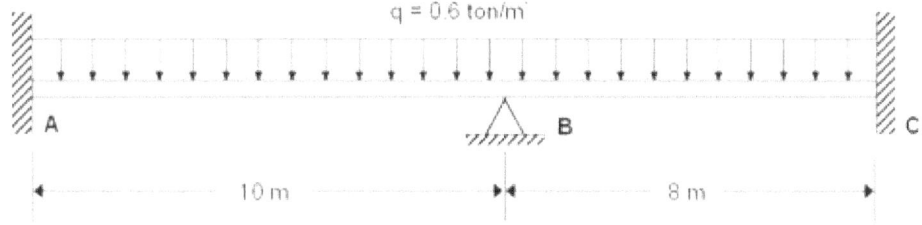

Figure 8.5: Beam with uniform load of q

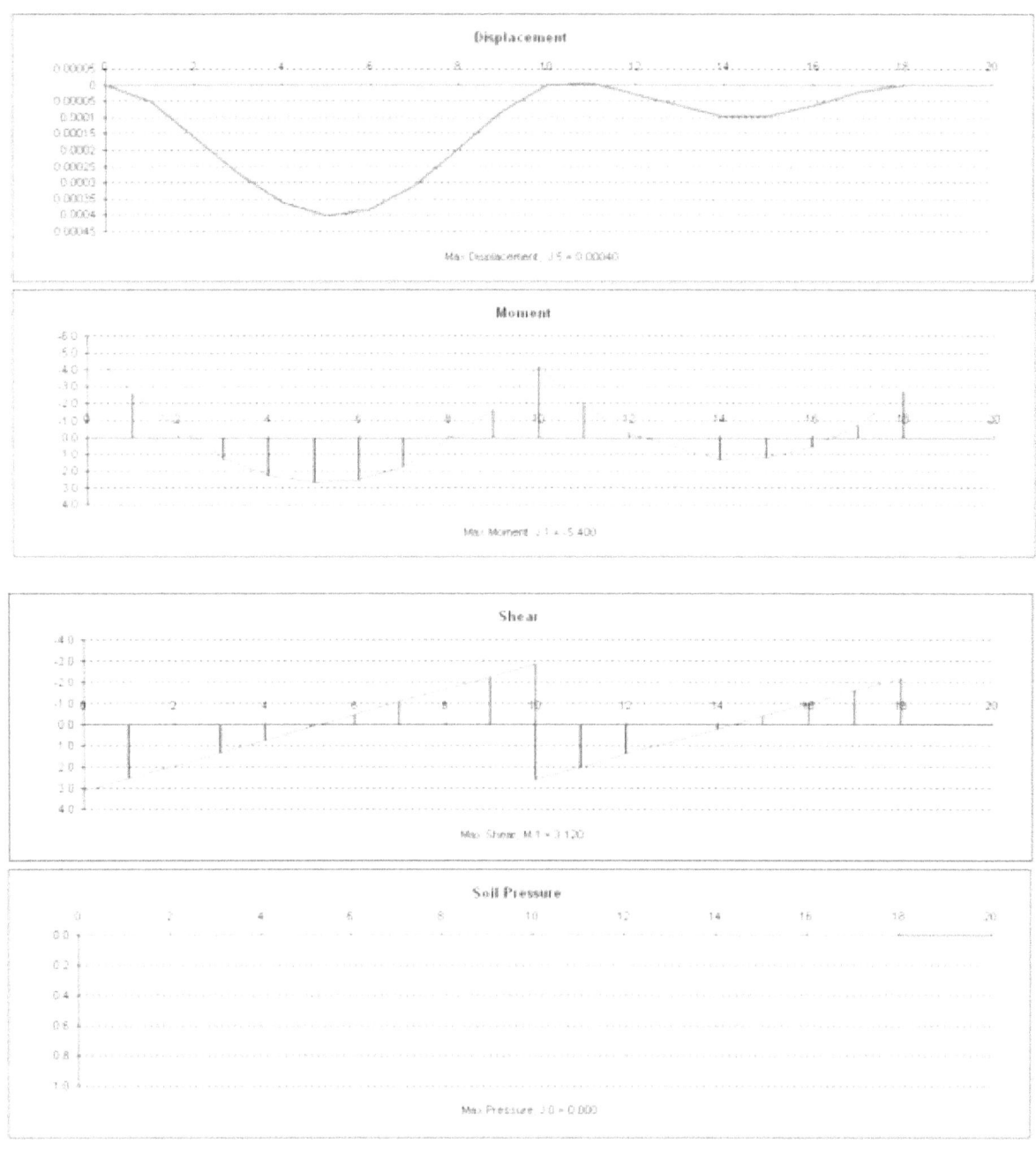

Figure 8.5: BOF solution for beam example

CHAPTER 9

LATERALLY LOADED STRUCTURE

Theory of beam on elastic foundation can also be applied for the analysis of structures subjected to lateral loads. Here, BOF program is slightly modified in which the orientation of the beam is now perpendicular to x-axis, and the external nodal forces – nodal displacements can be set whether lead to positive or negative axis. Load on nodes profile also to be displayed for a quick verification on inputted pressure magnitudes at both elements ends. The program for solution of laterally loaded structure is named XLAT.

9.1 CASE EXAMPLE

Figure 9.1 shows an example of retaining wall with given geometry, soil properties, pile, and anchor data. The figure also shows finite element (FE) model and numbering system.

Find:

- Magnitude of displacements, distribution of moments and shear forces along the wall for design purpose.
- Forces and stress acting on anchor for design purpose.

After the FE model (Figure 9.1) is established, next is to find lateral pressure behind the wall, acting from ground surface to the point O using Coulomb or Rankine active pressure coefficient. You can either input the lateral pressure to a node below the point O (referred to as either excavation point or dredge line).

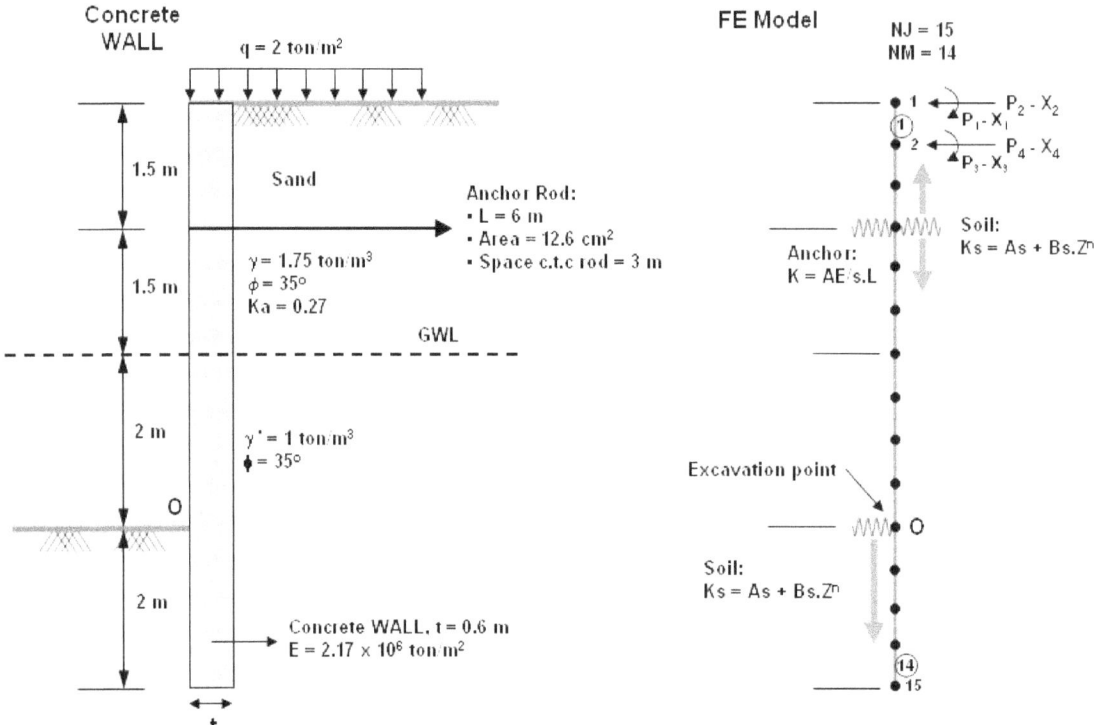

Figure 9.1: Model of retaining wall

Slight modifications were made in calculating fixed-end moments and forces of an element to take pressure profile that increases linearly with depth (triangular distribution) into account. The description is shown below:

The code:

```
'member fixed-end forces due to pressure
For i = 1 To NM
    With Member(i)
    d = Abs(.Pres1 - .Pres2)
```

An Introduction to Excel for Civil Engineers

```
            sq = Application.Min(.Pres1, .Pres2)
         'rectangular part
         w = sq * .bm
            Pa(Idm(1, i), i) = -w * .Lh ^ 2 / 12 'moment
            Pa(Idm(2, i), i) = -w * .Lh / 2 'horizontal
            Pa(Idm(3, i), i) = w * .Lh ^ 2 / 12 'moment
            Pa(Idm(4, i), i) = -w * .Lh / 2 'horizontal
         'triangular part & summing
         w = d * .bm
            Pa(Idm(1, i), i) = Pa(Idm(1, i), i) + (-w * .Lh ^ 2 / 30) 'moment
            Pa(Idm(2, i), i) = Pa(Idm(2, i), i) + (-w * .Lh * 3 / 20) 'horizontal
            Pa(Idm(3, i), i) = Pa(Idm(3, i), i) + (w * .Lh ^ 2 / 20) 'moment
            Pa(Idm(4, i), i) = Pa(Idm(4, i), i) + (-w * .Lh * 7 / 20) 'horizontal
      End With
Next i
```

Equivalent load at node due to pressure on element:

```
'equivalent joint load due to pressure
For i = 1 To NM
    For j = 1 To 4
        For n = 1 To 4
            Peq(Idm(j, i), i) = -Pa(Idm(j, i), i)
        Next n
     Next j
Next i
'sum load = joint load + eq.load
For i = 1 To NP
    Ps(i) = Pj(i)
Next i

'load superposition
For i = 1 To NM
    For j = 1 To 4
        Ps(Idm(j, i)) = Ps(Idm(j, i)) + Peq(Idm(j, i), i)
    Next j
Next i
```

Notes:

- The above code is the same as used in the previous programs to find the equivalent load on nodes.
- Variable Idm states nodal displacement indexes of element (member) ends. It has been also described earlier in the previous chapters.

To generalize program where variation in the physical characteristics of the structure can be incorporated into calculation, thus the input of height of beam, t, as in BOF is replaced by moment of inertia, I, in XLAT:

7	INPUT	
8	Joint Data:	
9	Joint No.	
10	X_coord	
11	Y_coord	
12	Ks*	
13	Spring**	
14	Element Data:	
15	No.	Inertia moment
16	J 1st	input
17	J 2nd	
18	I =	
19	B =	
20	Pressure1***	
21	Pressure2***	
22	Support Condition:	
23	No.	
24	Rotation	
25	Translation	
26		

The following chart window (Excel 2003) will appear by clicking on Plot Geometry button. It shows finite element geometry and pressure profile that have been inputted into the program refer to Figure 9.1.

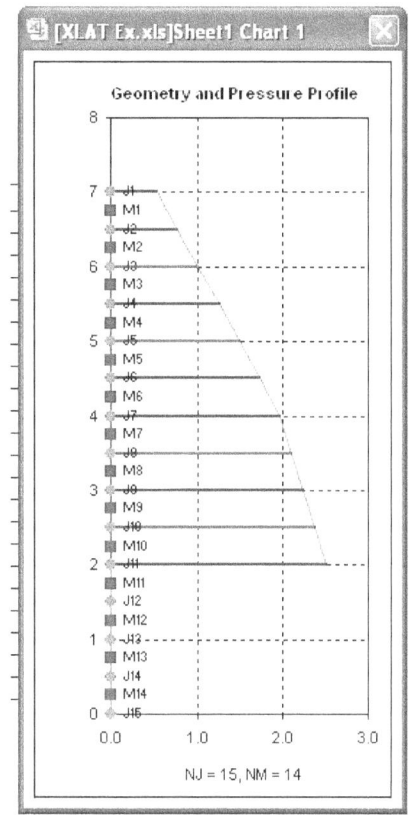

Modulus of subgrade reaction or spring constant of the soil of sand layer (Ks) in the front of the wall is assumed to increase with depth by the approach below:

ks = $A_s + B_s \cdot Z^n$. ton/m³,

= $1000 + 2000 \cdot Z^n$ → above GWL

= $600 + 1100 \cdot Z^n$ → below GWL

where,

As = $40(c \cdot N_c + 0.5\gamma \cdot B \cdot N\gamma)$

Bs = $40(\gamma \cdot N_q)$

z = depth from ground surface

Nc, Nγ, Nq = bearing capacity factors

n = 0.5, adopted exponent for non-linearity of Ks

Anchor rods are made of steel, with the specification shown in Figure 9.1. The input spring of anchor rod per meter width of wall is obtained from the following formula:

$K = \dfrac{AE}{sL}$, thus, for this case:

$K = \dfrac{12.6(2.0 \times 10^7)}{3(6)10^4} = 1400$ ton/m.

Input-output form of XLAT is shown in Figure 9.2 below:

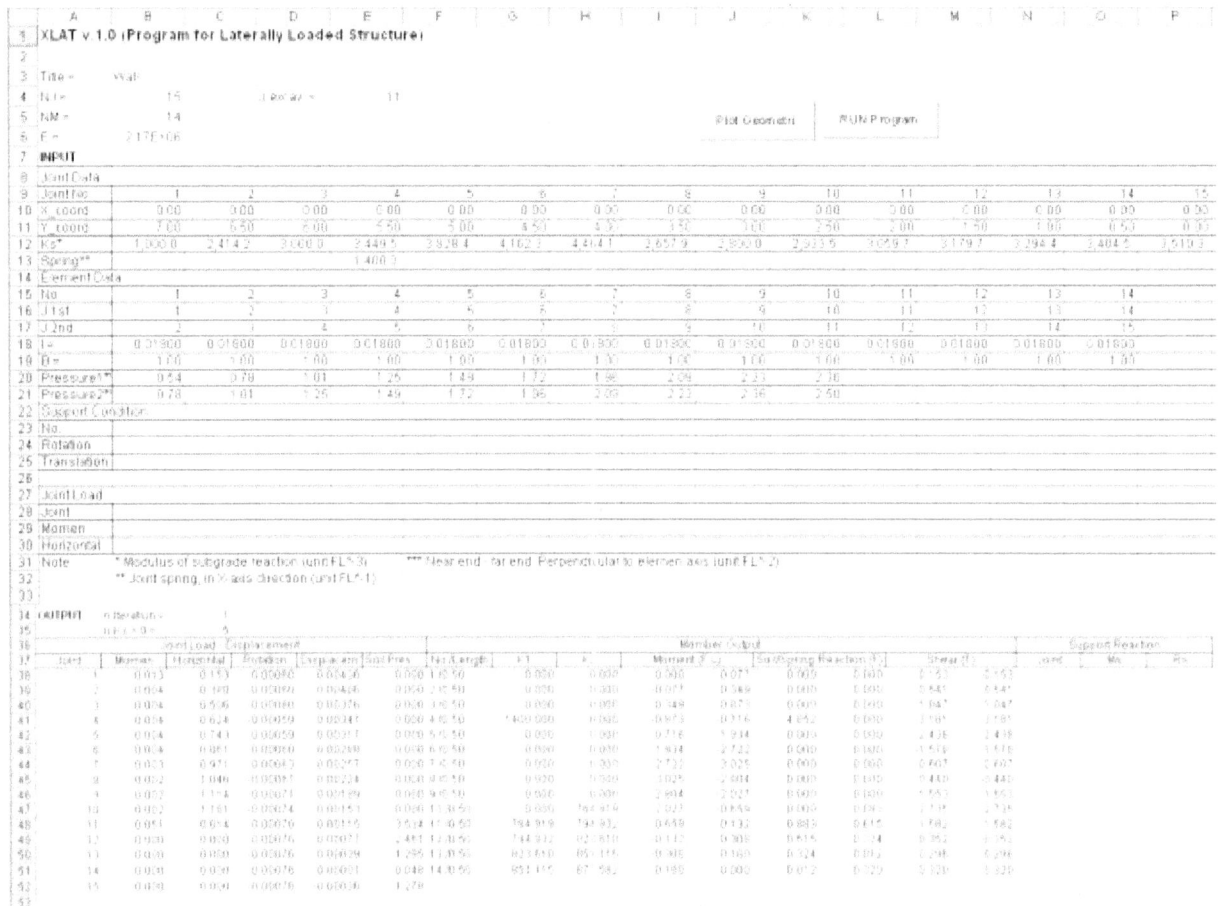

Figure 9.2: Input-output form of XLAT for retaining wall

Notes:

- Unit used in this example is ton – meter, to equalize the values resulted from the calculation.
- The data entered in "**J excav**" (stands for joint excavation) indicates that iterative process will be done from the top of the wall to this point. Note that, iteration will not be done below joint excavation because soil springs are present on both sides of wall. Definition of the iteration and its purpose are described in Chapter 8.

An Introduction to Excel for Civil Engineers

- To perform iterative process up until joint n (to check the soil spring direction), one should enter joint excavation = n + 1. Thus, in this relation, iteration will not be performed if joint excavation = 1 or n = 0.
- In designing anchor rod, the reaction forces acting on the anchor must be checked. The stress acting on the anchor is calculated as follows:

Member Output		Soil/Spring Reaction (F)		Shear (F)	
Moment (F.L)					
0.000	0.077	0.000	0.000	0.153	-0.153
-0.077	0.349	0.000	0.000	0.541	-0.541
-0.349	0.873	0.000	0.000	1.047	-1.047
-0.873	-0.716	4.852	0.000	-3.181	3.181
0.716	-1.934	0.000	0.000	-2.438	2.438
1.934	-2.722	0.000	0.000	-1.578	1.578
2.722	-3.025	0.000	0.000	-0.607	0.607
3.025	-2.804	0.000	0.000	0.440	-0.440
2.804	-2.027	0.000	0.000	1.553	-1.553
2.027	-0.659	0.000	0.883	2.735	-2.735
0.659	0.132	0.883	0.615	1.582	-1.582
-0.132	0.308	0.615	0.324	0.352	-0.352
-0.308	0.160	0.324	0.012	-0.296	0.296
-0.160	0.000	0.012	-0.320	-0.320	0.320

(Anchor spring reaction = 4.852)

Check:

$P_{axial} = 3 \times 4.852 = 14.557$ ton (c.t.c = 3 m)

$$f_s = \frac{P_{axial}}{A} = \frac{14.557}{12.6} = 1.155 \text{ ton/cm}^2$$

So, the specification chosen for the anchor rod must be adequate to resist the above force and stress.

The results of moment and shear force diagrams generated by XLAT program are presented in Figure 9.3. For wall design purposes, it can be taken the maximum positive bending moment (blue lines) that works below the anchor point, while negative moments (red lines) are located around the anchor and around the wall tip.

An Introduction to Excel for Civil Engineers

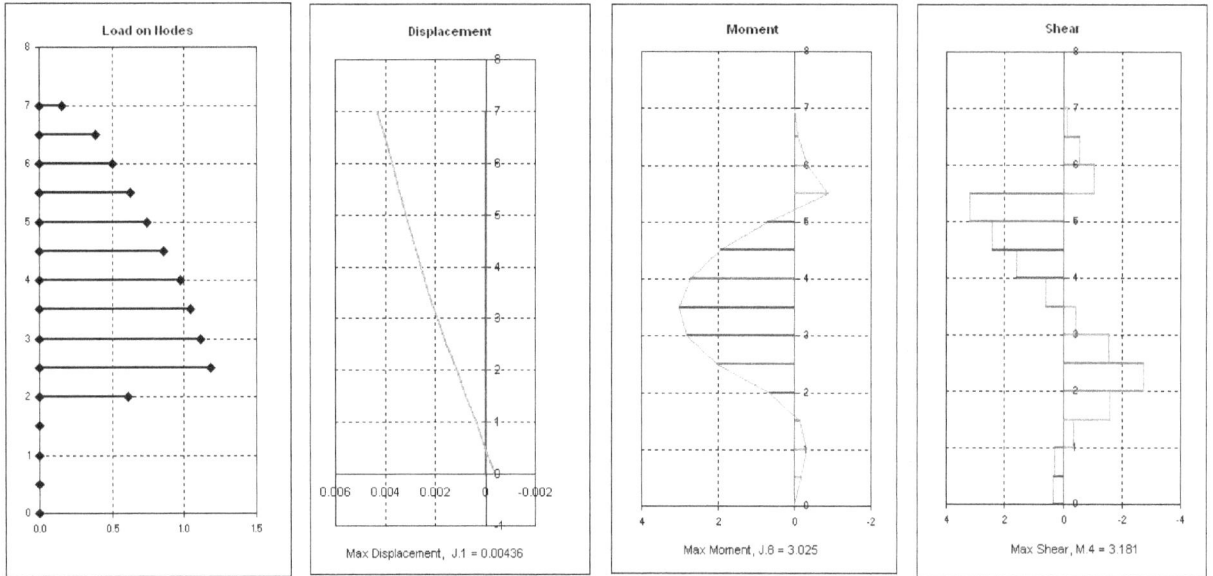

Figure 9.3: XLAT output chart

9.2 APPLICATION

Pile foundation with a diameter of 0.406 m embedded in sand layer to a depth of 16 meters. Pile and soil data are given in Figure 9.4. Pile head is assumed fixed against rotation but free to translate.

Find:

- Maximum load applied on the pile head for its limited magnitude of displacement of the pile head.

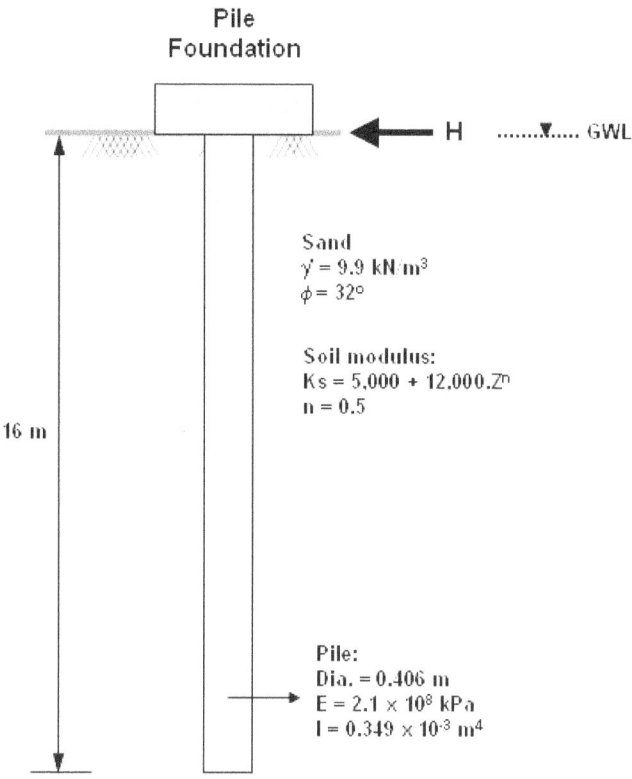

Figure 9.4: Pile foundation example

A chart generated by XLAT for this example is shown in Figure 9.5, where horizontal load H is taken 100 kPa. Displacement that occurs on the pile head is 0.0054 m (at joint 1, as shown in the figure). From load and displacement linear relationship, any load increases by 1 kPa will produce pile head displacement of 0.054 mm.

Therefore, for a case where pile head displacement is limited to 5 mm, the allowed maximum load = 5/0.054 kPa = 92.6 kPa.

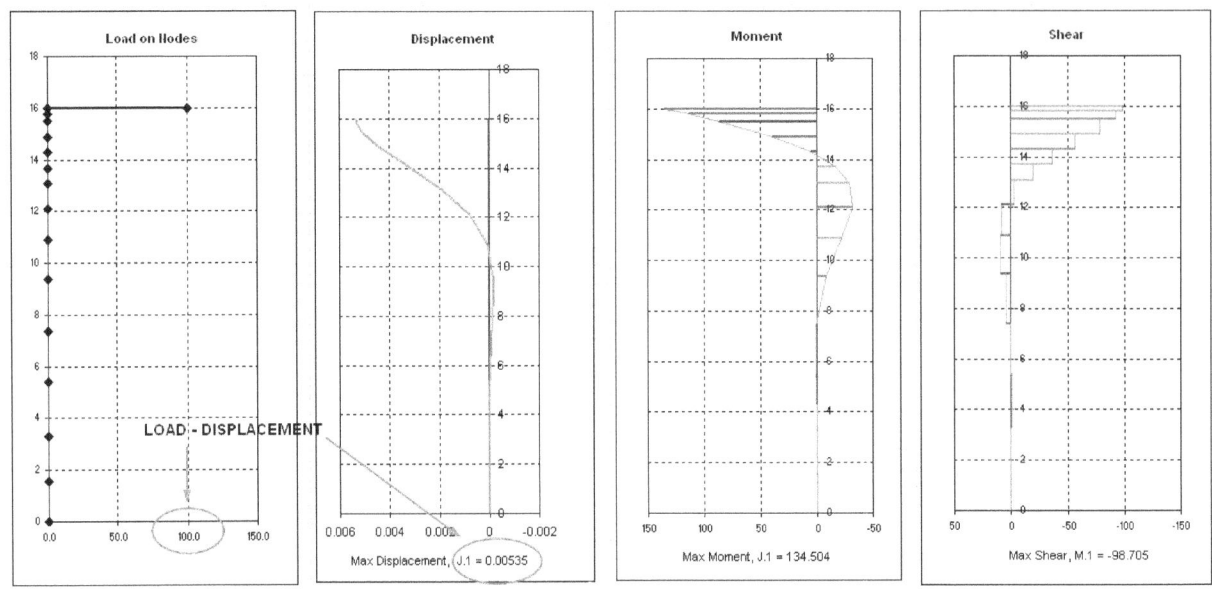

Figure 9.5: XLAT chart for pile foundation example

CHAPTER 10

ONE DIMENSIONAL CONSOLIDATION

In this chapter, we will apply numerical solution using finite difference (FD) method for Terzaghi's theory of one-dimensional consolidation. This method is based on a grid of time, t, versus depth, h, as shown in Figure 10.1. The depth of soil layer is divided into m equal parts of thickness Δz, while the period of time is divided to n equal parts of interval Δt.

The equation of one-dimensional consolidation according to Terzaghi's theory is:

$$\frac{\partial u}{\partial t} = c_v \frac{\partial^2 u}{\partial z^2} \qquad (10.1)$$

Finite difference forms of Taylor series for the first and second order derivatives of functions have been shown in Chapter 5, and for both sides of Equation 10.1 can be written:

$$\frac{\partial u}{\partial t} = \frac{u_{i+1,j} - u_{i,j}}{\Delta t}$$

$$\frac{\partial^2 u}{\partial z^2} = \frac{u_{i-1,j} - 2u_{i,j} + u_{i+1,j}}{\Delta z^2}$$

Substituting these values into Equation 10.1 obtains finite difference approach to one-dimensional consolidation equation as follows:

$$u_{i,j+1} = u_{i,j} + \beta(u_{i-1,j} + u_{i+1,j} - 2u_{i,j}) \qquad (10.2)$$

where,

$$\beta = \frac{c_v \Delta t}{(\Delta z)^2}$$

c_v coefficient of consolidation

$u_{i,j}$ excess pore pressure at depth i and time j.

β is referred to as a operator of Equation 10.2, and to make solution converge this value should not exceed ½. The value lies between 1/6 and ½ (R.F. Craig, 1987).

An Introduction to Excel for Civil Engineers

For a period of time t in an open layer:

$$T_v = \frac{c_v(n\Delta t)}{(\tfrac{1}{2}m\Delta z)^2} = 4\beta n/m^2 \tag{10.3}$$

In case of half-closed layer, the denominator becomes $(m\Delta z)^2$:

$$T_v = \beta n/m^2 \tag{10.4}$$

T_v is a time factor for consolidation

In case of impermeable boundary, where no flow across the boundary:

$\frac{\partial u}{\partial z} = 0$, or in FD form: $\frac{u_{i-1,j} - u_{i+1,j}}{2\Delta z} = 0$

For an impermeable boundary, Equation 10.2 becomes:

$$u_{i,j+1} = u_{i,j} + \beta(2u_{i-1,j} - 2u_{i,j}) \tag{10.5}$$

The degree of consolidation (U) at time t can then be obtained by finding area under initial isochrone (from initial excess pore pressure distribution) and area under isochrone at time t, given by the following equations:

half closed layer:

$$U = 1 - \frac{\int_0^d u\, dz}{\int_0^d u_i\, dz} \tag{10.6}$$

open layer:

$$U = 1 - \frac{\int_0^{2d} u\, dz}{\int_0^{2d} u_i\, dz} \tag{10.7}$$

where, d and z are respectively the thickness of a clay layer and any depth within a clay layer. Isochrones present the progress of consolidation where excess pore water pressures u plotted against the depths z for different time values t. Figure 10.2 shows an isochrone example. The blue line represents a variation of the initial u, while the magenta line represents u at time t.

Both Equation 10.2 and Equation 10.5 can be easily programmed, because the analysis is based on an equilaterally grid. This looks like to build an array of function values (u) with size of *m* x *n* (see Figure 10.1). The solution is done by simply taking a looping through a number of grid points, thus, to find of excess pore water pressures at a specified period of time (*n*) can be determined by giving a specified value in the looping.

If *m* and *n* refer to FD grid interval numbers according to Figure 10.1, then VBA code for half-closed layer can be written as follows:

```
'Finite difference approximation:
    For j = 0 To n
        For i = 1 To m - 1
        u(i, j + 1) = u(i, j) + Beta * (u(i - 1, j) + u(i + 1, j) - 2 * u(i, j))
        Next i
        'on impermeable boundary (at m points):
        i = m:  u(i, j + 1) = u(i, j) + Beta * (2 * u(i - 1, j) - 2 * u(i, j))
    Next j
```

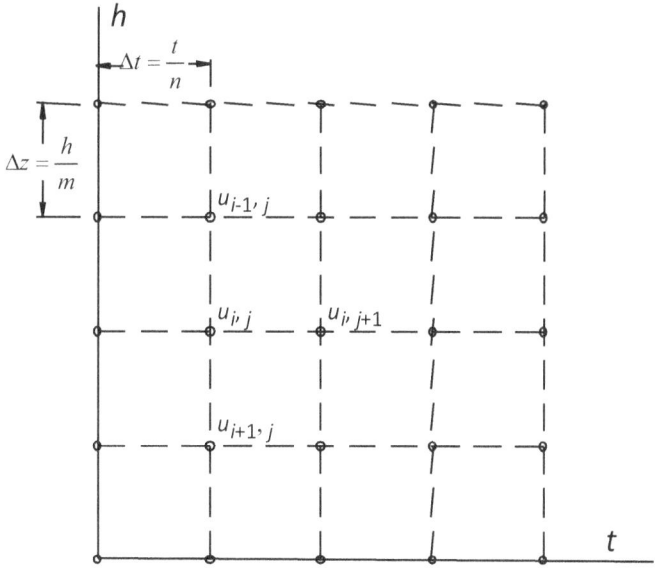

Figure 10.1: Grid of time versus depth

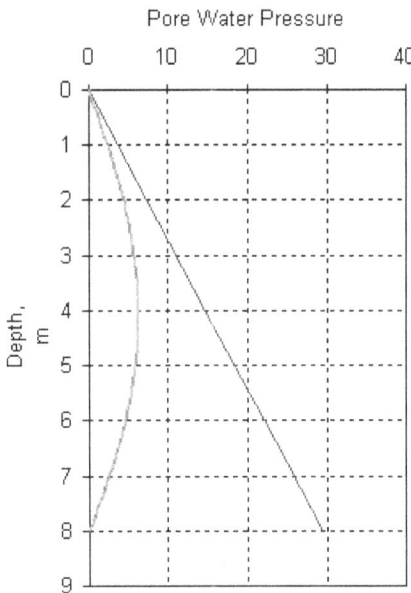

Figure 10.2: Isochrone example at specified time

In practice, the use of Taylor series adopts the first few terms omitting the higher order derivatives and the error due to truncation can be reduced to minimum when $\beta = 1/6$. Given this circumstance, *m* and *n* can be then determined directly to satisfy a fixed $\beta = 1/6$ for both layer conditions. Subsequently, Equation 10.3 and 10.4 are re-arranged to determine *n* and written as follows:

```
im = Cells(4, 2) 'no. of layer
    m = 10 * im
    h = Cells(3, 2) 'height of layer
    t = Cells(5, 5) 'time
    cv = Cells(5, 2) 'coef. of consolidation
    FDCCase = Cells(3, 5) 'Case of calculation


'open layered, re-Eq. 10.3
    Tv = cv * t / (h / 2) ^ 2
    n = 1.5 * m ^ 2 * Tv


'half closed layered, re-Eq. 10.4
    Tv = cv * t / h ^ 2
    n = 6 * m ^ 2 * Tv
```

In the process of finding *U*, the depth interval and the initial *u* input data are developed where are each multiplied by 10 (default by the Author) thus *m* = 10 x *im* as shown in the code. The interpolation technique is done to get the adjacent values, accordingly. The discussion of numerical methods in Chapter 5 demonstrates that dividing interval of the independent variable into smaller interval provides the result closer to the exact value, and it is similar to what will be doing here in the process of finding *U* (numerical integration) as well as final *u* (numerical differentiation).

Manipulation for getting smaller FD grid interval is as follows:

- Code to get initial depth input (*dz*) and initial *u* (*IP*).

    ```
    For i = 0 To im
        dZ(i) = i * h / im
        IP(i) = Cells(9 + i, 2)
    Next i
    ```

- Re-input *dz* and *IP* with a divisor 10 and performs interpolations to get new input values using variables named *rsdZ* and *rsIP*.

    ```
    n = 1
    rsdZ(0) = dZ(0)
    rsIP(0) = IP(0)
    For i = 0 To im - 1
        For j = 1 To 10
        rsIP(j) = j * (IP(i + 1) - IP(i)) / 10
        rsdZ(j) = j * (dZ(i + 1) - dZ(i)) / 10
        rsIP(n) = rsIP(j) + IP(i)
        rsdZ(n) = rsdZ(j) + dZ(i)
        n = n + 1
        Next j
    Next i
    ```

For an example, given below is initial pressure data:

Depth (H/m)	Initial Pressure
0.00	0.00
2.00	7.50
4.00	15.00
6.00	22.50
8.00	30.00

If the code runs, it will produce the following data:

Depth (H/m)	Initial Pressure
0.00	0.00
0.20	0.75
0.40	1.50
0.60	2.25
0.80	3.00
1.00	3.75
1.20	4.50
1.40	5.25
1.60	6.00
1.80	6.75
2.00	7.50
2.20	8.25
2.40	9.00
2.60	9.75
2.80	10.50
3.00	11.25
3.20	12.00
3.40	12.75
3.60	13.50
3.80	14.25
4.00	15.00
4.20	15.75
4.40	16.50

4.60	17.25
4.80	18.00
5.00	18.75
5.20	19.50
5.40	20.25
5.60	21.00
5.80	21.75
6.00	22.50
6.20	23.25
6.40	24.00
6.60	24.75
6.80	25.50
7.00	26.25
7.20	27.00
7.40	27.75
7.60	28.50
7.80	29.25
8.00	30.00

Figure 5 shows an open layer isochrone example with initial u increases linearly with depth. At time t, the area under isochrone curve between $y = 0$ and $y = 8$ is then sought. For this purpose, FDC uses trapezoidal method (in h/m unit) in which the total area = cumulative sum of h/m segment areas done in a looping through successive re-input dZ and IP values. The detailed code can be found in FDC program in the Attachment.

10.1 Application 1

The profile of excess pore water pressure (u) over depth in a saturated clay layer due to the applied loading are equal to vertical stress distribution below a foundation as described in Problem 4 of Chapter 3 that is shown below:

Depth (m)	u (ton/m^2)

0.0	10.00
0.5	9.76
1.0	8.63
1.5	7.01
2.0	5.49
2.5	4.28
3.0	3.36
3.5	2.68
4.0	2.17
4.5	1.79
5.0	1.49
5.5	1.26
6.0	1.08

Suppose that the clay layer is half-closed layer where water flows across the upper limit. The given $cv = 7.19$ m²/year and thickness of the layer is 6 m. Find the distribution of u and average degree of consolidation (U) at 6 months.

Answer

FDC result is shown as below:

Depth (H/m)	Initial Pressure	After (t) Pressure	ave U
0.00	10.00	0.00	46%
0.50	9.76	0.55	
1.00	8.63	1.06	
1.50	7.01	1.52	
2.00	5.49	1.89	
2.50	4.28	2.17	
3.00	3.36	2.35	
3.50	2.68	2.46	
4.00	2.17	2.51	

An Introduction to Excel for Civil Engineers

4.50	1.79	2.51	
5.00	1.49	2.50	
5.50	1.26	2.48	
6.00	1.08	2.47	

10.2 Application 2

From field piezometers measurement on a clay layer beneath embankment, the distribution of excess pore water pressure, u (after subtracted by its theoretical pressure) with depth is shown in the table below:

Depth (m)	u (kN/m^2)
0.0	39.00
2.0	44.40
4.0	50.50
6.0	45.50
8.0	42.40
10.0	40.00

Answer

The input-output form FDC is shown below:

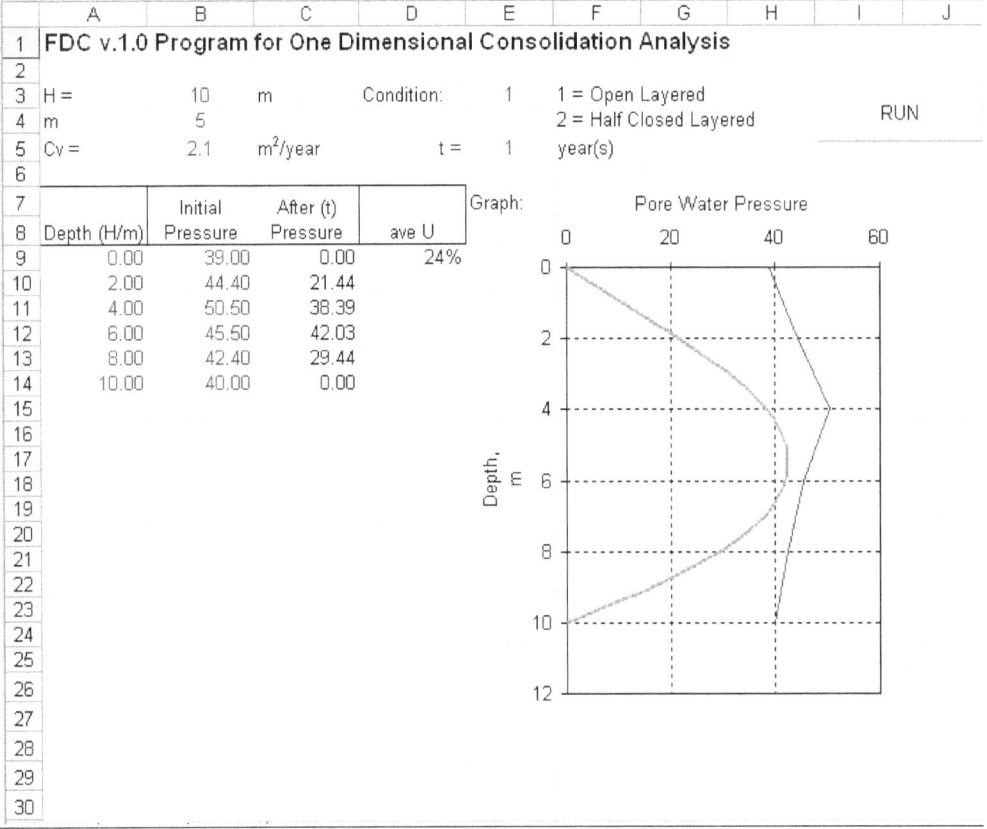

Notes:

- Keep in mind that FDC *initial* and *after pressure* refer to excess pore water pressures (*pwp*) distribution after subtracted by its theoretical pressures (water unit weight x depth). Thus, assuming soil is fully saturated, the initial excess *pwp* = applied load.
- The advantage of finite difference method is that any patterns of excess pore water pressure can be incorporated into calculation. The input data can be based on the initial observed values from a field or when load is applied gradually, for example, in consolidation problem below an embankment.
- The purpose of FDC programming for one-dimensional consolidation using numerical methods has actually been achieved, that is at the stage where the degree of consolidation based on areas under an isochrone at time t is found. However, if you wish to go further, a curve of U versus t as shown in Figure 10.3 can also be presented. This curve is created automatically by the program to include 10 different t values into a looping, and starts with t (years)= 0.1, then t = 0.5, 1, 2, and so on, and plotted on a semi-log chart.

An Introduction to Excel for Civil Engineers

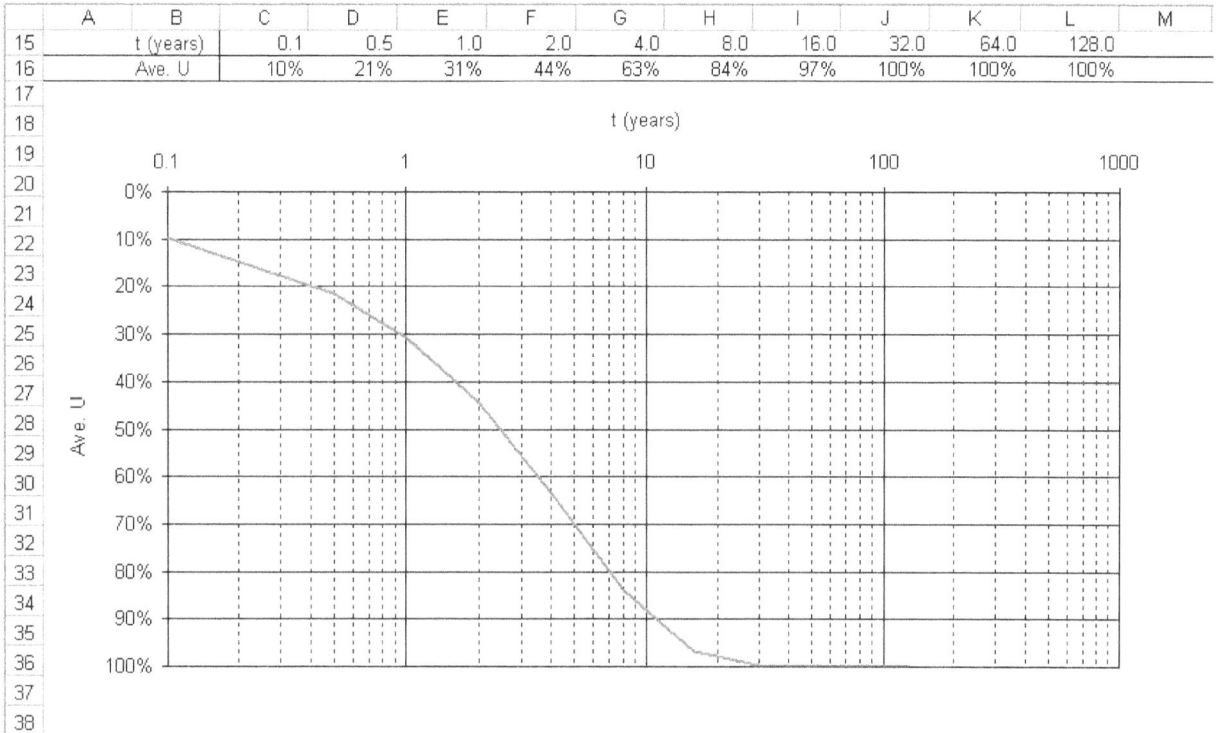

Figure 10.3: Relationship between average degree of consolidition (U) and specified time (t)

CHAPTER 11

AUTOCAD SCRIPT FILE

To graphically depict outputs of a program, alternatively, you can plot the outputs in AutoCAD software instead of using Excel chart. Here, you can work further with charts drawing with either a 2D or 3D model. The main advantage of AutoCAD is because this software is specifically built for composing drawings.

A script file meant here is a text file that contains a sequence of commands executed by AutoCAD. The sequence of commands can be made on a worksheet or in VBA to speed up and simplify the process of writing and executing the commands. The script file is made by a word processor such as Windows Notepad or Microsoft Word in ASCII format and is given with a .scr file extension.

In this chapter, we will be working with AutoCAD 2007.

11.1 Creating Scripts in Worksheet

Before creating a script, you should get familiar with AutoCAD **commands** and associated sequence of **entries** through **command prompt** (not remotely via menu button). For example, a command to create a line is **Line**, and followed by entries from coordinates of the first point, second and so on and ended by pressing **Enter**.

Example 1

The following is steps sequence in AutoCAD to create a drawing of 3 lines segments using the **Line** command through command prompt:

Command: line

Specify first point: 0,0

Specify next point or [Undo]: 1,1

Specify next point or [Undo]: 2,3

Specify next point or [Close/Undo]: 3,3

[Enter]

From the above steps, it can therefore be made the following text (script) replaces what was done above:

Line

0,0

1,1

2,3

3,3 [enter 2 blank spaces for an **Enter** to end the **Line** command]

Next, open Notepad program, type the script above, and remember to enter 2 blank spaces after the last point to end the **Line** command. Then, name and save it with .scr file extension, for example, **Line.scr**. Now, open your AutoCAD, type "**scr**" at the command prompt to display the **Select Script File** dialog box as below:

Select **Line.scr** file at the location that you have placed before and click **Open** to execute all commands in the script file. The result is shown below:

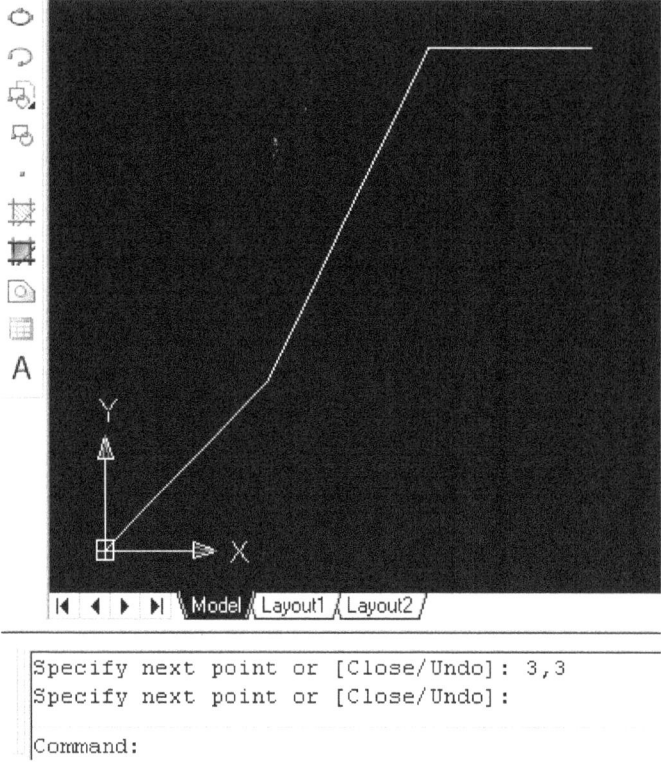

Notes:

- AutoCAD commands consist of prompt entries that include some options that must be entered in by the user. These options can also be 1). A command related to the main command and, 2). Attributes to an object, for example, properties of a line, circle or rectangle.
- The best way to understand a sequence of a command (e.g. **Line**) is by firstly trying out it in AutoCAD, and then note down all entries, including the requested options associated with the main command. This becomes the basis used for writing the script later.

The following is **Line** command and the required prompt entries:

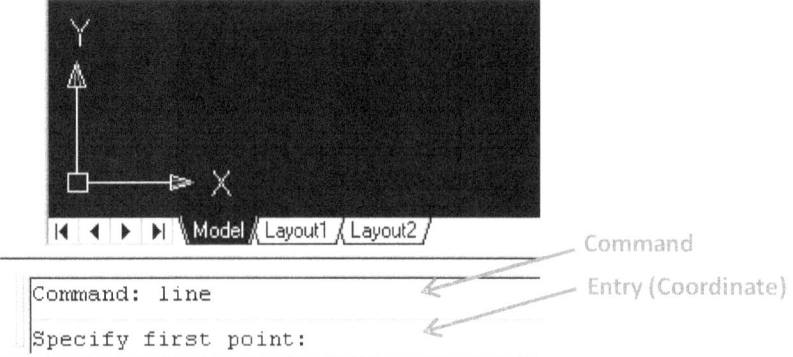

An Introduction to Excel for Civil Engineers   212

Options:

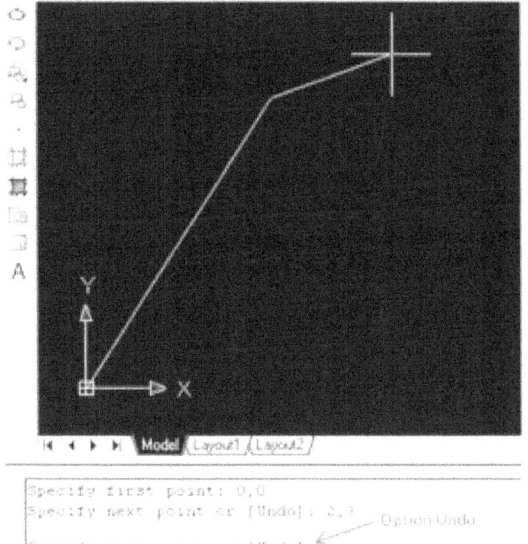

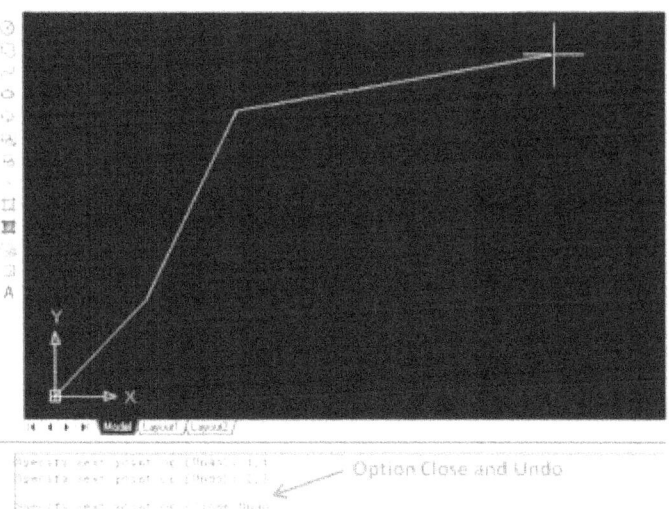

- Pressing **Enter** at the last line is to end the command, so lines are drawn up to the point coordinates of previous line. Pressing u is to do the **Undo** command, that is, undo the previous line segment, while c is to do the **Close** command, that is, close the last segment by connecting it to the first segment.
- Pressing **Enter** on keyboard is to end a command. In the script, it is done by giving a blank space or a blank line.

- Some AutoCAD commands display dialog boxes to enter data. To display prompt entries entered from keyboard (i.e. line by line through the command line), use a prefix "-" before a command, such as: **-Style**, **-Block** and **-Layer**.
- To joint data (either string or numeric) from two or more cells into one cell on a worksheet, you can use hyphen "&" (in quotation marks). This is the same as used in VBA to combine string and numerical data.
- AutoCAD script can be set horizontally or vertically. In the horizontal script writing, any data entered to the next data must be separated by an empty space, including for pressing **Enter**.
- Every time you run a script file, object snap must be inactive or in off mode, so that it gives the actual results. Click the **Osnap** button to make the mode on or off.

The other examples of AutoCAD commands and prompt entries:

- Below are options in **Text** command. The letter "j" stands for **Justify** command, taken from the first letter.

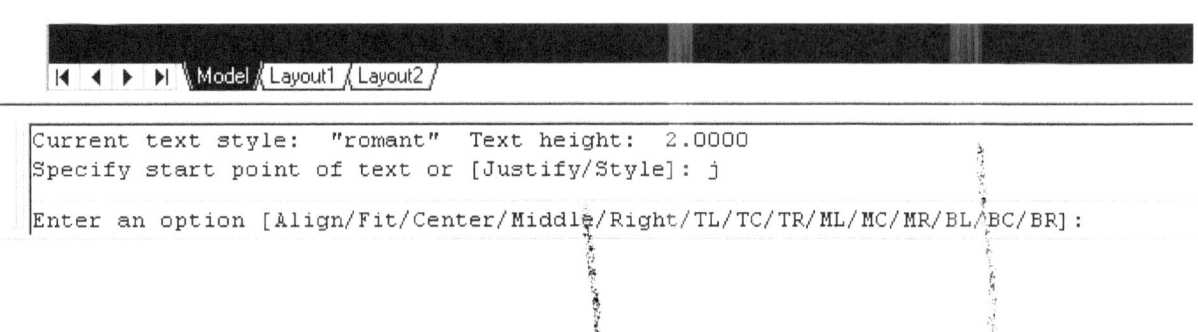

- Options in **Layer** command.

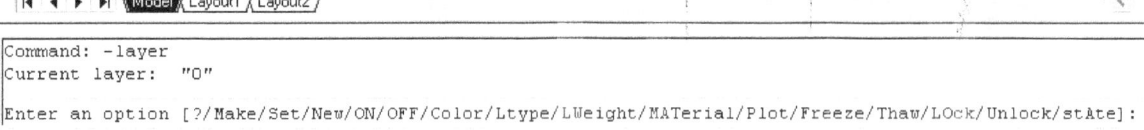

- Prompt entry for **Color** properties (**Layer** > **Color**).

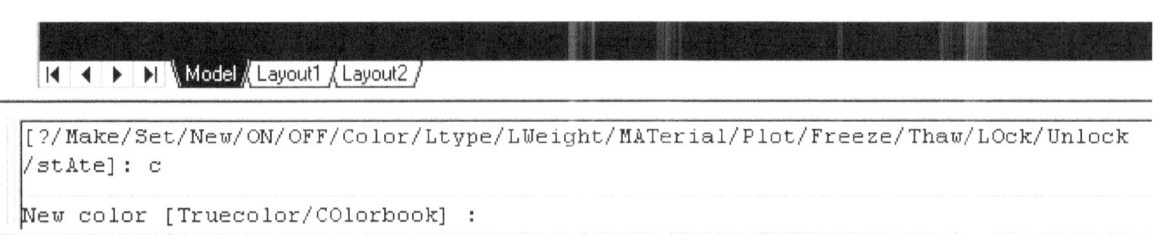

An Introduction to Excel for Civil Engineers

Creating AutoCAD script in a worksheet is a way to simplify and shorten the job of "creating" AutoCAD drawings by relying on Excel commands such as Copy and Paste, and its built-in functions. For line depiction which comprises many segments (tens or more), manual data entry through the command prompt is rarely used. Example 2 shows how to write AutoCAD script to a worksheet.

Example 2

The given example 1 can be made in a worksheet as follows:

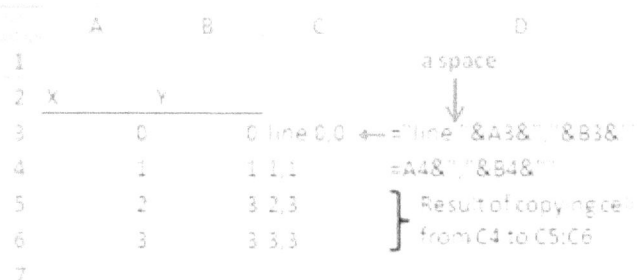

Prior to the first coordinates entry of (0,0) after the **Line** command, it must be given a blank space to execute the command, the same is done by pressing **Enter** in AutoCAD. The second coordinates of (1,1) and so on, should be placed in different line, that is, on cell C4, C5, and so on, so as to be able to write the next script by copying the formula on cell C4. The script for last point coordinates of (3,3) in cell C6 need to be added a blank space after the coordinates, to end the **Line** command:

=A6&","&B6&" "

Next is to create a script file with the following steps:

1. Select a cell range C3 to C6, then **Copy** by clicking the Copy icon on the toolbar or pressing Ctrl+C.

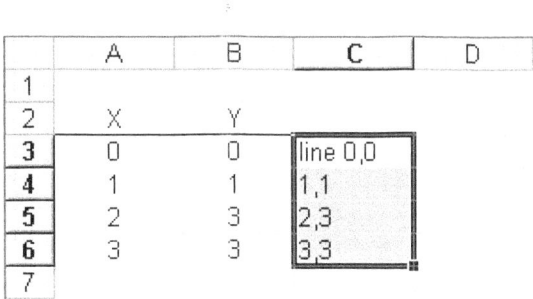

2. Open Notepad program, and then **Paste** (Ctrl + V) the values.

An Introduction to Excel for Civil Engineers

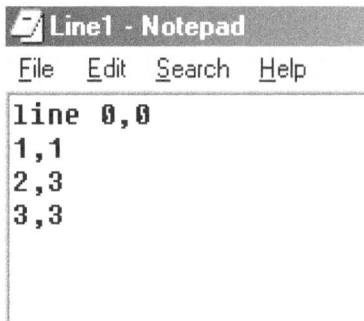

3. Save the file with the .scr file extension, for example, Line1.scr and place it, for example, in the directory C.

4. Open AutoCAD. Type "script" or "scr" at the Command prompt, or via **Tools** > **Run Script**.

5. From Directory C, select Line1.scr file, and click **Open**.

6. To fit the drawing on the screen, type **Zoom** > **Extents**.

The result is shown below:

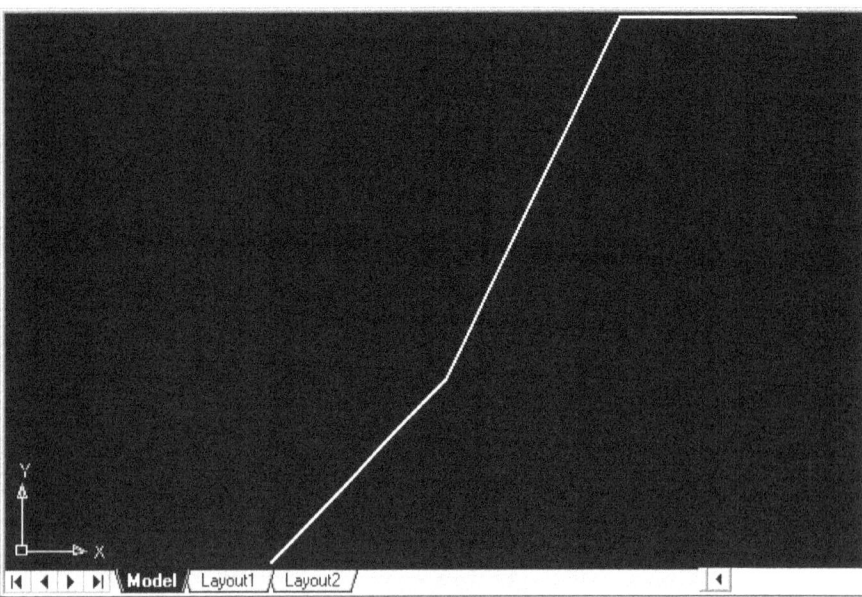

Example 3

In a pile foundation work, the number of blows from driving hammer to penetrate a pile until it reaches a depth of 28 meters is recorded. The data is presented in Table 10.1.

Table 10.1: Number of Blows versus Pile Penetration

Pile Penetration (m)	Number of blows/m'	Cumulative Blows
1	18	18
2	12	30
3	9	39
4	11	50
5	15	65
6	23	88
7	29	117
8	30	147
9	28	175
10	38	213
11	34	247
12	40	287
13	47	334
14	48	382
15	73	455
16	90	545
17	81	626
18	78	704
19	78	782
20	74	856
21	82	938
22	91	1029
23	101	1130
24	108	1238

25	120	1358
26	152	1510
27	163	1673
28	212	1885

Next is to present the data from Table 10.1 in a Cartesian coordinate system, where X-coordinate is the number of blows/meter and the Y-coordinate is the penetration of the pile in meter. Therefore, it requires a graph form, where the data have to fit with the form created. The penetration depth on the Y-axis is increased downward to state the depth below ground level, while the number of blows on the X-axis increases to the right. It is created as shown below.

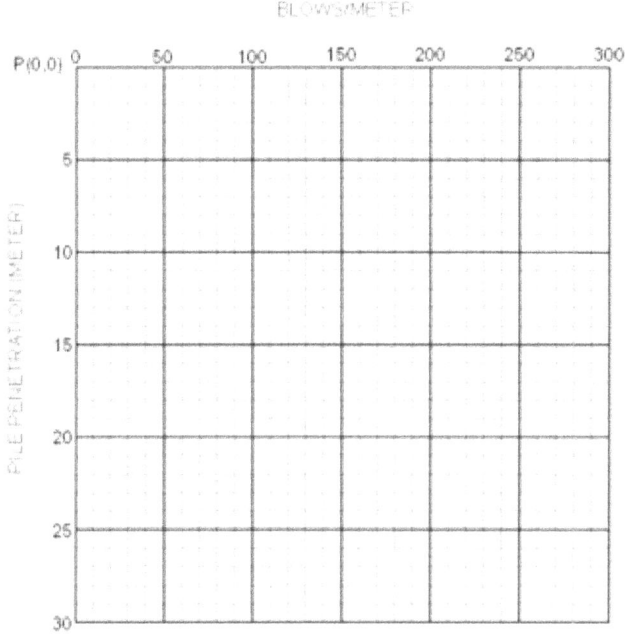

The origin point P(0,0) of the graph is located at point (0,0) in the drawing area, which is also called an insertion base point used as a base for locating any drawing objects on the graph. The scale is made as follows:

- X-coordinate: 1 unit = 10 blows
- Y-coordinate: 1 unit = 1 meter

With such scale, script for the data on the X-axis should be divided by 10, while the data on the Y-axis is divided by -1 for it has a negative direction from the origin P(0,0). Script is created in a worksheet as follows:

Pile No	Penetration (m)	Blow Count Blows/m	Accumulation Blows/m	Script
1	1	18	18	line 1.8,-1 ← = line (C5/10, -B5*-1)
	2	12	30	1.2,-2 ← = (C6/10, -B6*-1)
	3	3	33	0.3,-3
	4	17	50	1.7,-4
	5	15	65	1.5,-5
	6	23	88	2.3,-6
	7	29	117	2.9,-7
	8	30	147	3.0,-8
	9	28	175	2.8,-9
	10	38	213	3.8,-10
	11	34	247	3.4,-11
	12	40	287	4.0,-12
	13	47	334	4.7,-13
	14	48	382	4.8,-14
	15	73	455	7.3,-15
	16	90	545	9.0,-16
	17	81	626	8.1,-17
	18	78	704	7.8,-18
	19	78	782	7.8,-19
	20	74	856	7.4,-20
	21	82	938	8.2,-21
	22	91	1029	9.1,-22
	23	101	1130	10.1,-23
	24	105	1235	10.5,-24
	25	120	1355	12.0,-25
	26	155	1510	15.5,-26
	27	163	1673	16.3,-27
	28	212	1885	21.2,-28 ← = (C32/10, -B32*-1)

Result of copying cell from E6 to E7:E32

Now, save the script into a file with the .scr file extension. When the file runs, the following graph is shown in AutoCAD:

An Introduction to Excel for Civil Engineers   219

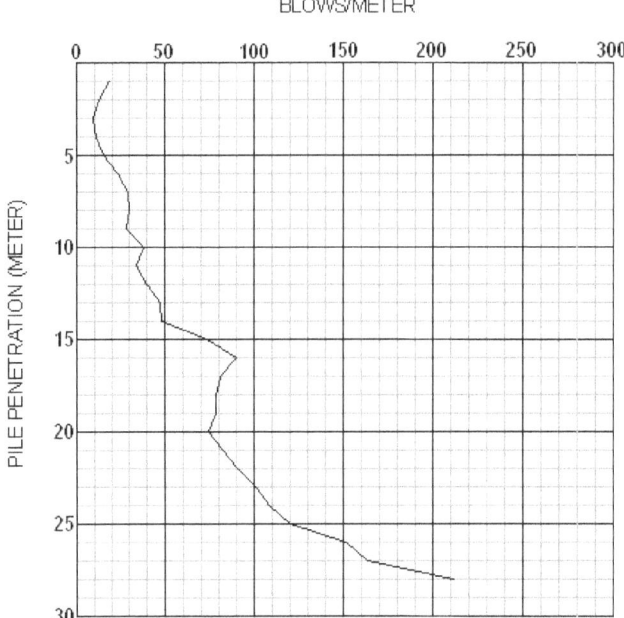

Example 4

In this example, a script will be created where the cumulative blows will also be plotted on the graph. Thus, both of the number of blows and the cumulative values are related to the same Y-axis (against pile penetration). Since the cumulative blows has a range of values up to thousands, a scale of 1 unit = 100 blows is given in order to conveniently fit the values in with the graph form.

The cumulative blows are drawn in chart using **Pline** with line thickness of 0.1 units. To complete of making the script, a new column has to be created (namely Script 2 next to the Script column), contains the formulas as shown below:

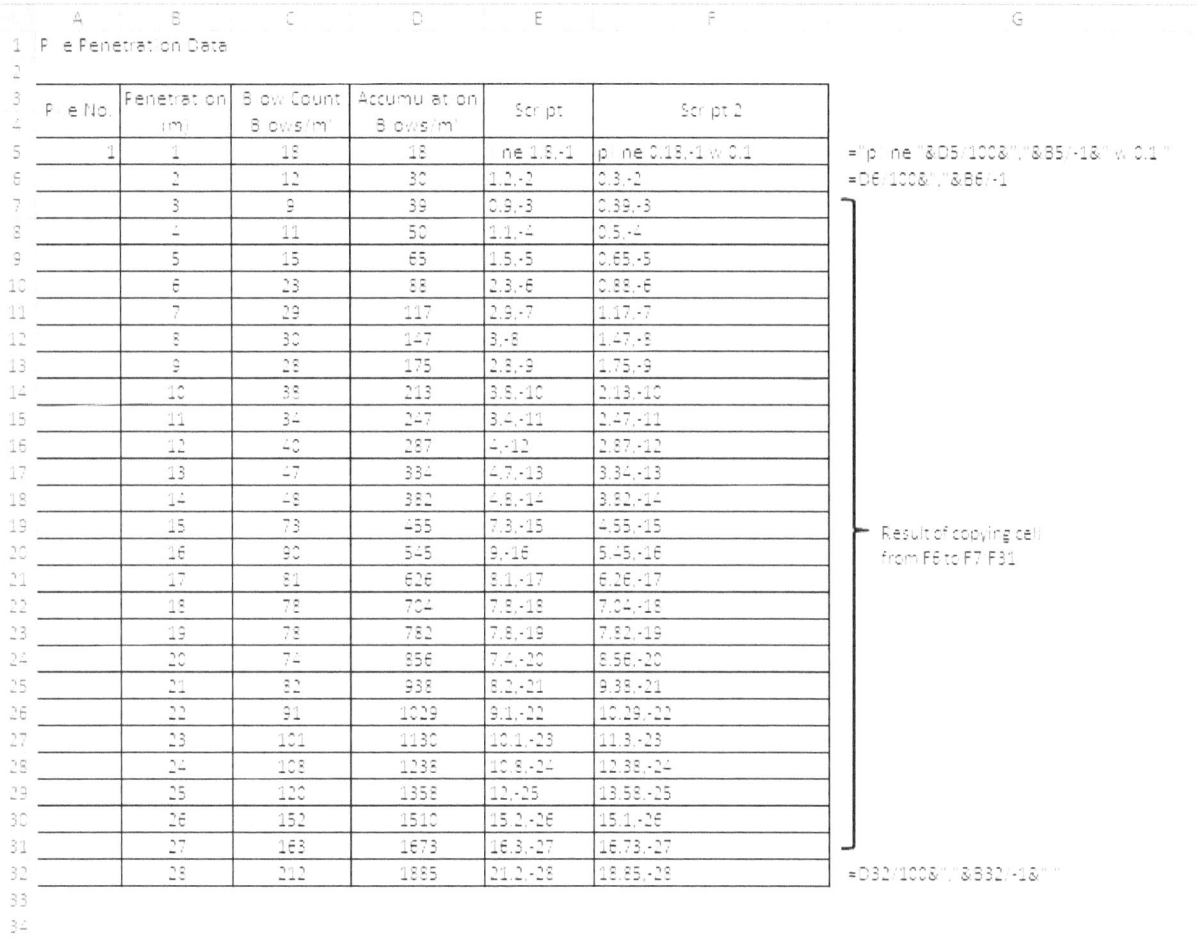

Next step is to combine both two scripts from blows count and its accumulation into a single file. At first, you have to select a cell range E5 to E32, then copy and paste it into Notepad program and then followed by cell range F5 to F32. The content of the script file is shown as below:

line 1.8,-1

1.2,-2

0.9,-3

1.1,-4

1.5,-5

2.3,-6

2.9,-7

3,-8

An Introduction to Excel for Civil Engineers   221

2.8,-9

3.8,-10

3.4,-11

4,-12

4.7,-13

4.8,-14

7.3,-15

9,-16

8.1,-17

7.8,-18

7.8,-19

7.4,-20

8.2,-21

9.1,-22

10.1,-23

10.8,-24

12,-25

15.2,-26

16.3,-27

21.2,-28

pline 0.18,-1 w 0.2

0.3,-2

0.39,-3

0.5,-4

0.65,-5

0.88,-6

1.17,-7

1.47,-8

1.75,-9

2.13,-10

2.47,-11

2.87,-12

3.34,-13

3.82,-14

4.55,-15

5.45,-16

6.26,-17

7.04,-18

7.82,-19

8.56,-20

9.38,-21

10.29,-22

11.3,-23

12.38,-24

13.58,-25

15.1,-26

16.73,-27

18.85,-28

When the file runs, the following graph is shown in AutoCAD:

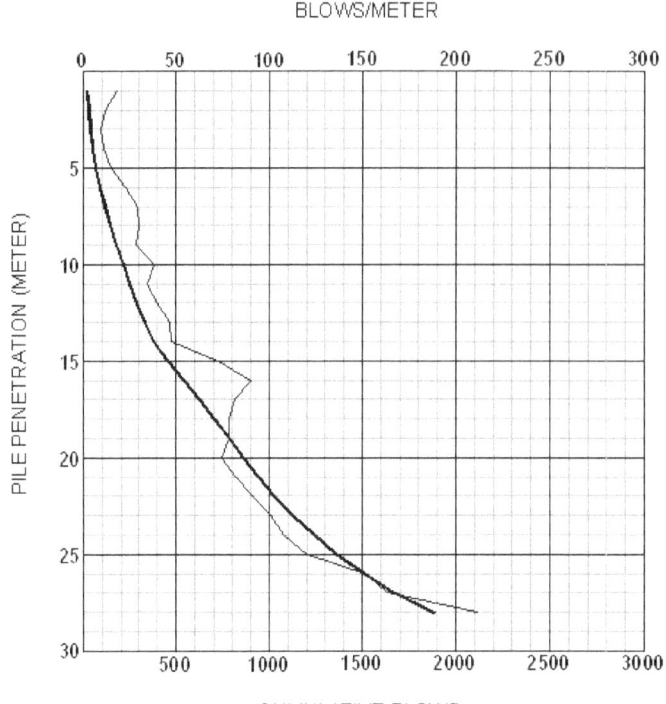

Example 5

In this example, we will be working with layers using the **Layer** command. It is now given 2 piles driving data, with location name PT-1 and PT-2 where a layer is used to group each driving data based on its location. The readers who are accustomed to use AutoCAD certainly understand the importance of working with layers.

To create a layer, click **Layer** > **Make** > enter a layer name. If the layer name is the location name and combined with the driving data, thus the script will be as follows:

"Layer make PT-1 line 1.8,-1"

The letter "m" can stand for **Make**, thus shortened to,

"Layer m PT-1 line 1.8,-1"

Each layer is then customized by giving a unique color. For this example, lines in layer PT-1 are blue, while lines in PT-2 are magenta. The script now becomes:

"layer m PT-1 c blue   line 1.8,-1"

The script created above is only written in the first line (row). The next line will only be the point coordinates entered into the layer. It is shown as below:

An Introduction to Excel for Civil Engineers

	A	B	C	D	E	F	G
1	Pile Penetration Data						
2							
3	Pile No.	Penetration (m)	Blow Count Blows/m'	Accumulation Blows/m'	Script	Script 2	
4							
5	1	1	18	18	layer m PT-1 c blue line 1.8,-1	pline 0.18,-1 w 0.1	Cell E5 ="layer m PT-1 c blue line "&C5/10&","&B5/-1
6		2	12	30	1.2,-2	0.3,-2	
7		3	9	39	0.9,-3	0.39,-3	
8		4	11	50	1.1,-4	0.5,-4	
9		5	15	65	1.5,-5	0.65,-5	
10		6	23	88	2.3,-6	0.88,-6	
11		7	29	117	2.9,-7	1.17,-7	
12		8	30	147	3,-8	1.47,-8	
13		9	28	175	2.8,-9	1.75,-9	
14		10	38	213	3.8,-10	2.13,-10	
15		11	34	247	3.4,-11	2.47,-11	
16		12	40	287	4,-12	2.87,-12	
17		13	47	334	4.7,-13	3.34,-13	
18		14	48	382	4.8,-14	3.82,-14	
19		15	73	455	7.3,-15	4.55,-15	
20		16	90	545	9,-16	5.45,-16	
21		17	81	626	8.1,-17	6.26,-17	
22		18	78	704	7.8,-18	7.04,-18	
23		19	78	782	7.8,-19	7.82,-19	
24		20	74	856	7.4,-20	8.56,-20	
25		21	82	938	8.2,-21	9.38,-21	
26		22	91	1029	9.1,-22	10.29,-22	
27		23	101	1130	10.1,-23	11.3,-23	
28		24	108	1238	10.8,-24	12.38,-24	
29		25	120	1358	12,-25	13.58,-25	
30		26	152	1510	15.2,-26	15.1,-26	
31		27	163	1673	16.3,-27	16.73,-27	
32		28	212	1885	21.2,-28	18.85,-28	
33	2	1	16	16	layer m PT-1 c magenta line 1.6,-1	pline 0.16,-1 w 0.1	Cell E33 ="layer m PT-1 c magenta line "&C33/10&","&B33/-1
34		2	8	24	0.8,-2	0.24,-2	
35		3	6	30	0.6,-3	0.3,-3	

To select script that has been made, take the following steps. At first, you have to copy the value of cell range E5 to E32 and then cell range D5 to D32. Afterward, select cell range E33 to E61 and D33 to D61. By doing these ways, the number of blow and the cumulative blow (that are related to the same Y-axis) are grouped into layers that correspond to their location, PT-1 and PT-2 respectively.

The script in Notepad is shown as below:

layer m PT-1 c blue   line 1.8,-1

1.2,-2

0.9,-3

1.1,-4

1.5,-5

2.3,-6

2.9,-7

3,-8

2.8,-9

3.8,-10

3.4,-11

4,-12

4.7,-13

4.8,-14

7.3,-15

9,-16

8.1,-17

7.8,-18

7.8,-19

7.4,-20

8.2,-21

9.1,-22

10.1,-23

10.8,-24

12,-25

15.2,-26

16.3,-27

21.2,-28

pline 0.18,-1 w 0.1

0.3,-2

0.39,-3

0.5,-4

0.65,-5

0.88,-6

1.17,-7

1.47,-8

1.75,-9

2.13,-10

2.47,-11

2.87,-12

3.34,-13

3.82,-14

4.55,-15

5.45,-16

6.26,-17

7.04,-18

7.82,-19

8.56,-20

9.38,-21

10.29,-22

11.3,-23

12.38,-24

13.58,-25

15.1,-26

16.73,-27

18.85,-28

layer m PT-2 c magenta   line 1.6,-1

0.8,-2

0.6,-3

1.3,-4

1.2,-5

1.6,-6

2.5,-7

2.9,-8

3.2,-9

3.6,-10

3.9,-11

4.1,-12

4.9,-13

4.7,-14

5.7,-15

7.4,-16

5.9,-17

5.6,-18

5.7,-19

5.9,-20

6.4,-21

6.9,-22

7.1,-23

7.7,-24

8.4,-25

9.3,-26

10.3,-27

11.4,-28

12.5,-29

pline 0.16,-1 w 0.1

0.24,-2

0.3,-3

0.43,-4

0.55,-5

0.71,-6

0.96,-7

1.25,-8

1.57,-9

1.93,-10

2.32,-11

2.73,-12

3.22,-13

3.69,-14

4.26,-15

5,-16

5.59,-17

6.15,-18

6.72,-19

7.31,-20

7.95,-21

8.64,-22

9.35,-23

10.12,-24

10.96,-25

11.89,-26

12.92,-27

14.06,-28

15.31,-29

The result is shown in AutoCAD as below:

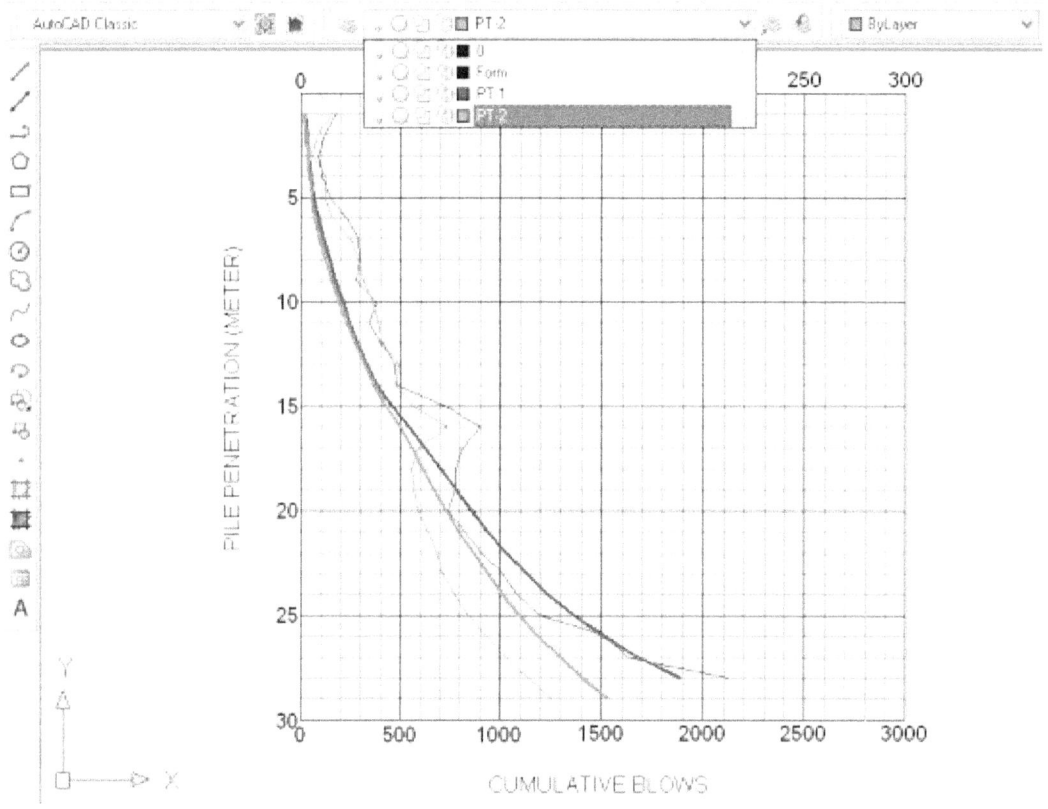

Layers created in AutoCAD can be seen in a combo-box for layers located at the top-middle of the drawing area. Each layer can be displayed individually or together with other layers. To turn layers On or Off, click on the light icon in the combo-box.

Note:

- Discussion about script of AutoCAD will take very long time for there are such many drawing features in AutoCAD. The detail is beyond the scope of this book. It is expected that the readers can get the ideas from the all examples above. The next lesson (recommended) could be started by associating objects with blocks in a drawing using the **Block** command. You can then insert blocks (that is, any objects that you have created) in your drawing as many as required.

11.2 CREATING SCRIPTS IN VBA

The advantage of VBA is its ability to create a file with ASCII format that contains text. The file is created using the CreateTextFile method with the following syntax:

object.**CreateTextFile(***filename*[, *overwrite*[, *unicode*]])

Description:

object	Name of FileSystemObject or Folder object
filename	String, name of a file to create
overwrite	Optional. Boolean value, if TRUE indicates that file can be overwritten, or vice versa. If omitted, the value is FALSE.
unicode	Optional. Boolean value, indicates whether that file is created as Unicode file (TRUE) or ASCII (FALSE). If omitted the value is FALSE.

Example

```
Sub Createfile()
    Set fso = CreateObject("Scripting.FileSystemObject")
    Set myfile = fso.CreateTextFile("c:\testfile.txt", True)
    myfile.WriteLine ("Write this text")
    myfile.Close
End Sub
```

For accessing the file that has been created, use the **Open** command. The **Open** syntax itself consists of several parts with the descriptions that are quite detailed, and it will not be fully covered here. For creating a script file, use the following syntax:

```
Open "c:\testfile.scr" For Output As #1
Print #1, "text"
Write #1, variable
Print #1, numeric & "text " & numeric
Close #1
```

Descriptions:

- **Open** command is used for accessing a file named "testfile" and to write script into the file. At the end of code, there is the **Close** command is to close the open file. If a file does not exist, it will be automatically created and named "testfile" and by the code above will be stored in directory C. File extension .scr is given to make the script file as an AutoCAD file.
- The **Print** and **Write** statements are used to write data into the file. The "&" sign after the Print statement is to merge text and numerical characters. Statement of Write #1, var x, y var, var z is to enter variables separated by commas.
- If a file in the directory does not exist, then a file will be automatically created. By this default, the **Open**...**Close** command is more practical to use than the CreateTextFile method, because it creates and accesses a file as well.
- If the existing file is in a folder, it must be completely written to include a folder and a file name (for example, c:\MyFolder\testfile.scr). If you want to create a new folder, use **MkDir** statement.

Example 1

Creating a file and accessing to write text.

```
Open "c:\testfile" For Output As #1 'open file
Print #1, "write this text" 'write text to file
Close #1
```

With the code above, a text, "write this text" will be written into file named "testfile" in directory C. When opened with Notepad program, the file shows:

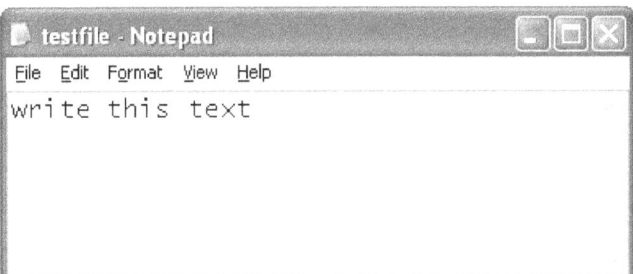

Example 2

Now, we will use VBA to create a script file for Example 2 of Section 11.1. For your convenience, it is re-presented here:

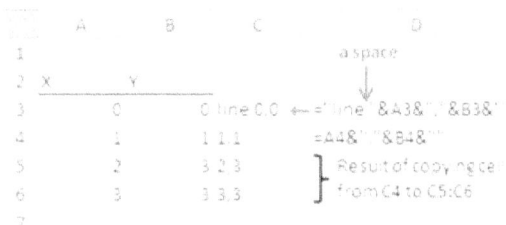

By using VBA, the Excel formulas in column C are no longer required. The worksheet form is now modified by adding a file name and a command button.

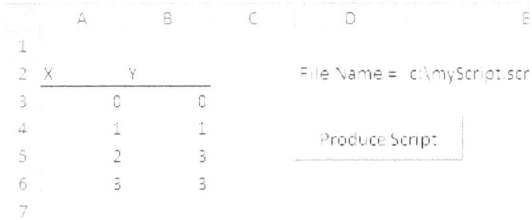

The code can be written as follows:

```
Private Sub CommandButton1_Click()
Dim myFile As String
myFile = Cells(2, 5)
Open myFile For Output As #1
For i = 1 To 3
   Print #1, "line " & Cells(2 + i, 1) & "," & Cells(2 + i, 2) _
   & " " & Cells(3 + i, 1) & "," & Cells(3 + i, 2)
   Write #1, 'an empty line for pressing Enter
Next i
Close #1
End Sub
```

To run the above code, click on the command button named **Produce Script**. The script file will contain the following text,

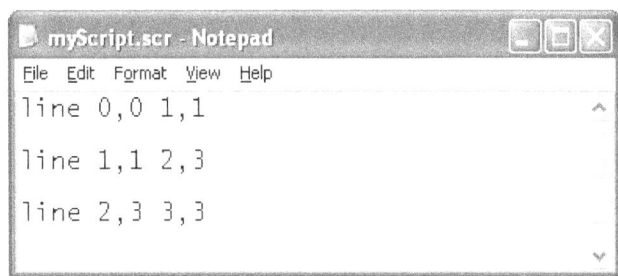

An Introduction to Excel for Civil Engineers

To run the script, at first open your AutoCAD, then type scr in the command prompt or via **Tools > Run Script**. From the **Select Script File** dialog box, select **myScript.scr**, and the line segments with the coordinates as in the script file will then be created in AutoCAD.

Example 3

In creating lines, it is highly recommended to create a table of joints, especially when it comprises many segments and not all of them are continuous. For the references, see the previous examples in Chapter 1. Next is an example of creating a script file to create lines where a new folder will be created for file storage.

	A	B	C	D	E	F	G	H	I	J	K
1	Create Lines								Folder Name =	c:\myScriptFolder	
2					Produce Script				File Name =	myScript.scr	
3	Joint	Coordinate									
4		x	y		Line	Joint					
5	1	1.0	1.0		1	1	2		Joint No. =	4	
6	2	2.0	3.0		2	2	3		Line No. =	3	
7	3	5.0	4.0		3	2	4				
8	4	3.0	1.0								
9											
10											

The code:

```
Dim npt, nln, i
Dim myFolder, myFile
myFolder = Cells(1, 10)
myFile = Cells(2, 10)
npt = Cells(5, 10)
nln = Cells(6, 10)
ReDim x(npt), y(npt)
ReDim x1(nln), y1(nln), x2(nln), y2(nln)

'Read joint coord
For i = 1 To npt
   x(i) = Cells(4 + i, 2)
   y(i) = Cells(4 + i, 3)
Next i

'Read lines data
For i = 1 To nln
```

An Introduction to Excel for Civil Engineers

```
    x1(i) = x(Cells(4 + i, 6))
    y1(i) = y(Cells(4 + i, 6))
    x2(i) = x(Cells(4 + i, 7))
    y2(i) = y(Cells(4 + i, 7))
Next i
Set fso = CreateObject("Scripting.FileSystemObject")
    If fso.FolderExists(myFolder) = True Then
        Filename = myFolder & "\" & myFile 'file with directory and folder
    Else
        MkDir (myFolder)
        Filename = myFolder & "\" & myFile
    End If

Open Filename For Output As #1

For i = 1 To nln
Print #1, "Line"
Write #1, x1(i), y1(i)
Write #1, x2(i), y2(i)
Write #1, 'an empty line for pressing Enter
Next i

Close #1
End Sub
```

The content of the script file is as below:

```
Line
1,1
2,3

Line
2,3
5,4

Line
2,3
3,1
```

When the script has run, the result shows as below:

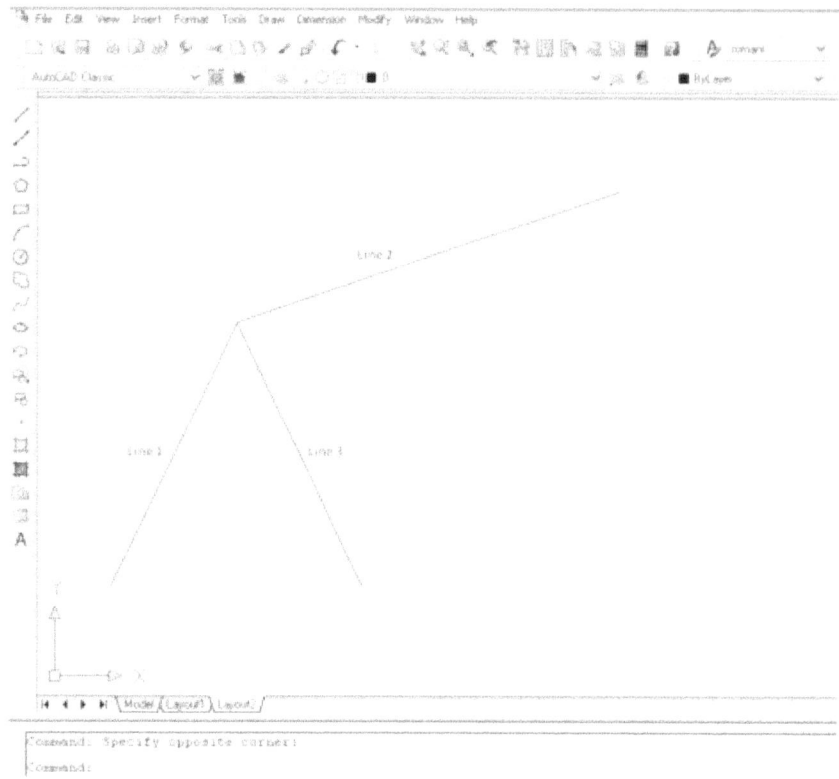

The use of script files for creating AutoCAD drawings in civil engineering field is quite popular because of its simplicity. You do not need to have advanced knowledge and great computer resources to produce any applications. Both Excel and AutoCAD are almost found in any computer owned by a civil engineer (who does not have?) and became must have software for civil engineers worldwide, thus, any applications created by Excel-VBA-AutoCAD are applicable to most computers.

Examples 4 to 7 in the next pages are AutoCAD drawings produced from script files that contain large amount of data. They are created for their respective interest.

Example 4 (next page):

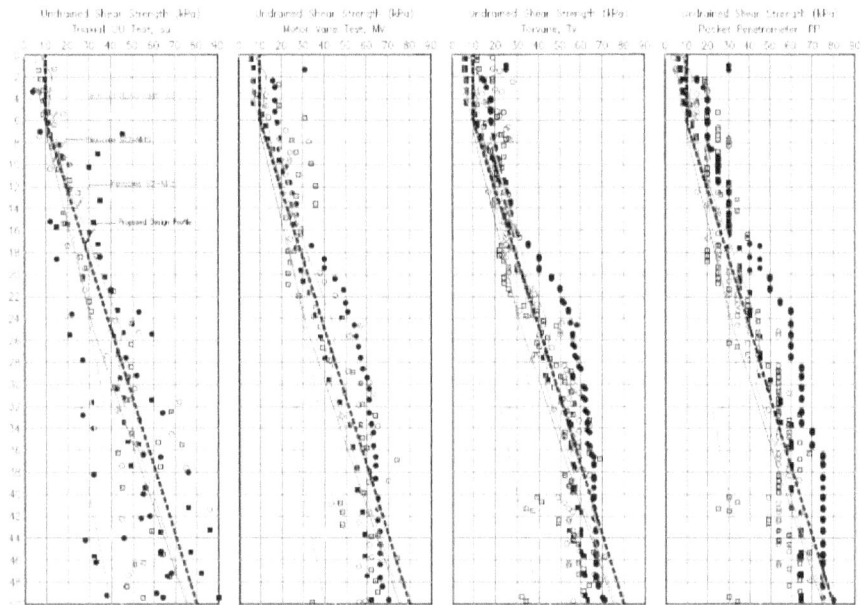

Figure 11.1: Profile of undrained shear strength of the soil versus depth from various test results

Example 5:

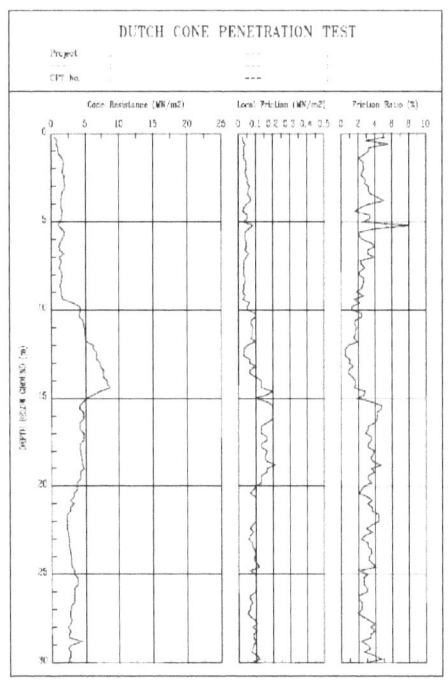

Figure 11.2: Result of Dutch Cone Penetration Test

An Introduction to Excel for Civil Engineers 237

Example 6

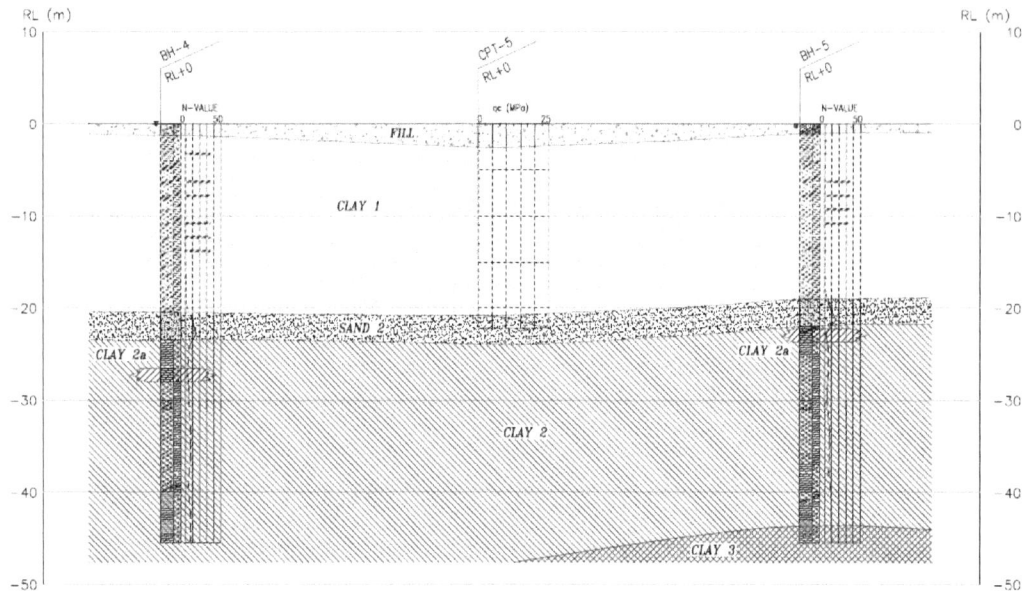

Figure 11.3: Long section of the soil profile

Example 7

Figure 11.4: Bending moment-Z diagram from 3D frame analysis result

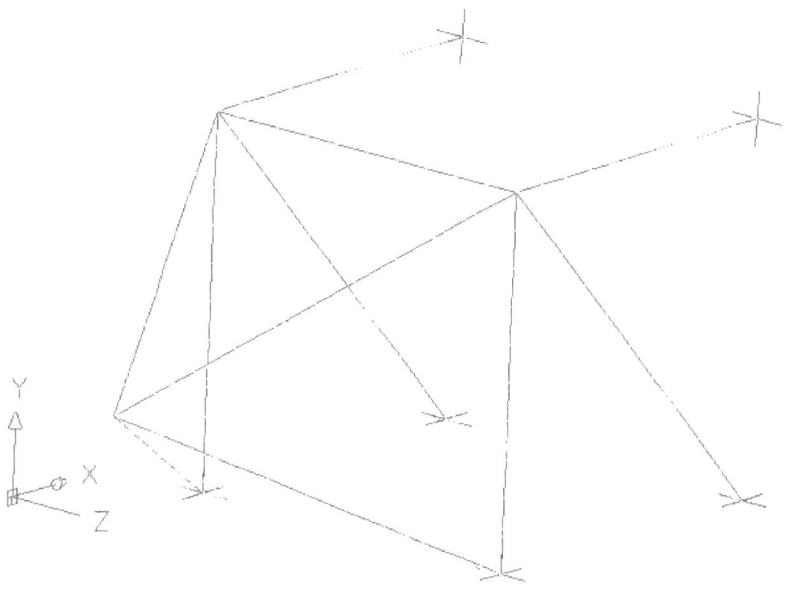

Figure 11.5: Bending moment-Y diagram from 3D frame analysis result

Figure 11.6: Diagram of bending moment-Z and bending moment-Y are displayed together

An Introduction to Excel for Civil Engineers

REFERENCES

Bambang Triatmodjo, *Metode Numerik*, Beta Offset, Yogyakarta, 2002.

Gunthar Pangaribuan, *Aplikasi Excel untuk Rekayasa Teknik Sipil*, Penerbit PT. Elex Media Komputindo, Jakarta, 2004.

Gunthar Pangaribuan, *Penggunaan VBA-Excel untuk Program Perhitungan*, Penerbit PT. Elex Media Komputindo, Jakarta, 2005.

Jean-Pierre Bardet, *Experimental Soil Mechanics*, Prentice-Hall Inc, 1997.

Joseph E. Bowles, *Foundation Analysis and Design*, Third Edition, International Student Edition, 1982.

R.F. Craig, *Soil Mechanics*, Fourth Edition, Spon Press, London, 1987.

Supartono, F.X Ir. dan Ir. Teddy Boen, *Analisa Struktur dengan Metode Matrix*, Penerbit Universitas Indonesia, 1984.

William Weaver, Jr., James M. Gere, *Matrix Analysis of Framed Structures*, Second Edition, Van Nostrand Reinhold Company, New York, 1980.

Wiryanto Dewobroto, *Aplikasi Sain dan Teknik dengan Visual Basic 6.0*, Penerbit PT. Elex Media Komputindo, Jakarta, 2003.

ATTACHMENT: PROGRAM CODE

Module1 (FRAME2D)

```vb
'================================================
'FRAME2D v.1.0 Program for 2D Frame Analysis, 2004
'by: Gunthar Pangaribuan - Refer to the book:
'An Introduction to Excel for Civil Engineers
'================================================
Option Explicit
Option Base 1
Public i As Integer, j As Integer, n As Integer
Type Joint_Data
    x As Double
    y As Double
End Type

Type Member_Data
    J1 As Integer
    J2 As Integer
    Dens As Double
    Ax As Double
    E As Double
    Iz As Double
    EI As Double
    lx As Double
    ly As Double
    Lh As Double
    Cx As Double
    Cy As Double
End Type

Public ChartWindow As Boolean
Public NP As Integer
Public DOF As Integer
Public NR As Integer
Public NJ As Integer
Public NM As Integer
```

```
Public Member() As Member_Data
Public Joint() As Joint_Data
Public NS As Integer 'no. of support
Public NUNI As Integer
Public UNI() As Double
Public GS() As Double 'global stiffness
Public Fm() As Double
Public Rs() As Integer
Public DFR() As Double
Public Idm() As Integer
Public Idj() As Integer
Public Irj() As Integer
Public Psum() As Double
Public Pmm() As Double
Public Pj() As Double
Public Xs() As Double
Public Xm() As Double
Public uscale As Integer
Public XAx_Wd As Double
Public YAx_Wd As Double

Sub FRAME2D()
On Error GoTo ErrMsg
Const NDJ = 3
Dim NLJ As Integer 'no of joint loads
NJ = Cells(4, 2)
NM = Cells(5, 2)
uscale = Cells(4, 5)
'X-range:
XAx_Wd = Application.Max(Rows("10:10")) - Application.Min(Rows("10:10"))
'Y-range:
YAx_Wd = Application.Max(Rows("11:11")) - Application.Min(Rows("11:11"))
NS = Application.Count(Rows("22:22"))
NLJ = Application.Count(Rows("27:27"))
NUNI = Application.Count(Rows("32:32"))
```

```
'Total number of joint displacements, NP:
NP = NDJ * NJ

ReDim Joint(NJ) As Joint_Data
ReDim Member(NM) As Member_Data
ReDim MS(6, 6, NM) As Double 'member stiffness matrix
ReDim spn(NS) As Integer

ReDim UNI(NM)
ReDim GS(NP, NP) 'global stiffness matrix
ReDim Idm(6, NM) 'displacement index
ReDim Pj(NP) 'joint load vector
ReDim Pmm(NP, NM) 'fixed-end forces
ReDim Psum(NP) 'sum load matrix vectors
ReDim Xs(NP) 'joint deformation vectors
ReDim Xm(6, NM) 'member deformations
ReDim Fm(6, NM) 'member forces
ReDim Rs(NP)
'===============
'Read Input Data
'===============
'Read joint coordinates
For i = 1 To NJ
    With Joint(i)
        .x = Cells(10, 1 + i)
        .y = Cells(11, 1 + i)
    End With
Next i

'Read member data
For i = 1 To NM
    With Member(i)
    .J1 = Cells(14, 1 + i)
    .J2 = Cells(15, 1 + i)
    .Dens = Cells(16, 1 + i)
    .Ax = Cells(17, 1 + i)
    .E = Cells(18, 1 + i)
```

```
            .Iz = Cells(19, 1 + i)
            .EI = .E * .Iz
            .lx = Joint(.J2).x - Joint(.J1).x
            .ly = Joint(.J2).y - Joint(.J1).y
            .Lh = Sqr(.lx ^ 2 + .ly ^ 2)
            .Cx = .lx / .Lh
            .Cy = .ly / .Lh
        End With
    Next i

    If ChartWindow = True Then Call PlotGeometry: Exit Sub
    Application.ScreenUpdating = False

    'Read joint loads
    For i = 1 To NLJ
        n = Cells(27, 1 + i)
        Pj(3 * n - 2) = Cells(28, 1 + i)
        Pj(3 * n - 1) = Cells(29, 1 + i)
        Pj(3 * n) = Cells(30, 1 + i)
    Next i

    'Read uniform loads
    For i = 1 To NUNI
        n = Cells(32, 1 + i)
        UNI(n) = Cells(33, 1 + i)
    Next i

    'restraint list and support (Rs) index
    For i = 1 To NS
        spn(i) = Cells(22, 1 + i)
        Rs(3 * spn(i) - 2) = Cells(23, 1 + i)
        Rs(3 * spn(i) - 1) = Cells(24, 1 + i)
        Rs(3 * spn(i)) = Cells(25, 1 + i)
    Next i

    DOF = 0
    For i = 1 To NP
```

```vba
        If Rs(i) = 0 Then DOF = DOF + 1
Next i

'#restrained joints
NR = NP - DOF

ReDim DFX(NDJ * NS, DOF) As Double '[Kbf]according to Eq. 4.12
ReDim DFR(DOF, DOF) As Double '[Kff]^-1 according to Eq. 4.9
ReDim RJ(NDJ * NS) As Double 'support reactions
ReDim Idj(DOF)   'free displacement index
ReDim Irj(NDJ * NS) 'support displacement index

'==================
'Structure Analysis
'==================
Call Mindex(Idm, Idj, Irj)
Call Stiff_Mtx(MS, GS)
Call MInvers(DFX, DFR)

'generate loads
Call Genload(Pmm, Psum)
'determine displacements
Call DISP(Xs, Xm)
'============
'Print Result
'============
'clear previous results
Dim LastRow
LastRow = ActiveSheet.UsedRange.Rows.Count
Range(Cells(39, 1), Cells(LastRow, 18)).ClearContents
'1.Print Loads
For i = 1 To NJ
    Cells(38 + i, 1).NumberFormat = "0"
    Cells(38 + i, 1) = i
    Cells(38 + i, 2).NumberFormat = "0.000"
    Cells(38 + i, 2) = Psum(3 * i - 2)
    Cells(38 + i, 3).NumberFormat = "0.000"
```

```
        Cells(38 + i, 3) = Psum(3 * i - 1)
        Cells(38 + i, 4).NumberFormat = "0.000"
        Cells(38 + i, 4) = Psum(3 * i)
Next i


'2. Print Joint displacements
For i = 1 To NJ
    Cells(38 + i, 5).NumberFormat = "0.00000"
    Cells(38 + i, 5) = Xs(3 * i - 2)
    Cells(38 + i, 6).NumberFormat = "0.00000"
    Cells(38 + i, 6) = Xs(3 * i - 1)
    Cells(38 + i, 7).NumberFormat = "0.00000"
    Cells(38 + i, 7) = Xs(3 * i)
Next i
'-------------
'Member Forces
'-------------
'{F}m=[K]m.{X}m

For i = 1 To NM
    For j = 1 To 6
    Fm(j, i) = 0
        For n = 1 To 6
            Fm(j, i) = Fm(j, i) + MS(j, n, i) * Xm(n, i)
        Next n
    Next j
Next i

'Print member forces
For i = 1 To NM
    With Member(i)
        Cells(38 + i, 8).NumberFormat = "0"
        Cells(38 + i, 8) = i & "./" & Format(.Lh, "0.0")
        Cells(38 + i, 9).NumberFormat = "0.000"
        Cells(38 + i, 9) = Pmm(Idm(1, i), i) + Fm(1, i)
        Cells(38 + i, 10).NumberFormat = "0.000"
        Cells(38 + i, 10) = Pmm(Idm(2, i), i) + Fm(2, i)
```

```vba
            Cells(38 + i, 11).NumberFormat = "0.000"
            Cells(38 + i, 11) = Pmm(Idm(3, i), i) + Fm(3, i)
            Cells(38 + i, 12).NumberFormat = "0.000"
            Cells(38 + i, 12) = Pmm(Idm(4, i), i) + Fm(4, i)
            Cells(38 + i, 13).NumberFormat = "0.000"
            Cells(38 + i, 13) = Pmm(Idm(5, i), i) + Fm(5, i)
            Cells(38 + i, 14).NumberFormat = "0.000"
            Cells(38 + i, 14) = Pmm(Idm(6, i), i) + Fm(6, i)
        End With
 Next i

'-----------------
'Support Reactions
'-----------------
For i = 1 To 3 * NS
    For j = 1 To DOF
        RJ(i) = RJ(i) + DFX(i, j) * Xs(Idj(j))
    Next j
Next i

For i = 1 To NS
    Cells(38 + i, 15).NumberFormat = "0"
    Cells(38 + i, 15) = spn(i)
    Cells(38 + i, 16).NumberFormat = "0.000"
    Cells(38 + i, 16) = RJ(3 * i - 2) - Psum(Irj(3 * i - 2))
    Cells(38 + i, 17).NumberFormat = "0.000"
    Cells(38 + i, 17) = RJ(3 * i - 1) - Psum(Irj(3 * i - 1))
    Cells(38 + i, 18).NumberFormat = "0.000"
    Cells(38 + i, 18) = RJ(3 * i) - Psum(Irj(3 * i))
Next i

'===========
'Draw charts
'===========
Call PlotGeometry
Call PlotDisplacement
Call PlotMoment
```

```
Call PlotShear
Call PlotAxial


Range("A1").Select
Application.ScreenUpdating = True
Exit Sub


ErrMsg: MsgBox "Error, please check input ...", vbOKOnly + vbExclamation, "FRAME2D"

Range("A1").Select
Application.ScreenUpdating = True
End Sub
```

Module2 (FRAME2D)

```
Option Explicit
Option Base 1
Public T() As Double 'transformation matrix,[T]
Public TT() As Double 'transpose [T], used in Module 3
'indexing for matrix subscript
Sub Mindex(dindex() As Integer, IFr() As Integer, IFx() As Integer)


'Member end-displacement indexes:
For i = 1 To NM
    With Member(i)
    dindex(1, i) = 3 * .J1 - 2
    dindex(2, i) = 3 * .J1 - 1
    dindex(3, i) = 3 * .J1
    dindex(4, i) = 3 * .J2 - 2
    dindex(5, i) = 3 * .J2 - 1
    dindex(6, i) = 3 * .J2
    End With
Next i


'Joint free displacement index, IFr and support index, IFx:
```

```
n = 1
j = 1
For i = 1 To NP
    If Rs(i) = 0 Then IFr(n) = i: n = n + 1
Next i

n = 1
For i = 1 To NS
    n = Cells(22, 1 + i)
    IFx(3 * i - 2) = 3 * n - 2
    IFx(3 * i - 1) = 3 * n - 1
    IFx(3 * i) = 3 * n
Next i
End Sub


Sub Stiff_Mtx(MK() As Double, S() As Double)
Dim sm1 As Double, sm2 As Double, sm3 As Double, sm4 As Double, sm5 As Double
ReDim M(6, 6, NM) As Double

'Building stiffness matrix
For i = 1 To NM
    With Member(i)
    sm1 = .Ax * .E / .Lh
    sm2 = 12 * .E * .Iz / (.Lh ^ 3)
    sm3 = 6 * .E * .Iz / (.Lh ^ 2)
    sm4 = 4 * .E * .Iz / .Lh
    sm5 = 2 * .E * .Iz / .Lh
    'Member stiffness
    MK(1, 1, i) = sm1: MK(1, 4, i) = -sm1
    MK(2, 2, i) = sm2: MK(2, 3, i) = sm3: MK(2, 5, i) = -sm2: MK(2, 6, i) = sm3
    MK(3, 2, i) = sm3: MK(3, 3, i) = sm4: MK(3, 5, i) = -sm3: MK(3, 6, i) = sm5
    MK(4, 1, i) = -sm1: MK(4, 4, i) = sm1
    MK(5, 2, i) = -sm2: MK(5, 3, i) = -sm3: MK(5, 5, i) = sm2: MK(5, 6, i) = -sm3
    MK(6, 2, i) = sm3: MK(6, 3, i) = sm5: MK(6, 5, i) = -sm3: MK(6, 6, i) = sm4
    'Member global stiffness
```

```
        M(1, 1, i) = sm1 * .Cx ^ 2 + sm2 * .Cy ^ 2: M(1, 2, i) = (sm1 - sm2) * .Cx * .Cy: M(1, 3, i) = -sm3 * .Cy
        M(1, 4, i) = -M(1, 1, i): M(1, 5, i) = -(sm1 - sm2) * .Cx * .Cy: M(1, 6, i) = M(1, 3, i)
        M(2, 1, i) = M(1, 2, i): M(2, 2, i) = sm1 * .Cy ^ 2 + sm2 * .Cx ^ 2: M(2, 3, i) = sm3 * .Cx
        M(2, 4, i) = M(1, 5, i): M(2, 5, i) = -M(2, 2, i): M(2, 6, i) = M(2, 3, i)
        M(3, 1, i) = M(1, 3, i): M(3, 2, i) = M(2, 3, i): M(3, 3, i) = sm4
        M(3, 4, i) = -M(1, 3, i): M(3, 5, i) = -M(2, 3, i): M(3, 6, i) = sm5
        M(4, 1, i) = M(1, 4, i): M(4, 2, i) = M(1, 5, i): M(4, 3, i) = -M(1, 3, i)
        M(4, 4, i) = M(1, 1, i): M(4, 5, i) = M(1, 2, i): M(4, 6, i) = -M(1, 3, i)
        M(5, 1, i) = M(1, 5, i): M(5, 2, i) = -M(2, 2, i): M(5, 3, i) = -M(2, 3, i)
        M(5, 4, i) = M(1, 2, i): M(5, 5, i) = M(2, 2, i): M(5, 6, i) = -M(2, 3, i)
        M(6, 1, i) = M(1, 3, i): M(6, 2, i) = M(2, 3, i): M(6, 3, i) = M(3, 6, i)
        M(6, 4, i) = -M(1, 3, i): M(6, 5, i) = -M(2, 3, i): M(6, 6, i) = M(3, 3, i)

        '==========================
        'Structure stiffness matrix
        '==========================
        'Storing members and superposition
        For j = 1 To 6
            For n = 1 To 6
                S(Idm(j, i), Idm(n, i)) = S(Idm(j, i), Idm(n, i)) + M(j, n, i)
            Next n
        Next j
        End With
Next i

End Sub
'Global matrix
Sub MInvers(SR() As Double, SD() As Double)
Dim n As Integer
```

```
'submatrix Stiffness, KBF
For i = 1 To DOF
    For j = 1 To 3 * NS
        SR(j, i) = GS(Irj(j), Idj(i))
    Next j
Next i

'submatrix Stiffness, KFF
For i = 1 To DOF
    For j = 1 To DOF
        SD(i, j) = GS(Idj(i), Idj(j))
    Next j
Next i

'Inverse []
   For i = 1 To DOF
    For j = 1 To DOF
        If j <> i Then SD(i, j) = SD(i, j) / SD(i, i)
    Next j
    For n = 1 To DOF
        If n = i Then GoTo 10
    For j = 1 To DOF
        If j <> i Then SD(n, j) = SD(n, j) - SD(i, j) * SD(n, i)
    Next j
10   Next n
    For n = 1 To DOF
        If n <> i Then SD(n, i) = -SD(n, i) / SD(i, i)
    Next n
    SD(i, i) = 1 / SD(i, i)
   Next i

End Sub
Sub Genload(Pa() As Double, Ps() As Double)
ReDim TT(6, 6, NM) As Double
ReDim Peq(NP, NM) As Double 'equivalent loads due to selfweight
Dim w As Double
```

```
'member fixed-end forces due to selfweight + uniform loads
For i = 1 To NM
    With Member(i)
    w = .Dens * .Ax
    Pa(Idm(1, i), i) = .Cy * w * .Lh / 2
    Pa(Idm(2, i), i) = .Cx * w * .Lh / 2 + (UNI(i) * .Lh / 2)
    Pa(Idm(3, i), i) = (.Cx * w * .Lh ^ 2 / 12) + (UNI(i) * .Lh ^ 2 / 12)
    Pa(Idm(4, i), i) = .Cy * w * .Lh / 2
    Pa(Idm(5, i), i) = .Cx * w * .Lh / 2 + (UNI(i) * .Lh / 2)
    Pa(Idm(6, i), i) = -(.Cx * w * .Lh ^ 2 / 12) - (UNI(i) * .Lh ^ 2 / 12)
    End With
Next i


'Transformation matrix (transpose)
For i = 1 To NM
    With Member(i)
    TT(1, 1, i) = .Cx: TT(1, 2, i) = -.Cy
    TT(2, 1, i) = .Cy: TT(2, 2, i) = .Cx
    TT(3, 3, i) = 1
    TT(4, 4, i) = .Cx: TT(4, 5, i) = -.Cy
    TT(5, 4, i) = .Cy: TT(5, 5, i) = .Cx
    TT(6, 6, i) = 1
    End With
Next i


'equivalent joint loads due to selfweight + UNI in global system (superposition)
For i = 1 To NM
    For j = 1 To 6
        For n = 1 To 6
            Peq(Idm(j, i), i) = Peq(Idm(j, i), i) + TT(j, n, i) * -Pa(Idm(n, i), i)
        Next n
     Next j
Next i



'sum loads = joint loads + eq.loads
```

An Introduction to Excel for Civil Engineers

```
For i = 1 To NP
    Ps(i) = Pj(i)
Next i

'load superposition
For i = 1 To NM
    For j = 1 To 6
        Ps(Idm(j, i)) = Ps(Idm(j, i)) + Peq(Idm(j, i), i)
    Next j
Next i

End Sub

Sub DISP(x() As Double, X2() As Double)
ReDim X2(6, NM) As Double
ReDim Xi(6, NM) As Double
ReDim T(6, 6, NM) As Double

'Joint Displacements {X} = [SD]^-1.{P}
For i = 1 To DOF
'x(Idj(i)) = 0
    For j = 1 To DOF
        x(Idj(i)) = x(Idj(i)) + DFR(i, j) * Psum(Idj(j))
    Next j
Next i

'Numbering of global {X}(NP) to global {Xi} element
For i = 1 To NM
    For j = 1 To 6
        Xi(j, i) = x(Idm(j, i))
    Next j
Next i

'Transforming {Xi} to local coordinates
'Transformation matrix:
For i = 1 To NM
    With Member(i)
```

```
        T(1, 1, i) = .Cx: T(1, 2, i) = .Cy
        T(2, 1, i) = -.Cy: T(2, 2, i) = .Cx
        T(3, 3, i) = 1
        T(4, 4, i) = .Cx: T(4, 5, i) = .Cy
        T(5, 4, i) = -.Cy: T(5, 5, i) = .Cx
        T(6, 6, i) = 1
    End With
Next i

'member deformations, transformed{X} = [T].{Xi}
For i = 1 To NM
    For j = 1 To 6
        X2(j, i) = 0
        For n = 1 To 6
            X2(j, i) = X2(j, i) + T(j, n, i) * Xi(n, i)
        Next n
    Next j
Next i

End Sub
```

Module3 (FRAME2D)

```
'This module consist of only code to create charts
Option Explicit
Option Base 1

Sub PlotGeometry()
On Error Resume Next
Dim Cx1, Cx2, Cy1, Cy2
ReDim mxVal(NM) As Variant
ReDim myVal(NM) As Variant
ReDim tagxVal(NM) As Variant
ReDim tagyVal(NM) As Variant
Dim am As Integer
```

```vba
'member coordinates
For i = 1 To NM
    With Member(i)
        Cx1 = Joint(.J1).x
        Cy1 = Joint(.J1).y
        Cx2 = Joint(.J2).x
        Cy2 = Joint(.J2).y
    End With
        mxVal(i) = Array(Cx1, Cx2)
        myVal(i) = Array(Cy1, Cy2)
        tagxVal(i) = Array((Cx1 + Cx2) / 2)
        tagyVal(i) = Array((Cy1 + Cy2) / 2)
Next i

    ActiveSheet.ChartObjects("Chart 1").Activate
    ActiveChart.ChartArea.Select
    Selection.ClearContents

'creating joints
For i = 1 To NJ
    With ActiveChart
        .SeriesCollection.NewSeries
        .SeriesCollection(i).XValues = Joint(i).x
        .SeriesCollection(i).Values = Joint(i).y
        .SeriesCollection(i).Name = "J" & i
    End With
    'node marker
    ActiveChart.PlotArea.Select
    ActiveChart.SeriesCollection(i).Select
    With Selection
        .MarkerBackgroundColorIndex = 3 'red
        .MarkerForegroundColorIndex = 3
        .MarkerStyle = xlCircle
        .MarkerSize = 6
        .Shadow = False
        .ApplyDataLabels AutoText:=True, LegendKey:= _
        False,         ShowSeriesName:=True,         ShowCategoryName:=False, ShowValue:=False, _
```

```
            ShowPercentage:=False, ShowBubbleSize:=False
    End With

    ActiveChart.SeriesCollection(i).DataLabels.Select
    With Selection
        .HorizontalAlignment = xlCenter
        .VerticalAlignment = xlCenter
        .ReadingOrder = xlContext
        .Position = xlLabelPositionRight
        .Orientation = xlHorizontal
    End With
    With Selection.Font
        .Name = "Arial"
        .FontStyle = "Regular"
        .Size = 8
    End With
Next i

    ActiveSheet.ChartObjects("Chart 1").Activate
    ActiveChart.ChartArea.Select

    n = NJ + NM
am = 1
'creating member lines
For i = NJ + 1 To n
    With ActiveChart
        .SeriesCollection.NewSeries
        .SeriesCollection(i).XValues = mxVal(am)
        .SeriesCollection(i).Values = myVal(am)
        .SeriesCollection(i).Name = "="""""
    End With
    ActiveChart.SeriesCollection(i).Select
    With Selection
        .MarkerBackgroundColorIndex = xlNone
        .MarkerForegroundColorIndex = xlNone
        .MarkerStyle = xlNone
        .Smooth = False
```

```
        End With
        With Selection.Border
            .ColorIndex = 5
            .Weight = xlThin
            .LineStyle = xlContinuous
        End With
am = am + 1
Next i


'creating member name tags
am = 1
For i = n + 1 To n + NM
    With ActiveChart
        .SeriesCollection.NewSeries
        .SeriesCollection(i).XValues = tagxVal(am)
        .SeriesCollection(i).Values = tagyVal(am)
        .SeriesCollection(i).Name = "M" & am
    End With
    ActiveChart.PlotArea.Select
    ActiveChart.SeriesCollection(i).Select
    With Selection
        .MarkerBackgroundColorIndex = 5
        .MarkerForegroundColorIndex = 5
        .MarkerStyle = xlSquare
        .Smooth = False
        .MarkerSize = 6
        .Shadow = False
        .ApplyDataLabels AutoText:=True, LegendKey:= _
        False,          ShowSeriesName:=True,          ShowCategoryName:=False,
ShowValue:=False, _
        ShowPercentage:=False, ShowBubbleSize:=False
    End With
    ActiveChart.SeriesCollection(i).DataLabels.Select
    With Selection.Font
        .Name = "Arial"
        .FontStyle = "Regular"
        .Size = 8
    End With
```

```
am = am + 1
Next i

    ActiveChart.ChartArea.Select
    With ActiveChart
        .Axes(xlCategory, xlPrimary).HasTitle = True
        .Axes(xlCategory, xlPrimary).AxisTitle.Characters.Text = _
        "NJ = " & Format(NJ, "0") & ", NM = " & Format(NM, "0")
    End With

ActiveChart.ShowWindow = True

End Sub

Sub PlotDisplacement()
On Error Resume Next

Dim Cx1, Cx2, Cy1, Cy2
ReDim mxValbf(NM) As Variant, myValbf(NM) As Variant
ReDim mxValaf(NM) As Variant, myValaf(NM) As Variant

Dim am As Integer, scale_Y As Single, scale_X As Single, scx As Single
Dim Xmax As Double, at_joint As Integer

    ActiveSheet.ChartObjects("Chart 2").Activate
    ActiveChart.ChartArea.Select
    Selection.ClearContents

'======================
'scale for displacements
'======================
'user scale: displacements are drawn up to max 10% of the axis range
'or X-range or Y-range * 10% = Xmax

'determine max. joint-X and Y displacement
'(user function UXMax written at the end of this module):
Xmax = Application.index(UXMax(Xs, NP), 1)
```

```
at_joint = Application.index(UXMax(Xs, NP), 2)
scx = (Application.Max(XAx_Wd, YAx_Wd) * 10 / 100) / Abs(Xmax)
If uscale = 1 Then
    scale_X = 1
    scale_Y = 1
ElseIf uscale = 0 Then
    scale_X = scx
    scale_Y = scx
Else
    scale_X = 0
    scale_Y = 0
End If


'member coordinates: before & after loading
For i = 1 To NM
    With Member(i)
        Cx1 = Joint(.J1).x
        Cy1 = Joint(.J1).y
        Cx2 = Joint(.J2).x
        Cy2 = Joint(.J2).y
    mxValbf(i) = Array(Cx1, Cx2)
    myValbf(i) = Array(Cy1, Cy2)
        Cx1 = Joint(.J1).x + scale_X * Xs(3 * .J1 - 2)
        Cy1 = Joint(.J1).y + scale_Y * Xs(3 * .J1 - 1)
        Cx2 = Joint(.J2).x + scale_X * Xs(3 * .J2 - 2)
        Cy2 = Joint(.J2).y + scale_Y * Xs(3 * .J2 - 1)
    mxValaf(i) = Array(Cx1, Cx2)
    myValaf(i) = Array(Cy1, Cy2)
    End With
Next i

    am = 1
    'creating member lines: before loading
    For i = 1 To NM
        With ActiveChart
            .SeriesCollection.NewSeries
            .SeriesCollection(i).XValues = mxValbf(am)
```

```
            .SeriesCollection(i).Values = myValbf(am)
            .SeriesCollection(i).Name = "="""""
        End With
        ActiveChart.SeriesCollection(i).Select
        With Selection
            .MarkerStyle = xlNone
            .Smooth = False
        End With
        With Selection.Border
            .ColorIndex = 5
            .Weight = xlThin
            .LineStyle = xlContinuous
        End With
    am = am + 1
    Next i

    n = NM + NM
    am = 1
    'creating member lines: after loading
    For i = NM + 1 To n
        With ActiveChart
            .SeriesCollection.NewSeries
            .SeriesCollection(i).XValues = mxValaf(am)
            .SeriesCollection(i).Values = myValaf(am)
            .SeriesCollection(i).Name = "="""""
        End With
        ActiveChart.SeriesCollection(i).Select
        With Selection
            .MarkerStyle = xlNone
            .Smooth = False
        End With
        With Selection.Border
            .ColorIndex = 7
            .Weight = xlMedium
            .LineStyle = xlContinuous
        End With
    am = am + 1
```

```
    Next i

    ActiveChart.ChartArea.Select
    With ActiveChart
        .Axes(xlCategory, xlPrimary).HasTitle = True
        .Axes(xlCategory, xlPrimary).AxisTitle.Characters.Text = _
        "Max Displacement,  J." & at_joint & " = " & Format(Xmax, "0.00000")
    End With

End Sub

Sub PlotMoment()
On Error Resume Next
Dim Cx1, Cx2, Cy1, Cy2
Dim Cmx1, Cmx2, Cmy1, Cmy2
ReDim mxVal(NM) As Variant
ReDim myVal(NM) As Variant
ReDim moxVal(NM) As Variant
ReDim moyVal(NM) As Variant
ReDim tagxVal(NM) As Variant
ReDim tagyVal(NM) As Variant

ReDim mjxVal(NM + NM) As Variant
ReDim mjyVal(NM + NM) As Variant
ReDim mcolor(NM + NM) As Variant
ReDim Pm_LM(3, NM) As Double
ReDim Pm_RM(3, NM) As Double
ReDim Pm_LT(3, NM) As Double
ReDim Pm_RT(3, NM) As Double

Dim am As Integer, scm As Single, scale_Y As Single, scale_X As Single
Dim Mmax As Double, at_joint As Integer, L_I As Integer, L_II As Integer

    ActiveSheet.ChartObjects("Chart 3").Activate
    ActiveChart.ChartArea.Select
    Selection.ClearContents
```

```vb
'analogous to plot displacement for scaling
Mmax = Application.index(UMMax(Pmm, Fm, NM), 1)
at_joint = Application.index(UMMax(Pmm, Fm, NM), 2)
scm = (Application.Max(XAx_Wd, YAx_Wd) * 15 / 100) / Abs(Mmax)

If uscale = 1 Then
    scale_X = 1
    scale_Y = 1
ElseIf uscale = 0 Then
    scale_X = scm
    scale_Y = scm
Else
    scale_X = 0
    scale_Y = 0
End If

'member moment, consider only 3rd and 6th vectors
For i = 1 To NM
    Pm_LM(2, i) = Pmm(Idm(3, i), i) + Fm(3, i)
    Pm_RM(2, i) = -(Pmm(Idm(6, i), i) + Fm(6, i))
Next i

'transform member moment to global axis by using [TT]
'the drawing should be in global coordinates
For i = 1 To NM
    For j = 1 To 3
        For n = 1 To 3
            Pm_LT(j, i) = Pm_LT(j, i) + TT(j, n, i) * Pm_LM(n, i)
            Pm_RT(j, i) = Pm_RT(j, i) + TT(j, n, i) * Pm_RM(n, i)
        Next n
    Next j
Next i

For i = 1 To NM
    With Member(i)
        Cx1 = Joint(.J1).x
        Cy1 = Joint(.J1).y
```

```
            Cx2 = Joint(.J2).x
            Cy2 = Joint(.J2).y
            'assign force coordinates
            Cmx1 = Cx1 + scale_X * Pm_LT(1, i) 'x direction
            Cmy1 = Cy1 + scale_Y * Pm_LT(2, i) 'y direction
            Cmx2 = Cx2 + scale_X * Pm_RT(1, i)
            Cmy2 = Cy2 + scale_Y * Pm_RT(2, i)
        End With
'member coordinates
        mxVal(i) = Array(Cx1, Cx2)
        myVal(i) = Array(Cy1, Cy2)
'moment coordinates
        moxVal(i) = Array(Cmx1, Cmx2)
        moyVal(i) = Array(Cmy1, Cmy2)
'member-joint coordinates
        mjxVal(2 * i - 1) = Array(Cx1, Cmx1)
        mjyVal(2 * i - 1) = Array(Cy1, Cmy1)
        'mcolor: define color for positive/negative value
        mcolor(2 * i - 1) = -(Pmm(Idm(3, i), i) + Fm(3, i))
        mjxVal(2 * i) = Array(Cx2, Cmx2)
        mjyVal(2 * i) = Array(Cy2, Cmy2)
        mcolor(2 * i) = (Pmm(Idm(6, i), i) + Fm(6, i))
Next i

'creating member lines
For i = 1 To NM
    With ActiveChart
        .SeriesCollection.NewSeries
        .SeriesCollection(i).XValues = mxVal(i)
        .SeriesCollection(i).Values = myVal(i)
        .SeriesCollection(i).Name = "="""""
    End With
    ActiveChart.SeriesCollection(i).Select
    With Selection
        .MarkerBackgroundColorIndex = xlNone
        .MarkerForegroundColorIndex = xlNone
        .MarkerStyle = xlNone
```

An Introduction to Excel for Civil Engineers

```
            .Smooth = False
        End With
        With Selection.Border
            .ColorIndex = 5
            .Weight = xlThin
            .LineStyle = xlContinuous
        End With
Next i

L_I = NM + NM
am = 1
'creating moment lines
For i = NM + 1 To L_I
    With ActiveChart
        .SeriesCollection.NewSeries
        .SeriesCollection(i).XValues = moxVal(am)
        .SeriesCollection(i).Values = moyVal(am)
        .SeriesCollection(i).Name = "="""""
    End With
    ActiveChart.SeriesCollection(i).Select
    With Selection
        .MarkerBackgroundColorIndex = xlNone
        .MarkerForegroundColorIndex = xlNone
        .MarkerStyle = xlNone
        .Smooth = False
    End With
    With Selection.Border
        .ColorIndex = 7
        .Weight = xlThin
        .LineStyle = xlContinuous
    End With
am = am + 1
Next i

L_II = NM + NM + NM + NM
am = 1
'creating joint lines to axis
```

```
For i = L_I + 1 To L_II
    With ActiveChart
        .SeriesCollection.NewSeries
        .SeriesCollection(i).XValues = mjxVal(am)
        .SeriesCollection(i).Values = mjyVal(am)
        .SeriesCollection(i).Name = "="""""
    End With
    ActiveChart.SeriesCollection(i).Select
    With Selection
        .MarkerBackgroundColorIndex = xlNone
        .MarkerForegroundColorIndex = xlNone
        .MarkerStyle = xlNone
        .Smooth = False
    End With
    With Selection.Border
        If mcolor(am) < 0 Then
        .ColorIndex = 3
        Else
        .ColorIndex = 5
        End If
        .Weight = xlMedium
        .LineStyle = xlContinuous
    End With
am = am + 1

Next i

    ActiveChart.ChartArea.Select
    With ActiveChart
        .Axes(xlCategory, xlPrimary).HasTitle = True
        .Axes(xlCategory, xlPrimary).AxisTitle.Characters.Text = _
        "Max Moment, J." & at_joint & " = " & Format(Mmax, "0.000")
    End With

End Sub
```

```vba
Sub PlotShear()

On Error Resume Next
Dim Cx1, Cx2, Cy1, Cy2
Dim Cmx1, Cmx2, Cmy1, Cmy2
ReDim mxVal(NM) As Variant
ReDim myVal(NM) As Variant
ReDim shxVal(NM) As Variant
ReDim shyVal(NM) As Variant
ReDim tagxVal(NM) As Variant
ReDim tagyVal(NM) As Variant

ReDim mjxVal(NM + NM) As Variant
ReDim mjyVal(NM + NM) As Variant
ReDim scolor(NM + NM) As Variant
ReDim Ps_LM(3, NM) As Double
ReDim Ps_RM(3, NM) As Double
ReDim Ps_LT(3, NM) As Double
ReDim Ps_RT(3, NM) As Double

Dim am As Integer, scs As Single, scale_Y As Single, scale_X As Single
Dim Smax As Double, at_joint As Integer, L_I As Integer, L_II As Integer

    ActiveSheet.ChartObjects("Chart 4").Activate
    ActiveChart.ChartArea.Select
    Selection.ClearContents

'analogous to with plot displacement for scaling
Smax = Application.index(USMax(Pmm, Fm, NM), 1)
at_joint = Application.index(USMax(Pmm, Fm, NM), 2)
scs = (Application.Max(XAx_Wd, YAx_Wd) * 15 / 100) / Abs(Smax)

If uscale = 1 Then
    scale_X = 1
    scale_Y = 1
ElseIf uscale = 0 Then
    scale_X = scs
```

```
        scale_Y = scs
Else
        scale_X = 0
        scale_Y = 0
End If


'member moment, consider only 2nd and 5th vectors
For i = 1 To NM
        Ps_LM(2, i) = (Pmm(Idm(2, i), i) + Fm(2, i))
        Ps_RM(2, i) = -(Pmm(Idm(5, i), i) + Fm(5, i))
Next i


'transform member shear to global axis by using [TT]
'the drawing should be in global coordinates
For i = 1 To NM
    For j = 1 To 3
        For n = 1 To 3
            Ps_LT(j, i) = Ps_LT(j, i) + TT(j, n, i) * Ps_LM(n, i)
            Ps_RT(j, i) = Ps_RT(j, i) + TT(j, n, i) * Ps_RM(n, i)
        Next n
    Next j
Next i


For i = 1 To NM
    With Member(i)
        Cx1 = Joint(.J1).x
        Cy1 = Joint(.J1).y
        Cx2 = Joint(.J2).x
        Cy2 = Joint(.J2).y
        'assign force coordinates
        Cmx1 = Cx1 + scale_X * Ps_LT(1, i) 'x direction
        Cmy1 = Cy1 + scale_Y * Ps_LT(2, i) 'y direction
        Cmx2 = Cx2 + scale_X * Ps_RT(1, i)
        Cmy2 = Cy2 + scale_Y * Ps_RT(2, i)
    End With
'member coordinates
        mxVal(i) = Array(Cx1, Cx2)
```

```
            myVal(i) = Array(Cy1, Cy2)
'shear coordinates
            shxVal(i) = Array(Cmx1, Cmx2)
            shyVal(i) = Array(Cmy1, Cmy2)
'member-joint coordinates
            mjxVal(2 * i - 1) = Array(Cx1, Cmx1)
            mjyVal(2 * i - 1) = Array(Cy1, Cmy1)
            scolor(2 * i - 1) = (Pmm(Idm(2, i), i) + Fm(2, i))
            mjxVal(2 * i) = Array(Cx2, Cmx2)
            mjyVal(2 * i) = Array(Cy2, Cmy2)
            scolor(2 * i) = -(Pmm(Idm(5, i), i) + Fm(5, i))
Next i


'creating member lines
For i = 1 To NM
    With ActiveChart
        .SeriesCollection.NewSeries
        .SeriesCollection(i).XValues = mxVal(i)
        .SeriesCollection(i).Values = myVal(i)
        .SeriesCollection(i).Name = "="""""
    End With
    ActiveChart.SeriesCollection(i).Select
    With Selection
        .MarkerBackgroundColorIndex = xlNone
        .MarkerForegroundColorIndex = xlNone
        .MarkerStyle = xlNone
        .Smooth = False
    End With
    With Selection.Border
        .ColorIndex = 5
        .Weight = xlThin
        .LineStyle = xlContinuous
    End With
Next i

L_I = NM + NM
am = 1
```

```
'creating shear lines
For i = NM + 1 To L_I
    With ActiveChart
        .SeriesCollection.NewSeries
        .SeriesCollection(i).XValues = shxVal(am)
        .SeriesCollection(i).Values = shyVal(am)
        .SeriesCollection(i).Name = "="""""
    End With
    ActiveChart.SeriesCollection(i).Select
    With Selection
        .MarkerBackgroundColorIndex = xlNone
        .MarkerForegroundColorIndex = xlNone
        .MarkerStyle = xlNone
        .Smooth = False
    End With
    With Selection.Border
        .ColorIndex = 7
        .Weight = xlThin
        .LineStyle = xlContinuous
    End With
am = am + 1
Next i

L_II = NM + NM + NM + NM
am = 1
'creating joint lines to axis
For i = L_I + 1 To L_II
    With ActiveChart
        .SeriesCollection.NewSeries
        .SeriesCollection(i).XValues = mjxVal(am)
        .SeriesCollection(i).Values = mjyVal(am)
        .SeriesCollection(i).Name = "="""""
    End With
    ActiveChart.SeriesCollection(i).Select
    With Selection
        .MarkerBackgroundColorIndex = xlNone
        .MarkerForegroundColorIndex = xlNone
```

```
            .MarkerStyle = xlNone
            .Smooth = False
        End With
        With Selection.Border
            If scolor(am) < 0 Then
            .ColorIndex = 3
            Else
            .ColorIndex = 5
            End If
            .Weight = xlMedium
            .LineStyle = xlContinuous
        End With
am = am + 1

Next i

    ActiveChart.ChartArea.Select
    With ActiveChart
        .Axes(xlCategory, xlPrimary).HasTitle = True
        .Axes(xlCategory, xlPrimary).AxisTitle.Characters.Text = _
        "Max Shear, J." & at_joint & " = " & Format(Smax, "0.000")
    End With

End Sub

Sub PlotAxial()

On Error Resume Next

Dim Cx1, Cx2, Cy1, Cy2
Dim Cmx1, Cmx2, Cmy1, Cmy2
ReDim mxVal(NM) As Variant
ReDim myVal(NM) As Variant
ReDim saxVal(NM) As Variant
ReDim sayVal(NM) As Variant
ReDim tagxVal(NM) As Variant
ReDim tagyVal(NM) As Variant
```

```
ReDim mjxVal(NM + NM) As Variant
ReDim mjyVal(NM + NM) As Variant
ReDim acolor(NM + NM) As Variant
ReDim Pa_LM(3, NM) As Double
ReDim Pa_RM(3, NM) As Double
ReDim Pa_LT(3, NM) As Double
ReDim Pa_RT(3, NM) As Double

Dim am As Integer, sca As Single, scale_Y As Single, scale_X As Single
Dim Amax As Double, at_joint As Integer, L_I As Integer, L_II As Integer

    ActiveSheet.ChartObjects("Chart 5").Activate
    ActiveChart.ChartArea.Select
    Selection.ClearContents

'analogous to plot displacement for scaling
Amax = Application.index(UAMax(Pmm, Fm, NM), 1)
at_joint = Application.index(UAMax(Pmm, Fm, NM), 2)
sca = (Application.Max(XAx_Wd, YAx_Wd) * 15 / 100) / Abs(Amax)

If uscale = 1 Then
    scale_X = 1
    scale_Y = 1
ElseIf uscale = 0 Then
    scale_X = sca
    scale_Y = sca
Else
    scale_X = 0
    scale_Y = 0
End If

'member axial, consider only 1st and 4th vectors
For i = 1 To NM
    Pa_LM(2, i) = -(Pmm(Idm(1, i), i) + Fm(1, i))
    Pa_RM(2, i) = (Pmm(Idm(4, i), i) + Fm(4, i))
Next i
```

```
'transform member axial to global axis by using [TT]
'the drawing should be in global coordinates
For i = 1 To NM
    For j = 1 To 3
        For n = 1 To 3
            Pa_LT(j, i) = Pa_LT(j, i) + TT(j, n, i) * Pa_LM(n, i)
            Pa_RT(j, i) = Pa_RT(j, i) + TT(j, n, i) * Pa_RM(n, i)
        Next n
    Next j
Next i

For i = 1 To NM
    With Member(i)
        Cx1 = Joint(.J1).x
        Cy1 = Joint(.J1).y
        Cx2 = Joint(.J2).x
        Cy2 = Joint(.J2).y
        'assign force coordinates
        Cmx1 = Cx1 + scale_X * Pa_LT(1, i)
        Cmy1 = Cy1 + scale_Y * Pa_LT(2, i)
        Cmx2 = Cx2 + scale_X * Pa_RT(1, i)
        Cmy2 = Cy2 + scale_Y * Pa_RT(2, i)
    End With
'member coordinates
        mxVal(i) = Array(Cx1, Cx2)
        myVal(i) = Array(Cy1, Cy2)
'axial coordinates
        saxVal(i) = Array(Cmx1, Cmx2)
        sayVal(i) = Array(Cmy1, Cmy2)
'member-joint coordinates
        mjxVal(2 * i - 1) = Array(Cx1, Cmx1)
        mjyVal(2 * i - 1) = Array(Cy1, Cmy1)
        acolor(2 * i - 1) = -(Pmm(Idm(1, i), i) + Fm(1, i))
        mjxVal(2 * i) = Array(Cx2, Cmx2)
        mjyVal(2 * i) = Array(Cy2, Cmy2)
        acolor(2 * i) = Pmm(Idm(4, i), i) + Fm(4, i)
Next i
```

```
'creating member lines
For i = 1 To NM
    With ActiveChart
        .SeriesCollection.NewSeries
        .SeriesCollection(i).XValues = mxVal(i)
        .SeriesCollection(i).Values = myVal(i)
        .SeriesCollection(i).Name = "="""""
    End With
    ActiveChart.SeriesCollection(i).Select
    With Selection
        .MarkerBackgroundColorIndex = xlNone
        .MarkerForegroundColorIndex = xlNone
        .MarkerStyle = xlNone
        .Smooth = False
    End With
    With Selection.Border
        .ColorIndex = 5
        .Weight = xlThin
        .LineStyle = xlContinuous
    End With
Next i

L_I = NM + NM
am = 1
'creating axial lines
For i = NM + 1 To L_I
    With ActiveChart
        .SeriesCollection.NewSeries
        .SeriesCollection(i).XValues = saxVal(am)
        .SeriesCollection(i).Values = sayVal(am)
        .SeriesCollection(i).Name = "="""""
    End With
    ActiveChart.SeriesCollection(i).Select
    With Selection
        .MarkerBackgroundColorIndex = xlNone
        .MarkerForegroundColorIndex = xlNone
```

```
            .MarkerStyle = xlNone
            .Smooth = False
        End With
        With Selection.Border
            .ColorIndex = 7
            .Weight = xlThin
            .LineStyle = xlContinuous
        End With
am = am + 1
Next i
L_II = NM + NM + NM + NM
am = 1
'creating joint lines to axis
For i = L_I + 1 To L_II
    With ActiveChart
        .SeriesCollection.NewSeries
        .SeriesCollection(i).XValues = mjxVal(am)
        .SeriesCollection(i).Values = mjyVal(am)
        .SeriesCollection(i).Name = "="""""
    End With
    ActiveChart.SeriesCollection(i).Select
    With Selection
        .MarkerBackgroundColorIndex = xlNone
        .MarkerForegroundColorIndex = xlNone
        .MarkerStyle = xlNone
        .Smooth = False
    End With
    With Selection.Border
        If acolor(am) < 0 Then
        .ColorIndex = 3
        Else
        .ColorIndex = 5
        End If
        .Weight = xlMedium
        .LineStyle = xlContinuous
    End With
am = am + 1
```

```
Next i
        ActiveChart.ChartArea.Select
    With ActiveChart
        .Axes(xlCategory, xlPrimary).HasTitle = True
        .Axes(xlCategory, xlPrimary).AxisTitle.Characters.Text = _
        "Max Axial, J." & at_joint & " = " & Format(Amax, "0.000")
    End With

End Sub


'user function to determine maximum value of
'X1 and X2 (rotation X3 is not included)


Function UXMax(Xs, NP) As Variant

Dim Abs_FXMax As Double
Dim FXMax As Double

Abs_FXMax = Abs(Xs(1))
FXMax = 0
n = 1
j = 3
For i = 2 To NP
    Select Case i
    Case j
        j = j + 3
        n = n + 1
    Case Else
        If Abs(Xs(i)) > Abs_FXMax Then
            Abs_FXMax = Abs(Xs(i))
            FXMax = Xs(i)
            UXMax = Array(FXMax, n)
            'UXMax keeps origin value(+ or - value)
        End If
    End Select
Next i
End Function
```

```
'user function to determine maximum value of
'moment, F3 (F1 and F2 are not included)

Function UMMax(Pmm, Fm, NM) As Variant
Dim Abs_FMMax As Double
Dim FMMax As Double

Abs_FMMax = 0
n = 0
For i = 1 To NM
    If Abs(Pmm(Idm(3, i), i) + Fm(3, i)) > Abs_FMMax Then
        Abs_FMMax = Abs(Pmm(Idm(3, i), i) + Fm(3, i))
        FMMax = -(Pmm(Idm(3, i), i) + Fm(3, i))
        n = Member(i).J1
        UMMax = Array(FMMax, n)
    End If
    If Abs(Pmm(Idm(6, i), i) + Fm(6, i)) > Abs_FMMax Then
        Abs_FMMax = Abs(Pmm(Idm(6, i), i) + Fm(6, i))
        FMMax = Pmm(Idm(6, i), i) + Fm(6, i)
        n = Member(i).J2
        UMMax = Array(FMMax, n)
    End If
Next i
End Function

'user function to determine maximum value of
'shear force, F2 (F1 and F3 are not included)
Function USMax(Pmm, Fm, NM) As Variant

Dim Abs_FSMax As Double
Dim FSMax As Double

Abs_FSMax = 0
n = 0
For i = 1 To NM
    If Abs(Pmm(Idm(2, i), i) + Fm(2, i)) > Abs_FSMax Then
        Abs_FSMax = Abs(Pmm(Idm(2, i), i) + Fm(2, i))
```

```
            FSMax = (Pmm(Idm(2, i), i) + Fm(2, i))
            n = Member(i).J1
            USMax = Array(FSMax, n)
        End If
        If Abs(Pmm(Idm(5, i), i) + Fm(5, i)) > Abs_FSMax Then
            Abs_FSMax = Abs(Pmm(Idm(5, i), i) + Fm(5, i))
            FSMax = -(Pmm(Idm(5, i), i) + Fm(5, i))
            n = Member(i).J2
            USMax = Array(FSMax, n)
        End If
Next i
End Function


'user function to determine maximum value of
'axial force, F1 (F2 and F3 are not included)
Function UAMax(Pmm, Fm, NM) As Variant

Dim Abs_FAMax As Double
Dim FAMax As Double

Abs_FAMax = 0
n = 0
For i = 1 To NM
    If Abs(Pmm(Idm(1, i), i) + Fm(1, i)) > Abs_FAMax Then
        Abs_FAMax = Abs(Pmm(Idm(1, i), i) + Fm(1, i))
        FAMax = -(Pmm(Idm(1, i), i) + Fm(1, i))
        n = Member(i).J1
        UAMax = Array(FAMax, n)
    End If
    If Abs(Pmm(Idm(4, i), i) + Fm(4, i)) > Abs_FAMax Then
        Abs_FAMax = Abs(Pmm(Idm(4, i), i) + Fm(4, i))
        FAMax = Pmm(Idm(4, i), i) + Fm(4, i)
        n = Member(i).J2
        UAMax = Array(FAMax, n)
    End If
Next i
End Function
```

Command Button (FRAME2D)

```
Private Sub CommandButton1_Click()
ChartWindow = True
    Call FRAME2D
End Sub

Private Sub CommandButton2_Click()
ChartWindow = False
    Call FRAME2D
End Sub
```

Module1 (TRUSS2D)

```
'==================================================
'TRUSS2D v.1.0 Program for 2D TRUSS analysis, 2004
'by: Gunthar Pangaribuan - Refer to the book:
'An Introduction to Excel for Civil Engineers
'==================================================

Option Explicit
Option Base 1

Public i As Integer, j As Integer, n As Integer

Type Joint_Data
    x As Double
    y As Double
End Type

Type Member_Data
    J1 As Integer
    J2 As Integer
    Dens As Double
    Ax As Double
    E As Double
```

```vba
    lx As Double
    ly As Double
    Lh As Double
    Cx As Double
    Cy As Double
End Type


Public ChartWindow As Boolean
Public NP As Integer
Public DOF As Integer
Public NR As Integer
Public NJ As Integer
Public NM As Integer
Public Member() As Member_Data
Public Joint() As Joint_Data
Public NS As Integer 'no. of support
Public GS() As Double 'global stiffness
Public Rs() As Integer
Public DFR() As Double
Public Idm() As Integer
Public Idj() As Integer
Public Irj() As Integer
Public Psum() As Double
Public Pmm() As Double
Public Pj() As Double
Public Xs() As Double
Public Xm() As Double
Public Fm() As Double
Public XAx_Wd As Double
Public YAx_Wd As Double



Sub TRUSS2D()
On Error GoTo ErrMsg

Const NDJ = 2
Dim NLJ As Integer 'no of joint loads
```

```
NJ = Cells(4, 2)
NM = Cells(5, 2)
'X-range:
XAx_Wd = Application.Max(Rows("10:10")) - Application.Min(Rows("10:10"))
'Y-range:
YAx_Wd = Application.Max(Rows("11:11")) - Application.Min(Rows("11:11"))
NS = Application.Count(Rows("22:22"))
NLJ = Application.Count(Rows("27:27"))
'Total number of joint displacements, NP:
NP = NDJ * NJ

ReDim Joint(NJ) As Joint_Data
ReDim Member(NM) As Member_Data
ReDim MS(4, 4, NM) As Double 'member stiffness matrix
ReDim GS(NP, NP) 'global stiffness matrix
ReDim Idm(4, NM) 'displacement index
ReDim Pj(NP) 'joint load vector
ReDim Pmm(NP, NM) 'fixed-end forces
ReDim Psum(NP) 'sum load matrix vector
ReDim Xs(NP) 'joint displacement vector
ReDim Xm(4, NM) 'member deformations
ReDim Fm(4, NM) 'member forces
ReDim Rs(NP)
ReDim spn(NS) As Integer

'===============
'Read Input Data
'===============

'Read joint coordinates
For i = 1 To NJ
    With Joint(i)
        .x = Cells(10, 1 + i)
        .y = Cells(11, 1 + i)
    End With
Next i
```

```
'Read element data
For i = 1 To NM
    With Member(i)
        .J1 = Cells(15, 1 + i)
        .J2 = Cells(16, 1 + i)
        .Dens = Cells(17, 1 + i)
        .Ax = Cells(18, 1 + i)
        .E = Cells(19, 1 + i)
        .lx = Joint(.J2).x - Joint(.J1).x
        .ly = Joint(.J2).y - Joint(.J1).y
        .Lh = Sqr(.lx ^ 2 + .ly ^ 2)
        .Cx = .lx / .Lh
        .Cy = .ly / .Lh
    End With
Next i

If ChartWindow = True Then Call PlotGeometry: Exit Sub
Application.ScreenUpdating = False

'Read joint loads
For i = 1 To NLJ
    n = Cells(27, 1 + i)
    Pj(2 * n - 1) = Cells(28, 1 + i)
    Pj(2 * n) = Cells(29, 1 + i)
Next i

'restraint list and support (Rs) index
For i = 1 To NS
    spn(i) = Cells(22, 1 + i)
    Rs(2 * spn(i) - 1) = Cells(23, 1 + i)
    Rs(2 * spn(i)) = Cells(24, 1 + i)
Next i

DOF = 0
For i = 1 To NP
    If Rs(i) = 0 Then DOF = DOF + 1
```

```
Next i

'#restrained joints
NR = NP - DOF

ReDim DFX(NDJ * NS, DOF) As Double '[Kbf]according to Eq. 4.12
ReDim DFR(DOF, DOF) As Double '[Kff]^-1 according to Eq. 4.9
ReDim RJ(NDJ * NS) As Double 'support reactions
ReDim Idj(DOF) 'free displacement index
ReDim Irj(NDJ * NS) 'support displacement index

'=================
'Structure Analysis
'=================

Call Mindex(Idm, Idj, Irj)
Call Stiff_Mtx(MS, GS)
Call MInvers(DFX, DFR)
'generate loads
Call Genload(Pmm, Psum)
'determine displacements
Call DISP(Xs, Xm)

'============
'Print Result
'============
'clear previous content
Dim LastRow
LastRow = ActiveSheet.UsedRange.Rows.Count
Range(Cells(35, 1), Cells(LastRow, 10)).ClearContents

'1.Print Loads
For i = 1 To NJ
    Cells(34 + i, 1).NumberFormat = "0"
    Cells(34 + i, 1) = i
    Cells(34 + i, 2).NumberFormat = "0.000"
    Cells(34 + i, 2) = Psum(2 * i - 1)
```

```vba
            Cells(34 + i, 3).NumberFormat = "0.000"
            Cells(34 + i, 3) = Psum(2 * i)
    Next i
    
    '2. Print Joint displacements
    For i = 1 To NJ
        Cells(34 + i, 4).NumberFormat = "0.00000"
        Cells(34 + i, 4) = Xs(2 * i - 1)
        Cells(34 + i, 5).NumberFormat = "0.00000"
        Cells(34 + i, 5) = Xs(2 * i)
    Next i
    
    '-------------
    'Member Forces
    '-------------
    '{F}m=[K]m.{X}m
    
    For i = 1 To NM
        For j = 1 To 4
        Fm(j, i) = 0
            For n = 1 To 4
                Fm(j, i) = Fm(j, i) + MS(j, n, i) * Xm(n, i)
            Next n
        Next j
    Next i
    
    'Print member forces
    For i = 1 To NM
        With Member(i)
            Cells(34 + i, 6).NumberFormat = "0"
            Cells(34 + i, 6) = i & "./" & Format(.Lh, "0.0")
            Cells(34 + i, 7).NumberFormat = "0.000"
            Cells(34 + i, 7) = Pmm(Idm(1, i), i) + Fm(1, i)
            Cells(34 + i, 8).NumberFormat = "0.000"
            Cells(34 + i, 8) = Pmm(Idm(3, i), i) + Fm(3, i)
        End With
    Next i
```

```
'-----------------
'Support Reactions
'-----------------
For i = 1 To 2 * NS
    For j = 1 To DOF
        RJ(i) = RJ(i) + DFX(i, j) * Xs(Idj(j))
    Next j
Next i

For i = 1 To NS
    Cells(34 + i, 9).NumberFormat = "0"
    Cells(34 + i, 9) = spn(i)
    Cells(34 + i, 10).NumberFormat = "0.000"
    Cells(34 + i, 10) = RJ(2 * i - 1) - Psum(Irj(2 * i - 1))
    Cells(34 + i, 11).NumberFormat = "0.000"
    Cells(34 + i, 11) = RJ(2 * i) - Psum(Irj(2 * i))
Next i

Call PlotGeometry
Call PlotDisplacement
Call PlotAxial

Range("A1").Select
Application.ScreenUpdating = True
Exit Sub

ErrMsg: MsgBox "Error, please check input ...", vbOKOnly + vbExclamation, "TRUSS2D"

Range("A1").Select
Application.ScreenUpdating = True

End Sub
```

Module2 (TRUSS2D)

```
Option Explicit
Option Base 1
Public T() As Double 'transformation matrix
Public TT() As Double 'transpose [T], used in Module 3

'Indexing for matrix subscript
Sub Mindex(index() As Integer, IFr() As Integer, IFx() As Integer)

'Member end-displacement indexes:
For i = 1 To NM
    With Member(i)
    index(1, i) = 2 * .J1 - 1
    index(2, i) = 2 * .J1
    index(3, i) = 2 * .J2 - 1
    index(4, i) = 2 * .J2
    End With
Next i

'Joint free displacement index, IFr and support index, IFx
n = 1
j = 1
For i = 1 To NP
    If Rs(i) = 0 Then IFr(n) = i: n = n + 1
Next i

n = 1
For i = 1 To NS
    n = Cells(22, 1 + i)
    IFx(2 * i - 1) = 2 * n - 1
    IFx(2 * i) = 2 * n
Next i

End Sub
```

```
Sub Stiff_Mtx(MK() As Double, S() As Double)
Dim sms As Double
ReDim M(4, 4, NM) As Double

'Building global stiffness matrix
For i = 1 To NM
    With Member(i)
    sms = .Ax * .E / .Lh
    'Member stiffness
    MK(1, 1, i) = sms: MK(1, 3, i) = -sms
    MK(3, 1, i) = -sms: MK(3, 3, i) = sms
    'Member global stiffness
    M(1, 1, i) = sms * .Cx * .Cx: M(1, 2, i) = sms * .Cx * .Cy: M(1, 3, i) = -M(1, 1, i): M(1, 4, i) = -M(1, 2, i)
    M(2, 1, i) = M(1, 2, i): M(2, 2, i) = sms * .Cy * .Cy: M(2, 3, i) = M(1, 4, i): M(2, 4, i) = -M(2, 2, i)
    M(3, 1, i) = M(1, 3, i): M(3, 2, i) = M(2, 3, i): M(3, 3, i) = M(1, 1, i): M(3, 4, i) = M(1, 2, i)
    M(4, 1, i) = M(1, 4, i): M(4, 2, i) = M(2, 4, i): M(4, 3, i) = M(3, 4, i): M(4, 4, i) = M(2, 2, i)
    'Storing members and superposition
    For j = 1 To 4
        For n = 1 To 4
            S(Idm(j, i), Idm(n, i)) = S(Idm(j, i), Idm(n, i)) + M(j, n, i)
        Next n
    Next j
    End With
Next i
End Sub
'Global matrix
Sub MInvers(SR() As Double, SD() As Double)
Dim n As Integer

'submatrix Stiffness, KRF
For i = 1 To DOF
    For j = 1 To 2 * NS
        SR(j, i) = GS(Irj(j), Idj(i))
    Next j
Next i
```

```
'submatrix Stiffness, KFF
For i = 1 To DOF
    For j = 1 To DOF
        SD(i, j) = GS(Idj(i), Idj(j))
    Next j
Next i

'Inverse []
   For i = 1 To DOF
    For j = 1 To DOF
        If j <> i Then SD(i, j) = SD(i, j) / SD(i, i)
    Next j
    For n = 1 To DOF
        If n = i Then GoTo 10
    For j = 1 To DOF
        If j <> i Then SD(n, j) = SD(n, j) - SD(i, j) * SD(n, i)
    Next j
10  Next n
    For n = 1 To DOF
        If n <> i Then SD(n, i) = -SD(n, i) / SD(i, i)
    Next n
    SD(i, i) = 1 / SD(i, i)
   Next i

End Sub

Sub Genload(Pa() As Double, Ps() As Double)
ReDim TT(4, 4, NM) As Double
ReDim Peq(NP, NM) 'equivalent loads due to selfweight
Dim Idx As Integer, W As Double

'member fixed-end forces due to selfweight
For i = 1 To NM
    With Member(i)
    W = .Dens * .Ax
    Pa(Idm(1, i), i) = .Cy * W * .Lh / 2
    Pa(Idm(2, i), i) = .Cx * W * .Lh / 2
```

```
            Pa(Idm(3, i), i) = .Cy * W * .Lh / 2
            Pa(Idm(4, i), i) = .Cx * W * .Lh / 2
        End With
Next i


'Transformation matrix (transpose)
For i = 1 To NM
    With Member(i)
    TT(1, 1, i) = .Cx: TT(3, 3, i) = TT(1, 1, i): TT(1, 2, i) = -.Cy: TT(3, 4, i) = TT(1, 2, i)
    TT(2, 1, i) = .Cy: TT(4, 3, i) = TT(2, 1, i): TT(2, 2, i) = .Cx: TT(4, 4, i) = TT(2, 2, i)
    End With
Next i


'equivalent joint loads due to selfweight in global system
For i = 1 To NM
    For j = 1 To 4
        For n = 1 To 4
            Peq(Idm(j, i), i) = Peq(Idm(j, i), i) + TT(j, n, i) * -Pa(Idm(n, i), i)
        Next n
     Next j
Next i


'sum loads = joint loads + eq.loads
For i = 1 To NP
    Ps(i) = Pj(i)
Next i


'load superposition
For i = 1 To NM
    For j = 1 To 4
        Ps(Idm(j, i)) = Ps(Idm(j, i)) + Peq(Idm(j, i), i)
    Next j
Next i


End Sub
```

```
Sub DISP(x() As Double, X2() As Double)
ReDim X2(4, NM) As Double
ReDim Xi(4, NM) As Double
ReDim T(4, 4, NM) As Double

'Joint Displacements {X} = [SD]^-1.{P}
For i = 1 To DOF
x(Idj(i)) = 0
    For j = 1 To DOF
        x(Idj(i)) = x(Idj(i)) + DFR(i, j) * Psum(Idj(j))
    Next j
Next i

'Numbering of global {X}(NP) to global {Xi} element
For i = 1 To NM
    For j = 1 To 4
        Xi(j, i) = x(Idm(j, i))
    Next j
Next i

'Transforming {Xi} to local coordinates
'Transformation matrix:
For i = 1 To NM
    With Member(i)
    T(1, 1, i) = .Cx: T(3, 3, i) = T(1, 1, i): T(1, 2, i) = .Cy: T(3, 4, i) = T(1, 2, i)
    T(2, 1, i) = -.Cy: T(4, 3, i) = T(2, 1, i): T(2, 2, i) = .Cx: T(4, 4, i) = T(2, 2, i)
    End With
Next i

'member deformations, transformed{X} = [T].{Xi}
For i = 1 To NM
    For j = 1 To 4
        X2(j, i) = 0
        For n = 1 To 4
            X2(j, i) = X2(j, i) + T(j, n, i) * Xi(n, i)
        Next n
```

```
    Next j
Next i

End Sub
```

Module3 (TRUSS2D)

```
'This module consist of only code to create charts
Option Explicit
Option Base 1
Sub PlotGeometry()

On Error Resume Next

Dim Cx1, Cx2, Cy1, Cy2
ReDim mxVal(NM) As Variant
ReDim myVal(NM) As Variant
ReDim tagxVal(NM) As Variant
ReDim tagyVal(NM) As Variant

Dim am As Integer

'member coordinates
For i = 1 To NM
    With Member(i)
        Cx1 = Joint(.J1).x
        Cy1 = Joint(.J1).y
        Cx2 = Joint(.J2).x
        Cy2 = Joint(.J2).y
    End With
        mxVal(i) = Array(Cx1, Cx2)
        myVal(i) = Array(Cy1, Cy2)
        tagxVal(i) = Array((Cx1 + Cx2) / 2)
        tagyVal(i) = Array((Cy1 + Cy2) / 2)
Next i

    ActiveSheet.ChartObjects("Chart 1").Activate
```

```
        ActiveChart.ChartArea.Select
        Selection.ClearContents


'creating joints
For i = 1 To NJ
    With ActiveChart
        .SeriesCollection.NewSeries
        .SeriesCollection(i).XValues = Joint(i).x
        .SeriesCollection(i).Values = Joint(i).y
        .SeriesCollection(i).Name = "J" & i
    End With
    'node marker
    ActiveChart.PlotArea.Select
    ActiveChart.SeriesCollection(i).Select
    With Selection
        .MarkerBackgroundColorIndex = 3 'red
        .MarkerForegroundColorIndex = 3
        .MarkerStyle = xlCircle
        .MarkerSize = 6
        .Shadow = False
        .ApplyDataLabels AutoText:=True, LegendKey:= _
        False,          ShowSeriesName:=True,          ShowCategoryName:=False,
ShowValue:=False, _
        ShowPercentage:=False, ShowBubbleSize:=False
    End With

    ActiveChart.SeriesCollection(i).DataLabels.Select
    With Selection
        .HorizontalAlignment = xlCenter
        .VerticalAlignment = xlCenter
        .ReadingOrder = xlContext
        .Position = xlLabelPositionRight
        .Orientation = xlHorizontal
    End With
    ActiveChart.SeriesCollection(i).DataLabels.Select
    With Selection.Font
        .Name = "Arial"
        .FontStyle = "Regular"
```

An Introduction to Excel for Civil Engineers

```
            .Size = 8
        End With
Next i


    ActiveSheet.ChartObjects("Chart 1").Activate
    ActiveChart.ChartArea.Select


    n = NJ + NM
am = 1
'creating member lines
For i = NJ + 1 To n
    With ActiveChart
        .SeriesCollection.NewSeries
        .SeriesCollection(i).XValues = mxVal(am)
        .SeriesCollection(i).Values = myVal(am)
        .SeriesCollection(i).Name = "="""""
    End With
    ActiveChart.SeriesCollection(i).Select
    With Selection
        .MarkerBackgroundColorIndex = xlNone
        .MarkerForegroundColorIndex = xlNone
        .MarkerStyle = xlNone
        .Smooth = False
    End With
    With Selection.Border
        .ColorIndex = 5
        .Weight = xlThin
        .LineStyle = xlContinuous
    End With
am = am + 1
Next i

'creating member name tags
am = 1
For i = n + 1 To n + NM
    With ActiveChart
        .SeriesCollection.NewSeries
```

```
            .SeriesCollection(i).XValues = tagxVal(am)
            .SeriesCollection(i).Values = tagyVal(am)
            .SeriesCollection(i).Name = "M" & am
        End With
        ActiveChart.PlotArea.Select
        ActiveChart.SeriesCollection(i).Select
        With Selection
            .MarkerBackgroundColorIndex = 5
            .MarkerForegroundColorIndex = 5
            .MarkerStyle = xlSquare
            .Smooth = False
            .MarkerSize = 6
            .Shadow = False
            .ApplyDataLabels AutoText:=True, LegendKey:= _
            False,          ShowSeriesName:=True,          ShowCategoryName:=False,
ShowValue:=False, _
            ShowPercentage:=False, ShowBubbleSize:=False
        End With
        ActiveChart.SeriesCollection(i).DataLabels.Select
        With Selection.Font
            .Name = "Arial"
            .FontStyle = "Regular"
            .Size = 8
        End With
am = am + 1
Next i

    ActiveChart.ChartArea.Select
    With ActiveChart
        .Axes(xlCategory, xlPrimary).HasTitle = True
        .Axes(xlCategory, xlPrimary).AxisTitle.Characters.Text = _
        "NJ = " & Format(NJ, "0") & ", NM = " & Format(NM, "0")
    End With

ActiveChart.ShowWindow = True

End Sub
```

```
Sub PlotDisplacement()
On Error Resume Next

Dim Cx1, Cx2, Cy1, Cy2
ReDim mxValbf(NM) As Variant, myValbf(NM) As Variant
ReDim mxValaf(NM) As Variant, myValaf(NM) As Variant

Dim am As Integer, scx As Single
Dim Xmax As Double, at_joint As Integer

    ActiveSheet.ChartObjects("Chart 2").Activate
    ActiveChart.ChartArea.Select
    Selection.ClearContents

'=======================
'scale for displacements
'=======================
'user scale: displacements are drawn up to max 10% of the axis range
'or X-range or Y-range * 10% = Xmax

'determine max. joint-X and Y displacement
'(user function UXMax written at the end of this module):
Xmax = Application.index(UXMax(Xs, NP), 1)
at_joint = Application.index(UXMax(Xs, NP), 2)
scx = (Application.Max(XAx_Wd, YAx_Wd) * 10 / 100) / Abs(Xmax)

'member coordinates: before & after loading
For i = 1 To NM
    With Member(i)
        Cx1 = Joint(.J1).x
        Cy1 = Joint(.J1).y
        Cx2 = Joint(.J2).x
        Cy2 = Joint(.J2).y
    mxValbf(i) = Array(Cx1, Cx2)
    myValbf(i) = Array(Cy1, Cy2)
        Cx1 = Joint(.J1).x + scx * Xs(2 * .J1 - 1)
        Cy1 = Joint(.J1).y + scx * Xs(2 * .J1)
```

```vb
                Cx2 = Joint(.J2).x + scx * Xs(2 * .J2 - 1)
                Cy2 = Joint(.J2).y + scx * Xs(2 * .J2)
        mxValaf(i) = Array(Cx1, Cx2)
        myValaf(i) = Array(Cy1, Cy2)
        End With
    Next i
    
     am = 1
    'creating member lines: before loading
    For i = 1 To NM
        With ActiveChart
            .SeriesCollection.NewSeries
            .SeriesCollection(i).XValues = mxValbf(am)
            .SeriesCollection(i).Values = myValbf(am)
            .SeriesCollection(i).Name = "="""""
        End With
        ActiveChart.SeriesCollection(i).Select
        With Selection
            .MarkerStyle = xlNone
            .Smooth = False
        End With
        With Selection.Border
            .ColorIndex = 5
            .Weight = xlThin
            .LineStyle = xlContinuous
        End With
    am = am + 1
    Next i
    
    n = NM + NM
    am = 1
    'creating member lines: after loading
    For i = NM + 1 To n
        With ActiveChart
            .SeriesCollection.NewSeries
            .SeriesCollection(i).XValues = mxValaf(am)
            .SeriesCollection(i).Values = myValaf(am)
```

```vb
                .SeriesCollection(i).Name = "="""""
            End With
            ActiveChart.SeriesCollection(i).Select
            With Selection
                .MarkerStyle = xlNone
                .Smooth = False
            End With
            With Selection.Border
                .ColorIndex = 7
                .Weight = xlMedium
                .LineStyle = xlContinuous
            End With
        am = am + 1
        Next i
        
        
        ActiveChart.ChartArea.Select
        With ActiveChart
            .Axes(xlCategory, xlPrimary).HasTitle = True
            .Axes(xlCategory, xlPrimary).AxisTitle.Characters.Text = _
            "Max Displacement,  J." & at_joint & " = " & Format(Xmax, "0.00000")
        End With

End Sub


Sub PlotAxial()
On Error Resume Next

Dim Cx1, Cx2, Cy1, Cy2
Dim Cmx1, Cmx2, Cmy1, Cmy2
ReDim mxVal(NM) As Variant
ReDim myVal(NM) As Variant
ReDim saxVal(NM) As Variant
ReDim sayVal(NM) As Variant
ReDim tagxVal(NM) As Variant
ReDim tagyVal(NM) As Variant


ReDim mjxVal(NM + NM) As Variant
```

```
ReDim mjyVal(NM + NM) As Variant
ReDim acolor(NM + NM) As Variant
ReDim Pa_LM(2, NM) As Double
ReDim Pa_RM(2, NM) As Double
ReDim Pa_LT(2, NM) As Double
ReDim Pa_RT(2, NM) As Double

Dim am As Integer, sca As Single
Dim Amax As Double, at_member As Integer, L_I As Integer, L_II As Integer

    ActiveSheet.ChartObjects("Chart 3").Activate
    ActiveChart.ChartArea.Select
    Selection.ClearContents

'analogous to plot displacement for scaling
Amax = Application.index(UAMax(Pmm, Fm, NM), 1)
at_member = Application.index(UAMax(Pmm, Fm, NM), 2)
sca = (Application.Max(XAx_Wd, YAx_Wd) * 10 / 100) / Abs(Amax)

For i = 1 To NM
    Pa_LM(2, i) = -(Pmm(Idm(1, i), i) + Fm(1, i))
    Pa_RM(2, i) = (Pmm(Idm(3, i), i) + Fm(3, i))
Next i

'transform member axial to global axis by using [TT]
'the drawing should be in global coordinates
For i = 1 To NM
    For j = 1 To 2
        For n = 1 To 2
            Pa_LT(j, i) = Pa_LT(j, i) + TT(j, n, i) * Pa_LM(n, i)
            Pa_RT(j, i) = Pa_RT(j, i) + TT(j, n, i) * Pa_RM(n, i)
        Next n
    Next j
Next i

For i = 1 To NM
    With Member(i)
```

```
            Cx1 = Joint(.J1).x
            Cy1 = Joint(.J1).y
            Cx2 = Joint(.J2).x
            Cy2 = Joint(.J2).y
            'assign force coordinates
            Cmx1 = Cx1 + sca * Pa_LT(1, i)
            Cmy1 = Cy1 + sca * Pa_LT(2, i)
            Cmx2 = Cx2 + sca * Pa_RT(1, i)
            Cmy2 = Cy2 + sca * Pa_RT(2, i)
      End With
'member coordinates
            mxVal(i) = Array(Cx1, Cx2)
            myVal(i) = Array(Cy1, Cy2)
'axial coordinates
            saxVal(i) = Array(Cmx1, Cmx2)
            sayVal(i) = Array(Cmy1, Cmy2)
'member-joint coordinates
            mjxVal(2 * i - 1) = Array(Cx1, Cmx1)
            mjyVal(2 * i - 1) = Array(Cy1, Cmy1)
            'mcolor: define color for positive/negative value
            acolor(2 * i - 1) = -(Pmm(Idm(1, i), i) + Fm(1, i))

            mjxVal(2 * i) = Array(Cx2, Cmx2)
            mjyVal(2 * i) = Array(Cy2, Cmy2)
            acolor(2 * i) = Pmm(Idm(3, i), i) + Fm(3, i)
Next i


'creating member lines
For i = 1 To NM
     With ActiveChart
          .SeriesCollection.NewSeries
          .SeriesCollection(i).XValues = mxVal(i)
          .SeriesCollection(i).Values = myVal(i)
          .SeriesCollection(i).Name = "="""""
     End With
     ActiveChart.SeriesCollection(i).Select
     With Selection
```

```
            .MarkerBackgroundColorIndex = xlNone
            .MarkerForegroundColorIndex = xlNone
            .MarkerStyle = xlNone
            .Smooth = False
        End With
        With Selection.Border
            .ColorIndex = 5
            .Weight = xlThin
            .LineStyle = xlContinuous
        End With
Next i

L_I = NM + NM
am = 1
'creating axial lines
For i = NM + 1 To L_I
    With ActiveChart
        .SeriesCollection.NewSeries
        .SeriesCollection(i).XValues = saxVal(am)
        .SeriesCollection(i).Values = sayVal(am)
        .SeriesCollection(i).Name = "="""""
    End With
    ActiveChart.SeriesCollection(i).Select
    With Selection
        .MarkerBackgroundColorIndex = xlNone
        .MarkerForegroundColorIndex = xlNone
        .MarkerStyle = xlNone
        .Smooth = False
    End With
    With Selection.Border
        .ColorIndex = 7
        .Weight = xlThin
        .LineStyle = xlContinuous
    End With
am = am + 1
Next i
```

```
L_II = NM + NM + NM + NM
am = 1
'creating joint lines to axis
For i = L_I + 1 To L_II
    With ActiveChart
        .SeriesCollection.NewSeries
        .SeriesCollection(i).XValues = mjxVal(am)
        .SeriesCollection(i).Values = mjyVal(am)
        .SeriesCollection(i).Name = "="""""
    End With
    ActiveChart.SeriesCollection(i).Select
    With Selection
        .MarkerBackgroundColorIndex = xlNone
        .MarkerForegroundColorIndex = xlNone
        .MarkerStyle = xlNone
        .Smooth = False
    End With
    With Selection.Border
        If acolor(am) < 0 Then
        .ColorIndex = 3
        Else
        .ColorIndex = 5
        End If
        .Weight = xlMedium
        .LineStyle = xlContinuous
    End With
am = am + 1
Next i

    ActiveChart.ChartArea.Select
    With ActiveChart
        .Axes(xlCategory, xlPrimary).HasTitle = True
        .Axes(xlCategory, xlPrimary).AxisTitle.Characters.Text = _
        "Max Axial, M." & at_member & " = " & Format(Amax, "0.000")
    End With

End Sub
```

```vb
'user function to determine maximum value of
'joint X1 and X2

Function UXMax(Xs, NP) As Variant

Dim Abs_FXMax As Double
Dim FXMax As Double
ReDim Idis(NP) As Double

'Joint displacement index
n = 1
For i = 2 To NP Step 2
    Idis(i - 1) = n
    Idis(i) = n
n = n + 1
Next i

Abs_FXMax = 0
n = 0
For i = 1 To NP
    If Abs(Xs(i)) > Abs_FXMax Then
        Abs_FXMax = Abs(Xs(i))
        FXMax = Xs(i)
        n = Idis(i)
        UXMax = Array(FXMax, n)
        'UXMax keeps origin value(+ or - value)
    End If
n = n + i
Next i

End Function

'user function to determine maximum value of
'axial force, F1
Function UAMax(Pmm, Fm, NM) As Variant

Dim Abs_FAMax As Double
```

```
Dim FAMax As Double

Abs_FAMax = 0
n = 0
For i = 1 To NM
    If Abs(Pmm(Idm(1, i), i) + Fm(1, i)) > Abs_FAMax Then
        Abs_FAMax = Abs(Pmm(Idm(1, i), i) + Fm(1, i))
        FAMax = -(Pmm(Idm(1, i), i) + Fm(1, i))
        n = i
        UAMax = Array(FAMax, n)
    End If
    If Abs(Pmm(Idm(3, i), i) + Fm(3, i)) > Abs_FAMax Then
        Abs_FAMax = Abs(Pmm(Idm(3, i), i) + Fm(3, i))
        FAMax = Pmm(Idm(3, i), i) + Fm(3, i)
        n = i
        UAMax = Array(FAMax, n)
    End If
Next i
End Function
```

Command Button (TRUSS2D)

```
Private Sub CommandButton1_Click()
ChartWindow = True
    Call TRUSS2D
End Sub

Private Sub CommandButton2_Click()
ChartWindow = False
    Call TRUSS2D
End Sub
```

Module1 (BOF)

```vb
'===========================================================
'BOF v.1.0 Program for Beam on Elastic Foundation, 2004
'by: Gunthar Pangaribuan - Refer to the book:
'An Introduction to Excel for Civil Engineers
'===========================================================

Option Explicit

Public i As Integer, j As Integer, n As Integer

Type Joint_Data
    x As Double
    y As Double
    Ks As Double
    Sp As Double
End Type

Type Member_Data
    J1 As Integer
    J2 As Integer
    tm As Double
    bm As Double
    EI As Double
    lx As Double
    ly As Double
    Lh As Double
    Cx As Double
    Cy As Double
    Km1 As Double
    Km2 As Double
    Pres As Double
End Type

Public ChartWindow As Boolean
Public NP As Integer
```

```
Public DOF As Integer
Public NR As Integer
Public NJ As Integer
Public NM As Integer
Public Member() As Member_Data
Public Joint() As Joint_Data
Public Em As Double
Public Km() As Double
Public NS As Integer 'no. of supports
Public GASAT() As Double 'global stiffness matrix
Public Rs() As Integer
Public DFR() As Double
Public Idm() As Integer
Public Idj() As Integer
Public Irj() As Integer
Public Psum() As Double
Public Pmm() As Double
Public Pj() As Double
Public Xs() As Double
Public Xm() As Double
Public Fm() As Double
Public mmomen1() As Double
Public mmomen2() As Double
Public shear1() As Double
Public shear2() As Double

Sub BOF()
On Error GoTo ErrMsg

Const NDJ = 2
Dim NLJ As Integer 'no of joint loads
Dim Ksn As Integer

NJ = Cells(4, 2)
NM = Cells(5, 2)
Em = Cells(6, 2)
```

```
NS = Application.Count(Rows("23:23"))
NLJ = Application.Count(Rows("28:28"))
Ksn = Application.Count(Rows("12:12"))

'Total number of joint displacements, NP:
NP = NDJ * NJ

ReDim Joint(NJ) As Joint_Data
ReDim Member(NM) As Member_Data
ReDim ESAT(4, 4, NM) As Double 'member matrix refer to the book
ReDim GASAT(NP, NP) 'global stiffness matrix refer to the book
ReDim Idm(4, NM) ' displacement index
ReDim Pj(NP) 'joint load vector

ReDim Pmm(NP, NM) 'fixed-end forces
ReDim Psum(NP) 'sum load vector
ReDim Xs(NP) 'joint displacement vector
ReDim Xm(4, NM) ' member deformations
ReDim Fm(4, NM) 'member forces

ReDim mmomen1(NM)
ReDim mmomen2(NM)
ReDim shear1(NM)
ReDim shear2(NM)
ReDim Rs(NP)
ReDim spn(NS) As Integer
Dim mshear As Double

'===============
'Read Input Data
'===============

'Read joint data - in order
For i = 1 To NJ
    With Joint(i)
        .x = Cells(10, 1 + i)
        .y = Cells(11, 1 + i)
```

```
                .Ks = Cells(12, 1 + i)
                .Sp = .Ks * Xs(2 * i) 'soil pressure
        End With
Next i

'Read member data
For i = 1 To NM
        With Member(i)
        .J1 = Cells(16, 1 + i)
        .J2 = Cells(17, 1 + i)
        .tm = Cells(18, 1 + i)
        .bm = Cells(19, 1 + i)
        .EI = Em * 1 / 12 * .bm * .tm ^ 3
        .lx = Joint(.J2).x - Joint(.J1).x
        .ly = Joint(.J2).y - Joint(.J1).y
        .Lh = Sqr(.lx ^ 2 + .ly ^ 2)
        .Cx = .lx / .Lh
        .Cy = .ly / .Lh
        .Pres = Cells(20, 1 + i)
        .Km1 = 0.5 * .Lh * .bm * Joint(.J1).Ks
        .Km2 = 0.5 * .Lh * .bm * Joint(.J2).Ks
        End With
Next i
'end spring:
With Member(1)
        .Km1 = .Lh * .bm * Joint(.J1).Ks
End With
With Member(NM)
        .Km2 = .Lh * .bm * Joint(.J2).Ks
End With

If ChartWindow = True Then Call PlotGeometry: Exit Sub
Application.ScreenUpdating = False

'Read joint load
For i = 1 To NLJ
    n = Cells(28, 1 + i)
```

```
        Pj(2 * n - 1) = Cells(29, 1 + i)
        Pj(2 * n) = Cells(30, 1 + i)
Next i

'restraint list and support (Rs) index
For i = 1 To NS
    spn(i) = Cells(23, 1 + i)
    Rs(2 * spn(i) - 1) = Cells(24, 1 + i)
    Rs(2 * spn(i)) = Cells(25, 1 + i)
Next i

DOF = 0
For i = 1 To NP
    If Rs(i) = 0 Then DOF = DOF + 1
Next i

'#restrained joints (zero displacement)
NR = NP - DOF

ReDim DFX(NDJ * NS, DOF) As Double '[Kbf]according to Eq. 4.12
ReDim DFR(DOF, DOF) As Double '[Kff]^-1 according to Eq. 4.9
ReDim RJ(NDJ * NS) As Double 'support reactions
ReDim Idj(DOF) 'free displacement index
ReDim Irj(NDJ * NS) 'support displacement index
ReDim nAs_Now(NJ) As Integer
Dim nAs_Last As Integer
Dim ITR As Integer
Dim ITR_Continue As Boolean
ITR_Continue = True

ITR = 1

'clear previous content
Dim LastRow
LastRow = ActiveSheet.UsedRange.Rows.Count
Range(Cells(38, 1), Cells(LastRow, 16)).ClearContents
```

```
'==================
'Structure Analysis
'==================
Do

Call Mindex(Idm, Idj, Irj)
Call FEM(ESAT, GASAT)
Call MInvers(DFX, DFR)
Call Genload(Pmm, Psum)
Call DISP(Xs, Xm)

    'Print used springs
    For i = 1 To NM
        With Member(i)
            Cells(37 + i, 8).NumberFormat = "0.000"
            Cells(37 + i, 8) = .Km1
            Cells(37 + i, 9).NumberFormat = "0.000"
            Cells(37 + i, 9) = .Km2
        End With
    Next i

    n = 0
    For i = 1 To NJ
    're-input joint's Ks and Sp if Xs < 0
        With Joint(i)
            If Xs(i * 2) < 0 And .Ks > 0 Then
            .Ks = 0
            .Sp = .Ks * Xs(2 * i)
            n = n + 1
            End If
        End With
    Next i

    're-input member's soil K
    For i = 1 To NM
        With Member(i)
            .Km1 = 0.5 * .Lh * .bm * Joint(.J1).Ks
```

```
            .Km2 = 0.5 * .Lh * .bm * Joint(.J2).Ks
        End With
    Next i
    With Member(1)
        .Km1 = .Lh * .bm * Joint(.J1).Ks
    End With
    With Member(NM)
        .Km2 = .Lh * .bm * Joint(.J2).Ks
    End With
    
    'check no. of active spring between 2 iterations
    nAs_Now(ITR) = NJ - n
    nAs_Last = nAs_Now(ITR - 1)
    
    If nAs_Now(ITR) = nAs_Last Or n = 0 Then
        ITR_Continue = False
        Cells(34, 3) = ITR - 1
        Cells(35, 3) = nAs_Now(ITR)
    End If
    
    ITR = ITR + 1

Loop Until ITR_Continue = False

'============
'Print Result
'============
'1. Print Loads
For i = 1 To NJ
    Cells(37 + i, 1).NumberFormat = "0"
    Cells(37 + i, 1) = i
    Cells(37 + i, 2).NumberFormat = "0.000"
    Cells(37 + i, 2) = Psum(2 * i - 1)
    Cells(37 + i, 3).NumberFormat = "0.000"
    Cells(37 + i, 3) = Psum(2 * i)
Next i
```

```
'2. Print Joint displacements and soil pressures
For i = 1 To NJ
    Cells(37 + i, 4).NumberFormat = "0.00000"
    Cells(37 + i, 4) = Xs(2 * i - 1)
    Cells(37 + i, 5).NumberFormat = "0.00000"
    Cells(37 + i, 5) = Xs(2 * i)
    Cells(37 + i, 6).NumberFormat = "0.000"
    With Joint(i)
    .Sp = .Ks * Xs(2 * i)
    Cells(37 + i, 6) = .Sp
    End With
Next i


'-------------
'Member Forces
'-------------
'{F}m=[S]m.{X}s or [F]m=[S].[A]T.[X]s
'there is already calculated S.A^T,
For i = 1 To NM
    For j = 1 To 4
    Fm(j, i) = 0
        For n = 1 To 4
            Fm(j, i) = Fm(j, i) + ESAT(j, n, i) * Xm(n, i)
        Next n
    Next j
Next i

'Print member forces
For i = 1 To NM
    With Member(i)
        'no/length
        Cells(37 + i, 7).NumberFormat = "0"
        Cells(37 + i, 7) = i & "./" & Format(.Lh, "0.00")
        'moment
        mmomen1(i) = Fm(1, i) + Pmm(Idm(1, i), i)
        Cells(37 + i, 10).NumberFormat = "0.000"
        Cells(37 + i, 10) = mmomen1(i)
```

```vba
            mmomen2(i) = Fm(2, i) + Pmm(Idm(3, i), i)
            Cells(37 + i, 11).NumberFormat = "0.000"
            Cells(37 + i, 11) = mmomen2(i)
            'spring
            Cells(37 + i, 12).NumberFormat = "0.000"
            Cells(37 + i, 12) = Fm(3, i)
            Cells(37 + i, 13).NumberFormat = "0.000"
            Cells(37 + i, 13) = Fm(4, i)
            'shear
            If Ksn = 0 Then
                'internal forces with supports
                mshear = (Fm(1, i) + Fm(2, i)) / .Lh
                shear1(i) = mshear + Pmm(Idm(2, i), i)
                shear2(i) = -mshear + Pmm(Idm(4, i), i)
            Else
                'as per reference - with springs
                mshear = (Fm(1, i) + Fm(2, i)) / .Lh
                shear1(i) = mshear
                shear2(i) = -mshear
            End If
            Cells(37 + i, 14).NumberFormat = "0.000"
            Cells(37 + i, 14) = shear1(i)
            Cells(37 + i, 15).NumberFormat = "0.000"
            Cells(37 + i, 15) = shear2(i)
        End With
    Next i

    '-----------------
    'Support Reactions
    '-----------------
    For i = 1 To 2 * NS
        For j = 1 To DOF
            RJ(i) = RJ(i) + DFX(i, j) * Xs(Idj(j))
        Next j
    Next i

    For i = 1 To NS
```

```
        Cells(37 + i, 16).NumberFormat = "0"
        Cells(37 + i, 16) = spn(i)
        Cells(37 + i, 17).NumberFormat = "0.000"
        Cells(37 + i, 17) = RJ(2 * i - 1) - Psum(Irj(2 * i - 1))
        Cells(37 + i, 18).NumberFormat = "0.000"
        Cells(37 + i, 18) = RJ(2 * i) - Psum(Irj(2 * i))
Next i

'draw charts
Call PlotGeometry
Call PlotDisplacement
Call PlotMoment
Call PlotShear
Call PlotSoilPressure

Range("A1").Select
Application.ScreenUpdating = True
Exit Sub

ErrMsg: MsgBox "Error, please check input ...", vbOKOnly + vbExclamation, "BOF"

Range("A1").Select
Application.ScreenUpdating = True
End Sub
```

Module2 (BOF)

```
Option Explicit
'Indexing for matrix subscript
Sub Mindex(index() As Integer, IFr() As Integer, IFx() As Integer)

'Member end-displacement indexes:
For i = 1 To NM
    With Member(i)
    index(1, i) = 2 * .J1 - 1
    index(2, i) = 2 * .J1
```

```
            index(3, i) = 2 * .J2 - 1
            index(4, i) = 2 * .J2
        End With
    Next i


    'Joint free displacement index, IFr and
    'restraint (support) index, IFx
    n = 1
    For i = 1 To NP
        If Rs(i) = 0 Then IFr(n) = i: n = n + 1
    Next i


    n = 1
    For i = 1 To NS
        n = Cells(23, 1 + i)
        IFx(2 * i - 1) = 2 * n - 1
        IFx(2 * i) = 2 * n
    Next i


End Sub


Sub FEM(SAT() As Double, GS() As Double)
ReDim ASAT(4, 4, NM) As Double


'Assembly of finite element matrix, Eq.4.16 & 4.17
For i = 1 To NM
    With Member(i)
    'member SA^T matrix:
    'from internal forces F - deformations d relationship, F = S.d or F = S.A^T.X
        SAT(1, 1, i) = 4 * .EI / .Lh: SAT(1, 2, i) = 6 * .EI / .Lh ^ 2
        SAT(1, 3, i) = 2 * .EI / .Lh: SAT(1, 4, i) = -6 * .EI / .Lh ^ 2
        SAT(2, 1, i) = 2 * .EI / .Lh: SAT(2, 2, i) = 6 * .EI / .Lh ^ 2
        SAT(2, 3, i) = 4 * .EI / .Lh: SAT(2, 4, i) = -6 * .EI / .Lh ^ 2
        SAT(3, 2, i) = .Km1
        SAT(4, 4, i) = .Km2
    'Member global stiffness (member ASA^T)
        ASAT(1, 1, i) = 4 * .EI / .Lh: ASAT(1, 2, i) = 6 * .EI / .Lh ^ 2
```

```
            ASAT(1, 3, i) = 2 * .EI / .Lh: ASAT(1, 4, i) = -6 * .EI / .Lh ^ 2
            ASAT(2, 1, i) = 6 * .EI / .Lh ^ 2: ASAT(2, 2, i) = 12 * .EI / .Lh ^ 3 +
.Km1
            ASAT(2, 3, i) = 6 * .EI / .Lh ^ 2: ASAT(2, 4, i) = -12 * .EI / .Lh ^ 3
            ASAT(3, 1, i) = 2 * .EI / .Lh: ASAT(3, 2, i) = 6 * .EI / .Lh ^ 2
            ASAT(3, 3, i) = 4 * .EI / .Lh: ASAT(3, 4, i) = -6 * .EI / .Lh ^ 2
            ASAT(4, 1, i) = -6 * .EI / .Lh ^ 2: ASAT(4, 2, i) = -12 * .EI / .Lh ^ 3
            ASAT(4, 3, i) = -6 * .EI / .Lh ^ 2: ASAT(4, 4, i) = 12 * .EI / .Lh ^ 3 +
.Km2
        'Storing members and superposition(global ASA^T)
        For j = 1 To 4
            For n = 1 To 4
                GS(Idm(j, i), Idm(n, i)) = GS(Idm(j, i), Idm(n, i)) + ASAT(j, n, i)
            Next n
        Next j
        End With
Next i

End Sub
'Global matrix
Sub MInvers(SR() As Double, SD() As Double)
Dim n As Integer

'submatrix Stiffness, KRF
For i = 1 To DOF
    For j = 1 To 2 * NS
        SR(j, i) = GASAT(Irj(j), Idj(i))
    Next j
Next i

'submatrix Stiffness, KBF
For i = 1 To DOF
    For j = 1 To DOF
        SD(i, j) = GASAT(Idj(i), Idj(j))
    Next j
Next i
```

```
'Inverse []
   For i = 1 To DOF
    For j = 1 To DOF
        If j <> i Then SD(i, j) = SD(i, j) / SD(i, i)
    Next j
    For n = 1 To DOF
        If n = i Then GoTo 10
    For j = 1 To DOF
        If j <> i Then SD(n, j) = SD(n, j) - SD(i, j) * SD(n, i)
    Next j
10  Next n
    For n = 1 To DOF
        If n <> i Then SD(n, i) = -SD(n, i) / SD(i, i)
    Next n
    SD(i, i) = 1 / SD(i, i)
   Next i

End Sub

Sub Genload(Pa() As Double, Ps() As Double)

ReDim TT(4, 4, NM) As Double
ReDim Peq(NP, NM) 'equivalent loads
Dim Idx As Integer, w As Double

'member fixed-end forces due to pressures
For i = 1 To NM
    With Member(i)
    w = .Pres * .bm
    Pa(Idm(1, i), i) = -w * .Lh ^ 2 / 12
    Pa(Idm(2, i), i) = -w * .Lh / 2
    Pa(Idm(3, i), i) = w * .Lh ^ 2 / 12
    Pa(Idm(4, i), i) = -w * .Lh / 2
    End With
Next i

'equivalent joint loads due to pressures
```

```
For i = 1 To NM
    For j = 1 To 4
        For n = 1 To 4
            Peq(Idm(j, i), i) = -Pa(Idm(j, i), i)
        Next n
     Next j
Next i

'sum loads = joint loads + eq.loads
For i = 1 To NP
    Ps(i) = Pj(i)
Next i

'load superposition
For i = 1 To NM
    For j = 1 To 4
        Ps(Idm(j, i)) = Ps(Idm(j, i)) + Peq(Idm(j, i), i)
    Next j
Next i

End Sub

Sub DISP(x() As Double, Xi() As Double)
ReDim T(4, 4, NM) As Double

'Joint Displacements {X} = [SD]^-1.{P}
For i = 1 To DOF
x(Idj(i)) = 0
    For j = 1 To DOF
        x(Idj(i)) = x(Idj(i)) + DFR(i, j) * Psum(Idj(j))
    Next j
Next i

'Numbering of global {X}(NP) to global {Xi} member
For i = 1 To NM
    For j = 1 To 4
        Xi(j, i) = x(Idm(j, i))
```

```
        Next j
Next i

End Sub
```

Module3 (BOF)

```
Option Explicit
Option Base 1
Sub PlotGeometry()


On Error Resume Next

Dim Cx1, Cx2, Cy1, Cy2
ReDim mxVal(NM) As Variant
ReDim myVal(NM) As Variant
ReDim tagxVal(NM) As Variant
ReDim tagyVal(NM) As Variant


Dim am As Integer

'member coordinates
For i = 1 To NM
    With Member(i)
        Cx1 = Joint(.J1).x
        Cy1 = Joint(.J1).y
        Cx2 = Joint(.J2).x
        Cy2 = Joint(.J2).y
    End With
        mxVal(i) = Array(Cx1, Cx2)
        myVal(i) = Array(Cy1, Cy2)
        tagxVal(i) = Array((Cx1 + Cx2) / 2)
        tagyVal(i) = Array((Cy1 + Cy2) / 2)
Next i

    ActiveSheet.ChartObjects("Chart 1").Activate
    ActiveChart.ChartArea.Select
```

```
    Selection.ClearContents

'creating joints + name tags
For i = 1 To NJ
    With ActiveChart
        .SeriesCollection.NewSeries
        .SeriesCollection(i).XValues = Joint(i).x
        .SeriesCollection(i).Values = Joint(i).y
        .SeriesCollection(i).Name = "J" & i
    End With
    'node marker
    ActiveChart.PlotArea.Select
    ActiveChart.SeriesCollection(i).Select
    With Selection
        .MarkerBackgroundColorIndex = 3 'red
        .MarkerForegroundColorIndex = 3
        .MarkerStyle = xlCircle
        .MarkerSize = 6
        .Shadow = False
        .ApplyDataLabels AutoText:=True, LegendKey:= _
        False,          ShowSeriesName:=True,          ShowCategoryName:=False,
ShowValue:=False, _
        ShowPercentage:=False, ShowBubbleSize:=False
    End With

    ActiveChart.SeriesCollection(i).DataLabels.Select
    With Selection
        .HorizontalAlignment = xlCenter
        .VerticalAlignment = xlCenter
        .ReadingOrder = xlContext
        .Position = xlLabelPositionAbove
        .Orientation = xlHorizontal
        .Font.Name = "Arial"
        .Font.FontStyle = "Regular"
        .Font.Size = 8
    End With
Next i
    ActiveSheet.ChartObjects("Chart 1").Activate
```

An Introduction to Excel for Civil Engineers

```
        ActiveChart.ChartArea.Select

    n = NJ + NM
am = 1
'creating member lines
For i = NJ + 1 To n
    With ActiveChart
        .SeriesCollection.NewSeries
        .SeriesCollection(i).XValues = mxVal(am)
        .SeriesCollection(i).Values = myVal(am)
        .SeriesCollection(i).Name = "="""""
    End With
    ActiveChart.SeriesCollection(i).Select
    With Selection
        .MarkerBackgroundColorIndex = xlNone
        .MarkerForegroundColorIndex = xlNone
        .MarkerStyle = xlNone
        .Smooth = False
    End With
    With Selection.Border
        .ColorIndex = 5
        .Weight = xlThin
        .LineStyle = xlContinuous
    End With
am = am + 1
Next i

'creating member name tags
am = 1
For i = n + 1 To n + NM
    With ActiveChart
        .SeriesCollection.NewSeries
        .SeriesCollection(i).XValues = tagxVal(am)
        .SeriesCollection(i).Values = tagyVal(am)
        .SeriesCollection(i).Name = "M" & am
    End With
    ActiveChart.PlotArea.Select
```

```
    ActiveChart.SeriesCollection(i).Select
    With Selection
        .MarkerBackgroundColorIndex = 5
        .MarkerForegroundColorIndex = 5
        .MarkerStyle = xlSquare
        .Smooth = False
        .MarkerSize = 6
        .Shadow = False
        .ApplyDataLabels AutoText:=True, LegendKey:= _
        False,         ShowSeriesName:=True,         ShowCategoryName:=False, ShowValue:=False, _
        ShowPercentage:=False, ShowBubbleSize:=False
    End With
    ActiveChart.SeriesCollection(i).DataLabels.Select
    With Selection
        .HorizontalAlignment = xlCenter
        .VerticalAlignment = xlCenter
        .Position = xlLabelPositionAbove
        .Orientation = xlHorizontal
        .Font.Name = "Arial"
        .Font.FontStyle = "Regular"
        .Font.Size = 8
    End With
am = am + 1
Next i

    ActiveChart.ChartArea.Select
    With ActiveChart
        .Axes(xlCategory, xlPrimary).HasTitle = True
        .Axes(xlCategory, xlPrimary).AxisTitle.Characters.Text = _
        "NJ = " & Format(NJ, "0") & ", NM = " & Format(NM, "0")
    End With

ActiveChart.ShowWindow = True

End Sub
```

```
Sub PlotDisplacement()
On Error Resume Next

Dim Cx1, Cx2, Cy1, Cy2
ReDim mxValbf(NM) As Variant, myValbf(NM) As Variant
ReDim mxValaf(NM) As Variant, myValaf(NM) As Variant

Dim Xmax As Double, At_joint As Integer, am As Integer

    ActiveSheet.ChartObjects("Chart 2").Activate
    ActiveChart.ChartArea.Select
    Selection.ClearContents

Xmax = Application.index(UXMax(Xs, NP), 1)
At_joint = Application.index(UXMax(Xs, NP), 2)

'member coordinates: before & after loading
For i = 1 To NM
    With Member(i)
        Cx1 = Joint(.J1).x
        Cy1 = Joint(.J1).y
        Cx2 = Joint(.J2).x
        Cy2 = Joint(.J2).y
    mxValbf(i) = Array(Cx1, Cx2)
    myValbf(i) = Array(Cy1, Cy2)
        Cx1 = Joint(.J1).x + .Cy * Xs(2 * .J1)
        Cy1 = Joint(.J1).y + .Cx * Xs(2 * .J1)
        Cx2 = Joint(.J2).x + .Cy * Xs(2 * .J2)
        Cy2 = Joint(.J2).y + .Cx * Xs(2 * .J2)
    mxValaf(i) = Array(Cx1, Cx2)
    myValaf(i) = Array(Cy1, Cy2)
    End With
Next i

    am = 1
    'creating member lines: before loading
    For i = 1 To NM
```

```
    With ActiveChart
        .SeriesCollection.NewSeries
        .SeriesCollection(i).XValues = mxValbf(am)
        .SeriesCollection(i).Values = myValbf(am)
        .SeriesCollection(i).Name = "="""""
    End With
    ActiveChart.SeriesCollection(i).Select
    With Selection
        .MarkerStyle = xlNone
        .Smooth = False
    End With
    With Selection.Border
        .ColorIndex = 5
        .Weight = xlThin
        .LineStyle = xlContinuous
    End With
am = am + 1
Next i

n = NM + NM
am = 1
'creating member lines: after loading
For i = NM + 1 To n
    With ActiveChart
        .SeriesCollection.NewSeries
        .SeriesCollection(i).XValues = mxValaf(am)
        .SeriesCollection(i).Values = myValaf(am)
        .SeriesCollection(i).Name = "="""""
    End With
    ActiveChart.SeriesCollection(i).Select
    With Selection
        .MarkerStyle = xlNone
        .Smooth = False
    End With
    With Selection.Border
        .ColorIndex = 7
        .Weight = xlMedium
```

```
                .LineStyle = xlContinuous
         End With
    am = am + 1
    Next i


    ActiveChart.ChartArea.Select
    With ActiveChart
        .Axes(xlCategory, xlPrimary).HasTitle = True
        .Axes(xlCategory, xlPrimary).AxisTitle.Characters.Text = _
        "Max Displacement,  J." & At_joint & " = " & Format(Xmax, "0.00000")
    End With

End Sub


Sub PlotMoment()
On Error Resume Next

Dim Cx1, Cx2, Cy1, Cy2
Dim Cmx1, Cmx2, Cmy1, Cmy2
ReDim mxVal(NM) As Variant
ReDim myVal(NM) As Variant
ReDim moxVal(NM) As Variant
ReDim moyVal(NM) As Variant
ReDim tagxVal(NM) As Variant
ReDim tagyVal(NM) As Variant

ReDim mjxVal(NM + NM) As Variant
ReDim mjyVal(NM + NM) As Variant
ReDim mcolor(NM + NM) As Variant


Dim Mmax As Single, At_joint As Integer, am As Integer, L_I As Integer, L_II As Integer, _
L_III As Integer, L_IV As Integer

    ActiveSheet.ChartObjects("Chart 3").Activate
    ActiveChart.ChartArea.Select
    Selection.ClearContents
```

```
Mmax = Application.index(UMMax(Pmm, Fm, NM), 1)
At_joint = Application.index(UMMax(Pmm, Fm, NM), 2)


For i = 1 To NM
    With Member(i)
        Cx1 = Joint(.J1).x
        Cy1 = Joint(.J1).y
        Cx2 = Joint(.J2).x
        Cy2 = Joint(.J2).y
        'assign coordinates
        Cmx1 = Cx1
        Cmy1 = Cy1 + mmomen1(i)
        Cmx2 = Cx2
        Cmy2 = Cy2 - mmomen2(i)
    End With
'member coordinates
        mxVal(i) = Array(Cx1, Cx2)
        myVal(i) = Array(Cy1, Cy2)
'moment coordinates
        moxVal(i) = Array(Cmx1, Cmx2)
        moyVal(i) = Array(Cmy1, Cmy2)
'member-joint coordinates
        mjxVal(2 * i - 1) = Array(Cx1, Cmx1)
        mjyVal(2 * i - 1) = Array(Cy1, Cmy1)
        'mcolor: define color for positive/negative value
        mcolor(2 * i - 1) = mmomen1(i)
        mjxVal(2 * i) = Array(Cx2, Cmx2)
        mjyVal(2 * i) = Array(Cy2, Cmy2)
        mcolor(2 * i) = mmomen2(i)
Next i


'creating member lines
For i = 1 To NM
    With ActiveChart
        .SeriesCollection.NewSeries
        .SeriesCollection(i).XValues = mxVal(i)
        .SeriesCollection(i).Values = myVal(i)
```

```
            .SeriesCollection(i).Name = "="""""
        End With
        ActiveChart.SeriesCollection(i).Select
        With Selection
            .MarkerBackgroundColorIndex = xlNone
            .MarkerForegroundColorIndex = xlNone
            .MarkerStyle = xlNone
            .Smooth = False
        End With
        With Selection.Border
            .ColorIndex = 5
            .Weight = xlThin
            .LineStyle = xlContinuous
        End With
    Next i

    L_I = NM + 1
    L_II = NM + NM
    am = 1
    'creating moment lines
    For i = L_I To L_II
        With ActiveChart
            .SeriesCollection.NewSeries
            .SeriesCollection(i).XValues = moxVal(am)
            .SeriesCollection(i).Values = moyVal(am)
            .SeriesCollection(i).Name = "="""""
        End With
        ActiveChart.SeriesCollection(i).Select
        With Selection
            .MarkerBackgroundColorIndex = xlNone
            .MarkerForegroundColorIndex = xlNone
            .MarkerStyle = xlNone
            .Smooth = False
        End With
        With Selection.Border
            .ColorIndex = 7
            .Weight = xlThin
```

```
            .LineStyle = xlContinuous
        End With
am = am + 1
Next i


L_III = L_II + 1
L_IV = L_II + NM + NM
am = 1
'creating joint lines to axis
For i = L_III To L_IV
    With ActiveChart
         .SeriesCollection.NewSeries
         .SeriesCollection(i).XValues = mjxVal(am)
         .SeriesCollection(i).Values = mjyVal(am)
         .SeriesCollection(i).Name = "="""""
    End With
    ActiveChart.SeriesCollection(i).Select
    With Selection
         .MarkerBackgroundColorIndex = xlNone
         .MarkerForegroundColorIndex = xlNone
         .MarkerStyle = xlNone
         .Smooth = False
    End With
    With Selection.Border
        If mcolor(am) < 0 Then
        .ColorIndex = 3
        Else
        .ColorIndex = 5
        End If
        .Weight = xlMedium
        .LineStyle = xlContinuous
    End With
am = am + 1

Next i

    ActiveChart.ChartArea.Select
```

```
    With ActiveChart
        .Axes(xlCategory, xlPrimary).HasTitle = True
        .Axes(xlCategory, xlPrimary).AxisTitle.Characters.Text = _
        "Max Moment, J." & At_joint & " = " & Format(Mmax, "0.000")
    End With

End Sub

Sub PlotShear()
On Error Resume Next

Dim Cx1, Cx2, Cy1, Cy2
Dim Cmx1, Cmx2, Cmy1, Cmy2
ReDim mxVal(NM) As Variant
ReDim myVal(NM) As Variant
ReDim tagxVal(NM) As Variant
ReDim tagyVal(NM) As Variant
ReDim shxval(NM) As Variant
ReDim shyval(NM) As Variant
ReDim sjxVal(NM + NM) As Variant
ReDim sjyVal(NM + NM) As Variant
ReDim mcolor(NM + NM) As Variant

Dim Smax As Double, At_member As Integer, am As Integer, L_I As Integer, _
L_II As Integer, L_III As Integer, L_IV As Integer

    ActiveSheet.ChartObjects("Chart 4").Activate
    ActiveChart.ChartArea.Select
    Selection.ClearContents

Smax = Application.index(USMax(Pmm, Fm, NM), 1)
At_member = Application.index(USMax(Pmm, Fm, NM), 2)

For i = 1 To NM
    With Member(i)
        Cx1 = Joint(.J1).x
        Cy1 = Joint(.J1).y
```

```
            Cx2 = Joint(.J2).x
            Cy2 = Joint(.J2).y
            'assign coordinates
            Cmx1 = Cx1
            Cmy1 = Cy1 - shear1(i)
            Cmx2 = Cx2
            Cmy2 = Cy2 + shear2(i)
        End With
'member coordinates
        mxVal(i) = Array(Cx1, Cx2)
        myVal(i) = Array(Cy1, Cy2)
'shear coordinates
        shxval(i) = Array(Cmx1, Cmx2)
        shyval(i) = Array(Cmy1, Cmy2)
'member-joint coordinates
        sjxVal(2 * i - 1) = Array(Cx1, Cmx1)
        sjyVal(2 * i - 1) = Array(Cy1, Cmy1)
        'mcolor: define color for positive/negative value
        mcolor(2 * i - 1) = -shear1(i)
        sjxVal(2 * i) = Array(Cx2, Cmx2)
        sjyVal(2 * i) = Array(Cy2, Cmy2)
        mcolor(2 * i) = shear2(i)
Next i

'creating member lines
For i = 1 To NM
    With ActiveChart
        .SeriesCollection.NewSeries
        .SeriesCollection(i).XValues = mxVal(i)
        .SeriesCollection(i).Values = myVal(i)
        .SeriesCollection(i).Name = "="""""
    End With
    ActiveChart.SeriesCollection(i).Select
    With Selection
        .MarkerBackgroundColorIndex = xlNone
        .MarkerForegroundColorIndex = xlNone
        .MarkerStyle = xlNone
```

```
            .Smooth = False
        End With
        With Selection.Border
            .ColorIndex = 5
            .Weight = xlThin
            .LineStyle = xlContinuous
        End With
Next i

L_I = NM + 1
L_II = NM + NM
am = 1
'creating shear lines
For i = L_I To L_II
    With ActiveChart
        .SeriesCollection.NewSeries
        .SeriesCollection(i).XValues = shxval(am)
        .SeriesCollection(i).Values = shyval(am)
        .SeriesCollection(i).Name = "="""""
    End With
    ActiveChart.SeriesCollection(i).Select
    With Selection
        .MarkerBackgroundColorIndex = xlNone
        .MarkerForegroundColorIndex = xlNone
        .MarkerStyle = xlNone
        .Smooth = False
    End With
    With Selection.Border
        .ColorIndex = 7
        .Weight = xlThin
        .LineStyle = xlContinuous
    End With
am = am + 1
Next i

L_III = L_II + 1
L_IV = L_II + NM + NM
```

```vba
am = 1
'creating joint lines to axis
For i = L_III To L_IV
    With ActiveChart
        .SeriesCollection.NewSeries
        .SeriesCollection(i).XValues = sjxVal(am)
        .SeriesCollection(i).Values = sjyVal(am)
        .SeriesCollection(i).Name = "="""""
    End With
    ActiveChart.SeriesCollection(i).Select
    With Selection
        .MarkerBackgroundColorIndex = xlNone
        .MarkerForegroundColorIndex = xlNone
        .MarkerStyle = xlNone
        .Smooth = False
    End With
    With Selection.Border
        If mcolor(am) < 0 Then
        .ColorIndex = 3
        Else
        .ColorIndex = 5
        End If
        .Weight = xlMedium
        .LineStyle = xlContinuous
    End With
am = am + 1
Next i

    ActiveChart.ChartArea.Select
    With ActiveChart
        .Axes(xlCategory, xlPrimary).HasTitle = True
        .Axes(xlCategory, xlPrimary).AxisTitle.Characters.Text = _
        "Max Shear, M." & At_member & " = " & Format(Smax, "0.000")
    End With

End Sub
```

```vba
Sub PlotSoilPressure()
On Error Resume Next

Dim Cx1, Cx2, Cy1, Cy2
Dim Cmx1, Cmx2, Cmy1, Cmy2
Dim Sp As Double
ReDim mxVal(NM) As Variant
ReDim myVal(NM) As Variant
ReDim spxVal(NM) As Variant
ReDim spyVal(NM) As Variant

ReDim spjxVal(NM + NM) As Variant
ReDim spjyVal(NM + NM) As Variant
ReDim mcolor(NM + NM) As Variant

Dim Spmax As Double, At_joint As Integer, am As Integer, L_I As Integer, L_II As Integer

    ActiveSheet.ChartObjects("Chart 5").Activate
    ActiveChart.ChartArea.Select
    Selection.ClearContents

Spmax = Application.index(USPMax(Pmm, Fm, NM), 1)
At_joint = Application.index(USPMax(Pmm, Fm, NM), 2)

For i = 1 To NM
   With Member(i)
        Cx1 = Joint(.J1).x
        Cy1 = Joint(.J1).y
        Cx2 = Joint(.J2).x
        Cy2 = Joint(.J2).y
        'assign coordinates
        Cmx1 = Cx1 + .Cy * Joint(.J1).Sp
        Cmy1 = Cy1 + .Cx * Joint(.J1).Sp
        Cmx2 = Cx2 + .Cy * Joint(.J2).Sp
        Cmy2 = Cy2 + .Cx * Joint(.J2).Sp
   End With
'member coordinates
```

An Introduction to Excel for Civil Engineers

```vb
            mxVal(i) = Array(Cx1, Cx2)
            myVal(i) = Array(Cy1, Cy2)
'soil pressure coordinates
            spxVal(i) = Array(Cmx1, Cmx2)
            spyVal(i) = Array(Cmy1, Cmy2)
'member-joint coordinates
            spjxVal(2 * i - 1) = Array(Cx1, Cmx1)
            spjyVal(2 * i - 1) = Array(Cy1, Cmy1)
            'mcolor: define color for positive/negative value
            mcolor(2 * i - 1) = Sp
            spjxVal(2 * i) = Array(Cx2, Cmx2)
            spjyVal(2 * i) = Array(Cy2, Cmy2)
            mcolor(2 * i) = Sp
Next i

'creating member lines
For i = 1 To NM
    With ActiveChart
        .SeriesCollection.NewSeries
        .SeriesCollection(i).XValues = mxVal(i)
        .SeriesCollection(i).Values = myVal(i)
        .SeriesCollection(i).Name = "="""""
    End With
    ActiveChart.SeriesCollection(i).Select
    With Selection
        .MarkerBackgroundColorIndex = xlNone
        .MarkerForegroundColorIndex = xlNone
        .MarkerStyle = xlNone
        .Smooth = False
    End With
    With Selection.Border
        .ColorIndex = 5
        .Weight = xlThin
        .LineStyle = xlContinuous
    End With
Next i
```

```
L_I = NM + NM
am = 1
'creating soil pressure lines
For i = NM + 1 To L_I
    With ActiveChart
        .SeriesCollection.NewSeries
        .SeriesCollection(i).XValues = spxVal(am)
        .SeriesCollection(i).Values = spyVal(am)
        .SeriesCollection(i).Name = "="""""
    End With
    ActiveChart.SeriesCollection(i).Select
    With Selection
        .MarkerBackgroundColorIndex = xlNone
        .MarkerForegroundColorIndex = xlNone
        .MarkerStyle = xlNone
        .Smooth = False
    End With
    With Selection.Border
        .ColorIndex = 7
        .Weight = xlThin
        .LineStyle = xlContinuous
    End With
am = am + 1
Next i

L_II = NM + NM + NM + NM
am = 1
'creating joint lines to axis
For i = L_I + 1 To L_II
    With ActiveChart
        .SeriesCollection.NewSeries
        .SeriesCollection(i).XValues = spjxVal(am)
        .SeriesCollection(i).Values = spjyVal(am)
        .SeriesCollection(i).Name = "="""""
    End With
    ActiveChart.SeriesCollection(i).Select
    With Selection
```

```
                .MarkerBackgroundColorIndex = xlNone
                .MarkerForegroundColorIndex = xlNone
                .MarkerStyle = xlNone
                .Smooth = False
        End With
        With Selection.Border
                If mcolor(am) < 0 Then
                .ColorIndex = 3
                Else
                .ColorIndex = 5
                End If
                .Weight = xlMedium
                .LineStyle = xlContinuous
        End With
am = am + 1
Next i

        ActiveChart.ChartArea.Select
        With ActiveChart
                .Axes(xlCategory, xlPrimary).HasTitle = True
                .Axes(xlCategory, xlPrimary).AxisTitle.Characters.Text = _
                "Max Pressure, J." & At_joint & " = " & Format(Spmax, "0.000")
        End With

End Sub

'user function to determine maximum value of joint translation
Function UXMax(Xs, NP) As Variant

Dim Abs_FXMax As Double
Dim FXMax As Double

Abs_FXMax = 0
n = 0
For i = 2 To NP Step 2
    If Abs(Xs(i)) > Abs_FXMax Then
        Abs_FXMax = Abs(Xs(i))
```

```
            FXMax = Xs(i)
            n = i / 2
            'UXMax keeps origin value(+ or - value)
            UXMax = Array(FXMax, n)
        End If
Next i

End Function


'user function to determine maximum value of member moment
Function UMMax(Pmm, Fm, NM) As Variant

Dim Abs_FMMax As Double
Dim FMMax As Double

Abs_FMMax = 0
n = 0
For i = 1 To NM
    If Abs(mmomen1(i)) > Abs_FMMax Then
        Abs_FMMax = Abs(mmomen1(i))
        FMMax = mmomen1(i)
        n = Member(i).J1
        UMMax = Array(FMMax, n)
    End If
    If Abs(mmomen2(i)) > Abs_FMMax Then
        Abs_FMMax = Abs(mmomen2(i))
        FMMax = -mmomen2(i)
        n = Member(i).J2
        UMMax = Array(FMMax, n)
    End If
Next i

End Function


'user function to determine maximum shear force
Function USMax(Pmm, Fm, NM) As Variant
```

```
Dim Abs_FSMax As Double
Dim FSMax As Double

Abs_FSMax = 0
n = 0
For i = 1 To NM
    If Abs(shear1(i)) > Abs_FSMax Then
        Abs_FSMax = Abs(shear1(i))
        FSMax = -shear1(i)
        n = i
        USMax = Array(FSMax, n)
    End If
    If Abs(shear2(i)) > Abs_FSMax Then
        Abs_FSMax = Abs(shear2(i))
        FSMax = shear2(i)
        n = i
        USMax = Array(FSMax, n)
    End If
Next i

End Function

'user function to determine maximum soil pressure
Function USPMax(Pmm, Fm, NM) As Variant

Dim Sp As Double
Dim Abs_FSPMax As Double
Dim FSPMax As Double

Abs_FSPMax = 0
n = 0
For i = 1 To NJ
    Sp = Joint(i).Ks * Xs(2 * i)
    If Abs(Sp) > Abs_FSPMax Then
        Abs_FSPMax = Abs(Sp)
        FSPMax = Sp
        n = i
```

```
        USPMax = Array(FSPMax, n)
    End If
Next i
End Function
```

Command Button (BOF)

```
Private Sub CommandButton1_Click()
ChartWindow = True
    Call BOF
End Sub


Private Sub CommandButton2_Click()
ChartWindow = False
    Call BOF
End Sub
```

Module1 (XLAT)

```
'=========================================================
'XLAT v.1.0 Program for Laterally Loaded Structure, 2004
'by: Gunthar Pangaribuan - Refer to the book:
'An Introduction to Excel for Civil Engineers
'=========================================================

Option Explicit

Public i As Integer, j As Integer, n As Integer

Type Joint_Data
    x As Double
    y As Double
    Ks As Double
    Spring As Double
    Sp As Double
End Type
```

```
Type Member_Data
    J1 As Integer
    J2 As Integer
    Im As Double
    bm As Double
    EI As Double
    lx As Double
    ly As Double
    Lh As Double
    Km1 As Double
    Km2 As Double
    Pres1 As Double
    Pres2 As Double
End Type

Public ChartWindow As Boolean
Public NP As Integer
Public DOF As Integer
Public NR As Integer
Public NJ As Integer
Public NM As Integer
Public Member() As Member_Data
Public Joint() As Joint_Data
Public Em As Double
Public Km() As Double
Public NS As Integer 'no. of supports
Public GASAT() As Double 'global stiffness matrix
Public Rs() As Integer
Public DFR() As Double
Public Idm() As Integer
Public Idj() As Integer
Public Irj() As Integer
Public Psum() As Double
Public Pmm() As Double
Public Pj() As Double
Public Xs() As Double
```

```
Public Xm() As Double
Public Fm() As Double
Public mmomen1() As Double
Public mmomen2() As Double
Public shear1() As Double
Public shear2() As Double

Sub XLAT()
On Error GoTo ErrMsg

Const NDJ = 2
Dim NLJ As Integer 'no of joint loads
Dim Jground As Integer 'excavation point

NJ = Cells(4, 2)
NM = Cells(5, 2)
Em = Cells(6, 2)
Jground = Cells(4, 5)

NS = Application.Count(Rows("23:23"))
NLJ = Application.Count(Rows("28:28"))
'Total number of joint displacements, NP:
NP = NDJ * NJ

ReDim Joint(NJ) As Joint_Data
ReDim Member(NM) As Member_Data
ReDim ESAT(4, 4, NM) As Double 'member matrix refer to the book
ReDim EASAT(4, 4, NM) As Double 'member matrix refer to the book
ReDim GASAT(NP, NP) 'global stiffness matrix refer to the book
ReDim Idm(4, NM) 'displacement index
ReDim Pj(NP) 'joint load vector

ReDim Pmm(NP, NM) 'fixed-end forces
ReDim Psum(NP) 'sum load vector
ReDim Xs(NP) 'joint displacement vector
ReDim Xm(4, NM) 'member deformations
ReDim Fm(4, NM) 'member forces
```

```
ReDim mmomen1(NM)
ReDim mmomen2(NM)
ReDim shear1(NM)
ReDim shear2(NM)
ReDim Rs(NP)
ReDim spn(NS) As Integer
Dim mshear As Double

'===============
'Read Input Data
'===============

'Read joint data - in order
For i = 1 To NJ
    With Joint(i)
        .x = Cells(10, 1 + i)
        .y = Cells(11, 1 + i)
        .Ks = Cells(12, 1 + i)
        .Spring = Cells(13, 1 + i)
        .Sp = .Ks * Xs(2 * i) 'soil pressure
    End With
Next i

'Read member data
For i = 1 To NM
    With Member(i)
    .J1 = Cells(16, 1 + i)
    .J2 = Cells(17, 1 + i)
    .Im = Cells(18, 1 + i)
    .bm = Cells(19, 1 + i)
    .EI = Em * .Im
    .lx = Joint(.J2).x - Joint(.J1).x
    .ly = Joint(.J2).y - Joint(.J1).y
    .Lh = Sqr(.lx ^ 2 + .ly ^ 2)
    .Pres1 = Cells(20, 1 + i)
    .Pres2 = Cells(21, 1 + i)
```

```
        .Km1 = 0.5 * .Lh * .bm * Joint(.J1).Ks + Joint(.J1).Spring
        .Km2 = 0.5 * .Lh * .bm * Joint(.J2).Ks
     End With
Next i

If ChartWindow = True Then Call PlotGeometry: Exit Sub
Application.ScreenUpdating = False

'Read joint loads
For i = 1 To NLJ
   n = Cells(28, 1 + i)
   Pj(2 * n - 1) = Cells(29, 1 + i)
   Pj(2 * n) = Cells(30, 1 + i)
Next i


'restraint list and support (Rs) index
For i = 1 To NS
    spn(i) = Cells(23, 1 + i)
    Rs(2 * spn(i) - 1) = Cells(24, 1 + i)
    Rs(2 * spn(i)) = Cells(25, 1 + i)
Next i

DOF = 0
For i = 1 To NP
    If Rs(i) = 0 Then DOF = DOF + 1
Next i

'#restrained joints
NR = NP - DOF

ReDim DFX(NDJ * NS, DOF) As Double '[Kbf]according to Eq. 4.12
ReDim DFR(DOF, DOF) As Double '[Kff]^-1 according to Eq. 4.9
ReDim RJ(NDJ * NS) As Double 'support reactions
ReDim Idj(DOF) 'free displacement index
ReDim Irj(NDJ * NS) 'support displacement index
ReDim nAs_Now(NJ) As Integer
Dim nAs_Last As Integer
```

```
Dim Ksn As Integer
Dim ITR As Integer
Dim ITR_Continue As Boolean
ITR_Continue = True
ITR = 1

'clear previous content
Dim LastRow
LastRow = ActiveSheet.UsedRange.Rows.Count
Range(Cells(38, 1), Cells(LastRow, 18)).ClearContents

'==================
'Structure Analysis
'==================
Do

Call Mindex(Idm, Idj, Irj)
Call FEM(ESAT, EASAT, GASAT)
Call MInvers(DFX, DFR)
Call Genload(Pmm, Psum)
Call DISP(Xs, Xm)

    'Print used springs
    For i = 1 To NM
        With Member(i)
            Cells(37 + i, 8).NumberFormat = "0.000"
            Cells(37 + i, 8) = .Km1
            Cells(37 + i, 9).NumberFormat = "0.000"
            Cells(37 + i, 9) = .Km2
        End With
    Next i

    n = 0
    For i = 1 To Jground - 1
    're-input joint's Ks and Sp if Xs > 0
        With Joint(i)
            If Xs(i * 2) > 0 Then
```

```
                .Ks = 0
                .Sp = .Ks * Xs(2 * i)
                n = n + 1
            End If
        End With
    Next i
    
    're-input member's soil K
    For i = 1 To NM
        With Member(i)
        .Km1 = 0.5 * .Lh * .bm * Joint(.J1).Ks + Joint(.J1).Spring
        .Km2 = 0.5 * .Lh * .bm * Joint(.J2).Ks
        End With
    Next i
    
    'check no. of active spring between 2 iterations
    nAs_Now(ITR) = NJ - n
    nAs_Last = nAs_Now(ITR - 1)
    
    If nAs_Now(ITR) = nAs_Last Or n = 0 Then
        ITR_Continue = False
        Cells(34, 3) = ITR - 1
        Cells(35, 3) = nAs_Now(ITR)
        Ksn = nAs_Now(ITR)
    End If
    
    ITR = ITR + 1

Loop Until ITR_Continue = False

'============
'Print Result
'============

'1.Print Loads
For i = 1 To NJ
    Cells(37 + i, 1).NumberFormat = "0"
```

```vb
        Cells(37 + i, 1) = i
        Cells(37 + i, 2).NumberFormat = "0.000"
        Cells(37 + i, 2) = Psum(2 * i - 1)
        Cells(37 + i, 3).NumberFormat = "0.000"
        Cells(37 + i, 3) = Psum(2 * i)
    Next i
    
    '2. Print Joint displacements and pressures
    For i = 1 To NJ
        Cells(37 + i, 4).NumberFormat = "0.00000"
        Cells(37 + i, 4) = Xs(2 * i - 1)
        Cells(37 + i, 5).NumberFormat = "0.00000"
        Cells(37 + i, 5) = Xs(2 * i)
        Cells(37 + i, 6).NumberFormat = "0.000"
        With Joint(i)
        .Sp = .Ks * Xs(2 * i)
        Cells(37 + i, 6) = .Sp
        End With
    Next i
    
    '-------------
    'Member Forces
    '-------------
    '{F}m=[S]m.{X}m or [F]m=[S].[A]T.[X]s
    'there is already calculated S.A^T,
    ReDim tshear(4, NM)
    
    'produce moments + soil pressures
    For i = 1 To NM
        For j = 1 To 4
        Fm(j, i) = 0
            For n = 1 To 4
                Fm(j, i) = Fm(j, i) + ESAT(j, n, i) * Xm(n, i)
            Next n
        Next j
    Next i
```

```vb
'Print member data
For i = 1 To NM
    With Member(i)
        'no/length
        Cells(37 + i, 7).NumberFormat = "0"
        Cells(37 + i, 7) = i & "./" & Format(.Lh, "0.00")
        'moment
        mmomen1(i) = Fm(1, i) + Pmm(Idm(1, i), i)
        Cells(37 + i, 10).NumberFormat = "0.000"
        Cells(37 + i, 10) = mmomen1(i)
        mmomen2(i) = Fm(2, i) + Pmm(Idm(3, i), i)
        Cells(37 + i, 11).NumberFormat = "0.000"
        Cells(37 + i, 11) = mmomen2(i)
        'spring
        Cells(37 + i, 12).NumberFormat = "0.000"
        Cells(37 + i, 12) = Fm(3, i)
        Cells(37 + i, 13).NumberFormat = "0.000"
        Cells(37 + i, 13) = Fm(4, i)
        'shear
        mshear = (Fm(1, i) + Fm(2, i)) / .Lh
        shear1(i) = mshear
        shear2(i) = -mshear
        Cells(37 + i, 14).NumberFormat = "0.000"
        Cells(37 + i, 14) = shear1(i)
        Cells(37 + i, 15).NumberFormat = "0.000"
        Cells(37 + i, 15) = shear2(i)
    End With
Next i


'-----------------
'Support Reactions
'-----------------
For i = 1 To 2 * NS
    For j = 1 To DOF
        RJ(i) = RJ(i) + DFX(i, j) * Xs(Idj(j))
    Next j
Next i
```

```
For i = 1 To NS
    Cells(37 + i, 16).NumberFormat = "0"
    Cells(37 + i, 16) = spn(i)
    Cells(37 + i, 17).NumberFormat = "0.000"
    Cells(37 + i, 17) = RJ(2 * i - 1) - Psum(Irj(2 * i - 1))
    Cells(37 + i, 18).NumberFormat = "0.000"
    Cells(37 + i, 18) = RJ(2 * i) - Psum(Irj(2 * i))
Next i

'draw charts
Call PlotGeometry
Call PlotDisplacement
Call PlotMoment
Call PlotShear
Call PlotLoad

Range("A1").Select
Application.ScreenUpdating = True
Exit Sub

ErrMsg: MsgBox "Error, please check input ...", vbOKOnly + vbExclamation, "XLAT"

Range("A1").Select
Application.ScreenUpdating = True

End Sub
```

Module2 (XLAT)

```
Option Explicit

'Indexing for matrix subscript
Sub Mindex(index() As Integer, IFr() As Integer, IFx() As Integer)

'Member end-displacement indexes:
```

```
For i = 1 To NM
    With Member(i)
    index(1, i) = 2 * .J1 - 1
    index(2, i) = 2 * .J1
    index(3, i) = 2 * .J2 - 1
    index(4, i) = 2 * .J2
    End With
Next i


'Joint free displacement index, IFr and
'restraint (support) index, IFx
n = 1
For i = 1 To NP
    If Rs(i) = 0 Then IFr(n) = i: n = n + 1
Next i


n = 1
For i = 1 To NS
    n = Cells(23, 1 + i)
    IFx(2 * i - 1) = 2 * n - 1
    IFx(2 * i) = 2 * n
Next i


End Sub


Sub FEM(SAT() As Double, ASAT() As Double, GS() As Double)


'Clearing array
For i = 1 To NP
    For j = 1 To NP
        GS(i, j) = 0#
    Next j
Next i


'Assembly of finite element matrix, Eq.4.16 & 4.17
For i = 1 To NM
    With Member(i)
```

```
    'member SA^T matrix:
    'from internal forces F - deformations d relationship, F = S.d or F =
S.A^T.X
        SAT(1, 1, i) = 4 * .EI / .Lh: SAT(1, 2, i) = 6 * .EI / .Lh ^ 2
        SAT(1, 3, i) = 2 * .EI / .Lh: SAT(1, 4, i) = -6 * .EI / .Lh ^ 2
        SAT(2, 1, i) = 2 * .EI / .Lh: SAT(2, 2, i) = 6 * .EI / .Lh ^ 2
        SAT(2, 3, i) = 4 * .EI / .Lh: SAT(2, 4, i) = -6 * .EI / .Lh ^ 2
        SAT(3, 2, i) = .Km1
        SAT(4, 4, i) = .Km2
    'Member global stiffness (member ASA^T)
        ASAT(1, 1, i) = 4 * .EI / .Lh: ASAT(1, 2, i) = 6 * .EI / .Lh ^ 2
        ASAT(1, 3, i) = 2 * .EI / .Lh: ASAT(1, 4, i) = -6 * .EI / .Lh ^ 2
        ASAT(2, 1, i) = 6 * .EI / .Lh ^ 2: ASAT(2, 2, i) = 12 * .EI / .Lh ^ 3 +
.Km1
        ASAT(2, 3, i) = 6 * .EI / .Lh ^ 2: ASAT(2, 4, i) = -12 * .EI / .Lh ^ 3
        ASAT(3, 1, i) = 2 * .EI / .Lh: ASAT(3, 2, i) = 6 * .EI / .Lh ^ 2
        ASAT(3, 3, i) = 4 * .EI / .Lh: ASAT(3, 4, i) = -6 * .EI / .Lh ^ 2
        ASAT(4, 1, i) = -6 * .EI / .Lh ^ 2: ASAT(4, 2, i) = -12 * .EI / .Lh ^ 3
        ASAT(4, 3, i) = -6 * .EI / .Lh ^ 2: ASAT(4, 4, i) = 12 * .EI / .Lh ^ 3 +
.Km2
    'Storing members and superposition(global ASA^T)
    For j = 1 To 4
        For n = 1 To 4
            GS(Idm(j, i), Idm(n, i)) = GS(Idm(j, i), Idm(n, i)) + ASAT(j, n,
i)
        Next n
    Next j
    End With
Next i

End Sub
'Global matrix
Sub MInvers(SR() As Double, SD() As Double)
Dim n As Integer

'submatrix Stiffness, KBF
For i = 1 To DOF
    For j = 1 To 2 * NS
        SR(j, i) = GASAT(Irj(j), Idj(i))
```

```
            Next j
Next i


'submatrix Stiffness, KFF
For i = 1 To DOF
    For j = 1 To DOF
        SD(i, j) = GASAT(Idj(i), Idj(j))
    Next j
Next i


'Inverse []
   For i = 1 To DOF
     For j = 1 To DOF
         If j <> i Then SD(i, j) = SD(i, j) / SD(i, i)
     Next j
     For n = 1 To DOF
         If n = i Then GoTo 10
         For j = 1 To DOF
             If j <> i Then SD(n, j) = SD(n, j) - SD(i, j) * SD(n, i)
         Next j
10   Next n
     For n = 1 To DOF
         If n <> i Then SD(n, i) = -SD(n, i) / SD(i, i)
     Next n
     SD(i, i) = 1 / SD(i, i)
   Next i


End Sub
Sub Genload(Pa() As Double, Ps() As Double)
ReDim Peq(NP, NM) As Double 'equivalent loads
Dim Idx As Integer, w As Double, d As Double, sq As Double


'member fixed-end forces due to pressures
For i = 1 To NM
    With Member(i)
    d = Abs(.Pres1 - .Pres2)
    sq = Application.Min(.Pres1, .Pres2)
```

```vb
        'rectangular part
        w = sq * .bm
        Pa(Idm(1, i), i) = -w * .Lh ^ 2 / 12 'moment
        Pa(Idm(2, i), i) = -w * .Lh / 2 'horizontal
        Pa(Idm(3, i), i) = w * .Lh ^ 2 / 12 'moment
        Pa(Idm(4, i), i) = -w * .Lh / 2 'horizontal
        'triangular part & summing
        w = d * .bm
        Pa(Idm(1, i), i) = Pa(Idm(1, i), i) + (-w * .Lh ^ 2 / 30) 'moment
        Pa(Idm(2, i), i) = Pa(Idm(2, i), i) + (-w * .Lh * 3 / 20) 'horizontal
        Pa(Idm(3, i), i) = Pa(Idm(3, i), i) + (w * .Lh ^ 2 / 20) 'moment
        Pa(Idm(4, i), i) = Pa(Idm(4, i), i) + (-w * .Lh * 7 / 20) 'horizontal
    End With
Next i

'equivalent joint loads due to pressures
For i = 1 To NM
    For j = 1 To 4
        For n = 1 To 4
            Peq(Idm(j, i), i) = -Pa(Idm(j, i), i)
        Next n
     Next j
Next i

'sum loads = joint loads + eq.loads
For i = 1 To NP
    Ps(i) = Pj(i)
Next i

'load superposition
For i = 1 To NM
    For j = 1 To 4
        Ps(Idm(j, i)) = Ps(Idm(j, i)) + Peq(Idm(j, i), i)
    Next j
Next i

End Sub
```

```
Sub DISP(x() As Double, Xi() As Double)
ReDim T(4, 4, NM) As Double

'Joint Displacements {X} = [SD]^-1.{P}
For i = 1 To DOF
x(Idj(i)) = 0
    For j = 1 To DOF
        x(Idj(i)) = x(Idj(i)) + DFR(i, j) * Psum(Idj(j))
    Next j
Next i

'Numbering of global {X}(NP) to global {Xi} member
For i = 1 To NM
    For j = 1 To 4
        Xi(j, i) = x(Idm(j, i))
    Next j
Next i

End Sub
```

Module3 (XLAT)

```
Option Explicit
Option Base 1
Sub PlotGeometry()
On Error Resume Next

Dim Cx1, Cx2, Cy1, Cy2
Dim Cmx1, Cmx2, Cmy1, Cmy2

ReDim mxVal(NM) As Variant
ReDim myVal(NM) As Variant
ReDim tagxVal(NM) As Variant
ReDim tagyVal(NM) As Variant
```

```
Dim am As Integer, L_I As Integer, L_II As Integer, L_III As Integer, L_IV As
Integer
Dim L_V As Integer, L_VI As Integer, L_VII As Integer, L_VIII As Integer


'member coordinates
For i = 1 To NM
    With Member(i)
        Cx1 = Joint(.J1).x
        Cy1 = Joint(.J1).y
        Cx2 = Joint(.J2).x
        Cy2 = Joint(.J2).y
    End With
        mxVal(i) = Array(Cx1, Cx2)
        myVal(i) = Array(Cy1, Cy2)
        tagxVal(i) = Array((Cx1 + Cx2) / 2)
        tagyVal(i) = Array((Cy1 + Cy2) / 2)
Next i


    ActiveSheet.ChartObjects("Chart 1").Activate
    ActiveChart.ChartArea.Select
    Selection.ClearContents


'creating joints + name tags
For i = 1 To NJ
    With ActiveChart
        .SeriesCollection.NewSeries
        .SeriesCollection(i).XValues = Joint(i).x
        .SeriesCollection(i).Values = Joint(i).y
        .SeriesCollection(i).Name = "J" & i
    End With
    'node marker
    ActiveChart.PlotArea.Select
    ActiveChart.SeriesCollection(i).Select
    With Selection
        .MarkerBackgroundColorIndex = 3 'red
        .MarkerForegroundColorIndex = 3
        .MarkerStyle = xlCircle
        .MarkerSize = 6
```

```
            .Shadow = False
            .ApplyDataLabels AutoText:=True, LegendKey:= _
            False,      ShowSeriesName:=True,      ShowCategoryName:=False,
ShowValue:=False, _
            ShowPercentage:=False, ShowBubbleSize:=False
        End With

        ActiveChart.SeriesCollection(i).DataLabels.Select
        With Selection
            .HorizontalAlignment = xlCenter
            .VerticalAlignment = xlCenter
            .ReadingOrder = xlContext
            .Position = xlLabelPositionRight
            .Orientation = xlHorizontal
            .Font.Name = "Arial"
            .Font.FontStyle = "Regular"
            .Font.Size = 8
        End With
Next i

    ActiveSheet.ChartObjects("Chart 1").Activate
    ActiveChart.ChartArea.Select

    L_I = NJ + 1
    L_II = NJ + NM
am = 1
'creating member lines
For i = L_I To L_II
    With ActiveChart
        .SeriesCollection.NewSeries
        .SeriesCollection(i).XValues = mxVal(am)
        .SeriesCollection(i).Values = myVal(am)
        .SeriesCollection(i).Name = "="""""
    End With
    ActiveChart.SeriesCollection(i).Select
    With Selection
        .MarkerBackgroundColorIndex = xlNone
        .MarkerForegroundColorIndex = xlNone
```

```
            .MarkerStyle = xlNone
            .Smooth = False
        End With
        With Selection.Border
            .ColorIndex = 5
            .Weight = xlThin
            .LineStyle = xlContinuous
        End With
am = am + 1
Next i

L_III = L_II + 1
L_IV = L_II + NM
'creating member name tags
am = 1
For i = L_III To L_IV
    With ActiveChart
        .SeriesCollection.NewSeries
        .SeriesCollection(i).XValues = tagxVal(am)
        .SeriesCollection(i).Values = tagyVal(am)
        .SeriesCollection(i).Name = "M" & am
    End With
    ActiveChart.PlotArea.Select
    ActiveChart.SeriesCollection(i).Select
    With Selection
        .MarkerBackgroundColorIndex = 5
        .MarkerForegroundColorIndex = 5
        .MarkerStyle = xlSquare
        .Smooth = False
        .MarkerSize = 6
        .Shadow = False
        .ApplyDataLabels AutoText:=True, LegendKey:= _
        False,        ShowSeriesName:=True,        ShowCategoryName:=False,
ShowValue:=False, _
        ShowPercentage:=False, ShowBubbleSize:=False
    End With
    ActiveChart.SeriesCollection(i).DataLabels.Select
    With Selection
```

An Introduction to Excel for Civil Engineers

```vba
            .HorizontalAlignment = xlCenter
            .VerticalAlignment = xlCenter
            .Position = xlLabelPositionRight
            .Orientation = xlHorizontal
            .Font.Name = "Arial"
            .Font.FontStyle = "Regular"
            .Font.Size = 8
        End With
am = am + 1
Next i

    ActiveChart.ChartArea.Select
    With ActiveChart
        .Axes(xlCategory, xlPrimary).HasTitle = True
        .Axes(xlCategory, xlPrimary).AxisTitle.Characters.Text = _
        "NJ = " & Format(NJ, "0") & ", NM = " & Format(NM, "0")
    End With


'Draw pressure
ReDim pxVal(NM) As Variant
ReDim pyVal(NM) As Variant
ReDim pjxVal(NM + NM) As Variant
ReDim pjyVal(NM + NM) As Variant


For i = 1 To NM
    With Member(i)
        Cx1 = Joint(.J1).x
        Cy1 = Joint(.J1).y
        Cx2 = Joint(.J2).x
        Cy2 = Joint(.J2).y
        'assign coordinates
        Cmx1 = Cx1 + .Pres1
        Cmy1 = Cy1
        Cmx2 = Cx2 + .Pres2
        Cmy2 = Cy2
    End With
```

```
'pressure coordinates
        pxVal(i) = Array(Cmx1, Cmx2)
        pyVal(i) = Array(Cmy1, Cmy2)
'member-joint coordinates
        pjxVal(2 * i - 1) = Array(Cx1, Cmx1)
        pjyVal(2 * i - 1) = Array(Cy1, Cmy1)
        pjxVal(2 * i) = Array(Cx2, Cmx2)
        pjyVal(2 * i) = Array(Cy2, Cmy2)
Next i

L_V = L_IV + 1
L_VI = L_IV + NM

am = 1
'creating pressure lines
For i = L_V To L_VI
    With ActiveChart
        .SeriesCollection.NewSeries
        .SeriesCollection(i).XValues = pxVal(am)
        .SeriesCollection(i).Values = pyVal(am)
        .SeriesCollection(i).Name = "="""""
    End With
    ActiveChart.SeriesCollection(i).Select
    With Selection
        .MarkerBackgroundColorIndex = xlNone
        .MarkerForegroundColorIndex = xlNone
        .MarkerStyle = xlNone
        .Smooth = False
    End With
    With Selection.Border
        .ColorIndex = 7
        .Weight = xlThin
        .LineStyle = xlContinuous
    End With
am = am + 1
Next i
```

```vba
L_VII = L_VI + 1
L_VIII = L_VI + NM + NM

am = 1
'creating joint lines to axis
For i = L_VII To L_VIII
    With ActiveChart
        .SeriesCollection.NewSeries
        .SeriesCollection(i).XValues = pjxVal(am)
        .SeriesCollection(i).Values = pjyVal(am)
        .SeriesCollection(i).Name = "="""""
    End With
    ActiveChart.SeriesCollection(i).Select
    With Selection
        .MarkerBackgroundColorIndex = xlNone
        .MarkerForegroundColorIndex = xlNone
        .MarkerStyle = xlNone
        .Smooth = False
    End With
    With Selection.Border
        .ColorIndex = 5
        .Weight = xlMedium
        .LineStyle = xlContinuous
    End With
am = am + 1
Next i

ActiveChart.ShowWindow = True

End Sub

Sub PlotDisplacement()
On Error Resume Next

Dim Cx1, Cx2, Cy1, Cy2
ReDim mxValbf(NM) As Variant, myValbf(NM) As Variant
ReDim mxValaf(NM) As Variant, myValaf(NM) As Variant
```

```vba
Dim Xmax As Double, At_joint As Integer, am As Integer

    ActiveSheet.ChartObjects("Chart 2").Activate
    ActiveChart.ChartArea.Select
    Selection.ClearContents

Xmax = Application.index(UXMax(Xs, NP), 1)
At_joint = Application.index(UXMax(Xs, NP), 2)

'member coordinates: before & after loading
For i = 1 To NM
    With Member(i)
        Cx1 = Joint(.J1).x
        Cy1 = Joint(.J1).y
        Cx2 = Joint(.J2).x
        Cy2 = Joint(.J2).y
    mxValbf(i) = Array(Cx1, Cx2)
    myValbf(i) = Array(Cy1, Cy2)
        Cx1 = Joint(.J1).x + Xs(2 * .J1)
        Cy1 = Joint(.J1).y + Xs(2 * .J1)
        Cx2 = Joint(.J2).x + Xs(2 * .J2)
        Cy2 = Joint(.J2).y + Xs(2 * .J2)
    mxValaf(i) = Array(Cx1, Cx2)
    myValaf(i) = Array(Cy1, Cy2)
    End With
Next i

    am = 1
    'creating member lines: before loading
    For i = 1 To NM
        With ActiveChart
            .SeriesCollection.NewSeries
            .SeriesCollection(i).XValues = mxValbf(am)
            .SeriesCollection(i).Values = myValbf(am)
            .SeriesCollection(i).Name = "="""""
        End With
```

```vba
        ActiveChart.SeriesCollection(i).Select
        With Selection
            .MarkerStyle = xlNone
            .Smooth = False
        End With
        With Selection.Border
            .ColorIndex = 5
            .Weight = xlMedium
            .LineStyle = xlContinuous
        End With
    am = am + 1
    Next i

    n = NM + NM
    am = 1
    'creating member lines: after loading
    For i = NM + 1 To n
        With ActiveChart
            .SeriesCollection.NewSeries
            .SeriesCollection(i).XValues = mxValaf(am)
            .SeriesCollection(i).Values = myValaf(am)
            .SeriesCollection(i).Name = "="""""
        End With
        ActiveChart.SeriesCollection(i).Select
        With Selection
            .MarkerStyle = xlNone
            .Smooth = False
        End With
        With Selection.Border
            .ColorIndex = 7
            .Weight = xlMedium
            .LineStyle = xlContinuous
        End With
    am = am + 1
    Next i

    ActiveChart.ChartArea.Select
```

```
    With ActiveChart
        .Axes(xlCategory, xlPrimary).HasTitle = True
        .Axes(xlCategory, xlPrimary).AxisTitle.Characters.Text = _
        "Max Displacement,  J." & At_joint & " = " & Format(Xmax, "0.00000")
    End With

End Sub

Sub PlotMoment()
On Error Resume Next

Dim Cx1, Cx2, Cy1, Cy2
Dim Cmx1, Cmx2, Cmy1, Cmy2
ReDim mxVal(NM) As Variant
ReDim myVal(NM) As Variant
ReDim moxVal(NM) As Variant
ReDim moyVal(NM) As Variant
ReDim tagxVal(NM) As Variant
ReDim tagyVal(NM) As Variant

ReDim mjxVal(NM + NM) As Variant
ReDim mjyVal(NM + NM) As Variant
ReDim mcolor(NM + NM) As Variant

Dim Mmax As Single, At_joint As Integer, am As Integer, L_I As Integer, L_II As Integer, _
L_III As Integer, L_IV As Integer

    ActiveSheet.ChartObjects("Chart 3").Activate
    ActiveChart.ChartArea.Select
    Selection.ClearContents

Mmax = Application.index(UMMax(Pmm, Fm, NM), 1)
At_joint = Application.index(UMMax(Pmm, Fm, NM), 2)

For i = 1 To NM
    With Member(i)
        Cx1 = Joint(.J1).x
```

```
            Cy1 = Joint(.J1).y
            Cx2 = Joint(.J2).x
            Cy2 = Joint(.J2).y
            'assign coordinates
            Cmx1 = Cx1 + mmomen1(i)
            Cmy1 = Cy1
            Cmx2 = Cx2 - mmomen2(i)
            Cmy2 = Cy2
        End With
'member coordinates
        mxVal(i) = Array(Cx1, Cx2)
        myVal(i) = Array(Cy1, Cy2)
'moment coordinates
        moxVal(i) = Array(Cmx1, Cmx2)
        moyVal(i) = Array(Cmy1, Cmy2)
'member-joint coordinates
        mjxVal(2 * i - 1) = Array(Cx1, Cmx1)
        mjyVal(2 * i - 1) = Array(Cy1, Cmy1)
        'mcolor: define color for positive/negative value
        mcolor(2 * i - 1) = mmomen1(i)
        mjxVal(2 * i) = Array(Cx2, Cmx2)
        mjyVal(2 * i) = Array(Cy2, Cmy2)
        mcolor(2 * i) = mmomen2(i)
Next i

'creating member lines
For i = 1 To NM
    With ActiveChart
        .SeriesCollection.NewSeries
        .SeriesCollection(i).XValues = mxVal(i)
        .SeriesCollection(i).Values = myVal(i)
        .SeriesCollection(i).Name = "="""""
    End With
    ActiveChart.SeriesCollection(i).Select
    With Selection
        .MarkerBackgroundColorIndex = xlNone
        .MarkerForegroundColorIndex = xlNone
```

```
            .MarkerStyle = xlNone
            .Smooth = False
        End With
        With Selection.Border
            .ColorIndex = 5
            .Weight = xlThin
            .LineStyle = xlContinuous
        End With
Next i

L_I = NM + 1
L_II = NM + NM
am = 1
'creating moment lines
For i = L_I To L_II
    With ActiveChart
        .SeriesCollection.NewSeries
        .SeriesCollection(i).XValues = moxVal(am)
        .SeriesCollection(i).Values = moyVal(am)
        .SeriesCollection(i).Name = "="""""
    End With
    ActiveChart.SeriesCollection(i).Select
    With Selection
        .MarkerBackgroundColorIndex = xlNone
        .MarkerForegroundColorIndex = xlNone
        .MarkerStyle = xlNone
        .Smooth = False
    End With
    With Selection.Border
        .ColorIndex = 7
        .Weight = xlThin
        .LineStyle = xlContinuous
    End With
am = am + 1
Next i
```

```vba
L_III = L_II + 1
L_IV = L_II + NM + NM
am = 1
'creating joint lines to axis
For i = L_III To L_IV
    With ActiveChart
        .SeriesCollection.NewSeries
        .SeriesCollection(i).XValues = mjxVal(am)
        .SeriesCollection(i).Values = mjyVal(am)
        .SeriesCollection(i).Name = "="""""
    End With
    ActiveChart.SeriesCollection(i).Select
    With Selection
        .MarkerBackgroundColorIndex = xlNone
        .MarkerForegroundColorIndex = xlNone
        .MarkerStyle = xlNone
        .Smooth = False
    End With
    With Selection.Border
        If mcolor(am) < 0 Then
        .ColorIndex = 3
        Else
        .ColorIndex = 5
        End If
        .Weight = xlMedium
        .LineStyle = xlContinuous
    End With
am = am + 1

Next i

    ActiveChart.ChartArea.Select
    With ActiveChart
        .Axes(xlCategory, xlPrimary).HasTitle = True
        .Axes(xlCategory, xlPrimary).AxisTitle.Characters.Text = _
        "Max Moment, J." & At_joint & " = " & Format(Mmax, "0.000")
    End With
```

```
End Sub

Sub PlotShear()
On Error Resume Next

Dim Cx1, Cx2, Cy1, Cy2
Dim Cmx1, Cmx2, Cmy1, Cmy2
ReDim mxVal(NM) As Variant
ReDim myVal(NM) As Variant
ReDim tagxVal(NM) As Variant
ReDim tagyVal(NM) As Variant
ReDim shxval(NM) As Variant
ReDim shyval(NM) As Variant
ReDim sjxVal(NM + NM) As Variant
ReDim sjyVal(NM + NM) As Variant
ReDim mcolor(NM + NM) As Variant

Dim Smax As Double, At_member As Integer, am As Integer, L_I As Integer, _
L_II As Integer, L_III As Integer, L_IV As Integer

    ActiveSheet.ChartObjects("Chart 4").Activate
    ActiveChart.ChartArea.Select
    Selection.ClearContents

Smax = Application.index(USMax(Pmm, Fm, NM), 1)
At_member = Application.index(USMax(Pmm, Fm, NM), 2)

For i = 1 To NM
    With Member(i)
        Cx1 = Joint(.J1).x
        Cy1 = Joint(.J1).y
        Cx2 = Joint(.J2).x
        Cy2 = Joint(.J2).y
        'assign coordinates
        Cmx1 = Cx1 - shear1(i)
        Cmy1 = Cy1
```

```vba
            Cmx2 = Cx2 + shear2(i)
            Cmy2 = Cy2
        End With
'member coordinates
        mxVal(i) = Array(Cx1, Cx2)
        myVal(i) = Array(Cy1, Cy2)
'shear coordinates
        shxval(i) = Array(Cmx1, Cmx2)
        shyval(i) = Array(Cmy1, Cmy2)
'member-joint coordinates
        sjxVal(2 * i - 1) = Array(Cx1, Cmx1)
        sjyVal(2 * i - 1) = Array(Cy1, Cmy1)
        'mcolor: define color for positive/negative value
        mcolor(2 * i - 1) = -shear1(i)
        sjxVal(2 * i) = Array(Cx2, Cmx2)
        sjyVal(2 * i) = Array(Cy2, Cmy2)
        mcolor(2 * i) = shear2(i)
Next i

'creating member lines
For i = 1 To NM
    With ActiveChart
        .SeriesCollection.NewSeries
        .SeriesCollection(i).XValues = mxVal(i)
        .SeriesCollection(i).Values = myVal(i)
        .SeriesCollection(i).Name = "="""""
    End With
    ActiveChart.SeriesCollection(i).Select
    With Selection
        .MarkerBackgroundColorIndex = xlNone
        .MarkerForegroundColorIndex = xlNone
        .MarkerStyle = xlNone
        .Smooth = False
    End With
    With Selection.Border
        .ColorIndex = 5
        .Weight = xlThin
```

```
            .LineStyle = xlContinuous
        End With
Next i


L_I = NM + 1
L_II = NM + NM
am = 1
'creating shear lines
For i = L_I To L_II
    With ActiveChart
        .SeriesCollection.NewSeries
        .SeriesCollection(i).XValues = shxval(am)
        .SeriesCollection(i).Values = shyval(am)
        .SeriesCollection(i).Name = "="""""
    End With
    ActiveChart.SeriesCollection(i).Select
    With Selection
        .MarkerBackgroundColorIndex = xlNone
        .MarkerForegroundColorIndex = xlNone
        .MarkerStyle = xlNone
        .Smooth = False
    End With
    With Selection.Border
        .ColorIndex = 7
        .Weight = xlThin
        .LineStyle = xlContinuous
    End With
am = am + 1
Next i


L_III = L_II + 1
L_IV = L_II + NM + NM
am = 1
'creating joint lines to axis
For i = L_III To L_IV
    With ActiveChart
        .SeriesCollection.NewSeries
```

```
                .SeriesCollection(i).XValues = sjxVal(am)
                .SeriesCollection(i).Values = sjyVal(am)
                .SeriesCollection(i).Name = "="""""
        End With
        ActiveChart.SeriesCollection(i).Select
        With Selection
            .MarkerBackgroundColorIndex = xlNone
            .MarkerForegroundColorIndex = xlNone
            .MarkerStyle = xlNone
            .Smooth = False
        End With
        With Selection.Border
            If mcolor(am) < 0 Then
            .ColorIndex = 3
            Else
            .ColorIndex = 5
            End If
            .Weight = xlMedium
            .LineStyle = xlContinuous
        End With
am = am + 1
Next i

    ActiveChart.ChartArea.Select
    With ActiveChart
        .Axes(xlCategory, xlPrimary).HasTitle = True
        .Axes(xlCategory, xlPrimary).AxisTitle.Characters.Text = _
        "Max Shear, M." & At_member & " = " & Format(Smax, "0.000")
    End With

End Sub


Sub PlotLoad()
On Error Resume Next

Dim Cx1, Cx2, Cy1, Cy2
Dim Cmx1, Cmx2, Cmy1, Cmy2
```

```
ReDim mxVal(NM) As Variant
ReDim myVal(NM) As Variant
ReDim lxVal(NM) As Variant
ReDim lyVal(NM) As Variant

ReDim ljxVal(NM + NM) As Variant
ReDim ljyVal(NM + NM) As Variant
Dim am As Integer, L_I As Integer, L_II As Integer

    ActiveSheet.ChartObjects("Chart 5").Activate
    ActiveChart.ChartArea.Select
    Selection.ClearContents

For i = 1 To NM
    With Member(i)
        Cx1 = Joint(.J1).x
        Cy1 = Joint(.J1).y
        Cx2 = Joint(.J2).x
        Cy2 = Joint(.J2).y
        'assign coordinates
        Cmx1 = Cx1 + Psum(2 * .J1)
        Cmy1 = Cy1
        Cmx2 = Cx2 + Psum(2 * .J2)
        Cmy2 = Cy2
    End With
'member coordinates
        mxVal(i) = Array(Cx1, Cx2)
        myVal(i) = Array(Cy1, Cy2)
'load coordinates
        lxVal(i) = Array(Cmx1, Cmx2)
        lyVal(i) = Array(Cmy1, Cmy2)
'member-joint coordinates
        ljxVal(2 * i - 1) = Array(Cx1, Cmx1)
        ljyVal(2 * i - 1) = Array(Cy1, Cmy1)
        ljxVal(2 * i) = Array(Cx2, Cmx2)
        ljyVal(2 * i) = Array(Cy2, Cmy2)
Next i
```

```
'creating member lines
For i = 1 To NM
    With ActiveChart
        .SeriesCollection.NewSeries
        .SeriesCollection(i).XValues = mxVal(i)
        .SeriesCollection(i).Values = myVal(i)
        .SeriesCollection(i).Name = "="""""
    End With
    ActiveChart.SeriesCollection(i).Select
    With Selection
        .MarkerBackgroundColorIndex = xlNone
        .MarkerForegroundColorIndex = xlNone
        .MarkerStyle = xlNone
        .Smooth = False
    End With
    With Selection.Border
        .ColorIndex = 5
        .Weight = xlThin
        .LineStyle = xlContinuous
    End With
Next i

L_I = NM + NM + NM
am = 1
'creating joint lines to axis
For i = NM + 1 To L_I
    With ActiveChart
        .SeriesCollection.NewSeries
        .SeriesCollection(i).XValues = ljxVal(am)
        .SeriesCollection(i).Values = ljyVal(am)
        .SeriesCollection(i).Name = "="""""
    End With
    ActiveChart.SeriesCollection(i).Select
    With Selection
        .MarkerBackgroundColorIndex = 1
        .MarkerForegroundColorIndex = 1
```

```
                .MarkerStyle = xlDiamond
                .Smooth = False
                .MarkerSize = 6
                .Shadow = False
            End With
            With Selection.Border
                .ColorIndex = 1
                .Weight = xlMedium
                .LineStyle = xlContinuous
            End With
am = am + 1
Next i

End Sub


'user function to determine maximum value of joint translation
Function UXMax(Xs, NP) As Variant

Dim Abs_FXMax As Double
Dim FXMax As Double

Abs_FXMax = 0
n = 0
For i = 2 To NP Step 2
    If Abs(Xs(i)) > Abs_FXMax Then
        Abs_FXMax = Abs(Xs(i))
        FXMax = Xs(i)
        n = i / 2
        'UXMax keeps origin value(+ or - value)
        UXMax = Array(FXMax, n)
    End If
Next i

End Function
```

An Introduction to Excel for Civil Engineers

```vb
'user function to determine maximum value of member moment
Function UMMax(Pmm, Fm, NM) As Variant

Dim Abs_FMMax As Double
Dim FMMax As Double

Abs_FMMax = 0
n = 0
For i = 1 To NM
    If Abs(mmomen1(i)) > Abs_FMMax Then
        Abs_FMMax = Abs(mmomen1(i))
        FMMax = mmomen1(i)
        n = Member(i).J1
        UMMax = Array(FMMax, n)
    End If
    If Abs(mmomen2(i)) > Abs_FMMax Then
        Abs_FMMax = Abs(mmomen2(i))
        FMMax = -mmomen2(i)
        n = Member(i).J2
        UMMax = Array(FMMax, n)
    End If
Next i

End Function

'user function to determine maximum shear force
Function USMax(Pmm, Fm, NM) As Variant

Dim Abs_FSMax As Double
Dim FSMax As Double

Abs_FSMax = 0
n = 0
For i = 1 To NM
    If Abs(shear1(i)) > Abs_FSMax Then
        Abs_FSMax = Abs(shear1(i))
        FSMax = -shear1(i)
```

```
            n = i
            USMax = Array(FSMax, n)
        End If
        If Abs(shear2(i)) > Abs_FSMax Then
            Abs_FSMax = Abs(shear2(i))
            FSMax = shear2(i)
            n = i
            USMax = Array(FSMax, n)
        End If
Next i

End Function


'user function to determine maximum soil pressure
Function USPMax(Pmm, Fm, NM) As Variant

Dim Sp As Double
Dim Abs_FSPMax As Double
Dim FSPMax As Double

Abs_FSPMax = 0
n = 0
For i = 1 To NJ
    Sp = Joint(i).Ks * Xs(2 * i)
    If Abs(Sp) > Abs_FSPMax Then
        Abs_FSPMax = Abs(Sp)
        FSPMax = Sp
        n = i
        USPMax = Array(FSPMax, n)
    End If
Next i

End Function
```

Command Button (XLAT)

```
Private Sub CommandButton1_Click()
ChartWindow = True
    Call XLAT
End Sub


Private Sub CommandButton2_Click()
ChartWindow = False
    Call XLAT
End Sub
```

Module1 (FDC)

```
Option Explicit
Public dZ() As Double
Public IP() As Double
Public rsdZ() As Double
Public rsIP() As Double
Public rsTP() As Double
Public m As Integer
Public im As Integer


Sub FDC()

'====================================================================
'FDC v.1.0 Program for One Dimensional Consolidation Analysis, 2004
'by: Gunthar Pangaribuan - Refer to the book:
'An Introduction to Excel for Civil Engineers
'====================================================================


On Error GoTo Check

Dim h As Double, t As Double, cv As Double, Tv As Double, n As Long
Dim FDCCase As Integer, i As Long, j As Long
Dim AIP As Double, ATP As Double
```

```vba
    im = Cells(4, 2) 'no. of layer
    m = 10 * im
    h = Cells(3, 2) 'height of layer
    t = Cells(5, 5) 'time
    cv = Cells(5, 2) 'coef. of consolidation
    FDCCase = Cells(3, 5) 'Case of calculation

ReDim dZ(0 To im) As Double, IP(0 To im) As Double
ReDim rsdZ(0 To m) As Double, rsIP(0 To m) As Double, rsTP(0 To m) As Double
Const Beta = 1 / 6

For i = 0 To im
    dZ(i) = i * h / im
    IP(i) = Cells(9 + i, 2)
Next i

're-input dZ and IP to obtain a smooth isochrone curve
n = 1
rsdZ(0) = dZ(0)
rsIP(0) = IP(0)
For i = 0 To im - 1
    For j = 1 To 10
    rsIP(j) = j * (IP(i + 1) - IP(i)) / 10
    rsdZ(j) = j * (dZ(i + 1) - dZ(i)) / 10
    rsIP(n) = rsIP(j) + IP(i)
    rsdZ(n) = rsdZ(j) + dZ(i)
    n = n + 1
    Next j
Next i

Dim LastRow
LastRow = ActiveSheet.UsedRange.Rows.Count
Range(Cells(9, 1), Cells(LastRow, 4)).ClearContents

If FDCCase = 1 Then
```

```
'open layered
    Tv = cv * t / (h / 2) ^ 2
    n = 1.5 * m ^ 2 * Tv

    ReDim u(0 To m + 1, 0 To n + 1) As Double

u(0, 0) = 0

    For i = 0 To n
        u(0, i + 1) = 0 'first row = 0
        u(m, i + 1) = 0 'last row = 0
    Next i

    For i = 1 To m - 1
        u(i, 0) = rsIP(i) '> first row to < last row
    Next i

    'Finite difference approximation:
    For j = 0 To n
        For i = 1 To m - 1
            u(i, j + 1) = u(i, j) + Beta * (u(i - 1, j) + u(i + 1, j) - 2 * u(i, j))
        Next i
    Next j

ElseIf FDCCase = 2 Then

'half closed layered
    Tv = cv * t / h ^ 2
    n = 6 * m ^ 2 * Tv

    ReDim u(0 To m + 1, 0 To n + 1) As Double

u(0, 0) = 0

    For i = 0 To n
        u(0, i + 1) = 0 'first row = 0
    Next i
```

```
    For i = 1 To m
        u(i, 0) = rsIP(i)
    Next i


    'Finite difference approximation:
    For j = 0 To n
        For i = 1 To m - 1
            u(i, j + 1) = u(i, j) + Beta * (u(i - 1, j) + u(i + 1, j) - 2 * u(i, j))
        Next i
        'on impermeable boundary (at m points):
        i = m:  u(i, j + 1) = u(i, j) + Beta * (2 * u(i - 1, j) - 2 * u(i, j))
    Next j

Else
    GoTo Check
End If
    'Result: after t pressure
    For i = 1 To m
    rsTP(i) = u(i, n + 1)
    Next i

    'Result
    For i = 0 To im
    Cells(9 + i, 1).NumberFormat = "0.00"
    Cells(9 + i, 1) = dZ(i)
    Cells(9 + i, 2).NumberFormat = "0.00"
    Cells(9 + i, 2) = IP(i)
    Cells(9 + i, 3).NumberFormat = "0.00"
    Cells(9 + i, 3) = rsTP(10 * i)
    Next i

    'Determine area under Isochrone
    'using trapezoidal approximation
    'in H/m unit
    AIP = 0
```

```
        ATP = 0
        For i = 0 To m - 1
            AIP = AIP + (rsIP(i) + rsIP(i + 1)) / 2  'area of initial pressure
            ATP = ATP + (rsTP(i) + rsTP(i + 1)) / 2  'area of after t pressure
        Next i
        'Print degree of consolidation, U
        Cells(9, 4).NumberFormat = "0%"
        Cells(9, 4) = 1 - ATP / AIP


'Produce FDC Chart
Call FDCchart


ActiveSheet.Range("A1").Select
Exit Sub


Check: MsgBox "Please check the input data ...", vbOKOnly + vbExclamation, "FDC Error!"

End Sub
```

Module2 (FDC)

```
Sub FDCchart()


On Error Resume Next
Dim Cx1, Cx2, Cy1, Cy2
ReDim mxValbf(0 To im) As Variant, myValbf(0 To im) As Variant
ReDim mxValaf(0 To m + m) As Variant, myValaf(0 To m + m) As Variant


Dim am As Integer

    ActiveSheet.ChartObjects("Chart 1").Activate
    ActiveChart.ChartArea.Select
    Selection.ClearContents

    'creating series lines: initial pressure
    am = 1
```

```
For i = 0 To im - 1
    mxValbf(am) = Array(IP(i), IP(i + 1))
    myValbf(am) = Array(dZ(i), dZ(i + 1))
    With ActiveChart
        .SeriesCollection.NewSeries
        .SeriesCollection(am).XValues = mxValbf(am)
        .SeriesCollection(am).Values = myValbf(am)
        .SeriesCollection(am).Name = "="""""
    End With
    ActiveChart.SeriesCollection(am).Select
    With Selection
        .MarkerStyle = xlNone
        .Smooth = False
    End With
    With Selection.Border
        .ColorIndex = 5
        .Weight = xlThin
        .LineStyle = xlContinuous
    End With
am = am + 1
Next i

j = im + m
am = 0
'creating series lines: after t pressure
For i = im + 1 To j
    mxValaf(i) = Array(rsTP(am), rsTP(am + 1))
    myValaf(i) = Array(rsdZ(am), rsdZ(am + 1))
    With ActiveChart
        .SeriesCollection.NewSeries
        .SeriesCollection(i).XValues = mxValaf(i)
        .SeriesCollection(i).Values = myValaf(i)
        .SeriesCollection(i).Name = "="""""
    End With
    ActiveChart.SeriesCollection(i).Select
    With Selection
        .MarkerStyle = xlNone
```

```
            .Smooth = False
        End With
        With Selection.Border
            .ColorIndex = 7
            .Weight = xlMedium
            .LineStyle = xlContinuous
        End With
    am = am + 1
    Next i

End Sub
```

Command Button (FDC)

```
Private Sub CommandButton1_Click()
    Call FDC
End Sub
```

Files associated with this book are available and can be downloaded freely from http://xl4eng.blogspot.co.id. You will receive exercise files that correspond to each chapter as the following:

- Chapter 1: Regression.xlsx and Charts.xlsx (Chapter 1.10)
- Chapter 2: Interpolation.xlsx
- Chapter 3: Chart Macro.xlsm and User Defined Function.xlsm
- Chapter 4: Inverse.xlsm and MMULT.xlsm
- Chapter 6: Frame2D.xls - Program for 2D Frame Structure Analysis
- Chapter 7: TRUSS2D.xls - Program for 2D Truss Structure Analysis
- Chapter 8: BOF.xls - Beam on Elastic Foundation Program
- Chapter 9: XLAT.xls - Laterally Loaded Structure Program
- Chapter 10: FDC.xls - One Dimensional Consolidation Program
- Chapter 11: Folders of Example 3, 4, 5 (Section11.1) and VBA script examples, include 3 AutoCAD DWG files, plus 3 script files.

To purchase your own print book please visit: https://amzn.to/2TeMPkC

www.ingramcontent.com/pod-product-compliance
Lightning Source LLC
Chambersburg PA
CBHW080616190526
45169CB00009B/3196